education in transition

Altgeld, circa 1903

eｏｕｃａｔíｏｎ íｎ ｔｒａｎｓíｔíｏｎ

The History of
Northern Illinois
University

Earl W. Hayter

NORTHERN ILLINOIS
UNIVERSITY PRESS
DEKALB

The publication of this book
was made possible by a grant from
the NIU Foundation.

Earl W. Hayter is Professor Emeritus in History and the University
Historian at Northern Illinois University at De Kalb, Illinois

Library of Congress Cataloging in Publication Data
Hayter, Earl W
Education in transition.
"A seventy fifth anniversary history."
Includes bibliographical references.
1.   Illinois.   Northern Illinois University,
De Kalb—History.   I.   Title.
LB1861.D42H39   378.773′28   73-15098
ISBN 0-87580-047-5

To the thousands of students
who have passed through this
institution, the author dedicates
this book with the hope that it may
rekindle some of the happier moments
of their student days as well as a
stronger faith in their university
in the years to come.

Contents

Contents

Contents

Lowden Hall, 1965

First College Avenue bridge, Spring of 1900

Foreword

IN A NATION mature enough to be approaching the celebration of its bicentennial, a seventy-fifth anniversary for an institution can seem somewhat awkward and contrived. In many instances perhaps it represents little more than the fact that it is half-way between its fiftieth and centennial anniversaries.

At Northern Illinois University, however, I believe there are two reasons why our seventy-fifth has a special meaning. Unlike most institutions of similar background and vintage, Northern Illinois University never has been the subject of a history, nor has a biography of any of its leaders ever been written. So the occasion of this anniversary has given inspiration to an undertaking that was long overdue. We are particularly fortunate that an historian with the background of Dr. Earl W. Hayter undertook the assignment of writing the story of Northern. He is a native of the Midwest and has been associated with Northern Illinois University since 1936, or for half the period of the school's existence.

The second reason that makes our seventy–fifty anniversary a special one is that it is within the third quarter-century of our being that our institution grew more than tenfold. Put another way, in the first fifty years of Northern's existence 8,180 degrees were awarded compared to 53,940 in the next twenty-five.

In an era when new campuses for thousands of students have been developed almost overnight, our growth may not have been singular. I submit, however, that coping with a growth increment of 1,500 students per year in the decade of the '60s was a more difficult task than planning initially for a full-blown facility. There are times when the problems of dealing with a physical plant that was planned and built piecemeal are highly frustrating. However, when one considers the problems our predecessors had in dealing with financial commitments that never extended beyond a biennium, and shibboleths such as "You don't bank land," one can only reflect on how impressive it is that the campus layout we have is as rational and coherent as it is.

One thing I particularly like about Dr. Hayter's history is that it is honest and candid. The warts and blemishes are all there. It was comforting to find out that the men whose stern portraits daily stare me down on the third floor of Lowden Hall were human after all.

Although our growth and development to date has been remarkable, it is clear that Northern, along with many other similar institutions, has entered a new era. Our enrollment peaked, at least for a while, two years ago. It seems clear at this point that much of our growth potential in the years immediately ahead will be in our extension and adult education programs. I am confident that our faculty and staff have the imagination and resilience to adapt to the new challenges. We are reassured by the vitality and growth of the geographical area we serve.

As our alumni grow in numbers, we hope that they will join in making it possible for the University to do some of the extra things that will distinguish it as a true university with a character and a personality, if you will, of its own.

Richard J. Nelson
President

DeKalb, Illinois
January 9, 1974

Preface

NORTHERN Illinois University is approaching the seventy-fifth anniversary of continuous service since it opened in the fall of 1899 as a normal school for the education of elementary teachers. Over this span of time, it has broadened its program to prepare teachers for the secondary schools and, finally, instructors for colleges and universities. Today, Northern fits the description of what is called a multi-purpose university, although hardly in the sense of the older universities with their various professional colleges. It should be compared to similar institutions which have suddenly been thrust into university status but which are still in search of their identity as well as their future.

In spite of this spectacular growth and development, little is known, and less has been written, of N.I.U.'s past, even though all of its sister schools in the state have had over the years from one to five separate histories. The initiative for this history of Northern was largely provided by a young historian by the name of James Connor who came to the campus as associate provost in 1965. Connor received his doctorate from the University of Wisconsin, where a classic history of that institution had been written by two prominent history professors. Upon arriving here, he soon set the wheels in motion for a history of N.I.U. Upon discovering that my wife, Beulah, and I had written a short article on the founding of Northern for the *Northern Alumnus* (December 1958) and also noting that I would soon be retiring from teaching, he managed in 1968 to maneuver me into the position of University Historian.

There had been a few previous efforts to write a history of the school, but for reasons unknown no major work was ever attempted. President John W. Cook was the first with his short "History of Northern Illinois State Normal School on Its

Twenty-First Birthday"; and three former faculty members, Swen F. Parson, Norma Stelford, and Charles W. Whitten, collaborated in compiling a brief "History of Northern Illinois State Teachers College" in 1949 for the fiftieth anniversary.

For one who had spent the major part of his professional life researching and writing on specialized topics in agricultural history, this assignment was indeed a vastly new experience. During the better part of five years, this project has commanded my constant attention, and it has been a subject that has grown in interest to me partly because of my close relationship with the institution for thirty-three years as a faculty member and also because it had served as an interesting challenge to me, after I had reached the end of my teaching career in 1969.

Throughout the writing of this history I have tried to develop the various phases that the University has passed through, to deal with its principal aims and ideals, its tensions, conflicts, and controversies in situations over which men and women differed, to discuss the qualities and capacities of its leadership, its financial support by the state, its growth and expansion, the nature of the students and faculty, and, where possible, to include bits of amusement for the alumni. In my interpretations of the sensitive areas of differences existing among administration, faculty, and students, I have attempted to balance my judgments as fairly as possible, realizing that some of the more recent periods have had excessive tensions and confrontations and that, therefore, the judgments are still in the process of being formed.

Particular items, events, and quotations—where it seems necessary—have been documented, but there is no bibliography of materials used since most of the documents (both cited and uncited) are available in the N.I.U. Archives. The study does unfortunately suffer from the loss of two major sources of historical materials belonging to John W. Cook and Dean Romeo M. Zulauf, both of whose collections of papers were irresponsibly destroyed before the project was initiated.

I cannot begin to acknowledge my indebtedness to all those who personally contributed in some way to this work, for any such effort would be certain to have numerous omissions. I am greatly indebted to the institution itself for affording me the opportunity to instruct some of the thousands of students who passed through its halls during my years as an instructor. Some of these students and especially the graduate assistants who aided me in researching various topics I recall with pleasure: Kathleen Clark, Scott Davis, Jean Humphrey, William Lamperes, William Leighly, and Ronald Rezny. Moreover, it would have been difficult to complete the manuscript without the excellent services of the Personnel Office and its secretary, Beverly Arison, who week after week sent me typists such as Marcia Westerman.

President Smith during his four years and President Nelson during his as yet brief administration encouraged this project and gave some financial support to it until economic cutbacks finally forced curtailment of such projects. I also owe much to my worthy colleagues, Emory Evans and Patrick White, of the History Department, for providing several graduate assistants to aid me as well as to Darla Woodward, Departmental secretary, for the necessary office supplies.

The complete manuscript was examined by a few active faculty members and various sections by others. Hugh Jameson, retired head of the Social Science Department; John Lloyd, retired member of the Economics Department; Howard Gould, retired head of the Physical Science Department; F. R. Geigle, vice president for Development and Alumni Relations; Paul Burtness, dean, Liberal Arts and Sciences; Ruth Haddock, director, Student Assistance and Information; Emory Evans, chairman, History Department; Clara Sperling, University Secretary; Michael McDermott, director, University Programming and Activities; and Owen "Bud" Nangle, director, Sports Information—all were willing to scrutinize the areas dealing with their competency. Thomas Woodstrup, former director, Alumni Relations, gave helpful comments throughout the writing of the book and two students, Michael Maibach and Charles Stanley, read parts pertaining to their time at Northern. A former student and president of the Student Association Board, Ray L. Steele, offered remarks on the years he was at Northern. J. Robert Hainds, a former vice president and director of the Graduate School under President Holmes, took

time out from his retreat in the Arizona desert to read the section on the development of the graduate programs.

Other individuals have been helpful with their memories that reached back into distant years where only scanty evidence now remains. Beatrice Gurler, daughter of a prominent, early DeKalb family, unraveled several of the knotty events that took place when the school began. Eleanor Zulauf, daughter of Swen Parson and a graduate of the Normal School who had spent most of her life within the shadows of the "Castle," also contributed freely from her recollections and source materials.

The late Judge J. Warren Madden took time from his illustrious career to write two long letters relating his experiences at Northern from 1906 to 1908. Jennie Whitten, daughter of Professor Charles Whitten, unearthed important sources relating to his career, which she donated to the University Archives. Edward Fitzgerald, Thomas "Tuck" Huntzicker, and Stanley Gritzbaugh shared their knowledge of the difficult times during the presidency of J. Stanley Brown. I wish also to thank Howard Gould; Jacob E. Alschuler, Board member during the Adams administration; Clyde Lyon, a former professor of reading and oratory; and Olive Johnson, who for many years was bookkeeper at Northern, for their important tape-recorded interviews.

My deepest appreciation goes to Joseph Bauxar, N.I.U. Archivist, for his untiring assistance from the inception of the project. He has always been most willing to share the burden of researching many of the difficult phases of this history as well as to serve as a consultant in solving its myriad problems. Moreover, he has provided not only free access to the University Archives but also working space that he sorely needed for his expanding section of the library. During the early phase of the project, he was especially helpful in securing valuable sources from the descendents of John W. Cook, Waite W. Embree, and Charles A. McMurry.

Finally, there are two young women who have played an enormous role in this enterprise from its beginning and whose efforts and interests have only increased as the deadline grew nearer; to them I owe more than words can express. Patsy Kelley Lundberg, assistant in the University Archives, and Mary Dale Wiley, former university publications editor, can never be sufficiently thanked for their ideas and criticisms so willingly offered as the task unfolded. Their only possible reward for this service would be the merit that others may see in the finished product. It is my hope that in future years they will reflect upon this cooperative enterprise as "our" book in every respect.

I am deeply obligated to my wife, Beulah, who has willingly sacrificed her interests by foregoing vacations, entertaining, lectures, recitals, and even desired foreign travel as well as managing the home so as to provide conditions under which maximum work is possible. She never hesitated to man the typewriter or to give abundantly of her time advising, criticizing, and editing the various drafts so often found on her desk—and sometimes even endured a certain amount of testy temperament on the part of her husband.

Earl W. Hayter

DeKalb, Illinois
October 1973

An aerial view of campus, 1956

Introduction

A PROPER perspective over the growth and destiny of an educational institution should include a brief description of its physical and cultural setting.

Geographically DeKalb and its environs are set in a typical prairie. These immense stretches of prairie lands, often called by the early settlers "God's Meadows," were formed "in the laboratory of Nature; inexorable forces have uplifted and depressed them, molding them to a form ideally adapted for the home of man." [1] The area receives an excellent annual amount and distribution of rainfall and the range of temperature and humidity during the summer months are ideal for agriculture, producing a lengthy, warm, humid growing season. This combination of natural factors has created in this part of Illinois one of the great food-producing sections of the nation. After the frontier period of producing various kinds of cereal crops on these prairies, the farmers finally settled upon the cultivation of corn and soybeans, and with few modifications this practice has continued into the present.

Early in the history of DeKalb, small industries began to develop. Labor to assist this process came in several migrations, some from northern Europe and others from the eastern United States. Skilled craftsmen settled in the DeKalb area, putting their inventive minds to work in small shops and producing numerous items for use on the farm. A few of the important implements manufactured here were farm wagons, manure spreaders, gasoline engines, barbed wire fencing, smooth and woven wire fences, nails, and fence staples. In addition, there were other factories producing such commodities as shoes, gloves, mittens, brick, and dairy products, and by 1894 one could count as many as 150 small business houses in the city. [2] The population nearly doubled during the next four

1

years between 1895 and 1899, reaching 5,904 inhabitants in the census of 1900.[3]

Ecologists who study the relationship between man and his environment would have been impressed by the fortunate location of this town on the edge of the great western prairies, where the ongoing settlers moved through into the broad treeless expanses of the West. A few early residents with inventive proclivities were soon to sense the economic demands of the area; new demands stirred the inventors' minds to action, and before many years a new type of fencing material was created that would in time help to revolutionize the West.

Only a few of the inventors of barbed wire fencing in the 1870s were to achieve any lasting success. Joseph F. Glidden, on his DeKalb homestead, perfected a form of barbed wire that eventually became the standard for manufacturers and consumers throughout the world. Jacob Haish, a DeKalb lumber dealer, developed simultaneously in his shop an "S"–type barb that was a close competitor for a few years. Isaac L. Ellwood, a hardware merchant in DeKalb, also invented a style of fence which soon proved quite ineffective; but, seeing the economic possibilities of his neighbor's patent, he purchased a half interest from Glidden for a few hundred dollars. They formed a partnership and began producing by hand for commercial use several thousand pounds per year.[4] Haish too set up a small factory and from these two little plants other companies were in time licensed to produce barbed wire in many parts of the country. By 1895, as many as 157,000 tons of various types were manufactured annually. Glidden, who was not particularly interested in the manufacture of fencing, sold his half interest rather early, leaving Ellwood and a new Eastern partner the task of consolidating all the patents into one company; this they did through a long period of costly litigation. The wire producers were finally merged into what became known as the American Steel and Wire Company, which, in 1901, became a subsidiary of the United States Steel Corporation.[5]

Barb City, as DeKalb was called, also had a wide reputation for another kind of industry. This was the buying, selling, and breeding of horses. There were several dealers in horses in

DeKalb but it was through the Ellwood family that this business, especially, took on national importance. Percheron draft horses predominated in the venture, but in time coach and trotting breeds were also introduced. DeKalb was known in northern Illinois for its monthly horse market held every third Friday on the main section of the business street. It was for the local buyers chiefly; but the Ellwood enterprise was of such mammoth proportions that his horses were handled from the large "Ellwood Green" stables on the outskirts of the city and from his large ranches in Texas. William L. Ellwood, his eldest son, was placed in charge of the business, and by 1890 it was estimated that this family had invested more than a million dollars in the industry, bringing into DeKalb and sending to the western states in that year 367 carloads of horses, many of which had been imported from France.[6]

With the development of these major and minor industries, DeKalb was soon to become, as its citizens liked to think of it, the "live wire" city. The editor of the *Chronicle* in 1894 extolled its greatness by proudly saying, "DeKalb is the largest manufacturing center in the west in proportion to population"; less than a year later his boastfulness was extended to DeKalb County: "Its fertile soil, nearness to markets, its churches, schools, its beautiful women, good society and in all other things that go to make up the sense of human happiness, it is doubtful if DeKalb county is excelled anywhere in the world."[7]

DeKalb demonstrated this civic pride by installing a few of the modern conveniences and improving the general quality of living. In 1893, an electric light and power plant was constructed by two leading citizens, and the city was able to have the full length of Main Street lighted at night.[8]

The unpaved parts of Main Street in DeKalb, according to local citizens of this period, were impossible for pedestrians to cross during the rainy season, and during dry and windy weather they were often dusty. It was finally completely paved with brick as a part of the agreement with the trustees of the normal school when they made the decision to locate in DeKalb.[9]

DeKalb was not known in its formative years as a healthful place to live. It was not until about 1891 that "the necessity. . . forced itself upon the minds of the authorities" that there was a desperate need for a sewage system. That year the people decided something had to be done, so they employed a first-class engineer from Minneapolis and had a comprehensive and complete system laid out, with the necessary maps and charts; by the close of that year they expected to begin construction.[10]

Railway transportation facilities by the early 1900s were quite satisfactory, with the Chicago and North Western Railway Company's east-west double-track trunk line and its two branches running north and south from DeKalb. Passenger trains were available on the main line each day, east and west, and at least one train ran daily on the north and south branches. The North Western morning "milk train" was also requested to build platforms just west of the Kishwaukee River to assist students who commuted to the college from nearby towns. In 1895, the Chicago and Great Western Railway Company extended a branch line into DeKalb that later made it possible for students to travel to Wisconsin and the northwestern states.[11] Moreover, an electric inter-urban system, connecting the normal school with Sycamore, was chartered in the fall of 1899 and completed in 1902. It ran from the west entrance of the present Altgeld Hall down Normal Road to Lincoln Highway, east to Fourth Street, north to Oak, east to Tenth, north to Pleasant, east to Thirteenth, and north to Sycamore Road, which it followed to the end of the line in front of the County Courthouse in Sycamore.[12]

This description of a few of the economic and physical characteristics of DeKalb offers a brief profile of the midwestern city in which the people of Illinois chose to establish another normal school where they would send their young people to live and to prepare for teaching in the common schools. A few observations on the beliefs, values, traditions, and origins of the townspeople might be interesting in light of the rural dynamics and philosophy that had been and was the most powerful influence in rural and small-town America at the turn of the century and which permeated the life of its institutions.[13]

An excellent example of this philosophy is found specifically in the fact that Illinois lawmakers chose out-of-the-way communities in which to locate normal schools. This procedure was hardly new in the United States but it was a marked contrast to the practice followed in most foreign countries, where, as a rule, educational institutions were established in or near large cities where students could have the cultural advantages of an urban center. This idea of isolating such institutions was, no doubt, deliberate and conformed to the basic belief that those people who lived in towns and small cities where it was quiet, safe, and free of urban social evils were also those people who were stable, hard-working, law-abiding, moral, patriotic, healthy, and religious and who would naturally experience the highest fulfillment of human nature. On the other hand, inhabitants of the large cities were subject to the wickedness and social sins that beset the prodigal son. This ruralistic philosophy, in spite of the rapidly growing urban population, was able to maintain its political grip upon state and local governments well into the twentieth century when the Supreme Court finally established the rights of urban dwellers in the ruling commonly called "one man, one vote."

The social structure of DeKalb was stratified: a few wealthy families at the top, a few poverty cases at the bottom, and in between, a sizeable number at all levels of the middle class, white collar, and factory workers. Most, if not all, of the upper establishment, being mostly of the first generation, had made their wealth by their own hard work and industry, combining this respected trait with perhaps a high degree of economic acumen, common sense, and good luck. Add to this capitalistic ethic a personal philosophy of rugged individualism and it generally meant financial success. Hard work and self-reliance were almost a religion. Under no circumstances should the government be asked to help or support the individual even in the most difficult situations, unless it might be in the form of the poorhouse—and then only when one had reached old age. This philosophy, nevertheless, did concede among other things that it was perfectly permissible for the government to assist the industrial interests through protective tariffs or monetary policy, for in so doing, the government was helping to develop American business and this in turn created more jobs and raised the standard of living for all sections of society. These entrepreneurs apparently ignored the conflicting elements in their philosophy of government; most of the leading manufacturers were members of the Republican party, which advocated these industrially oriented economic policies of the post-Civil War period.

The DeKalb wire mills employed around four hundred laborers during the most prosperous years. Each manufacturer pursued a paternalistic welfare policy with his employees; when wage rates were to be modified or employment reduced or when problems arose pertaining to health, accidents, seniority, and retirement, it was the employers who made the final decisions. It was customary on Thanksgiving and Christmas holidays for employers to parcel out something in the form of a bundle of food, a sack of flour, or a fine turkey; this generous gesture was usually well received by the laborers, for they considered it not just a gesture or habit on the part of their employers but rather an outpouring of personal benevolence and sacrifice. In this period, labor was peaceful and strikes were rare.

The whole city had a high regard and deep respect for the three illustrious capitalists of DeKalb, even though (or perhaps because) many were dependent upon them. If they were to be ranked as to the order they held in public esteem, they would probably have been judged in the following order: Joseph Glidden first, Isaac Ellwood second, and Jacob Haish third.

These important citizens were certainly unlike each other in personality traits, yet they were surely alike in having a common belief in the philosophy and virtues of the American system—the system that had afforded them their wealth and prestige. Glidden and Haish were members of the Democratic party, while Ellwood was a Republican; however, in matters

Joseph F. Glidden

regarding the community those differences were rarely noticed. They were intensely patriotic and truly self-made men; and with the exception of Glidden, who "had been through the public schools at home [New York] as well as an academy and seminary," they were almost completely self-educated.

Joseph Farwell Glidden, frequently known as "Uncle" Joe, was looked upon by the people of DeKalb as their first citizen, something of an elder statesman. He lived alone for some years in his hotel suite on Main Street, and served as the city's host for important guests and dignified affairs, appearing on various occasions on his hotel balcony to say a few words to his townspeople. His invention—at one time considered among the ten most important by the patent office—had made him world-renowned, and there was no question that he was a celebrated personage who attracted important people. A few lines from his eulogy by John W. Cook, the first president of Northern, indicates some of the many facets of Glidden's personality:

What he has been to this community it would be idle for me to attempt to describe. . . . He was here quite at the beginning.

7

Isaac E. Ellwood

. . . He helped to build the first school house and has always been a tireless friend of . . . education. . . . He was the largest contributor to the erection of one of the churches. He and Jacob Haish were the cunning inventors who explain the prosperity of the town. His party nominated him for the General Assembly and for the National Congress. . . . He was many-sided . . . in his endowments. . . . Intellectually, it was a sort of penetration to the heart of things. I soon saw that this was the quality that made him an inventor . . . .

He was always interested in public affairs. . . . While he was a partisan in politics . . . he seemed to be indebted to no one but himself. I was always instructed by his conversation on political questions. His criticisms were often biting . . . and in general I believed him to be substantially right. . . . Withal there was a simplicity . . . about him that carried conviction . . . .

Like most inventors he was rather a visionary. . . . He was more interested in ideas than in money. . . . I have always suspected that his wealth came to him because of his connection with men who were . . . superiors in administrative ability.

Jacob Haish

With his holdings he should have had a princely income yet. . . . Rumor has it that the statue [sic] of limitation paid many a debt that was due him . . . . I have often imagined that he loved his fields less for the rents they brought him than the companionship they gave him. . . . I suspect that [he was] . . . more a poet than a money getter.

I have hinted at the independence of his character. . . . I do not mean that he lacked in affection. . . . I have seen him deeply touched by a simple song. . . . Although he kept a hotel he never solicited patronage. If a guest complained he advised him to go elsewhere.

And so the chapter has come to its end at last. The good old man passes into history.

Isaac Leonard Ellwood had become, in spite of his lack of schooling, an effective leader. On numerous occasions he performed as a public speaker and to most listeners he was impressive, probably because of his early experience as an auctioneer. His speeches were generally on favorite subjects that permitted him the opportunity to orate and emphasize with emotion his deep-seated personal values. One survivor of the period remembers going as a child every year to one of the city parks to hear the Colonel (honorary rank in the Illinois guard) make the same speech on Memorial Day. Ellwood's wife, however, related that it was uncomfortable for her to attend these speaking engagements, for his grammatical errors were too embarrassing. Ellwood was an impressive man in size and demeanor as well as in voice. He had an assurance and confidence in his abilities that brought him into financial and political relationships with the greatest names of the nation. He enjoyed the amenities of life to the fullest, living like other wealthy entrepreneurs of his day with many servants and chauffeurs, the finest selection of food, drink, clothes, furniture, carriages, horses, and automobiles, as well as membership in the noted clubs. He entertained senators, governors, and even Theodore Roosevelt in his home. In his later years, he traveled more, making occasional trips to his large ranches in Texas, to Florida, where he had his private yacht and winter home, then back to his Lake Geneva, Wisconsin, summer residence. On occasion he traveled abroad, where his wife collected many rare pieces of china and other precious items for her personal museum. He was a lover of fine horses and spent many hours in his carriage, driving over his large expanse of land near the city, and he also raised for sale one of the best herds of Percherons in America.

Jacob Haish, the third member of the triumvirate, was quite different from his associates—physically as well as personally. He was a short man and generally gruff. Some of his barbed wire associates considered him a "noisy and provocative Dutchman" who was able to stir up all kinds of dissension. During his productive years as a manufacturer he was noted in the trade as an unusually independent person, fearing no man and beholden to none, characteristics that may have been his salvation at a time when few were able to survive the predatory practices of the marketplace. He came to this country when he was quite young and had the difficult problem of learning English. He had a particularly hard time pronouncing words properly and his heavy German accent remained with him all his life.

Underneath this stern exterior, however, was a generous nature. One of his most gracious gestures was his effort to instill a love of nature in the minds of the local children by passing out in the spring of the year "small and healthy chrysanthemum plants" to the lower- and upper-level pupils who would volunteer to plant and care for them until they bloomed, at which time a contest would be held and prizes awarded. After an active career in industry, Haish lived for many years in his large and singularly quaint if not eccentric home. These were quiet years and his regular daily routine was to make his way to Main Street where the people of DeKalb were in the habit of seeing the "old man . . . sitting in the Haish Bank at the corner of Third and Lincoln Highway . . . ."[14]

These three men were highly honored for their leadership in the community, and those who were familiar with the over-all public spirit of DeKalb and the proud "willingness of all hands to pull together for the common good" credited this spirit to the "united efforts and harmonious labors" of these leaders who invested their millions in productive enterprises. It takes the journalistic gift of the editor of the *Chronicle* to sum up the significance of these three men to all the people in DeKalb:

A city possessing men of such energies and pluck and unity of purpose, and determination to secure what they undertake, has something better than capital. It is something which not only makes capital, but it makes men more than the representatives of wealth. It makes them respected everywhere . . . and it gives them a power and an influence which money cannot buy.

In this respect the citizens of DeKalb are to be congratulated upon the class of public spirited men who are in command of its vast capital.[15]

DeKalb had many churches and exhibited a variety of religious beliefs, but without exception all church denominations were representatives of the Christian faith. It was predominantly a Protestant town with the relatively large Methodist church towering over the other four denominations. One rather large Catholic church served the city.[16]

In 1895, most of the middle-class people of all denominations were still traditional believers in their institutional doctrines. The faith of only a few of the more sophisticated intellectuals was plagued by the then current Darwinian concept and other such conflicting theories emerging in America—criticism of the Bible, secularism, agnosticism, and emphasis on the Social Gospel which held that the "principles of Christianity were sufficient upon which to construct a just social order."[17] Theological seminaries at this time were hardly aware of the new role of the church in the myriad of social problems brought about by the growth of urban and industrial society. Protestant ministers were a mobile group, and it was not unusual for one of the churches in the community to find itself with a pastor who might have been exposed to some of the newer thoughts and more liberal interpretations found in the writings and speeches of Robert Ingersol, Clarence Darrow, John William Draper, Andrew D. White, and Walter Rauschenbusch. These "heresies" often created a disturbance in the more conservative churches and there were cleavages within congregations.

However, few social problems or conflicting issues were present in this rather homogeneous community when the normal school opened its doors in the fall of 1899. Although ethnic-racial differences were a source of irritation in many communities at this period, this was not the case in DeKalb, for its population was predominantly Anglo-Saxon and Caucasian. By the turn of the nineteenth century fairly large groups of immigrants arrived from Sweden and Finland, and a few years later a smaller number arrived from middle and southeastern Europe, but few difficulties arose and they were all soon assimilated into the pattern of living.

Such might not have been the case had there been any attempt by Blacks to establish their homes and rear their families in DeKalb, as many did in the more sophisticated city of Sycamore. In DeKalb, there was always a conspicuous absence of them and for decades there was a rather effective rumor that they were not welcome; for years it was almost impossible for Black students to secure rooms in the city. With only one dormitory on the campus—which was not built until 1915—and only one Black family for many years in the city, it becomes quite understandable that there were so few of that race in attendance at Northern until almost the present day.

Public spirit was high during the late 1890s, but in respect to partisan politics there were so few Democrats in the town or county that in election years there never was a serious contest. The only time a real political campaign did develop was on occasions such as city contests for the mayor's office. Since 1852, when Glidden was elected sheriff, DeKalb County has never elected a Democrat to county office. The Republican party did have a serious split in 1912 when Theodore Roosevelt ran on the Progressive ticket, and defeated each of his opponents in DeKalb county by margins of two to one.[18]

Military, fraternal, literary, and benevolent clubs and societies as well as improvement associations were a part of the social fabric, and this was the period throughout the nation that many of these organizations experienced rapid growth and were embraced by all levels of society.[19] Each was unique in purpose, and each afforded much needed services to its members in the form of "fraternal feelings of good fellowship," a degree of economic security, and opportunities for personal service and development. The one that stood out particularly in the community was the Grand Army of the Republic, which for years saw itself as the watchdog of the "American Way of Life" and whose many chapters were a powerful lobby to influence legislation in the form of pension laws for the veterans and to perpetuate the memory of the heroes of the Civil War.

Special attention should be given to the literary societies, two of which consisted wholly of the more prominent women. The aim and purpose of one was specifically to exert "a genuine love of culture and knowledge" and also to be a "positive factor throughout the social life of the city." The DeKalb Ladies' Literary and Social Circle was organized in 1888 and was the pride of the community; its members were those especially interested in the study of American and British authors and English literature.[20]

13

The second ladies' improvement society was called the Chautauqua Literary and Scientific Circle; the name indicates that it had somewhat the same general purpose as its sister circle; however, the means of attaining the goal was somewhat different. This circle was connected with a national society that had its headquarters on Chautauqua Lake in western New York, whereas the other was purely a local study club. This organization had regular meetings of their class, as they called themselves,

every alternate Saturday afternoon . . . . The reading and study is done by each individual member at home and the exercises for each session of the class are arranged by a program committee and consist of character sketches of prominent persons connected with the history of the country under consideration; papers upon subjects connected with the lesson with discussions upon the same; and class drill by questions and answers upon the required study.[21]

A further development of the literary improvement societies occurred on 4 May 1895, only a few days before the chartering of the new normal school. In the parlors of the Glidden house members of the two ladies' organizations joined a smaller number of prominent men in the community for the purpose of organizing what they chose to call the University Association. The aim of the Association was to apply their intellectual energies systematically to the "study of the world's history." [22]

For years DeKalb had maintained an active municipal band, and by 1892 it consisted of twenty regular members. It was well known in the region, for it had gone "out as regimental band in the Douglas Brigade at the opening of the [Civil] War," and also earlier had "caught the Pikes Peak fever, and went west in 1858, and . . . was the first band that ever played on the streets of Denver, Colorado." [23] In 1876, early in his career, Jacob Haish built an Opera House which for many years served as a center for artistic endeavors.

The local citizens also began in 1893 to feel the lack of a public library, and as a result one was organized and located on the second floor in the City Hall, occupying the space long used as a reading room. Because there was no library fund, books were collected from the local citizens. In 1895, a movement was inaugurated to secure a Carnegie library, but for various reasons the project fell through; as a result the mayor and council established a library by ordinance. Mrs. E. B. Murray was engaged as librarian for a salary of $20 per month; she served until 1927. In 1909, another attempt was made for a Carnegie library but, before the matter had been consummated, negotiations were cancelled when Swen Parson reported that he had been informed that a wealthy man in DeKalb had provided $100,000 for such an institution in his will. However, the matter was to be kept a secret. Before too long this wealthy man (Haish) had some misunderstanding with the city council and destroyed his will. Negotiations with the Carnegie Corporation failed again, for the corporation had placed Illinois under a ban prohibiting any further grants because some library boards in the state had been careless in handling the libraries. Some time later, word came to Parson that Haish had reconsidered the matter of a library and a new will was drawn restoring the original sum of money.

This secret item in Haish's will was known to only three or four individuals in DeKalb, and since they could not reveal it to the public, these delays in securing a library caused considerable criticism of the city officials and Library Board. This they were unable to justify until the reading of the will after Haish's death. The Haish Memorial Library was finally dedicated on 15 February 1931—many years after the establishment of the normal school.[24]

The enthusiasm that came with the normal school was also expressed when one of the DeKalb women's clubs engaged Professor Otto Cohahn, M.A., to teach them French and German. No doubt he pleased his prospective pupils by saying that he would require no "outside work" but that he chose to instruct by what he called the "Natural Method." The ladies were eager and optimistic about this learned professor and they were sure they would find his work most interesting; he would fit in perfectly with the "educational spirit . . . just now permeating our community."[25]

"The Castle" under construction, July 1896

Forging A Normal School
In Northern Illinois

THE RAPID growth of public education in Illinois in the
later part of the nineteenth century created a real demand
for trained teachers which the three existing Illinois normal
schools at Normal, Carbondale, and Chicago were unable to
supply. As a result many school districts were compelled to
employ teachers who were totally unfit to teach or who were at
best only partially prepared. This situation stimulated interest
on the part of schoolmen and many Illinois laymen in the
establishment of additional training schools. More and more
people were unwilling to place the education of their children,
as they had in earlier days, under the guidance of any ill-
equipped person who would take the job. As President Edwin
C. Hewitt of Illinois State Normal University observed in 1888:

*It is the sole legitimate purpose of Normal Schools to give this
special preparation. . . . And yet it remains true that thousands
enter our schools as teachers every year, with no special
preparation whatever. Two things the people should do, as fast
as the growth of public sentiment will permit,—they should
demand such special preparation in those who propose to*

teach, and they should provide increased facilities for obtaining such preparation.[1]

Numerous attempts were made to get the Illinois General Assembly to appropriate funds for additional normal schools during the 1870s and 1880s. In 1877, one of the leading rural journals published in Chicago reported that the prospects looked bright for "A Normal School in Northern Illinois to be supported by legislative appropriations."[2] At the time, Senator D. D. Hunt, who resided in DeKalb, was chairman of an Illinois Senate committee whose duty it was to report on the "policy to be pursued in regard to State normal schools." From this forum, he took the opportunity to plead with the state that it not only properly support the already existing schools but also provide additional institutions.[3]

In September 1894, three months before the opening of the state legislature, John W. Cook, one of the strongest advocates of additional normal schools and at that time president of Illinois State Normal University, likewise appealed to the state officials:

While other states are marching along in this particular we are remaining stationary. New York is now supplementing the work of her 12 normal schools . . . [and] the new . . . four state normal schools [added] to the five already existing in Massachusetts is a striking proof of the public faith in the professional preparation of teachers in that historic commonwealth. Wisconsin is perhaps outstripping all the rest of the states when her population is considered. Why shall Illinois be content to remain indifferent to this great interest? . . . There is great and immediate need of a normal school in northern Illinois.[4]

In time, however, this situation changed, primarily due to the growing strength of teachers' organizations and to a rather substantial gubernatorial defeat for the Republican party in 1892. The Democrats had not held the governor's office for several decades, and with the organization of the Northern Illinois Teachers Association in 1882 and the efforts of the Illinois State Teachers Association, there soon developed an articulate group of teachers and city and county super-intendents in every county of the state who campaigned vigorously for additional normal schools. To see to it that the idea was not overlooked, they established a "policy . . . to keep up a perpetual agitation of the subject" and a standing commit-tee to bring the matter before each annual meeting of the Teachers Association.[5]

The role of the new governor, John Peter Altgeld, was an important one in the educational development of the state during his four years in office. In fact, the whole educational system of the state was expanded in the number of normal schools as well as in an enlarged building program for other institutions. His deep concern for education never waned throughout his incumbency.[6]

A subscriber to the populist and progressive traditions, Governor Altgeld had a deep concern for those who did not enjoy the benefits of the expanding economy of the post-Civil War period but who were instead victims of a system—the laborers, farmers, immigrants, and other deprived elements of society. To all these he gave his attention, and he saw in the expansion of normal schools the possibility of upgrading the educational level of the masses through better trained teachers, for the majority of teachers at this time were seldom even high-school graduates but had rather "from six to eight grades in the common schools."[7]

In making political appointments following his inaugura-tion, Governor Altgeld became interested in Clinton Rosette, editor of the *DeKalb Chronicle* in northeastern Illinois. Even though his city and section were predominantly Republican, Rosette was of that vanishing breed of editor known for independent, tough-minded courage. He had a bold and on occasion personal style of reporting, not infrequently challeng-ing the community to intense feelings of anger or to high levels of enthusiasm for some worthy cause. There was no doubt of his partisanship, for he displayed it where everyone could see it—on the masthead of his paper: "Democrat in All Things and Under All Circumstances." He was fearless in his attacks on Republican heroes, and President Grant especially was one of his favorite targets. Rosette illustrated his capacity for excoria-

Governor John P. Altgeld

tion in journalism on 12 June 1880, not only thanking God for Grant's last defeat at the national convention but also describing the president as a "whiskey-soaked Demagogue" and consigning him to the "Deepest Recesses of Hell."[8]

Rosette, however, was more than a partisan editor. With his alertness, imagination, and directness of purpose, he was able frequently to communicate his ideas persuasively to the local leadership in spite of his intractable nature. He received a certain respect from them; for after all he was a local boy who had grown up in the county, taught school as a young man, and had risen from apprentice in the town print shop to become editor of the *Chronicle*. In 1893, he was chosen president of the Illinois Press Association, a highly respected success story in any American community.[9] John W. Cook, his longtime friend, gave the eulogy upon his death in 1909:

He had as his absorbing ambition a greater DeKalb. He was a man of unusual intellectual gifts. In a way he was a visionary of visionaries, but he had a way of enlisting others in the realization of his visions. His highest ambition first, last and all the time was a greater DeKalb.[10]

Clinton Rosette

The governor, believing that Rosette should be compensated for his effective contribution in the election of 1892, gave him his choice of several positions.[11] Rosette was a former schoolmaster and there was a vacancy at the time on the Board of Education of the State of Illinois—the board whose function it was to control the Illinois State Normal University at Normal. This position seemed to represent Rosette's interests and also to serve as an excellent opportunity for him to become thoroughly acquainted with the functioning of a normal school.

Within a few months, he was completely absorbed in the board's activities and the inner workings of normal-school education. One of the first moves he made was to join with prominent educators who had been endeavoring to secure additional normal schools but whose annual resolutions had had little effect upon Republican governors and legislative bodies.

It was evident that what they needed was a different type of leadership, one that embodied the characteristics of a man like Rosette. Through his relationship with these educational leaders and with President Cook of Illinois State Normal University, by whom Rosette had been encouraged to proceed, he quickly discovered that an additional normal school was possible in northern Illinois. With the support of such groups and individuals as well as a favorable response from Governor Altgeld, he formulated his plans to enlist some powerful Republican interests in his home town. Here lived one of the noted barbed wire millionaires, Isaac L. Ellwood, who was known by rural people throughout the middle west and in Illinois especially for his Republican influence on both the local and state levels.[12] The *Oregon Republican* reported of Ellwood that he was "one of the largest hearted men that Illinois soil has ever developed, and who a few years ago was in what may be termed moderate circumstances . . . but one of the few men who money does not spoil. There is no man who thinks more of his friends or will go farther to do them a kindness than Mr. Ellwood." His personal appearance was so much in favor "that it takes little argument for him to carry his point"; also in his favor at this time were the many senators and representatives of the state as well as influential industrialists who were beholden to him for past favors.[13]

Colonel Ellwood was an extremely active businessman with widespread financial enterprises, but in spite of these demands he immediately cancelled most of his appointments and for over three months threw himself into the contest with his characteristic energy. He spent days at a time at the Leland Hotel in Springfield, and when he was not there he had his worthy co-worker, Rosette, take his place.

A number of leading educators and county and city superintendents were conscripted to assist in drawing up the bill. President John W. Cook wrote in his history of the northern normal that he "spent all of the time . . . on the scene of battle" during the critical hours. Cook was well known and no doubt had more expertise than others, and his active presence also gave an added assurance that there would be no opposition from Illinois State Normal University.[14]

The strategy used was to have Senator Daniel D. Hunt, a member of the Committee on Education, in charge of the bill. On 10 January 1895, he introduced Senate Bill No. 2, titled "An Act to establish and maintain the Northern Illinois State Normal School." A definite location was deliberately omitted to increase the chances for winning support from other Republicans who controlled the Assembly.[15] Another favorable factor that aided in moving the bill through the legislature was a second bill introduced 7 February by Senator Isaac B. Craig of Mattoon to locate a sister normal in the eastern part of the state. Although the northern sponsors were somewhat opposed to the idea of trying to get two normal-school bills through the Assembly in one session, the move did prove a benefit, for it placed forty counties in a bloc that could be relied upon to support the bills. They played tag through the legislature, with the Northern bill breaking the ice for the Eastern bill. The pattern seemed to be that the Northern bill had to have the support of Eastern people; the Eastern bill was the reward for those who supported the Northern one.[16]

Opposition was not slow in coming, however, for as soon as the bill was introduced, the governor discovered that some members of his own party disagreed with the whole idea of additional normal schools. Cook records that he actually overheard the governor admonish these party members: "If you think you are advancing the interests of the democratic party by opposing this addition to educational forces I want to say to you that you are distinctly on the wrong track."[17]

Some of the larger cities in northern Illinois were fully aware that with Ellwood behind the measure his city would naturally have an advantage over theirs as a site; as a result, they were in a difficult position, for they all realized the need for such an institution. Dixon, Illinois, being in somewhat different circumstances, made an overt attempt to block the legislation by sending a delegation of prominent citizens to Springfield, for their town already had a private institution called the Northern Illinois Normal School and Dixon Business College, which was advertised as "One of the Largest and Most Thoroughly Equipped Colleges in the West." It boasted an enrollment of 2,063 in 1899, and had students "from almost every state."[18] Rockford, too, was alarmed about DeKalb's role in this undertaking, and there was considerable disputation in Rockford newspapers, pointing out with pride the advantages of their city with special emphasis upon the scenic grandeur of the historic Rock River. However, no interference was exerted in Springfield to prevent passage of the bill. The plan Rockford decided upon, as was also the case with the other northern rivals, was to wait and make its bid to the Board of Trustees that would be appointed to select the site when the bill was made law. Moreover, it became the opinion of most of the cities that Ellwood would have a difficult "job on his hands when he undertakes to convince his associates [the Board of Trustees] that DeKalb should have the school.[19]

The struggle in the General Assembly varied in the two houses; in the Senate, after the initial confrontation with a few minor amendments and a reduction of the appropriation to $50,000, the bill passed by a vote of 33 to 2 on 14 March. It was then sent to the House of Representatives for their concurrence.[20] In the House, however, it was a different story. Ellwood found it necessary to use all of his influence, especially when the bill came up on 2 May for the second reading. There was determined opposition; according to the *Chicago Herald*, "it was one of the hardest witnessed there in recent years." Everyone knew that this was the turning point in the fight against the normal-school bills. A Springfield reporter stated:

About four hours were consumed in discussion of this measure. Almost every member seemed anxious to amend the bill. At least seventy-five amendments were offered, but only two or three of them were adopted. A motion was made to recommit the bill to the appropriations committee, for the purpose of killing it, but the motion was voted down by a majority of about two to one. This indicates that the measure will go through the house easily when it comes up on third reading.[21]

Two of these amendments would have forced the trustees to locate the school "upon some river . . . where plenty of pure water and good sewage can be had" or, specifically, upon the "Fox river, Pecatonica river, Mississippi river or Rock river."[22] These two amendments would have assured the prize to one of the principal competitors of DeKalb. Everyone was aware that DeKalb was located on the small Kishwaukee River, which was certainly no match for these larger waterways and which even had to have a community face-lifting in order to prepare it for the trustees when they came to examine the DeKalb site.[23]

President Cook, noting the victory in the House, remarked that the arguments concerning subsequent stages of the bill were largely a matter of form and that opposition had dwindled to only a few voices from Dixon who were still holding out in order to protect their private school. On 15 May the bills were finally called up on third reading and the Northern Normal School bill passed the House by a majority of 97 to 29; the Eastern Normal School bill even had a slightly larger margin of 96 to 24. With the amendments finally agreed upon, the privilege of taking the bills to Governor Altgeld was afforded Clinton Rosette in recognition of his devoted service. The governor signed them on 22 May 1895, and the General Assembly adjourned *sine die* on 14 June.[24]

Reporters who witnessed the movement of these two normal-school bills through the legislature were of one opinion, that their success was due to the political influence that Ellwood was able to exert when necessary. One illustration serves to show how he was able to apply his thrust. Knowing that 2 May, when the bill would come before the House on second reading, would be the real test of his strength, he wrote in a short space of time three letters to Albert J. Hopkins, a close friend and Republican congressman from Aurora. He revealed to him a maneuver whereby he planned to buy $50,000 of "stock in the [Chicago] Inter-Ocean enterprise," for, as he said, "I believe that this paper will exert the greatest influence . . . in your behalf," but he also stated that he hoped to utilize "this scheme in a considerable extent in behalf of our Normal School Bill and . . . if some of the leaders down there [Springfield] think the scheme is going through I can continue to use it to good advantage. Hence, a word to the wise is sufficient." Moreover, in one of the letters he added a postscript for Hopkins to have the Speaker of the United States House of Representatives, "Uncle" Joe Cannon of Danville, Illinois, "in Springfield Tuesday morning, [for] besides helping your interests he could do me a personal favor in the matter of the Craig and Hunt School Bills, if he felt so disposed."[25] Sometime after the Normals were

25

November 1896

established, Colonel Ellwood indicated in another letter to the congressman that his "scheme" must have been effective, for he said: "It is very gratifying that we had so many and such influential friends at a time when their assistance was so much needed, enabling us to accomplish our purpose. I thank you from the bottom of my heart."[26]

A few of the more important provisions of the charter are as follows:

The object . . . shall be to qualify teachers for the common schools of the State by imparting instruction in the art of teaching in all branches of study which pertain to a common school education, in the elements of the natural and of the physical sciences, in the fundamental laws of the United States and of the State of Illinois, in regard to the rights and duties of citizens.

The powers of this institution were placed in a Board of Trustees of five members to be appointed by the governor with the advice and consent of the Senate. Two members were to serve for two years and three for four years; "no two members . . . shall be residents of any one county, or in one congressional district. The Superintendent of Public Instruction shall be a trustee . . . *ex officio.*"

The Board of Trustees were empowered to

appoint instructors . . . fix their respective salaries and prescribe their several duties. They shall also have the power to remove any of them for proper cause after having given ten days notice of any charge which may be duly presented, and reasonable opportunity of defense. They shall also prescribe the text-books, apparatus and furniture to be used in the school, and provide the same, and shall make all regulations necessary for this management.

27

Another important provision was the one that committed the trustees, as soon as possible following their appointment, to

arrange to receive from the localities desiring to secure the location of said school, proposals for the donation of a site, of not less than forty acres of ground, and other valuable considerations, and shall locate the same in the place offering the most advantageous conditions, all things considered, as nearly central as possible in that portion of the State lying north of the main line of the C.R.I. & P.R.R., with a view of obtaining a good water supply and other conveniences for the use of the institution. (Emphasis added.)

Once this site had been selected, the trustees were to have plans submitted and contracts let for the erection of a sufficient number of buildings in which

to furnish educational facilities for such number of students as hereinafter provided for, . . . also for the improvement of the land so as to make it available for the use of the institution. The buildings shall not be more than two stories in height, and be constructed upon the most approved plan for use, and shall be of sufficient capacity to accommodate not less than one thousand students, with the officers and necessary attendants.

Finally each county of the state was entitled to free instruction for two pupils, and each senatorial district, the number of pupils equal to the number of representatives in that district. The superintendents of schools in the counties, in cooperation with the Board of Trustees, were responsible for the selection of these students. A final provision was that each student wishing to attend at the fees prescribed by the Board of Trustees must "sign and file with the secretary of the Board a declaration that he or she will teach in the public schools within the State not less than three years in case that engagements can be secured by reasonable efforts." If the student failed to fulfill these conditions, he or she would be required to pay a tuition fee of one dollar a week for the time of attendance.[27]

With the long struggle over in the Assembly, the remaining problem was to secure appointees to the Board of Trustees who would favor DeKalb as the site of the school. Who they would be was entirely in the hands of Governor Altgeld, and immediately there developed an astonishingly active contest for these five positions on both normal boards. As the *Chicago Tribune* noted in respect to the northern normal, Colonel Ellwood's problems were now over as far as the legislature was concerned but his other troubles were just beginning. "A number of cities that did little or nothing toward the passage of the bill have swooped down on Gov. Altgeld for the purpose of capturing the location."[28] There were over two hundred applications for these ten positions on the two boards. The governor took his task seriously and gave selection of the trustees "unusual attention. Today [18 May] he did nothing but receive delegations who called in support of candidates. The largest number of applications . . . came from the eastern school district."[29]

A number of cities in the north had designs on the prize but the principal contenders were Rockford, Freeport, Polo, Dixon, Oregon, Fulton, and DeKalb; for the eastern school there were at least a dozen cities "warmly contesting for the Honor" but it finally ended in a hotly drawn-out contest between Mattoon and Charleston. The former city, which had exerted most of the leadership in passage of the normal school bill, soon discovered that the contest was by no means settled; in fact Mattoon, realizing how formidable the contest was, made some appeals to Ellwood for help. One was written by James Clark on 23 July:

I want to ask you, if you can conveniently, . . . to come down to Springfield Friday to help us out. Our trustees meet in the State Superintendents office . . . to receive propositions and locate the Normal. We are to have a hot contest. We think, however, that we have the advantage in location and we are prepared to make excellent propositions in sight [sic] and cash money. . . . Hoping you will be there . . . .[30]

Ellwood, in his generous manner, replied to an earlier letter from another citizen in Mattoon that he recognized the justice of the request but "I do not feel that it would be prudent on my part to take any part in the location of the school in that district. . . . I think your own good judgement will appreciate the prudence of my keeping out of the contest."[31]

Political partisanship did not seem to be a major concern in the appointment of the trustees even though the Democrats had been out of office for many years. After serious consideration the governor placed three Democrats and two Republicans on the Northern Board, which, with the Republican *ex-officio* member, State Superintendent of Public Instruction S. M. Inglis, was equally divided. Ellwood was selected almost immediately as the first appointee, no doubt a gesture on the part of the governor in recognition of his untiring efforts. As it turned out he was the only appointee from a city contending for the site. Three others were appointed without any repercussions from northern Illinois cities: Judge A. A. Goodrich, a lawyer in Chicago, was elected chairman; Charles Deere, president of the John Deere Plow Company of Moline, a member; and W. C. Garrard, secretary of the Illinois Board of Agriculture, Springfield, was elected secretary. The governor wanted the fifth appointee to be from one of the two more prominent interested cities, Freeport and Rockford. This appointment was delayed since both had a candidate, "and neither city would agree on either of them." Since these two towns were only about thirty miles apart the governor suggested that they get together and agree upon one delegate to represent the region. This precipitated a mild sectional quarrel and in the end the governor was ready to break the deadlock by appointing Rockford's candidate, Mayor Warner. But a delegation from that city, headed by the postmaster, called on the governor protesting that choice; the ruffled governor voiced his dissatisfaction: "I am not going to settle your local quarrels," and forthrightly appointed Thomas Sparks, a lawyer from Bushnell and a former member of the legislature, whose name had not even been mentioned previously. It was a surprise to the appointee himself. The Senate promptly confirmed the appointments.[32] With no one on the Board from these two prominent cities DeKalb had a real advantage.

So elated was he with his appointment and confirmation to the Board that Ellwood dispatched a message to the governor extending his sincere appreciation for this honor

as well as the many courtesies extended to me during the time this bill was pending before the legislature, which have placed me under obligations that I find it hard to express, but hope to be able to show my appreciation . . . more fully in the future.

If nothing happens in the meantime to make it impossible, I will call on you next Tuesday morning [June 4th] at your office, in compliance with your wishes.[33]

A few weeks later, after the adjournment of the legislature, Ellwood addressed another letter to the governor in which he said:

I am anxious to renew the invitation I gave you personally while in Springfield recently for you and your kind lady to come to my place here and spend a few days in quiet country rest. I sincerely feel that it will do you good, and prove a tonic that you require, and will promise you that you shall not be burdened by making speeches or anything of that sort, but be allowed to take a full measure of rest.[34]

There is no record to show that the governor was able to enjoy this respite from his busy office, but he did visit DeKalb on 1 October 1895, when he spoke at the laying of the cornerstone for the normal school.

Probably 1898

2

DeKalb Wins
the Prize

ONCE the Board of Trustees had been appointed by the governor, one of its first duties was to select a site for the school within a circumscribed area of northern Illinois. All interested cities were invited to file with the secretary of the Board by 15 June 1895, their applications for site inspections and such listings of "other valuable considerations" as each was willing to contribute.[1] Even though a sizeable number of towns "held up their hands for the prize" when the invitation was announced, as the time drew near for them to assemble an attractive financial offer, several suddenly lost enthusiasm. Some who would have been expected to enter the contest began to "feel that the location . . . was a foregone conclusion at the beginning; that the measure creating it was engineered by a millionaire citizen of DeKalb in the interest of that particular city."[2] The few that remained, feeling they had superior qualifications to those of DeKalb, and prepared "written propositions" were Dixon, Rockford, Polo, Oregon, Fulton, and Freeport. Five of these were the principal competitors for most of the race; however, in the final showdown the decision was made between DeKalb and Rockford.[3]

Aurora was the first to drop out, but not before the selection committee had arrived for its inspection. A letter had been sent to the committee by the mayor which "led them to believe Aurora was really seeking the plum."[4] They remained in that city but a few hours since the mayor soon made it clear that they did not wish to be "counted as a competitor." As a Rockford editor remarked, Aurora made this weak gesture merely "as a sort of handle for something better in the future."[5]

The Freeport people were also uncertain about the idea. Early in the contest they were among the few who had sent a delegation to Springfield, before the commissioners were even appointed, to get the governor to appoint one of their citizens to the Board. Failing at this and being told "at the capitol that DeKalb had a cinch on the school . . . [Freeport] let the matter go by default" and prepared no proposal. Trustee Goodrich at the eleventh hour before the final decision thought that Freeport should be brought into contention, so they half-heartedly and hurriedly assembled a committee for the 15 July meeting in Chicago. Again they vacillated and arrived on the scene too late; the commissioners finally ruled them out of the contest.[6]

Once the remaining contenders were alerted to the importance and magnitude of this state institution and what it would mean to them, they began serious campaigns to mobilize their community resources. They knew full well that they needed large monetary gifts as well as an excellent tract of land of not less than the minimum requirement of forty acres and preferably one that would be donated by some local benefactor. Paved roads, sidewalks, sewers, waterlines, telephones, electricity, housing additions for faculty and students, railway connections, bridges, and a minimum number of children for a model school were all obligations that would fall upon the winner of this coveted prize. The combined energies of each city's organizations feverishly went toward securing as many valuable resources as were available. The local newspapers carried on, in part for outside consumption, vigorous campaigns in favor of their locations. Some of the neighboring cities who made no bids, or who were early drop-outs like Freeport and Aurora, threw in their lot with one or more of the other contenders.

In reviewing the assets of the various locations, the publicity tended to emphasize those points of physical and cultural interest that would create a contrast to DeKalb, which they all knew they must ultimately outbid. Those that were located on the "inimitable Rock River"—Rockford, Oregon, and Dixon—wrote eloquently of its scenic beauty of "wooded hills and bluffs," its historic and artistic background, and its peaceful settings where students would not be distracted from their studies. Contrasting the natural possessions of these three cities with those of DeKalb, the *Franklin Reporter* said:

DeKalb is a hustling little city . . . built up and is sustained by large barb wire plants and other manufacturing establishments, and is favorably located for that class of industries. The country . . . is a low, level plain, undiversified by hill or dale, woodland or stream, from which the lover of nature might gain an inspiration, or the weary brain worker find an occasional hour of rest and pleasant recreation. The mind of the student is . . . impressed by his surroundings, and grimy smoke stacks and the din and hum of machinery are not incentives to healthful study. A more pleasing prospect is presented in the quiet woodland, the beautiful hill, the grassy dell, the bold and picturesque cliff, or the winding stream. . . . Added to these are opportunities for the embryo geologist to study the mysterious work of the ages, the wonderful formation of the earth in its various strata . . . while the young botanist finds in the varied forms of plant life a perfect paradise for research.

For such buildings as would be required the location here is unsurpassed. The situation is elevated, the drainage perfect; and for a water supply . . . a never failing abundance of the purest and best. In comparison with these advantages what has DeKalb to offer?[7]

In Rochelle, DeKalb's neighbor, the editor of the *Register* wrote one of the commissioners a personal letter warning him of the unhealthful conditions in DeKalb:

Thinking that perhaps I possessed a little information which had not been given you and which might assist you materially in giving your final decission [sic] . . . I take the liberty to address you. Knowing that a most important matter . . . was the water and drainage, I say that at DeKalb they have a woful [sic] lack of both, while at Polo and Oregon or Rockford they have a fine

35

supply of good, pure water and good drainage. It was only last winter that DeKalb had an epidemic of a contagious disease which took off thirty-seven people within a month, there being nine funerals in one day, . . . caused by the . . . impurity of the water and the poor drainage. . . . As to DeKalb . . . I believe it would be a grevious [sic] mistake to locate the school at that place.[8]

The *Oregon Republican,* in praising "Poor little Polo" and its skimpy proposal, mentioned that it had assets other than material ones. For instance, this homogeneous rural town would be an excellent place for parents to send their young people to school, for it was, among other things, a "solid temperance" community, while DeKalb was not so fortunate in this respect. In fact, the Oregon editor stated, if the normal school were to be located in DeKalb, it would be not only morally wrong but also illegal, for the law required that all such institutions be "a mile distant from saloons."[9] Moreover, it was true that Polo was not blessed with a beautiful river nor with great wealth, but what it lacked in these material matters it made up for in enthusiasm. So noticeable was Polo's dynamic spirit that one of the commissioners during the inspection trip was heard to remark: "Such self-denial and open-handed generosity is worthy of the reward it seeks." Polo even attracted the sympathy of the Freeport community about twenty-five miles away, who had failed to file a bid themselves but who decided that it might be wise to throw their influence to Polo; for as they said, if "we cannot have it [ourselves] let us strive to keep the school as near us as possible."

Rockford, the largest of the contenders, carried on an extensive campaign, believing that since it had a perfect combination of physical, cultural, and financial assets as well as a highly reputed public school system there was no reason that the decision should not be made in its favor. "If the scholars could select the location," observed one of the commissioners, "there would be no doubt about the choice they would make." Rockford's publicity emphasized its beautiful river valley, its "cultivated and united people," and its surrounding atmosphere as a most desirable location for an institution of learning.

Lamenting their one deficiency, when compared with DeKalb, they did not hesitate to remind the public that their "city has no millionaire backer, it is true," but, if this contest is an open one and not "a cut and dried affair" between Governor Altgeld and Colonel Ellwood, there is no question that Rockford and its environs are superior to the barbed wire city.[10] Even Ellwood himself, when viewing the Rockford site with the commissioners, had to admit that it was "certainly a magnificent location and I must confess that you people up here don't half appreciate your beautiful river. . . . If DeKalb can't get it I am in favor of Rockford."

During this period of publicity, when DeKalb was more or less the focal point of attack, its reaction to the campaign was quite reasonable and tolerant, expressing generally a spirit of confidence:

The [DeKalb] CHRONICLE has no bricks to throw at competing towns or space to spare on jealous neighbors who are not in the fight. But it believes that DeKalb will secure the school on the merits of its offer as well as on its prior claim by right of creating the school. It would not hesitate to place the matter in the hands of the legislature that passed the bill, or the governor who signed it, or the teachers of the state who did so much for it, or the trustees who have the matter in charge. The question will be settled on its merits and not on the desires or false charges of individuals or cities who came into the fight at the last moment.[11]

This confidence as to the outcome did not engender good will but rather a sense of futility and pessimism among the other contenders. But even with the criticism and personal attacks upon DeKalb and its popular millionaire citizen, it was not without friends during this struggle. The *Dwight Star and Herald Tribune* in discussing the various rivals stated: "We know of no better place for the school than DeKalb—except Dwight of course." The *Rochelle Herald* had a number of favorable words to say in DeKalb's behalf, and also the *St. Charles Chronicle* noted that since her citizens had made no concerted effort for the school, "we may as well hustle for some deserving city, . . . and follow the course marked out by the rules of justice and hurrah for DeKalb." [12]

Between 22 May, when the governor signed the normal school bills into law, and 24 June, when the Board of Trustees began their search for a site, five cities filed proposals for consideration. To evaluate these sites properly the trustees left Chicago by special train on that date, stopping first at Aurora only to discover that this city was not interested in being a contender. During the afternoon, which was "dry, sultry, and dusty," they journeyed on to Rockford and were shown the two sites that were offered for inspection.[13] The commissioners were pleased with both, but the Harlem Park area of forty-four acres was the favorite, since it was on the Rock River. Following the inspection trip they were presented a "most superb banquet," finishing just in time to attend the presentation of Rockford's total offerings. Besides the beautiful acreage with street car lines to and from the city, Rockford agreed to construct water mains or an artesian well on the school grounds. The use of the public library in the city, a $10,000 cash offering for a gymnasium, and model schools necessary for the training of teachers were also part of the total proposition. A reporter for the Rockford press, commenting on the presentation, said: "Nothing was left undone by the local committee to show the advantages of Rockford . . . and the claim presented certainly could not have failed to make a lasting impression. . . . Rockford's site is the ideal one of the state." The trustees left early the next morning for the other inspections.

At Polo the commissioners found every "man, woman and child . . . enlisted in the work of bringing the constituted authorities to see that Polo is the ideal spot for the institution." In spite of the inclement weather, which forced the committee "during a blinding rain" to take cover in the shelter house of Barber's Park, there was no lack of interest. Polo offered a site of forty acres of the "finest land, both for quality and location, in the state." An additional six acres of land located elsewhere were also promised; the community had collected pledges of $20,000 to apply toward purchase of equipment for the model school; and finally various public improvements were presented which would have a direct bearing upon the "convenience and prosperity" of the entire normal school. Geographically the location was excellent, and there were other substantial factors in Polo's favor, such as a pure and excellent water supply, superior sanitary conditions, and railroad facilities as well as a people with a high level of refinement and culture.[14] In fact, the commissioners all had a deep respect for the efforts of this little town.

With Rockford and DeKalb in such keen competition with each other, there was little chance for towns such as Oregon, Dixon, or Fulton to succeed; and there is little evidence that the commissioners actually considered any of their proposals very seriously. Oregon had little to offer other than the "inimitable summer resort" section of the Middle West with its "wooded hills and bluffs." No doubt it would have been a paradise for students. In the end, however, Oregon was unable to qualify as it did not have enough children in its schools for the model school.[15] The trustees had a somewhat different attitude toward Dixon because from the very beginning of the movement to secure an additional normal school in northern Illinois its role had been one of opposition. Dixon leaders had fought hardest in Springfield against Ellwood and Rosette; now they offered to transfer their private normal and business college to the State of Illinois in exchange for the new normal.

The commissioners, however, accompanied by Senator C. B. Farwell and Superintendent of Public Instruction Samuel M. Inglis, moved on to Fulton where a committee of citizens met them with carriages and took them around the city. They were shown several sites, two of which were on the bluffs in the northern part of the city overlooking the Mississippi River. Besides a gift of one of these sites, the city offered to lay water mains, put in electric lights, and build a temporary building for the school as well as to grant riparian rights along the river for a boathouse.[16]

When the commissioners arrived in DeKalb that Wednesday, 26 June, the city that was to be their last inspection was ready and waiting. It had been preparing for this occasion since 22 May when it was certain that northern Illinois was to have another normal school, and certainly no stone was left unturned in making preparations.[17] The "founding fathers"— Ellwood, Haish, and Glidden—along with a number of other prominent leaders in the city had hurriedly begun to improve DeKalb's physical features and had put a great deal of effort into the preparation of financial proposals that would attract the commissioners. Ellwood was fully convinced that whatever had to be done and whatever the cost might be, he and the city must meet it or they would forfeit all the time and money they had already spent to secure the legislation and executive approval. Haish also shared this view and was ready to increase his donation from $10,000 to $25,000 if necessary "to secure the school."[18]

The DeKalb proposal was considerably larger than the others in the number of acres to be given for the campus. Glidden, who was publisher of the *DeKalb Chronicle* as well as DeKalb's most respected citizen and the principal developer of the most successful and widely sold barbed wire fencing in America, had landholdings of some 787 acres in DeKalb township. Of this amount there was a tract of sixty-three acres in his original homestead adjoining the northwest side of the city. This was the city's first choice for the site.[19] It was an excellent field with prairie grass and a nice grove of trees that Glidden had used for his horse pasture and a race track, and was the grounds for the annual county fair.

A second site was sugested by Rosette. When one considers the development of the last seventy-five years in the particular area that he suggested, it is not difficult to see how perceptive and imaginative his idea was. He recommended the following location:

How would it do for DeKalb to locate the Normal School on the Sycamore road about two miles out. Let the county build a new court house about two miles south of Sycamore and then proceed to build one of the finest cities in the whole of America on the intervening territory? . . .

40

It could be done and then the cruel war would be over [between the two cities] and all the world would be at peace. 20,000 people in the two places—would build a town from DeKalb to Sycamore. DeKalb is ready to contract to furnish its half and build the school. What say you neighbors? . . . The street from DeKalb to Sycamore could be made as fine as was ever seen and a . . . scheme could be engineered to furnish the cash to do it with—why not try it?[20]

There is no record of any reply from the Sycamore citizens to this proposal.

Since there is no original contract preserved that sets forth the official figures in cash and "other valuable considerations," one must rely on scattered available sources. In the case of Ellwood, it appears quite certain that he contributed more than what has been attributed to him. On the final day, when the decision was to be made, the competition from Rockford and the efforts on the part of Freeport to get back into competition had increased to such an extent that Ellwood was given a real scare; so much so that he made the assertion later that "he stood ready to increase his bid to any amount necessary."

The following inquiry from Ellwood's attorney to the secretary of the Board of Trustees, when the total package from DeKalb was being legally assembled, seems to indicate that Ellwood did increase his original contribution. His attorney wrote as follows:

I understand that Mr. Ellwood personally made some agreements with the Board of Trustees, outside of the general proposition that was made by the city, and while I do not know what he may have done about it, as I have not had an opportunity to talk with him in regard to it, it seems to me that we should have copies of whatever he may have submitted in writing of this nature, for our files. I have a copy of the general proposition executed by Mr. E [llwood], Mr. Haish, Mr. Lett [Lott] and Bradt & Shipman, but of nothing else, and if there is anything further in which Mr. E. is directly interested I would be pleased if . . . we are furnished with a copy.[21]

41

The gift of land from Glidden and a small tract from Ellwood exceeded land gifts offered by other towns by more than twenty-one acres; it was without doubt the most valuable single gift of all the entire listings. To this generous gift Jacob Haish added $10,000 in cash for the construction of a gymnasium; it was used later, however, for books along with an additional $1,400 for library equipment.[22] The City Council, for their part of the proposal, agreed to lay sewers and pave the main street with brick as far west as the Kishwaukee bridge, and the county road commissioners agreed to extend the pavement along the south side of the proposed campus as far as the main entrance. The city also obligated itself to improve parts of the new addition with walks, drives, and landscape gardening from designs furnished by the Board of Trustees. The city councilmen consented to construct sidewalks from the railway station to the school grounds, and also made a cash offering of $10,000 to pay for the transportation of building materials so that there could be a better structure. The city also promised to donate $20,000 toward the building for electric lights and steam heating. One of the most important articles, dictated somewhat by the law itself, was the model school; and on this point the DeKalb School Board offered the best arrangement and facilities for student teaching. It was stated that their proposition was regarded by the trustees as "better than a perpetual endowment of $100,000 in the saving it will effect the state."[23]

Of all the DeKalb contributions, no doubt the ones that impressed the commissioners most were those of Colonel Ellwood. The *DeKalb Chronicle* reported that his promises consisted of $20,000 in cash and a $50,000 loan without interest as well as the development of a residential subdivision in his "horse pasture" adjoining the campus on the east side of the river.[24] Plans for the addition were designed in the form of a horseshoe by a landscape architect from Lincoln Park in Chicago.

The streets were to be macadamized between concrete curbs, and . . . concrete side walks and two-inch elm trees twenty-five feet apart were to be planted in the parking. The lots were to have at least an eighty-foot frontage. Just a fair price for a lot was all Mr. Ellwood wanted. It was not to be a real-estate boom. He also promised to build a suitable residence for the president and to build three "club-houses" for accommodation of students. Also, he was to build three residences suitable for faculty members. These were all to be had at a nominal rental.[25]

The DeKalb offering could certainly not compare with the picturesque scenery offered by Rockford and other Rock River cities, which all of these cities continually referred to as the decisive factor for the Board to use in making their decision. DeKalb, on the other hand, was fully aware that the one thing that would be more likely to decide the issue was not an attractive bluff overlooking a scenic river but rather the hard cold cash raised by the DeKalb citizens, which the others from the beginning were unable to match. Thus throughout the five weeks of competition it was DeKalb's primary emphasis on the pecuniary advantages that were so attractive to the Board, since the legislative appropriation of $50,000 was inadequate and circumscribed—none of it could be spent before 1 July 1896, and thereafter only in sums not to exceed $10,000 per month. The restrictions in the original legislation apparently reflect the lawmakers' intention to encourage the trustees to secure as large a cash contribution as possible from the city selected for the site. Without additional funds architectural plans could not be drawn and the new building could not be begun before 1 July 1896. It was without doubt the "jingle of the millionaire's gold" that eliminated Rockford when the trustees finally decided.[26]

When the Board of Trustees arrived in DeKalb after visiting the Fulton site, they were met by a number of DeKalb citizens and were shown the advantages of DeKalb as a location. Following their inspection of the Glidden land, they retired to the Ellwood home, where they were served a banquet.

Everything had been done by the local citizens to create a favorable impression. Knowing how much emphasis had been placed throughout the struggle upon the need for an attractive fresh-water stream, they made a concerted effort to give the Kishwaukee River a complete face-lifting. Anyone who has seen this river in mid-summer can fully appreciate how dry it gets and how poorly it impresses the sightseer. Fortunately nature had given some help in the process of brightening up not only the river but the grass and foliage as well, for on the night of 24 June and the afternoon and night of 25 June, the day before the trustees arrived, 1.83 inches of rain fell in the DeKalb area.[27]

This welcome rain coming at such a propitious time helped to change the general picture of the river and its environs. However, it was not sufficient to raise it to any extent, for at this time of year it required many inches of rainfall to change appreciably the water level, and besides, it had been so dry during the spring months that "observers were reporting dry wells and wheat failure." So thus a number of DeKalb individuals contrived a plan to transform a small section of the river into a picturesque sight of nature. They installed near the waterworks, which was located on the riverbank, a small dam across the "Kish" near the bridge and out of sight of the trustees, who were to be escorted over this route on their way to inspect the prospective campus. With this device the river could be raised several feet by draining the city water supply from its tank into the stream at the prearranged moment when the commissioners were crossing the bridge.[28]

Many embellishments of this event have survived in early recollections as well as belated reports in several neighboring newspapers; just how much is fact and how much is fiction is difficult to determine from the records. It is true that some of these newspaper accounts were published in derision by competing cities to point out the methods the DeKalb people had used to deceive the Board of Trustees; however, others who were not actively involved in the contest also published reports of it.[29]

The following account of how they carried out this effective transformation in time for the inspection tour is taken from the *Chadwick Items* and was reprinted in the *DeKalb Chronicle* more than a month after the occasion:

44

While it is not the best place for the school, having no natural advantages whatever, the devotion and self-sacrificing spirit displayed by the people excites admiration and all join in congratulating the barb city of the flats and unlimited mud. Two days before the commissioners visited the city on their tour of inspection, the people turned out en masse regardless of sex and scooped up all the slime and mud of the Kishwaukee slough, covered the bottom with gravel and pebbles, and then went without water two days so that the water supply from the water works could be turned into the "river." A large quantity of fine fish were introduced and the park put in proper shape, so that when the commissioners came they were surprised to find semi-tropical trees and vegetation growing in profusion in the park, and the inhabitants pulling fine brook trout from the Kishwaukee and using the water of the stream for culinary purposes.[30]

The *Oregon Republican* editor turned to satire to discuss the incident; however, he was not certain of its authenticity, for he did note that the whole story was only "rumored." His main interest was in the part dealing with the fishing scene. The city water had raised the river sufficiently so that it could hold a rowboat with a man equipped with fishing tackle. "It just happened that the day the Normal commissioners were at DeKalb this lone fisherman had a vigorous bite, and as . . . [they] were driving over the bridge he succeeded in landing a handsome fish. . . . Just where the fish hailed from is unknown, but it looked haggard and footsore, like it had tramped a long distance. . . . There is some talk of stocking the Kishwaukee with summer cured cod. They stand the pressure all right in either a wet or dry season." In his final words he turned to a more serious vein and thought this whole occurrence unfortunate since it proved conclusively to the Board of Trustees that there was good fishing in DeKalb.[31]

The Board of Trustees, following the DeKalb inspection, returned to Judge Goodrich's office in Chicago to begin the difficult task of making the final site selection. Delegations were requested to meet with the Board at 11 A.M. on 15 July so that each city representative could have a private audience. Nearly two hundred people from Rockford, Polo, Oregon, Fulton, Freeport, and DeKalb were present. The Board took nearly four hours listening and discussing the various propositions. In the case of Freeport, a controversy had developed over whether her delegations should be heard and also whether the Board should postpone the decision in order to make an inspection of the Freeport site. The Freeport delegation had arrived several hours late; one bid had already been opened; and there was a question as to the propriety of giving them a hearing. The commissioners divided on the issue. Ellwood, "sensing that a delay might be dangerous, called attention to the fact that Freeport had plenty of time in which to invite the commissioners to that city." He also pointed out that if exceptions were made in this case a number of other towns might want the same prerogative. By using his influence on the Freeport delegation and especially his old friend in the wire business, Daniel C. Stover, he was able to win his argument not to postpone action on the other bids.[32]

After this long discussion, the commissioners recessed for a half-hour lunch and then returned in secret session to make the long-awaited decision.

Excitement ran high with the Rockford and DeKalb delegations, especially since they were the two most serious contenders. It was obvious that the length of time spent in this session indicated that the commissioners had reached a deadlock. C. H. Deere and W. C. Garrard favored Rockford and I. L. Ellwood and Judge Goodrich were for DeKalb. The fifth member, Thomas J. Sparks, was undecided.[33] A Rockford newspaper reporter, in this tense moment of indecision, wrote, "A great deal of ante-room work is going on between Ellwood and the other commissioners." By 5 P.M., on the first regular ballot, they were able to secure a unanimous vote in favor of DeKalb.

With the long struggle for the location now over, it was time for the people of DeKalb to celebrate. News of the decision in Chicago was immediately dispatched to them, and

at once the town was in an uproar. Flags were displayed, fireworks exploded, horns tooted and every citizen alternately hugged himself and his neighbor. At six o'clock every factory whistle in the city turned loose and for fifteen minutes the din was so great that the denizens of sleepy old Sycamore, six miles away, were aroused from their accustomed torpor and straight way fell to wondering what it was all about. The racket at night was such as only a crowd of DeKalb enthusiasts can make. It was indescribable![34]

When Ellwood returned home from Chicago he was given a great reception, an outpouring of the people's gratitude to the one they honored most for this tremendous achievement. The procession was headed by a brass band which escorted him from the depot to his home and was described as the biggest affair ever seen in the town, embracing citizens from all walks of life.[35] Because of rain on 16 July, a "jubilation" triumph had to be postponed until the night of 20 July, at which time more than five thousand people were present. Many came by train from different cities, and most of DeKalb's civic and social organizations participated with plenty of fireworks.[36]

With this sudden outburst of community spirit and pride changes were soon made and new ideas suggested overnight. On the day of the final decision, Glidden and Rosette, publisher and editor of the *DeKalb Chronicle*, decided that if the citizens were going to have telephones, an interurban railway, electric lights, paved streets, and a normal school, certainly the time "is ripe for a daily paper." Popular subscriptions were also suggested by Rosette in order to engage an artist to execute paintings of Glidden, Ellwood, and Haish so that they could be placed, as a tribute, in the main reception room of the new building.[37] The city of DeKalb, always proud of its successful baseball team, also decided to honor the new school by changing the team's name to the "DeKalb Normals."

It was proposed by many DeKalb citizens as well as the Republican press in the Eighth Congressional District that Ellwood should be rewarded with a seat in Congress. The following press account testified as to how he was esteemed by his party:

Mr. Ellwood is a true and staunch republican, loyal to the cause of [tariff] protection and a safe man to be put in the halls of congress. The rousing republican majority that the Eighth district rolls up at every election comes largely from his persistent and watchful efforts. No one could be truer to the party of Lincoln, Grant, Logan and Garfield than that big hearted I. L. Ellwood.[38]

And to be sure that Jacob Haish was not overlooked by the DeKalb people in the melee of excitement, the *Aurora Blade* carried a special tribute to him which was reprinted in the *DeKalb Chronicle.*

[He is a] quiet, unassuming gentleman who has by his liberality, business enterprise and love of home done as much for the good name and business interests of DeKalb as anyone within its borders. He is also a barb wire millionair [sic]. . . . But he is not a politician and consequently he is not coated over so thick with newspaper gush. In politics Mr. Haish is a democrat.[39]

DeKalb also did what other American cities generally do: the names of these illustrious citizens were given to streets, buildings, and schools.

Letters of commendation poured in from all over the country and Rosette claimed that he received three hundred at the *Chronicle* office alone. Prominent schoolmen and women were lavish in their praise; a brief quote from two of them will illustrate their attitude toward this educational achievement. Cook, who was to be the school's first president, wrote to Rosette: "Three cheers and a tiger for DeKalb! Accept my sincere congratulations." O. T. Bright, Cook County superintendent of schools, congratulated Rosette for his "splendid services to the cause of education in this state. . . . We are fully aware of the fact that we never could have secured the . . . Normal School . . . without the work which you and Mr. Ellwood have rendered."[40]

Cities too sent congratulatory messages, knowing full well what tremendous effort was necessary to secure the legislation as well as the site. From Aurora came such liberal praise: "Your site is beautiful. Your donations are princely. Your people are loyal and enterprising and you deserve the prize." The *Harvard Herald* also said: "It is a great victory for DeKalb, as well as Col. I. L. Ellwood, it's [*sic*] public-spirited and generous-hearted citizen, whose gallant fight won the day. . . . The *Herald* is glad that DeKalb proved victorious." [41]

Those cities who competed for the prize, however, were disappointed, and a few were caustic and extremely bitter; some blamed the governor and some accused Ellwood of using his millions to buy the legislature as well as the trustees. Immediately following the decision a number of editors, including those at Oregon, Polo, and Rochelle, urged their readers to take legal action on the normal-school location, claiming that it was a put-up job and that the "school was fixed for DeKalb before it was boodled [bribed] through the legislature." [42] Cooler minds prevailed, however, and they changed their attack upon DeKalb from the courts to the columns of their newspapers.

"Poor Polo" had a double sorrow to bear; she not only lost the prize that seemed within her grasp at one time but also had the misfortune of receiving a false notification during the closing moments of the final decision that she was victorious. The *Dixon Sun* reported that "some ungodly scamp sent a telegram to Polo that Polo had secured the Normal School, and signed the name of . . . one of the committee. . . . Thereat the populace became wild with enthusiasm" and enormous preparations were arranged to meet the victorious representatives when they returned. But when the train pulled into the station the "assembled thousands furled their flags . . . and like the Arab silently melted away to weep . . . for 'The Lost Cause.'" [43]

Governor Altgeld and the trustees also came in for some criticism in the press. The *Rockford Republican,* when the decision was announced, carried these harsh words: "The fact that Altgeld had anything to do with it was enough to prove it was rotten. . . ." This same paper declared that there were "several high grade ornamental liars on the normal school board." [44] The *Rockford Daily Register-Gazette,* in citing adverse press reactions, quoted the *Chicago Post:* "The location . . . at DeKalb is calling forth all kinds of ridicule of the commissioners for selecting such a site, when picturesque locations and as great inducements were offered" by some other towns. Moreover, they believed "that legislators who make vast appropriations of money for state schools in towns where millionaires live are very stupid, to put it mild."

The one item in the DeKalb offering that caused the most criticism by the Rockford people was the high evaluation figure given the Glidden acreage—a figure of $700 per acre or a total of about $46,000. When this large sum was combined with the other contributions of the city, township, and citizens, it placed the total DeKalb proposal "$50,000 more than any other town." This incensed the Rockfordites, for they insisted that the Glidden tract was highly inflated and that $100 per acre would have been a good price for this "marshy land." [45] Rockford had placed an evaluation on their "superior" tract of forty-four acres at $40,000; if the Board had reduced the DeKalb land evaluation to about $7,000, it would have placed the Rockford proposal in a much better light. But no changes were made and even though Rockford had lost the normal she still retained her pride; in defeat their dignified state senator David Hunter was led to boast: "Rockford did not need the school as much as the school needed Rockford." Other Rockford citizens were less antagonistic than the senator and expressed more charitable sentiments for the "live wire" city.

The *Rochelle Herald* criticized the selection by stating that "there was not a city that the committee visited but what offered a more beautiful and attractive location than the one offered by DeKalb." Polo complained that the trustees picked the lowest spot in northern Illinois where "health and sanitary conditions were completely lost sight of. It was a money consideration and how easily accomplished."[46] Dixon, however, accepted the inevitable: "We have no complaints, DeKalb is a good place for the school. Mr. Ellwood is a very pleasant gentleman."

In reflecting upon this decision to build the normal school in DeKalb, one might question the advisability of placing such an institution in a small and out-of-the-way rural town, especially when a large and more culturally advanced city like Rockford was an alternative. DeKalb possessed no libraries or art galleries or learned people who might serve both the college and community as inspirational leaders—all of which were necessary if the school were to succeed and develop intellectually and culturally. DeKalb, moreover, not only lacked these essentials but had also been built around a major industry under the firm control of the three "patriarchs." In fact the normal-school students had to wait thirty-two years before having an adequate public library in the community.

A normal school, perhaps more than the traditional academic college, needed community assets in order to offer some supplementary sources of enlightenment and stimulation in various fields of the arts for the students and faculty alike. Such training institutions were not academically inclined, since their curricula were mainly directed toward preparing young people, often with limited background, to teach in the common schools.

In recent years the University has had difficulty in trying to expand into the professional areas of law, medicine, engineering, and agriculture as well as to accommodate various types of institutes. These important branches of a university are generally the most expensive and require the facilities of an urban center; in places like DeKalb they suffer for want of staff and support.

Crowd gathered to watch cornerstone laying, 1 October 1895

Launching
the New Normal

A FINAL burst of community energy and enthusiasm came
during the months before the opening of the school. For
nearly four years the people had waited in anticipation of this
event, but never were they certain when the state legislature
would finally furnish the necessary funds. Each biennial appropriation after 1895 made it possible to complete a little
more construction, but now it was hoped that the 1899 session
of the General Assembly would not only provide funds to
complete the building but also to finance the opening and
operation of the Normal. Day by day, from the opening of the
Assembly in January until the middle of April, DeKalb waited,
realizing that if sufficient funds were made available, it would
be "a day and night race for five months" in order "to finish and
equip the school by Oct. 1st." [1]

Appropriation matters were moving toward a decision in
the legislature. On 31 March 1899, the Chicago newspapers
were certain that sufficient funds to finish the building and
open the school would pass, even though DeKalb people had
no information at the time. But by 13 April, word was received
in DeKalb that the Board of Trustees had let all contracts to

finish the building, and an appropriation of $165,000 had passed both houses of the Assembly and had gone to Governor Tanner's desk for his signature.

With the assurance of this appropriation, the city began at once to organize for the opening. Rosette was still in the forefront, pleading that "every good citizen of DeKalb should do all in his power to advertise" the coming of the big event in spite of the few "calamity howlers. . . . Now is the time to commence to boom DeKalb."

A great deal of work had to be done before several hundred students could find a college home in DeKalb; no dormitories existed and only a few new houses had been built for them. Moreover, new faculty members as well as the usual influx of individuals in search of business opportunities made it evident that the housing problem would be critical.

During the spring and summer, surveys were made for additional living quarters; no families in any part of town were overlooked. More families wanted students to house than to feed. By early summer there was still a serious shortage of "cottages" and this condition seemed critical to the editor of the *Chronicle*, enough so at least to stir him into action. He made an appeal to the citizens on the basis of what might happen if board and rooms were not supplied for these young people. In his opinion, he predicted, there would be no doubt "one or two big dormitories or apartment houses built to accommodate them"; this, he believed, would not serve the best interests of the city or the school, and to prevent this from happening he urged those who were able to get "busy and build 150 six to eight room cottages."[2] Construction was moving along in Colonel Ellwood's addition with three large homes—one for the president of the new normal school; one for the Colonel's son, E. Perry; and one for Professor Charles McMurry, who was to head the training school—and several others of less pretentious character were being planned, mostly for prospective faculty members. DeKalb was waiting and working toward the opening day of their school in September.

Soon after the Board of Trustees had been appointed, it began to call for plans for the main building.[3] Five or six architects had been working nearly two months, and at the Chicago meeting on 15 July 1895, a subcommittee of three members was appointed to select one of the plans. The architects sought suggestions from several prominent normal school leaders in Illinois, especially from John W. Cook, who was to be the new school's first president. Cook's insistence that the interior arrangements match his particular theories of education helped to make the building one of the "finest structures for Normal School purposes thus far built in this country."[4]

The exterior design of the building was not left entirely in the hands of the architect. Governor Altgeld took an enthusiastic, if not arbitrary, interest in the architecture that was used for a number of public buildings built during his four years in office. He not only requested the opportunity to sit in judgment of such plans but, in some cases where opposition to his views was expressed, he would use his personal influence and the expertise he had in building construction to achieve his particular wishes.[5] As one writer has noted, the governor was "particularly fond of a certain style of architecture, usually referred to as Tudor Gothic, or the English-castle style. It resembled the old castles along the Rhine River in Germany."

Governor Altgeld, in order to substantiate his interest in the subject, called attention to the travesty that had already been perpetrated upon the people of Illinois—that of the 160-odd public buildings already built, scarcely one had any character and "nearly all of them look like warehouses or shops." His basic recommendations, in order to redress this deficiency, were that buildings should first of all be completely fire-proofed, since the original building at Southern Illinois State Normal University was lost by fire in 1883; and secondly, that separate and unattached structures such as these individual school buildings should have an impressive architectural exterior which could be obtained "by simply carrying . . . the wall, above the cornice line, and there breaking the lines in such a way as to produce small towers, battlements, etc."[6]

There seems no evidence of opposition to the governor's ideas about the appearance of the northern Normal such as he experienced with President Draper at the University of Illinois, where in spite of his persistent zeal, he finally was obliged to admit defeat. Colonel Ellwood in three letter exchanges with the Board and the governor on this matter indicates a willingness on the part of the trustees to cooperate. On 19 July 1895, four days after the site selection, Ellwood wrote to one of his colleagues on the Board expressing his desire to consult with the governor about the plans:

While I know the matter of showing the plans for the proposed school building to Governor Altgeld was spoken of at our meeting . . . I desire to mention it once more, as I think it is very essential that this is done, as he has had a great deal of experience in building and is in position to give us valuable advice upon the subject.

By 10 August, the Board had decided to have its next meeting in Springfield so that they might "call upon the Governor for the purpose of looking over the plans and specifications." It is not known whether they saw him personally, but Ellwood replied as follows on 19 August to a letter from the executive secretary which set forth the governor's desires:

On my return here I find your kind letter containing suggestions of the Governor with reference to the school buildings, which I assure you would have been acknowledged before this but for my absence. However, I now wish you to thank him for me, assuring him that I not only appreciate his kindness in this matter, but esteem him highly for the interest he is evincing in having these buildings worthy of the great state of Illinois. I am obliged to leave here again almost immediately . . . but it shall be my purpose to see that his wishes are followed as closely as possible in this matter.[7]

The Board of Trustees at their Chicago meeting on 26 August found that the subcommittee had selected two sets of plans from the sixteen submitted, leaving the final choice to the Board. After some deliberation they accepted the plans of Charles E. Brush of Chicago and also engaged him as the supervising architect.[8] The Board received bids from six contractors, and on 10 October they accepted the bid of $145,155.44 submitted by William J. McAlpine of Dixon, Illinois.[9] Excavation was to begin as soon as possible.

With these major decisions resolved, the Board now moved with all speed to begin construction. Tentative dates had been selected for the ground-breaking and cornerstone-laying ceremonies; one for 17 September and the other on 3 October, later changed to 1 October. On 11 September, Judge Goodrich of the Board, architect Brush, and the landscape gardener, assisted by Ellwood, Glidden, Haish, and Hunt, staked out the site for the new building a half-mile from the center of DeKalb on the fringe of a beautiful grove of trees.

Breaking the ground was a brief exercise; yet it stirred the imagination. It would be difficult to improve upon the unknown author who reported the event on that day of 17 September 1895, from the highest knoll in the Glidden pasture. Here the "Castle on the Hill" was to be built about equidistant from the Kishwaukee River and its tiny tributary to the west.

At 11 o'clock today Mr. Glidden, Mr. Haish, Senator Hunt, W. L. Ellwood [the Colonel's son], Mr. Fisk, Clinton Rosette, of the Committee on Ceremony, Architect Bush [sic], Landscape Gardener Nelson, Engineer Merriam, Joseph Bale of the Chicago Times-Herald, and about 200 citizens of DeKalb made their way to the site of the new school building. Mr. Haish, always original had a plan for having the ground broken with a lead pencil. He had the pencil all prepared. Senator Hunt took it and asked Mr. Glidden to break the sod. He did so with a neat speech, the most impressive part of which was when he said: "I bought this land from the government in 1850. I have lived upon it ever since. I now surrender it for the benefit of future generations." He broke the ground and the pencil he used will be deposited in the corner stone. Active work has now begun and will not stop until the Northern Illinois Normal is done.[10]

Much activity in the city and county during the summer and fall of 1895 was concerned with the mobilization of the citizens into numerous committees to prepare for the laying of the cornerstone on Tuesday, 1 October. It would be difficult to find a better example of the American committee system or a more baroque spirit than was demonstrated during this period in advertising and promoting the coming event. Yet the avowed purpose of this elaborate system was surely for no other reason than to promote the welfare of the new normal school.[11]

The entire effort was concentrated in the hands of an executive committee composed of seven of the most prominent citizens in the community. Clinton Rosette was the president, and there were at least fifty auxiliary committees, to which were assigned the essential activities dealing with the parade, speeches, press, housing, food and refreshments, transportation, sports, fireworks, police, receptions, and publicity, to mention only the more important ones. A. W. Fisk, executive secretary of the Ceremony Committee, had as many as fifteen aides, and during this period he carried on a vast correspondence as well as extensive travels in order to handle the numerous activities and to secure the talent. This was all to be done on a budget of $6,000, mostly raised in the community. Special trains had to be arranged weeks in advance; hundreds of tents had to be borrowed from various armories and camp grounds to be used by organizations, township groups, and dignitaries as their headquarters for a predicted attendance of 35,000 to 40,000 people. Chicago, according to the *Times-Herald*, was requested to supply a team of detectives to keep an eye on uninvited guests of the light-fingered variety.[12]

The townships of the county were all organized into committees of representative men to aid in publicizing the event, and even the editors of the other counties in northern Illinois were brought to DeKalb as a group so they could be properly entertained and encouraged to support the occasion. The county school teachers were given a holiday, and many civic societies, ball teams, marching fraternal bands, and military groups were also given special invitations. And again Colonel Ellwood issued a personal invitation to the governor and his wife, as he had done at the close of the legislative session, to be his special guest at his home and also to "let me know upon

Tents set up for cornerstone laying, 1 October 1895

what train you will arrive [so] that we may meet you at the station." [13]

The biggest event in the history of DeKalb finally arrived on a clear but windy and slightly chilly day. People began to arrive by the thousands, surging all over the city. In fact, one of the observers reported that there were so many milling about that the sidewalks would not contain them and "for blocks the side streets were jammed with rigs and wagons used by the neighboring visitors in flocking into the city. The railroad yards were 'full-up' with emptied passenger coaches and still the excursion trains continued to arrive."

Activities began early and continued throughout the entire day and on into the night. The first event was at 9 A.M. when Governor Altgeld was escorted by the fraternal orders and other civic societies to the fairgrounds where he delivered his speech before a 1,000–seat grandstand which had been erected for the occasion. Other speakers were John W. Cook; Judge Goodrich; Orville T. Bright, Cook County superintendent of schools; Rev. Frank W. Gunsaulus, president of Armour Institute; and I. L. Ellwood, who gave the welcome address. Several musical numbers were performed by the Schumann Lady Quartette, the Imperial Quartette, the Pullman Band, and the DeKalb Choral Society. Special deference was shown to the two General Assembly members, Michael Stoskopfs and David T. Littler, who were the legislative leaders responsible for the normal school legislation; both were also speakers on this occasion. [14]

The governor's speech placed much emphasis upon the nonmaterial values of life: "something that cannot be purchased across the counter, and does not depend upon the market; something that does not grow in a night, but must be nurtured by truth and illuminated by wisdom." He noted with some pride the progress that Illinois was making in the field of education and the superior position her institutions had attained: "The intellectual and literary activity is already being shifted from the hills of New England to the prairies of Illinois, and the time is near at hand when from this State will go out the most advanced ideas in all the fields of human knowledge. . . . In education we have laid the foundations for institutions that will grow stronger with the centuries."

Cornerstone laying crowd, 1 October 1895

From these convictions on the value of education, he turned his attention to his immediate task:

We have met to lay the corner-stone of an institution that is designed to produce the perfect teacher, who shall in the school-room make of the young, as near as human effort can, perfect men and women. If this institution shall instill the right spirit, it shall teach the diversity of toil, if it shall make of the youth of the land strong, independent and liberty-loving men and women, then only the centuries can measure the good that will flow from it.

Institutions frequently partake of the character of the people whose influence surrounds them. When the question arose last winter of founding a new institution . . . in the northwestern part of the State we favored the measure, not simply because it was just to this great section of the State, but for the higher reason that here was found, . . . the industry, intelligence, the sturdy character and the high aim which would make an institution a success. Above all things, we want this institution to stand on the basic principle that all men are born equal, and that only industry, intelligence and effort shall lead to preferment.

If I had not believed that here a university would be free from a weakening dilettanteism, that here industry and character would rank above all other things, then the bill would have been vetoed. . . . Let me say to you now that should it at any time in the future be used as a convenience by the trustees to furnish places for a living for relatives and favorites so that the standing of the university would be lowered, then go to the Executive at Springfield, no matter who he may be, and demand a change. . . .

Now, my fellow citizens, . . . I care not for your politics, I care not what you think of this or that public man, I care not to what sect you belong, or at what shrine you kneel, but I do ask that you bring your best offering to the . . . future of this country.[15]

Noon was a real test for the local citizens. They had literally thousands to feed, even though large numbers brought their own lunch baskets and many vendors were on Main Street selling hot dogs and sandwiches. It was, in fact, an old-fashioned family picnic on a grand scale. A force of 150 people was conscripted to hand out tons of food to the multitude from the huge central tent. No one was to be left out, and the oft-repeated cry, "Are you hungry?" was constantly heard throughout the woods along the south edge of the campus. All food was served free of charge to those on the normal school grounds, refreshment stands were set up to quench their thirst, and there was plenty of food left over. Bands played throughout the noonday period.[16]

Following the lunch, the "Grand Parade" began to form to march to the building site to lay the cornerstone. The Pullman Band led the march in which twenty-five other bands were dispersed among the nine divisions made up of various organizations and fifty beautiful floats. The entire Masonic Grand Lodge of the Illinois A.F. and A.M. marched with 700 delegates in white aprons. The Knights Templar were there, representing 713 lodges in the state—all in full regalia. The ninth division, consisting of the Grand Marshal of the Grand Lodge, Governor Altgeld and his staff, and members of the legislature, all in carriages, led the parade.[17]

The Grand Lodge had been in convention in Chicago and came as a body in special trains to perform the ceremony. Some 2,500 or more other Masons were also in DeKalb. By 3 P.M. the miles-long parade finally arrived at the spot where the stone was already hanging by a derrick above a completed section of the normal-school building. Swen F. Parson and his large chorus opened the ceremonies with the singing of "America."

After a few brief speeches, Joseph Glidden opened the formal exercises by inviting the Grand Lodge to lay the cornerstone. Leroy A. Goddard, the Grand Master, along with his officers, performed the appropriate ritual using the "corn, wine and oil brought from Jerusalem for the purpose." The customary box was deposited in the cavity of the stone and a list of its contents read; since no record has been preserved, all that is known today are the few items mentioned by the newspaper reporters: the Prayer Book of the Episcopal Church, a copy of the *Inter-Ocean* for 1 October, several war relics, a history of

DeKalb, the pencil used to break the ground, a set of United States coins and fractional currency, and the first shoe produced by the Leonard-Atkinson shoe factory in DeKalb.[18] Governor Altgeld was given a silver trowel and was asked to assist in spreading the cement that was to encase the box. After this ceremony as many as five thousand spectators moved to the ball field to watch a baseball game between Pullman and DeKalb and the football game between Armour and Rush Medical College.

The evening program was an all-musical one featuring the quartets, the Pullman Band, and the DeKalb Choral Society. Immediately after these exercises an enormous display of fireworks which lasted for nearly an hour was presented to about twenty thousand spectators. "One set piece entitled 'The Falls of the Kishwaukee' blazed away for 45 minutes, while $300 went up in smoke," observed a reporter. At the close of the pyrotechnics the executive committee concluded "Ceremony Day" with a reception and dance with music by the Pullman Band at the Chronicle Hall. No one doubted that it was the greatest day in the history of DeKalb.

After the cornerstone ceremony, when only a few mounds of stone were in evidence, construction of the building went forward as planned. Specifications in the original legislation outlined the following restrictions:

The buildings shall not be more than two stories in height, and be constructed upon the most approved plan for use, and shall be of sufficient capacity to accommodate not less than one thousand students, with the officers and necessary attendants. The outside walls to be of hewn stone or brick; partition walls of brick, or equally good fire-proof material; roof of slate, and the whole buildings made fire resisting, and so constructed as to be warmed in the most healthful and economical manner, with ample ventilation in all of its parts.[19]

Some of the main features of this large building were its library accommodations; laboratories; gymnasium (eighty by eighty-five feet and furnished with baths); a large study hall; museum room; art room; literary society rooms; as well as thirty-six school and class rooms and a suitable number of cloak and lunch rooms. But with all of these it was the auditorium that should be especially noted, for it was not only spacious but capable of seating as many as twelve hundred people and was decorated with the hope of inspiring the students who would gather there daily for general exercises. Around the cornice of the hall "appear heads of such notable characters in government and war as Washington, Lincoln, Grant and Logan; in education Pestalozzi, Froebel, Herbart, Comenius, Agassiz, our own Dr. [William T.] Harris, and the reverend Dr. [Edward A.] Sheldon, for so many years the president of the great normal school at Oswego, New York." [20] A few other distinguished faces, representing various fields of learning, were also there.

Construction of the building was vigorously pressed the first year until the $50,000 non-interest-bearing loan from Colonel Ellwood was expended. The legislative session in 1897 made an additional appropriation of $75,000. This, by the spring of 1899, had brought construction to such a stage that the legislature decided to add to the nearly $100,000 biennial appropriation an additional $66,000 in order to allow the school to open and to finance the operating expenses for the two succeeding years, 1899–1901. [21]

The school was officially opened on 12 September 1899, in spite of the many unfinished parts of the building. On 2 January 1900, the Board of Trustees met and accepted the completed edifice from the architect and contractor, "paying them in full" and releasing them from all further obligations. The trustees were generous in their praise of these two individuals for the fine manner and sense of responsibility they showed during those four years and were "unanimous in the opinion that the building was in every respect up to the agreement entered into. . . ." There had been absolutely no friction from the beginning to the completion of the building. The trustees had only the highest praise for the builders, claiming that it was not only their unanimous opinion that "it is the best piece of public work for the money ever constructed in the United States" but that this judgment was also "supported by expert opinion" as well. All bills against the institution were audited and paid, and the building stood absolutely clear of any encumbrances.

Once plans for the building and bids for construction had been accepted, the next big step in opening the school was the selection of a president. As was the practice in those days, the trustees assumed entire responsibility. The problem was somewhat simplified, however, since there appeared to be but one choice in the minds of most people. John Williston Cook, president of Illinois State Normal, had been closely connected with the new normal-school movement before it had reached the legislative stage and thereafter as an advisor for the four years of its construction. His further credentials were that he was considered an outstanding schoolman, and he was well known as a teacher, lecturer, writer, and administrator. There was no doubt from the beginning on the part of the trustees that he was their choice and that they would make every effort to secure him for this position. On the day the bill passed the committee on appropriations in the House of Representatives at Springfield, Senator D. D. Hunt was the first to put forward his name; Colonel Ellwood and other DeKalb leaders had always thought of Cook as their favorite candidate. As early as 11 August 1895, sentiment was building in his favor; the editor of the *Chronicle* expressed it as follows:

President Cook is recognized as one of the very best equipped Normal School men in the United States, and the trustees of the Northern school are going to pay very close attention to any suggestion they may obtain from him about . . . their school. If President Cook should find himself in a position to entertain a proposition from them, there is little doubt that he would be tendered the presidency of this school. . . . It would be a great hit for the Northern Illinois Normal School if it could put John W. Cook and the faculty that he would select, at the head of this new school.[22]

Altgeld, probably 1898

The Board, a group of professional and business men who knew little or nothing of how such a school operated, was eager to find a person whose reputation as a schoolman was established so that the school could get a good start. Cook was without doubt the best qualified schoolman; when Senator Cullom was asked his opinion, he remarked: "If I had had to select a President for a Normal School, I should have gone straight as a railroad could carry me to John W. Cook." Cook continued to gain favor in succeeding years among prominent schoolmen of the state; and as the normal building neared completion, the Board of Trustees on 18 April 1899, finally interviewed and offered him by unanimous vote the presidency of the school. Cook was not completely uninterested in this position, and the Board was quite confident that he would finally accept after he had had a week or so to consider it thoroughly.[23]

It was a major decision and not an easy one for Cook, for there were a number of factors involved. One of these was that unless he could convince his colleague, Charles A. McMurry, to come with him and take command of the Practice School, he did not want to make the change. McMurry was recognized as one of the leading authors, lecturers, and authorities on principles and methods of teaching. He had received his doctorate from Halle University in Germany, and he also had an enviable personality for this sensitive and often troublesome phase of pedagogy. With his years of experience as administrator and teacher in the public schools, he was, according to Cook, the one who could make the greatest contribution at the new Normal. After some discussion and persuasion, McMurry finally decided to make the move. But this was only the first hurdle and Cook continued to seek things of "extraordinary inducement other than pecuniary" from the Board.

With the exception of one year in a public school at Brimfield, Illinois, Cook had spent his entire academic life and professional career at Illinois State Normal. During those thirty-six years—three as a student, twenty-four as a teacher, and nine as a president—he was completely satisfied with every aspect of the institution with the exception of one. In his own words,

Altgeld, another view, probably 1898

The practice school was too small to permit him to work out one problem in which he had become profoundly interested. Because of the small size of the ordinary practice school the practice work has usually been limited to the instruction of classes, hence the Normal Pupils had no practical experience in taking charge of rooms. The ideal practice school will contain not only opportunities for class teaching but also for opportunities for room charge until they have been carefully prepared to enter upon the complete work of the public school with every assurance of success. With such a practice school a Normal school can settle the question of one's ability to become a teacher and thus save their pupils from the disastrous failures that so many graduates make. If it appears that one lacks the natural adaptation to the work of the teacher he can prepare for some other calling.

For such a practice school nothing less than a system of public schools would be adequate. If Normal students could have a system of public schools in which to do their practice work, the situation would be ideal, for they would be anticipating their life work under trained experts.[24]

Cook outlined a proposal incorporating such a system to the DeKalb School Board. They were to place their public elementary schools at the disposal of the normal school for the purpose of practice teaching. This proposal was discussed at length by DeKalb citizens and their board, and it met with their approval; however, for some years there was discontent among various groups in the city. It was either the long distance and difficulties involved in getting to and from the normal school or the more persistently controversial issue of having normal-school students practicing upon DeKalb's children that was disturbing. Under this revolutionary idea, as Cook conceived it, there would be two practice schools—one in the normal building and another in one of the city schools—each comprising all eight grades. The practice work was to be supervised by critic teachers, all of whom were under the general charge of the director of the training schools and all of whom were members of the Normal faculty. The superintendent of the school system would be employed by the city and would be a member of the Normal staff.[25]

A third demand was made on the Board before Cook would accept the position and that was that he "have the selection of the faculty, without interference on the part of anyone." The Board without hesitation assured him of this privilege in a unanimous resolution stating "that no one would be considered as an employee unless nominated by the president of the school." This was an empty gesture, for several of them tried to influence his decisions.[26] Ellwood especially was embarrassed, for he had made personal promises to a legislator at Springfield when it was necessary to secure votes. He had received many letters from prospective candidates for positions in the school but with the exception of one or two cases he forthrightly mailed them on to Cook. In the case of Senator C. F. Berry, a Republican from Hancock County, he did make a genuine effort to influence Cook's judgment:

Is there any prospect of taking care of Mr. Berry's candidate for a position with the faculty in some way that he may be reconciled, in view of the promises that were made to him? You are aware of the condition of things at the time these promises were made to him, and the fact is, that Mr. Berry has a right to accuse me personally perhaps more than anyone else, . . . But of course, I shall stand with the balance of the trustees to confirm any appointments you may make, but have a lingering hope that this being the only unpleasant thing resulting from promises I have made, that in some way it can be adjusted.[27]

A number of letters were exchanged among Ellwood, Berry, and Cook before this matter was resolved. The senator had a candidate from his school in Carthage for the mathematics position that Cook was trying to fill, and he expected Cook to accept her, since Ellwood had promised him a position. The numerous exchanges between the senator and Cook were long and at times rather heated; finally, to please Ellwood, he agreed to examine this woman's credentials and teaching experience. If he found that she was unqualified, he would reserve the right to refuse her the position. This was the case and he forthrightly notified the senator that he would have to refuse. In a letter to Ellwood he said that this "Berry business gives me a good deal of trouble. It wouldn't if his candidate were only suitable but she is of limited scholarship, lack of culture and would be wholly out of place on our faculty. . . . I would accept one of his if she were suitable." [28]

Ellwood in one other case tried to influence Cook indirectly through the office of Governor Tanner, who had succeeded Altgeld; but as he said to his correspondent, he was not too hopeful "for as you are aware I was not a Tanner man in the convention and he knows it, for I have told him that as between him and Mr. Hopkins I am a Hopkins man." The record does not show whether the governor appealed in behalf of Ellwood or not. It does show, however, that a strong effort was made for a certain "Mr. Smith of Fulton County" and after some discussion, the governor agreed to the same understanding as the one made with Senator Berry.

Cook carefully reviewed the credentials and then informed the governor that he must decline his candidate in order to protect the normal school from such unmeritorious people. The governor's reply indicated the faith he had in Cook's leadership: "It is not my purpose to cripple you in the slightest . . . degree." He assured Cook that he would accept his judgment, for "you are in a better position to judge." [29]

When Cook accepted the offer from the Board of Trustees at Northern, to take effect on 1 July 1899, he was so well known among educational leaders and especially normal-school presidents that he was often referred to as the "Crown Prince of Teacher Education." He was born on 20 April 1844, in Oneida County, New York. When he was seven years old, his family came west to McLean County, Illinois, where they resided before moving to Kappa, Illinois. In this small town he spent his boyhood, finishing what education was available and then starting to work at various jobs within the community before finally deciding in 1862 to enter Illinois State Normal University. He was graduated from there in 1865, taught one year in the Brimfield, Illinois, public schools, and then returned to his alma mater, where he rose gradually from principal of the grammar department of the Model School to the presidency

John W. Cook
first president, 1899–1919

before being invited to Northern in 1899. At fifty-five years of age he had already given thirty-three years of service to the cause of normal-school education at various levels. During that time he became one of the most popular educational leaders at conventions, institutes, and public forums. He was a person of many talents, and his achievements were quite remarkable, especially for one who had only a normal-school education and three honorary degrees.[30]

He took pride in his versatility. He could preach sermons, sing about "cockles and mussels" in his tenor voice, compose poems, write books, tell stories and jokes, and exhort his audiences, especially students and faculty, with adages, aphorisms, epigrams, and proverbs, or "Cookisms," as some called them. He was also able to associate with all classes of society, from the flagman at the railroad crossing to the governors of the state.

In his relationships with students and faculty alike he was a perfectionist—straightforward, sometimes stern and sarcastic—in his demands. No one was likely to try to circumvent his wishes; however, he was never personal or vindictive when dealing with those under his jurisdiction. In fact, his over-all professional attitude was hopeful and optimistic, all of which helped to build the respect of those who worked with him during his many years as an administrator. He insisted on meeting all students individually and talking over their backgrounds and intentions when they entered the Normal as freshmen, thus making it possible for him to know them personally as well as to keep a tight rein on their future activities. There was no doubt that he was a firm believer in the theory and practice of *in loco parentis.*

The new students and faculty, upon entering the Normal, were soon to learn the fundamental rules and regulations laid down and enforced by him, and in case some might forget he periodically called attention to them. According to some early faculty remembrances he did not hesitate to reprimand students and faculty alike for not leaving their rubbers at the outside door—for he had an equal abhorrence of dirt or mud or tardiness. Faculty or student participation in the establishment or enforcement of institutional codes of behavior had not yet arrived. He had no fear of his students; in most cases it was just the reverse, for he gave the impression that he was the master of any situation, and at no time did he shy away from a controversy or an opportunity to enforce his ideas. His physical image also reinforced the students' feelings toward him, for he was overweight and walked with his stomach thrust forward, tending to produce an image of a dominant individual. He worked long hours on his many speeches, class lectures, letters, and publications, often until the wee hours of the morning. On occasion his wife had to remind him that it was time to come home. He was not only a hard worker himself but he expected everyone else in the institution to be the same. All his life he drove himself relentlessly and rarely did he avail himself of a vacation; in fact he utterly disdained them and much preferred teaching in summer institutes or traveling long distances to give a series of lectures.[31]

During his long tenure as a teacher, it was his firm conviction that teaching was the primary function for his faculty as well as for himself; all other phases of college life, including that of administering the Normal, were secondary in importance. In his classes of senior students he did much more than just instruct in psychology, philosophy, or the history of education; he also had a vital interest in their personal lives. His teaching techniques created some anxiety among his students, for he had a system of recitation in his classroom that caused some fear, especially upon the first encounter. One former student recalled that Cook loved to delve into the minds of the students—especially the younger ones—to see how little they knew; another student claimed that many were afraid of him in or out of the classroom but they were not certain why.

At the opening of his class sessions he would usually lecture for a few minutes on the topic of the day. Then he would pick a certain paragraph and ask one of his students to rise and read the selection, after which she was to explain the passage. While she was still standing, President Cook might take over the discussion at any moment and present some of his ideas, which could keep the student standing for several minutes longer. At this time, if he was satisfied with the recitation, he would permit her to sit down; if not, he would commence a probing exercise in order to secure further insights, maybe even sending her to the blackboard. Immediately following each individual recitation, often lasting as long as ten to fifteen minutes, he would proceed to record the grade immediately in the record-book which always lay visible on his desk for the whole class to ponder. The marks they received from these exercises—sometimes two or three in a quarter—were vitally important in determining their final grades.[32]

Even with these austere and somewhat harsh mannerisms, he radiated a fatherly image and a certain charisma that captivated the faculty and students and increased as they learned to know him. It was difficult not to be fascinated by him, for he was constantly doing things for them; he attended the literary societies, plays, sports, receptions, and never were his faculty members' offices or his office or home closed to a student. Moreover, he frequently reminded them that all students in the Normal were "members of the same guild." At social and informal receptions, of which there were many since so little entertainment existed outside the campus, he would on occasions please the students by accompanying himself on the piano while singing "Annie Laurie" and other favorite songs. These pleasantries were part of the "mental album" of treasured incidents of school life that he wished the students to carry away when they graduated.

Cook had a genuine fascination for automobiles, and when they came into vogue, he was one of the first to buy one. Not many years thereafter, Professor E. C. Page followed suit; however, it was a number of years before other faculty members could afford one. But even in this "get out and get under" hand-cranking era and with only two cars on the campus, a parking problem soon developed, and it was, of course, resolved in favor of the president. According to Olive Swift Johnson, Cook's clerk at the time, each day Cook drove up the plank road and parked his car in the exclusive, sheltered spot, under the "Castle" arch, leaving Page to park his just beyond this protective cover.

With the country roads still undeveloped for the automobile and with mechanical services still mainly available only in the cities, it was not an unusual experience for Cook, when driving

President Cook with granddaughter outside his College Avenue residence (1905 Norther)

to neighboring towns, either to get stuck or to have a break-down and have to be hauled back to DeKalb by some kind-hearted farmer. Students, long after they had gone from the campus, still remembered how they had received their first auto ride from Cook when he drove them up the hill to school. Others, with not such fond memories, could recall the time he flashed his headlights on them while they were romancing on one of the secluded window sills of the Castle.[33]

Cook was also a man with deep religious feelings, though not in the strict denominational sense. Before coming to DeKalb he was a leading member and worker in the Congrega-tional and later the Unitarian churches in Bloomington, taking an active interest in the Sunday School activities of the children. At the general exercises each morning at Northern, over which he presided, there was always a part that contained a definite religious spirit. He was not averse to having the Bible read in the public schools and he believed that prospective teachers should be exposed in these exercises to scriptural readings, prayers, hymns, and an occasional sermon. In DeKalb he took an interest in ministers and choirs of various denominations.

As for his political persuasion there is ample evidence that he was a faithful member of the Republican party throughout his lifetime. Even in the election of 1912, when many an educated party member defected to the Progressive party, he remained within the fold. After this particular election he made the following comment in a letter to his old friend, President Felmley, "I am gratified to see that the bellowing Bull Moose is in captivity. I cannot but feel that Taft has been treated very shabbily indeed." Cook himself made financial contributions to the party at election time, but on those occasions when the party tried to assess him and his faculty members a definite amount it became a different matter, and he became irate and stubborn in denouncing such an outrageous practice. On such occasions he went directly to the governors and convinced them that the introduction of politics into the normal schools would be the end of their usefulness, for capable men and women would absolutely refuse to become regular faculty members.[34]

During his first weeks in the presidency at DeKalb, Cook also continued in his old position at Normal. He commuted back and forth, spending three days a week at Normal and returning to DeKalb for the other four. Since the new building was still unfinished, he established a temporary office at the Chronicle Hall until the first week of September when his new office was completed. He made his living quarters at the Glidden House while his wife remained at Normal until their new home in the Ellwood Addition was finished. Their adult children, Agnes and John, were then living in Chicago.

One of Cook's first major tasks was to assemble a faculty that would as nearly as possible meet his basic qualifications. He had believed for years that the teaching personnel for such institutions should be recruited from those who had been identified with normal-school work. Such restrictions confined his recruitment to some extent to his former students and faculty at Normal or instructors from the public and other normal schools, thus excluding candidates from academic institutions. This basic criterion for faculty membership in the normal schools was fairly well observed and continued well into the teachers college period. He also insisted that if the candidates were unknown to him, he must have knowledge of their teaching ability.

The faculty member who was to be director of the practice department was considered by Cook as next to the president in importance, and this position was already filled, for Charles McMurry had earlier promised to leave Illinois State Normal and become the first supervisor of practice teaching. He brought with him to Northern not only several years of practical experience in public and normal schools but also a rich background in the whole revolution in educational development in Europe. McMurry's doctorate from a German university always gave Cook a real sense of pride, for none of the other normals in Illinois had such a showpiece in their training departments.

The next in importance in the hierarchy of his faculty was someone who could assist Cook in the teaching of psychology as well as take over completely the courses in pedagogy, the science of teaching. He secured one of his former students, John A. H. Keith, who had, after graduating from Normal, served two years as principal of one of the departments in the practice school there. Keith had then left for Harvard University, where he received his M.A. degree just at the time Cook was selected as president of Northern.

For the field of mathematics his choice was unquestionably one of his favorite students, Swen F. Parson, who had graduated from Normal in 1892 and had taught there in the practice school before coming to DeKalb, where he was employed in the public schools. Since this discipline was so important in the teacher-training program, an assistant to Parson was also felt necessary. Thus, after the political conflict was resolved with Senator Berry, Anna Parmelee, principal of Sterling High School for the preceeding ten years, was discovered for this position. Some years later when evaluating this appointment, Cook felt that securing her for his faculty "was a piece of the rarest fortune. She was not only an excellent class room teacher but was greatly interested in all the pedagogical problems of the school."

To teach the history courses Cook engaged Edward C. Page, a graduate of Northwestern University and a student and faculty member at the University of Chicago for nearly five years. He was experienced in rural and high-school teaching and at one time was an assistant county superintendent of Ogle County.

To teach his nature study and biology courses Cook selected Fred Lemar Charles, a young man with two academic degrees from Northwestern University. He had also attended the University of Chicago for a year and had taught science courses for three years at a Chicago high school before coming to Northern. He was selected on the basis of "the interest he had manifested in nature study in [the] elementary grades," Cook said, "and . . . I wished to accentuate that kind of work."

John A. Switzer, the second science instructor, was engaged to teach physics and chemistry. He had attended the University of Wisconsin in the department of civil engineering and had obtained a degree in electrical engineering from Cornell University in 1895. He remained at Cornell as a graduate student

Northern's first parking lot, circa 1913

for another year, after which he was appointed science teacher in the East Aurora High School where he taught until coming to Northern.

For geography, Katherine P. Williamson was chosen. She had a variety of experiences; she had graduated from, attended, or had taught in a number of schools: State Normal at Winona, Minnesota (one of Cook's favorite normals); Cook County Normal; Kindergarten Training School, St. Louis; and the University of Chicago.

For the ancient and modern languages, one of the better-trained and more sophisticated candidates was secured from Illinois State Normal. She was Mary R. Potter, who had an M.A. degree in comparative philology from Boston University and several years' teaching experience. To assist her in the language courses Alice Patten, a member of a prominent local family, was selected. She had a diploma from Normal and a degree from the University of Michigan. For the preparation of teachers in reading, Cook chose Sue D. Hoaglin, a graduate of the Kansas Normal, who had also done some graduate work at the University of Chicago.

Emma Stratford was selected for the position of drawing teacher. She had received her training in the Normal Art Department of Pratt Institute and had taught in one of the Michigan state Normals and in the Des Moines public schools. The two librarians, Elma Warrick as head and Grace E. Babbitt as assistant, were chosen to operate the Haish Library. Andrew H. Melville was given the principalship for the Practice School; because of illness he was compelled to discontinue his work after two months, and W. E. King substituted as a temporary replacement.[35]

A final and most important selection was still to be made and that was superintendent of DeKalb schools. This position depended upon the city school board, since it had been agreed earlier that in order to satisfy Cook's demands and to fit his normal-school plan the board would reorganize their school system. This they did by discontinuing the services of their superintendent as well as their regular teachers with the exception of three who were graduates of Illinois State Normal and who were qualified to fit into the Cook plan. Since the plan

Haish Library, circa 1901. Librarians Jandell and Milner are at desks in rear; bust of Jacob Haish is above fireplace mantel

was that the new superintendent was also to be a member of the Normal faculty, the school board appealed to Cook to recommend a satisfactory replacement. This he did in the person of Newell D. Gilbert, who was recommended by Clinton Rosette. According to the available records, he had not taught in or attended a normal school although he did have two academic degrees from Illinois Wesleyan and eight years of successful experience as an administrator in a number of small town and city schools. The choice proved a satisfactory one. After he had successfully combined the city schools with the normal schools in a "hearty cooperation," he became a full member of the teaching faculty in 1907 and served in various important capacities until his death in 1924, at which time he was dean of the faculty and professor of psychology and sociology. He was certainly one of the most respected members of the faculty, and a dormitory was later given his name.[36]

Cook's faculty list was now complete and accepted by the Board for the opening of school. This was indeed a commendable achievement since he had not accepted the presidency until 1 May. With such a short time before the opening of school in September and with the added responsibilities of carrying on the Illinois State Normal presidency for a few months, he was under great stress and strain and was compelled to work with persistent exertion. In one of his letters he mentioned that he had two to three hundred applicants for the fifteen faculty positions and that during this period of recruitment he had "not slept more than four or five hours a night." In addition to selecting the faculty he had to create a curriculum, enroll a student body, secure facilities for their room and board, and finally push forward with all speed for the completion of the building—all in a period of about four months. Only his long experience in educational administration enabled him to make the progress that he did.

Since Cook was more concerned with the ability of normal-school teachers to demonstrate a high degree of skill in teaching pupils, he tended to place less weight on their academic training. This rather low level was noticeable in his first faculty and he was fully aware of it, for some years later he had an occasion to mention it to one of his Board members. One

President Cook presides over 1904 faculty meeting

faculty member and a long-time friend, Clyde Lyon, stated that there was no doubt that Cook "was suspicious of one who had advanced degrees" because such a person was too "specialized and thus found it harder to fit into the Normal program." He also felt that Cook was opposed to them, though he never said so, because he did not have an earned degree of his own.[37]

Cook placed a high premium on a candidate's interest in teaching, how "thoroughly . . . they were on fire with enthusiasm." He often illustrated the importance of this quality by citing a remark once made by President Gregory of the University of Illinois: "You can bore a hole through a 2-inch oak plank with an iron poker if the poker is red hot." He believed that he had selected such a faculty.

Even though he was firmly convinced of the merit of these qualifications for his faculty, he nevertheless failed to escape the ridicule of the more academic institutions, such as the liberal arts colleges, which were for years "the sharpest critics of the normal schools."

Two examples of critical comments from representatives of the college people illustrate the chasm then developing between these two groups of educators: the rebuke of Charles Francis Adams that "it is devoutly to be hoped that, some day, a glimmer of true light will effect an entrance into the professional educator's head"; and Nicholas Murray Butler's characterization of normal schools as "academies or high schools with a slight infusion of pedagogic instruction."[38]

President Cook's basic requirements for Northern's first faculty were met completely with the fifteen teachers selected. Six of these appointees had been associated with him as teachers or students at Illinois State Normal; three more had taught in other state normals; and the remaining six had had various teaching experience in public schools. As far as it is possible to determine, there were three members with some form of bachelor's degree, four with the master's, one with a doctorate.

Cook displayed no prejudice between the sexes in his selection, for they were nearly equally divided; however, some difference in salaries is quite distinguishable.[39] Of the original faculty members whom he recruited, only four chose to remain

Auditorium by electric light, with oil portraits of Ellwood (left) and Glidden
(1903 Norther)

at Northern until retirement. Five others rose to more prominent positions—one as a normal-school president, one as a
university dean of women, and three as professors at various
other colleges and universities.

The teaching load and "program of recitations" were set up
so that most faculty members taught four days a week, four to
five forty-five minute periods a day; those in the minor
subjects, such as music and drawing, had a twelve-hour teaching load with six sections of two hours each. All classes began at
nine in the morning, following the general exercises; each
faculty member had office hours of about the same length of
time, generally forty-five minutes, spread out during different
times of the day. Cook taught one or two sections of seniors and
had an office hour in the morning and one in the afternoon. He
had many administrative duties which he performed to the
most minute detail, such as ordering all library books and
issuing all excuses and grades from his office. Grades were
computed, during the early years, on the basis of written
examinations during the class periods on materials gleaned
from the text-book assignments and were based on single digit
numbers: seven was considered passing, eight a good mark,
and nine equivalent to an "A" grade. By 1919, according to
Julia Stipe Ostergaard, a number system using two digits had
been introduced; and by 1926, letter grades were used.

Cook also observed and supervised each faculty member's
teaching duties. The turnover of faculty members took place
for various reasons, for, as Professor Lyon related in an
interview, "occasionally, one or two would find the atmosphere
not to their liking." According to Cook the turnover of faculty
was mainly due to the wretched salaries and the complete
failure, year in and year out, of the state government to finance
the normal schools properly. Staff salaries increased almost
imperceptibly.

The next major task for the president was to organize and
publicize his admission requirements and the courses of study;
since it was not possible at this late date to publish a catalog, he

*Northern's gymnasium in 1902; now houses Printing and Duplicating
Department*

resorted to leaflets and the *DeKalb Chronicle* to reach the public. He notified all prospective students that the "courses at first offered [at Northern] will be similar to those in force at the Illinois State Normal, whose catalogue will give much desired information." He adopted his alma mater's plan of dividing the school year into three quarters, with an additional term during the summer months. Pupils were not permitted any selection in their studies but were required to take the classes prescribed in the "Courses of Study." This was somewhat contrary to the national trend in academic institutions, which for some years had been abandoning the prescription idea and expanding the number of elective courses.[40]

The four courses of study chosen by Cook consisted of a one-year course for college or normal-school graduates; a two-year course for graduates from accredited high schools; a three-year course for those with less than three years of high school; and a four-year course for those without any high-school training.

Certain persons in these courses of study were required to take an admission examination. All candidates were required to "present with their papers a certificate of good moral character, signed by some well-known person." This was something which Cook insisted upon in all cases. It is interesting to note, however, how many of these in the first class were signed by him. He also made it clear to all that this new normal school was a professional school; that it existed for no other purpose than the preparation of teachers for the schools of Illinois. The first term was for fifteen weeks; the second and third for twelve each, making a total of thirtynine. It was not until 1918 that the academic year was reduced to thirtysix weeks.

It was fortunate that he displayed the interest he did in the three- and four-year-course students; they were, he said, often

older than either of the other groups and, while inferior to them in scholarship, are harder workers, more serious in disposition and more willing to endure the comparative inconvenience of country life. A highly respectable percentage of them take high rank in their classes and in the work of the practice school. They understand country ways, are satisfied with country living and get on well with country people. Many of them have farm work through the long vacation and teach fall and winter. They become resident teachers continuing their work in the same locality for several years. It is to be regreted [sic] . . . that there are not more of this class of teachers and before we can have the best kind of schools in the country the farmers will have to see to it that there are more.[41]

It was from the two groups with the least education that he received the preponderance of his first student body, and without them he surely would have had an unimpressive beginning. Of the 173 students who were finally registered that first quarter, 106 were deficient in some basic requirements. An analysis of the 220 students who were enrolled at the close of the first year shows the following distribution of status: special, 3; seniors, 16; juniors, 68; three-year course, 120; and four-year course, 13.[42]

The first quarter's enrollment consisted of 146 women and 27 men with over 45 percent ranging in age from twentyone to forty years. It was often possible, however, for some of these three- and four-year enrollees to shorten the period by a year, and a few could even secure a diploma in one year. Several had taught for ten years or more in rural and town schools. There were forty in the first year's classes who had attended Illinois State Normal, but, since the new normal was nearer their homes, had decided to transfer to it. The first graduating class consisted of sixteen members, thirteen of whom had followed the president from Illinois State to Northern. There were twentynine different occupations and professions represented among the parents, with farming by far the most common one. The student body in the first year represented some thirtyfour Illinois counties with two students coming from other states; nearly one-fourth were from DeKalb County.[43]

Fees for this type of education were extremely low, for the Illinois normal schools gave free tuition to those who were willing to teach a prescribed period of time in Illinois schools. The only fee was an incidental instructional one of $6.00 per year. The usual cost for textbooks and stationery for the academic year of thirty-nine weeks was about $10.00; board and room was estimated at $124.00, making a total of $140.00 for the school year. Boarding clubs in the Ellwood Addition were constructed soon after the school opened, and by the beginning of the second year many students were living in them. Others found living quarters at private homes and had their meals at the clubs, while still others secured both their board and room from private families. These places were mostly within easy walking distance of the school with only an occasional muddy street, a narrow footbridge, and the never-to-be-forgotten plank sidewalk to encounter on the way to classes.

The school's instructional organization was modest for the first few years, with no identifiable departments, only subject fields with teachers associated with them. There were no major or minor courses of study. The following courses were listed in the first catalog as offered in all courses of study:

TEACHER TRAINING:
History of education, philosophy of education, psychology and pedagogy, observation and teaching, school organization and management.
ENGLISH:
English grammar, reading, oratory, literature, composition, rhetoric.
LANGUAGES:
Latin, German, Greek.
SOCIAL SCIENCES:
History, sociology, political economy, civics.
GEOGRAPHY:
Geography, physical geography.
SCIENCES:
Biology, geology, physics, chemistry, astronomy.
FINE ARTS:
Music, drawing.
PHILOSOPHY:
History of philosophy, ethics.
MATHEMATICS:
Arithmetic, algebra, geometry.

Requirements for graduation were determined according to number of credits: the one-year graduate was required to earn twelve credits in professional studies and teaching; a graduate of the two-year course had to have a total of thirty credits; the three- and four-year sequences required a total of forty-eight and fifty-seven credits respectively. In addition to these credit hours an educational thesis of at least fifteen hundred words was required during the senior year; these were considered so important that the better ones were read at commencement exercises.

On Monday, 11 September 1899, the first students arrived to participate in an historic event. Many had already registered by mail or in DeKalb during the late summer months while still others were yet to come; a few were even to be admitted as late as November. Many still had the difficult task of finding places to board and room. So scarce were these facilities that even the president devoted some of his time to room-hunting for the students.

The opening days were not pleasant, for either students or faculty; the building was by no means completed and there was the constant din of sawing and pounding, and scraping and filing, with mortar boxes, stepladders, and sawhorses everywhere. Carpenters, masons, and other craftsmen were busy in the halls and the "swarthy Italians" were diligently laying the mosaic tile. The gray stone building was impressive to most of the students, although one remarked, "I was a little disappointed when I saw the Normal building standing out in a field with stones and bare ground around it." Another remembered this first day as long as she lived because of the noise and bags of cement and workmen's tools littering the hallways, which were dark, for there was not yet electricity in the unfinished part. Things in general were in such disarray that in order to hold recitations the teachers and pupils "shut themselves up in a few rooms and," as Cook remarked, "waited patiently for deliverance." Only half-day sessions were held during the period that the building was being completed.

The campus also was much less attractive than many had expected. Cook had mailed out several thousand announcements to teachers, prospective students, leading newspapers, and prominent school and educational journals containing the architect's drawing of a beautiful edifice with wide walks and a nice lawn with trees, shrubs, and vines; and these were what the students had seen. Instead, a plank walk from the bridge to the building was the only sidewalk; and instead of vines and shrubs, the campus was strewn with stones, piles of earth, and other debris from this immense construction. To add to the unsightly view, the Glidden half-mile race track and several old wooden structures of an obsolete fairground "graced the campus" and were, as the president noted, "anything but decorative in their effect." Some of these depressing sights and sounds on the first few days may have contributed to what the *Chronicle* reported as a plague of homesickness among many of the students.

The next morning, Tuesday, 12 September, at eight o'clock sharp, "Dr. Cook with watch in hand" assembled everyone in the study hall for the opening exercise. President Cook in a brief ceremony had the students begin by singing "America," then followed it with the Twenty Third Psalm, and concluded with the Lord's Prayer. Standing before this audience, who seemed to sense the significance of the occasion, he offered a few words of greeting, "stressing the idea that in future years every one present would recall with great satisfaction the fact that he had been present on this occasion of this 'first day of school' in the Northern Illinois State Normal School."[44] The exercise closed with Swen Parson leading the group in some popular songs, after which the students were directed to their classrooms for instruction. The seniors were directed to Room 18, where they had to wait for two hours before Cook was able to meet them and deliver his first lecture in psychology. While they were waiting, the Italian workers inspired Minnie A. Hausen, in spite of the disorder, to compose the first poem at the Normal. She chose to call it "Mosaics," and the third verse illustrates the quality and content of this poetical composition:

These lone, Etruscan workmen labor on;
They spend the body for the wage it wins.

The school and teachers o'er the lessons con,
The shrine of thought its potent life begins.
One hears the fall of wave by Florence's feet,
One hears the future statehood's onward beat.

During the first ten days of school the students and faculty rapidly fell into a regular pattern of organization until it came time to dedicate the opening of their school. Three days were set aside for that purpose—21–23 September. These "Crimson Days," as they were called, were to have a somewhat carnival nature. The city, as it had done earlier in 1895 with the laying of the cornerstone, had spent months with many committees preparing for the occasion. It was to be, as Ellwood said, "the most elaborate . . . [celebration ever] attempted in northern Illinois."

The Crimson Days began on Thursday at 9 A.M. with whistles and bells. Main Street downtown was draped and festooned with lights, and the local merchants and manufacturers had decorated booths. A street fair with tent shows, parades, trapeze performers, merry-go-rounds, and vaudeville acts was all free to the public. Some of these acts turned out to be slightly too entertaining: some oriental dancing girls were over-zealous in welcoming the new Normal to DeKalb and thus invited the local priest and some church women to have them arrested on morals charges. Pickpocket artists were also overtaken and "shipped back to Chicago." These were insignificant parts of the Main Street entertainment but they drew front-page headlines in the Rockford and Sycamore press. During the day the Pullman Military Band, along with other local bands, gave concerts, and in the evening there was a procession of elaborate floats. Uniformed equestrians as well as masked individuals marched to the campus. There, under the trees, Mrs. Jessie Ray, Ellwood's daughter, was crowned Queen of the Crimson Days. Following this ceremony all those in masks returned to the Chronicle Hall where a masked ball ended the first day.[45]

Friday, "Dedication Day," was to be the climax of the celebration, but rain marred the proceedings, taking away the color and excitement and giving the "town a thoroughly dilapidated look." Parts of the scheduled program were either cancelled or postponed until Saturday. In the forenoon the children's parade was to feature large numbers of children along with their teachers and superintendents from many northern counties, where a holiday had been declared. But it had only a small representation carrying umbrellas; they were followed by Governor Tanner and his staff in carriages escorted by a company of national guard. Instead of halting at the woods or the school grounds to eat their lunches, they continued to the Normal building, where they could eat out of the rain. The dedication ceremony was held inside but limited space forced many to crowd into the gymnasium where they "stood up for two mortal hours" to hear the lengthy program of special music and speeches. Featured as a speaker was Governor Tanner, who talked briefly on educational matters, but poor health prevented him from giving a major address. Other speakers also had to abandon their prepared speeches. Following Tanner were the two U.S. senators from Illinois, Cullom and Mason; Congressman Hopkins; state senators D. D. Hunt and O. F. Berry; and Judge C. A. Bishop, who represented the interests of the general public. Superintendents of the Chicago and Cook County schools, E. B. Andrews and O. T. Bright, both spoke for educational interests, and the ceremony concluded with remarks by President Draper of the University of Illinois. A pleasing incident in closing was the presentation of a special gift in behalf of Jacob Haish in the form of an expensive cane to all those who were instrumental in the founding of the school. The canes had a miniature picture of the Normal framed in gold with the name of the owner inscribed. Part of the cane was made from Osage orange wood, which was used, because of its thorns, for fencing and which had suggested the invention of barbed wire, the material that gave DeKalb its wealth for the establishment of the normal school.[46]

A later parade for Friday, to be reviewed by the governor, had to be abandoned, and the fireworks postponed until Saturday night. But at nine o'clock the Queen's Ball and the reception for the governor, the most prominent feature of the Crimson Days, were held in the Normal Auditorium with music

Students pose around "Freshman Bench" which was constructed in 1903

furnished by the Pullman Band and some of the professional vocalists. Following this elaborate affair a tour was given of the building. So great was the enthusiasm over the ball and tour that the street fair downtown became a secondary matter, much to the sorrow of its promoters.

By Saturday morning the weather had cleared and efforts were made to put some of the events that were left off Friday back on the program. A floral parade took place in the afternoon featuring twenty elaborately decorated vehicles in which were seated some of the prominent men and women of the county; a number of equestriennes in white and pink; bicyclists trimmed with flowers escorted by a miniature queen and pony and led by the Pullman Band. At the close of this striking display of flowers, the fireworks were touched off on the college grounds with a piece that symbolized the "Three Crimson Days" and an equally appropriate finale, one called "Good Night."

At this moment, the people in DeKalb could rightfully feel that their normal school was legitimate: it had been founded, located, constructed, and dedicated. Now, beginning Monday morning, 25 September, it was ready to commence what some of its earliest alumni have chosen to call "The Twenty Golden Years."

Original Castle Drive gatepost, as it stood on campus woods from 1926–1966 to mark site of 1900 Theodore Roosevelt speech

Altgeld Hall about 1913

The Twenty-Year Mission

UPON assuming the presidency of the new normal school at DeKalb, John W. Cook made it amply clear that he had a definite mission to fulfill. It was to establish in northern Illinois the first normal school that would have under its supervision a town's elementary school system that could be used for the purpose of training teachers.

The local school board agreed to this cooperative arrangement, not only because it wanted to encourage Cook to come to DeKalb, but also because the proposition was financially attractive to them. It would lower considerably the budget for teachers' salaries and it would also provide the entire cost of construction and operation of one school, which would be located on the campus.

Cook's unique teacher-training program was almost an obsession with him; he was constantly reiterating its values and achievements in his innumerable letters, public speeches, classroom lectures, and scholarly writings. There was no doubt in his mind that this partnership afforded certain benefits for the student teachers not found in other normal schools, the most important being "the fact that these practicing students are actually city teachers . . . and in this relation . . . they are not only getting the technical training under trained critics but they are also getting the social training that is necessary for superior community service."[1]

Under these educational beliefs of President Cook, the Practice School (the name was changed to Training School in 1904) became the body and soul of Northern Illinois State Normal School, and around it developed his single-purpose concept. This meant that all faculty members must believe in and give their allegiance to this central theme; however, this did not preclude differences of opinion on matters of methodology and theory. In fact, there was at times plenty of discussion at the demonstrations, faculty meetings, and educational conventions. On some occasions students were pleasantly awed by the lively debates between Cook and McMurry in the Practice School. An individual faculty member who found this normal-school view slightly too restrictive would soon move on. This rarely happened, however, for the careful screening process that took place at the time of recruitment was designed to select faculty members who concurred with the principles of Cook's philosophy.

The members of the normal-school faculty were considered actual members of the Practice School staff and they knew that they must be ready at all times to step into a training class and demonstrate their ability to teach their subject matter to children. Cook held the view that nothing would have a greater influence upon the character of instruction in their classrooms than this experience. "Theory," he said, "will soon reduce itself to usable form and will test itself by its value as a schoolroom procedure. There will be little talk about method; but there will be a [great] deal of thinking accomplished in the way of getting material into shape for use with children."[2]

The procedure of using the faculty in this manner was generally in the form of a technique called the critique lesson, which was offered regularly each week with a class in the Practice School taught by one of the faculty members or by a regular critic teacher and observed by the student teacher. On occasions, it might be held at a faculty meeting or even before the whole student body in the general exercises, with Cook closing the demonstration with his evaluation. Everyone could enter into the discussion and criticism during the periods that followed these lessons. They were looked upon as a means of testing both the theory and the skill of the teacher—a model form of recitation which could help the prospective teacher "to avoid a whole family of blunders which are commonly made by . . . teachers who have never been subjected to criticism." Thus one might find on a certain day of the week Swen Parson demonstrating to the student teachers methods of teaching fractions in arithmetic to a sixth-grade class or Fred L. Charles offering to the fourth graders one of his fascinating studies of animal life or Lida McMurry presenting to one of her elementary classes a demonstration in the teaching of children's literature. So important was this aspect of discussion and criticism in Cook's philosophy that he considered it the essential foundation for all normal schools.

Such experiences were not altogether happy ones, for all students knew that sooner or later the day would come when they must embark upon this frightening path to becoming a teacher. It was an ordeal to look forward to, and to some it was a nightmare; even some of the faculty had fearful thoughts when they anticipated their annual session before their colleagues. Older alumni, who were children in attendance at the Practice School when these critiques were held, can still remember their anxiety while sitting before the faculty, waiting to be called upon to recite. Clyde Lyon, a teacher of reading and drama, related in an interview that when it came time for his first critique he became so unnerved that he gave a wholly unsatisfactory demonstration; in the case of Professor Charles, his, too, was so poorly done that he requested an opportunity to redeem himself.

This exercise was a common subject of discussion among the students from the day they entered the institution. As the time drew nearer, the anxiety grew greater. The following lines, "On Teaching My First Critique," by Charles Murtagh reveal his anxiety:

Oft in the silent night,
'Ere I had passed to sleep,

There loomed before my mind,
The thoughts of that critique.

The people there
Who come to stare,
The critic teachers, too,
The music master
With his stick,
To see what I should do.

So in the silent night,
'Ere I had passed to sleep
There loomed before my mind,
The thoughts of that first critique

Once both faculty and students had gone through these traumatic experiences, and the hours of dread and anxiety were left behind, only thoughts of achievement and victory remained, finally to grow into acknowledgement of the significance and importance of the exercise.

This technique for training teachers may have been, in the eyes of the president, students, and faculty, the best in the country, but it had its critics among some prominent educators. President E. A. Sheldon of the Oswego Normal School, who was considered one of the outstanding normal-school leaders in America, was in disagreement on some points. In replying to one of Cook's letters asking for a judgment on the proposed new teacher-training program in DeKalb, he stated that his criticism was not so much of the critique lessons as it was of the role of the critic teacher who, according to Cook, was "supposed to be present at all times to look after the control and order of the room and to criticise the work of the pupil teacher." He opposed this method, for

few teachers can do their best under such conditions. They have no sense of freedom. They work under restraint . . . the responsibility of the school is not thrown upon them. . . . What I contend for . . . is that the pupil teachers shall be left alone . . . not merely to hear the lessons . . . teach the branches of study, but to show their power to find out what the children

104

are . . . and to so direct them as to get growth. In other words,
I want their power to govern tested. . . . I would have the
critics go in occasionally, quite as much . . . to find out what is
good in the teacher, as to find out her faults.

Our practice rooms are so arranged that the critics may
observe . . . without exposing themselves to the teacher or
pupils, and so go only occasionally into the rooms.[3]

President Livingston C. Lord of Eastern Illinois also built a
national reputation as a normal-school leader, but his emphasis
was less upon the centrality of the training school and more
upon the recruitment of highly qualified faculty members with
the potential for creative teaching. Lord differed somewhat
with Cook in that he was constantly working for more scholarship and higher salaries for his staff, and in many of his reports
to his Board of Trustees he called to their attention the
importance of both these factors in securing and retaining
good faculty members.[4]

Of the faculty members who aided most in making the
normal school prominent, none did more than Charles and
Lida McMurry. Cook brought them both to Northern with Dr.
McMurry as director of the Practice Schools and his sister-in-
law as critic teacher for the elementary grades. McMurry
structured the two training schools and equipped them with a
regular staff to his liking—three critic teachers on the campus
and eight at Glidden School in town. He worked closely with
Newell D. Gilbert, the first city superintendent, and with the
principals of the practice schools under this new arrangement.
He brought to this work a rich background of travel and
experience from his years in Europe as well as a specialized
knowledge of the Herbartian pedagogical principles that were
then being explored by numerous American educators.[5] His
German doctorate also gave him an eminent position among
these educational leaders.

He immediately gained a high reputation in the city and on
the campus, expressing his ideas in lectures and writings. But

by the second year in DeKalb, he began to find the work too exacting and asked the president for a leave of absence so that he might devote full time to scholarship—more specifically to the writing of books embodying the application of his theories that were then being discussed in many of the normal schools. Cook reluctantly stretched this year and a half leave into a period of more than five years, one of which McMurry spent as president of a Pennsylvania normal school. In 1907, he returned to the campus as a professor of pedagogy, assuming John A. H. Keith's position, which was made vacant when Keith became president of the Wisconsin State Normal School at Oshkosh. McMurry held this position until 1911 when he accepted the superintendency of schools in DeKalb and the position of director of the training department with no teaching assignments.

McMurry was a prolific writer who, according to one reporter, had authored or coauthored by the time of his death in 1929 at least forty books, some of which were widely used as texts. With his proficiency in the German language, he also found time to translate some of the more important treatises on educational theory and practice as well as to serve as editor of the National Herbart Society yearbooks.[6]

Moreover, he was a socially conscious individual and took an active role in community affairs, using his broad knowledge in teaching Bible classes, preaching in churches, and serving on the local school board. On the campus he was asked to serve as president in the absence of Cook and was constantly involved with students in their various activities. As a teacher he was rated superior by his colleagues and his classes were very popular with students. He was in great demand by other educational institutions to speak or to join their faculties, and during his long and productive career he served as lecturer at many of the prestigious universities of the nation.

By 1915, the pressures for his services elsewhere proved too attractive. The decision to leave the Normal was indeed a difficult one for McMurry and his family, as it had been a most satisfying period for them. He finally accepted the alluring inducements from the rapidly rising George Peabody College for Teachers at Nashville, Tennessee.

His departure, along with Keith's at an earlier date, was indeed a severe loss to the institution, relieving it of two of its better educationists; unfortunately, they were not replaced with scholars of comparable reputation or experience. Their courses were reshuffled, giving Gilbert psychology and pedagogy and elevating Floyd R. Ritzman from principal of the Glidden School to director of the training department. Cook took over completely the history of education courses.

So highly were the McMurrys respected by the faculty and alumni at Northern that the first new building erected in 1911 was later given the name McMurry Training School to honor both Charles and Lida Brown McMurry.

During her seventeen years at Northern, no faculty member was sought after more eagerly by the student teachers to work under than Mrs. McMurry; as a rule she had twice as many students training with her than any other critic teacher. She was especially adept in working with small children, for she knew how to select and how to use materials to develop a child's interest. She authored and coauthored children's literature and poems (one book with Cook's daughter, Agnes Cook Gale) and she adapted various teaching materials to the Herbartian theories. Her maiden name of Brown was a well-known one, for she came from a family that had produced some prominent educators. However, she had a certain distinction in her own right, not only as an educator, but as the founder of the first student Y.W.C.A. chapter in the United States, at Illinois State Normal on 12 November, 1872.[7]

A third person who rendered creative service in building the Normal's reputation was Luther A. Hatch, who, in 1900, became the principal and also critic teacher of the Practice School, serving in that capacity until 1907 when he accepted the city superintendency of schools which he held until his untimely death in 1911. He was tireless in his work with children, both in and out of the schoolrooms, in his efforts to keep them interested in school life. In his dual capacity, he organized many creative projects, especially for the teenage boys who had at this time few activities in school. Manual arts programs were developed for the noon hour periods. He financed these mainly by donations. They were continued as part of the regular curriculum of the Normal School Industrial Arts Department, a phase of vocational instruction for children that increased in importance in many of the public schools throughout the country. Girls, too, were encouraged during these noonday sessions to create needlework under the guidance of the critic teacher, "Addie" McLean.

Hatch had been a farmer in his earlier years, and often took the children on field trips to farms, dairies, and industries; he developed the idea of growing gardens and planting flowers and trees, along with the study of wild animals, birds, and Indian lore. These outdoor activities were part of the larger program then being encouraged by President Theodore Roosevelt's conservation and rural life movements, and they found a perfect laboratory on Northern's untouched campus with its beautiful virgin trees, small shallow lake, and the popular Kishwaukee River.

Since nature study and biology were to have an important place in his curriculum, Cook was able to secure Fred Lemar Charles as his teacher for these courses. This rather gifted young man joined the first faculty and remained until 1909 when he left to take an important position at the University of Illinois. He was the faculty advisor who inaugurated the student newspaper, the *Northern Illinois,* with a first printing of fifteen hundred copies, to be used as souvenirs two months after school opened. He was the supervisor of the senior circuses, director of the junior plays, with their take-offs on senior and faculty individuals, and also the captain of the first tennis organization. In the spring of 1900, he was listed on the baseball team as pitcher and shortstop as well as manager. His interest in the teaching of natural history to children also led him to organize a small zoo for the Practice School.

From the start he was considered by the first faculty a promising scholar, being its only member of the prestigious Phi Beta Kappa honorary fraternity as well as having a wide interest in many aspects of the intellectual spectrum. He had an unexpected fascination for poetry, which he indulged by publishing a volume of his own in 1896, *Sunshine and Zephyrs.*

Many of his students who went on to universities owed "their ambition . . . and their subsequent success to his encouragement; many others learned to see a more wonderful and beautiful world through his eyes." One of his students stated that he started her out on a long life of bird watching; another recalled with real enthusiasm how he was able to get the students to rise cheerfully at the "crack of dawn to go on bird trips . . . or spend hours, voluntarily, keeping watch—and careful notes—on a mother robin all through the time she was brooding, hatching, and raising her babies. Relays of students kept up the watch each day from dawn until the mother no longer left the nest at night." [8]

So highly was Charles respected by his former students and colleagues at Northern that within a few years after his life was tragically ended in 1911, a beautiful, bas-relief, bronze plaque was hung in the foyer of the administration building.[9] Necessary funds for the memorial were contributed; the full-bust, side-view portrait was executed by a former DeKalb resident, John G. Prasuhn. During this time his widow set up a student loan fund for science students. By 1943, however, it was the wish of the family that the balance of this fund be used to build the memorial seat which today graces a shady nook beneath the Scotch pines near the Swen Franklin Parson Library.

Upon assuming his position under Cook, another professor, John Alexander Hull Keith, fresh out of Harvard University with an A.B. degree, threw himself into the process of creating a first-class normal school. He taught psychology and pedagogy with a freshness and enthusiasm that soon made him second to Cook in popularity with the students. Besides organizing the first golf club and laying out a nine-hole course, he acted as coach and player on the first football team. He also participated in state and national educational meetings, and early in his career found time to publish some of his ideas concerning the processes and problems of elementary education.[10]

Edward Carleton Page was another faculty member who made a genuine contribution to the Normal. He came with a solid background of academic training and experience, and throughout his thirty years of service in the training of teachers he never lost touch with the academic aspect of his discipline as did so many when they became involved in a pedagogical environment. In fact, consistently throughout his career he

109

participated in local, state, and national history societies by reading papers, reviewing books, and serving as chairman of program sections. He was privileged also to be the president of the history teachers section of the American Historical Association in 1912 as well as to be a long-time associate with the Illinois State Historical Society.

At this period in the teaching of U.S. history, historians were still generally conservative, patriotic, and moralistic in their interpretations, and Professor Page was no exception in this regard. In his lectures, he showed great loyalty and devotion for the founding fathers and he had a lifetime propensity for emphasizing the stories, essays, letters, documents, and biographies that magnified their contributions. Moreover, he was a firm believer in the use of primary sources in his classes, and this approach often had a tendency to cause many of the students to dislike his style and to consider him too dull and conventional. But in spite of their aversion to his style, he was nevertheless respected for the immense amount of time he gave to the students and their activities, serving many years as chairman on the board of managers of the *Northern Illinois.* He also acted as president when J. Stanley Brown, Cook's successor, was absent from the campus.

The activity that brought some renown to this teacher, for both the school and himself, was his early interest in collecting memorabilia of early America in order to make the teaching of history more real for practice teachers and school children alike. At first his interest was in collecting objects that were of historical significance, and he would borrow items from various owners for display in the hallways. The idea of a permanent museum occurred to him when the Training School was moved into its new building in 1911, leaving two offices available for the project; then the objects were assembled into what became known as the Page Museum.

Children from distant schools came to see the museum as well as to hear Page lecture, and he made many of the collections available on loan to the regional schools. Moreover, the museum was highly publicized through the dissemination of his several pamphlets, and the *DeKalb Review* observed that nothing aside from the Normal had done more to give prominence to DeKalb than the Page Museum.[11]

With Page's retirement in 1929, the museum, as so often happens to such creations, soon became a collection of "cobwebs, dirt and dead flies on the two top floors of the Old Main Tower," where one could find "disused and outdated articles of convenience" from the past. No one had any interest in becoming its director, and thus it soon became a place few visited, and those who did were often either young lovers looking for a secret rendezvous or perhaps others with lower motivations such as the appropriation of some curio or Indian relic.

The disposition of this valuable collection was a problem, and the museum continued to deteriorate until President Adams requested of the Normal School Board that they either restore the museum to a useable condition or dispense with it entirely. The decision was finally made to have the materials arranged in some order so they could be useful for teaching purposes. Some of the more massive items, however, such as farm machinery, were donated by President Adams to the Museum of Science and Industry in Chicago.

The effort to make the remaining materials useful to elementary teachers was unsuccessful and the museum was kept under lock and key by Milo E. Whittaker, head of the Social Science Department, until 1940, when Professor Charles E. Howell and a group of student assistants took over the museum as a project. Working with curricula classes, they cataloged and classified it according to grade levels and for a brief time the idea proved a success; however, with the outbreak of the war it was decided to abandon the project entirely and turn it over to the Training School. There it remained until the opening of the new University School, where it was moved and stored for a few years. Now the collection is in the University Historical Committee storage room. The number of old guns slowly dwindled; according to one informant, a few of them found their way to a Board member's rumpus room wall.

Swen Franklin Parson was the one member of the original faculty whose life conforms more to the Horatio Alger pattern of success than any of his colleagues. He came to this country as a fourteen-year-old "Green Swede," according to his own description, with practically no formal education and unable to speak English. But after going through the typical process of

Americanization—studying in the lower grades with children and working at shamefully low-paying tasks—he finally found himself teaching at a country school. After a few years of this experience he attended Illinois State Normal, where he was graduated (with a two-year diploma) in 1892. When Cook came to Northern in the summer of 1899, he selected Parson, who was at the time connected with the local school system, as his mathematics teacher. Parson had a long and fruitful career as an arithmetic teacher at Northern.

Faculty members held him in high esteem for his rare quality of fairness in dealing with people. He never permitted himself to be drawn into faculty quarrels or to make hasty judgments of his colleagues. The writer recalls on several occasions one of his characteristic remarks: "If I am not absolutely certain of a man's motives, I shall certainly not wish to impugn them." Clyde Lyon, one of his close friends, stated that Parson was a man who shied away from making personal judgments and was not one to join any factions, always maintaining a somewhat detached philosophical point of view. In fact, Lyon said that he felt that Parson should have been a judge.

These personal qualities of leadership elevated him to important assignments in the town for civic improvements: he was a member of the high-school board of education, and both he and his wife served as officers on the first parent-teachers association. However, his greatest service to the community was perhaps his long and profitable efforts spent in securing the Jacob Haish Memorial Library for DeKalb. The alumni honored him in 1937 with a portrait to hang in the foyer of the administration building next to that of President Cook. Edgar Miller, of Chicago, was the artist, and all alumni chapters were invited to join in the enterprise.[12] Parson was further honored after his death when his name was given to the new college library.

Ida S. Simonson joined the Northern faculty at the beginning of the third year as the teacher of rhetoric and English literature, in which position she remained continuously without leave until 1933, when she retired with emeritus status. She soon demonstrated her ability to arouse a love for literature in her students as well as a creative capacity for writing. She gave unstintingly of her time to her classes, and for over thirty years served as faculty advisor for the *Norther* yearbook. So much did students appreciate this "sweet, gentle, soft-spoken lady of kindly eyes" that in a sophomore class poll taken in 1925 she was listed as the most popular and most admired of the faculty. Perhaps the nicest tribute to this inspiring lady was an unsigned sonnet written in 1927 by a student in her literature class. The following is an excerpt:

As the wall of time crumbles into years
And the grey dust of unremembered days,
I will forget the dead philosophy
Of Shakespeare, Wordsworth, and the ages' peers,
But I'll recall your many gentle ways
And how your eyes would often smile at me.[13]

After Mary Ross Potter resigned as teacher of foreign languages to assume a deanship at Northwestern University, Mary Ross Whitman followed in that position, which she continued to hold until her retirement in 1930. Somewhat unlike her women colleagues, she was a stern disciplinarian. She was highly respected by the faculty for her superior training in the classics at universities in Rome, Paris, and Ann Arbor, at the latter of which she had completed most of her doctoral requirements. She was especially talented in giving travelogues and lectures based on her travels. During summer vacations she frequently took students to see the English Lake Country, castles on the Rhine, and passion plays, cathedrals, and Roman antiquities. One of the most publicized of these trips was at the outbreak of World War I, when they found themselves in Germany near the battlefront. Her efficient manner in finally returning her charges home safely won her high praise.

As for this person's ability in the classroom, she excelled with the few who were able to go beyond the required course in English grammar. Norma Stelford, a 1914 graduate and valedictorian of her class, was so pleased with her instruction that she was able to secure Cook's permission to take an extra course in Latin so that she could enter the University of Chicago as a junior. Some found Whitman an unforgettable instructor. She had high standards, precise methods, and anything but leniency in her testing and grading. Dorothy Youngblood, a former student who had her the last year she taught at Northern, remembered her as rather awesome, but nevertheless a person with infinite patience and one who "gave me an excellent foundation in French grammar."

For eighteen of Cook's twenty years at Northern he served under the trustees of the Northern Illinois State Normal School, which consisted of five members appointed by the governor for four-year terms plus the state superintendent of public instruction who served as an *ex-officio* member. Its president, secretary, and treasurer were chosen by the appointed members, and the secretary drew an annual salary of $300. Cook's final two years were served under the Normal School Board, which consolidated all five of the normal schools in an attempt to reduce the number of administrative boards in charge of the public institutions in the state. It consisted of nine members appointed by the governor, with the state superintendent of public instruction and the director of the Department of Registration and Education as *ex-officio* members; the latter officials were made secretary and director, respectively.[14]

From the beginning of Cook's presidency he was always among friends on his Board of Trustees, for he was well acquainted with most of the twenty-three members who served at one time or another during this period, and his reputation and ability as a normal-school president enhanced his standing with them. No doubt his closest friend, the one responsible for bringing him to Northern, was Isaac L. Ellwood, who served on the Board until his death in 1910. After that, Ellwood's son, William, was appointed and served until 1913. The senior Ellwood's son-in-law, John H. Lewis, also served as the Board's treasurer until the Board was abolished in 1917. Following William L. Ellwood, John A. Dowdall, an attorney and judge from DeKalb, was appointed in 1915 for the remaining years of the Board.[15]

With such a close relationship, Cook had little trouble in securing his budgets and his boards did little to supervise his activities, giving him a contingent fund to use freely for many things, including books for the library as well as faculty salaries. On the other hand, he was never a president to give the Board much concern, for he was very careful and cautious in requesting funds; in fact, on one or more occasions he was too careful, for his appropriations were inadequate to meet emergencies and he found it necessary to borrow from the Williston Hall rental fees. Because of his parsimonious ways, he was treated with real deference by state legislators and even governors when he journeyed to Springfield with his budgetary requests. In 1914, the Board expressed in their report to the governor their evaluation of his sense of economy at Northern:

Your attention is respectfully called to the record which the institution has made in the fifteen years of its existence in the matter of appropriations. The most rigid economy has marked its administration. Its budgets have met the approval of the General Assembly and of the successive Chief Executives.[16]

In spite of this cordial relationship, Cook had in his more confidential moments misgivings about the financial support the state gave the normal school. He always felt that his type of institution was neglected in favor of the University of Illinois. Moreover, in respect to his sister normal schools, he was somewhat embarrassed with his smaller enrollments, for he had no high-school department as some of the others had and no extension courses or rural school programs.

This made a difference of several hundred fewer students in his enrollment figures. In order to rationalize his lower attendance records in respect to the others, he insisted that his students were of a higher caliber, thus giving him "a very satisfactory school in quality." These various competitive differences among the five institutions had a tendency to "array the interests of one against those of another"; however, with the reorganization under a single board in 1917, some of these nagging problems were minimized.

The presidents soon found that the new Normal School

Board had a number of disadvantages not present in its predecessors. One which Cook especially disliked was the physical strain of traveling over the entire state to attend the meetings. After returning from a long trip to Carbondale, he confided in a letter to his sister Dell that he was "not caught up into the 7th heaven by this running about business"; and in another letter he noted that "we have all convened at the sites of the several Normal Schools now so that we have completed the circumference of the heavens. . . . It is anything but an easy job to run one of these institutions. The anxieties of the situation are worse than . . . the labor." [17]

Other grievances the presidents had about the new Board were that it had taken away some of the privileges they had had and created other problems such as preparation of financial forms, difficulties in the Civil Service regulations, and delays in the construction of buildings. Under the old boards, the presidents were given a large measure of administrative control with a free hand to go ahead on their own; they were able to use their various fees to pay bills, meet emergencies, and raise salaries without having it listed in their budgets or securing Board approval. Now this had all changed, and there was so much dissatisfaction that the Chairman of the Board and Director of Registration and Education F.W. Shepardson reported that he had received fifteen hundred letters of complaints covering a range of subjects, including the horribly low salaries that were depleting the normal-school faculties, shortages of fuel and freeze-ups, and a host of other problems brought on by the new bureaucracy. Cook illustrated this unhappy condition by noting an entry in his Board reports that he had recently had to get permission to purchase an item as small as a flag for his main building!

One of the interesting changes in the process of training teachers was the development of the institute and the summer session of the normal school, both for the purpose of upgrading the poorly trained public-school teacher. In earlier times, the presence of a middle-aged man or woman in college was unheard of, for schooling was supposed to end during the period of youth; but public sentiment was changing rapidly in favor of adult education, and by the time Northern opened its doors both of these practices were well established. For those older teachers who had taught with little training for many years and who did not wish credit for their work, the institute generally offered a series of ten lectures; but if teachers wished to pursue work toward a diploma or for certification purposes, they would enter the summer session.

President Cook arranged for a short session the first summer with a two-week institute; but a regular six-week session plus the institute was the pattern for many years thereafter. Efforts were made to entertain the students after the class sessions with receptions, games, sports, lectures, recitals, and the daily general exercises. For several summers the famous Ben Greet Players gave Shakespearean plays in the Normal Woods, attracting large audiences from outlying towns. The Jacob Haish and George Gurler families, both with spacious lawns, held large receptions for faculty, students, and townspeople, for several summers.[18]

At the opening session of the summer school, Cook followed his regular procedure with the full-time students in the general exercises, by "institutionalizing" the summer students in respect to "disorderliness in the halls or cloak-rooms . . . the peculiarities of plate glass . . . also . . . where not to leave their foot prints in the halls." Housing was no problem, for the students could live in the vacated club houses and private homes.

Enrollment in the first institute was twenty teachers, and 135 attended the first summer session; the ratio of men to women was generally about one to ten. Total enrollment increased gradually to a high of 775 in the summer of 1915; then declined precipitously until it reached 548 in 1919 at the time of Cook's retirement. Only one term was offered until the summer of 1921, when two sessions were started.[19]

The first building to be added on campus after the "Castle on the Hill" was the greenhouse in 1907. The need for this structure grew in part out of the interest that developed for landscaping the virgin campus. This sixty-seven-acre tract was

117

rich in natural beauty and comprised diversified areas: in the southwest corner was a large grove of trees, in the central section lay a large prairie meadow, and in the southeastern part was a lake that was usually low in water during part of the year since it was fed by a drainage ditch with rain water from the fields to the west of the campus. Along the eastern border ran the narrow, winding Kishwaukee River. This variety of physical features afforded excellent possibilities for a beautiful campus once the creative imagination could be found, as well as the necessary financial resources.

During the first few school years the campus remained mainly in its natural state since finances were so scarce that not even sidewalks, bridges, pavements, or electric lights could be installed. Such primitive conditions were not convenient for students or faculty since they had to walk long distances, often through mud and water, in order to get to the main building or to find a place to eat, since there was only one bridge and that was on Main Street. The first roads and sidewalks were made of plank, one leading to the building from the south entrance gate for the use of carriages and a sidewalk that led up the hill from the three-foot-wide wooden bridge built across the river on College Avenue. Ascending the knoll from the Ellwood Addition over this precarious contrivance was neither easy nor pleasant, for the planks were loose enough so that a step on one end would lift the other end and into the mud would go the pedestrian with horrendous thoughts of his reception by Cook when he reached the building. Imagine also the students' anxiety walking up the hill on very dark nights before the installation of lights, which was delayed until as late as 1917. In time, with increased appropriations, the board walks and plank roads gave way to concrete and brick and the risky wooden bridge was replaced in 1902 with one of steel, thus ending a heroic phase in Northern's early history that was so often recalled with pleasure at alumni gatherings.

In one of the biennial budgets, funds were listed for a fence to separate the campus from the street beginning at the main entrance and extending east to the river bank; as so often happens, it was eliminated by the legislature. However, Colonel Ellwood, as he had on so many occasions, demonstrated his

The first College Avenue bridge, Spring 1900

benevolence by furnishing the necessary funds to complete it. The *Chicago Tribune* described it as a "work of real art . . . with posts at intervals of 200 feet . . . bear[ing] wrought iron candelabra for electric lights." The main entrance had a double drive gate with two walk gates of ornamental wrought iron, and with circular seats of stone. The stone posts were elaborately carved.[20]

In 1906, the transformation of the virgin campus was begun. Two individuals were mainly responsible for its design and landscaping. Before this time only a few plantings of trees, windbreaks, and flowers were made, but through

the instrumentality of a sympathetic member of the state legislature (whose name is unknown) funds were secured for beginning the present scheme. An expert landscape architect, Mr. Walter Burley Griffin, of Chicago, later the winner in the international contest for supplying plans for the new capitol site of Australia, was given the commission. Upon Mr. Griffin's first visit to the site he found that the foundation of the building was not, in his opinion, of sufficient strength. He therefore conceived the idea of offering some support by building a series of terraces, which also afforded opportunity for formal planting. The large terraces, which support the upper plateau, are eight feet high and extend 384 feet along the front of the building.[21]

At the southeast corner, near the lake, was placed a large octagon with walks and flower beds, and the lower plateaus were used for formal and natural styles of gardens. The lower plateau, in front of the "Castle," was laid out in a series of sunken gardens which became one of the beauty spots of the campus until brick and mortar pre-empted the spot for the present Lowden Hall.

To make the right plantings of flowers, vines, shrubs, and trees for this design, various beds, drives, and terraces were created by Frank K. Balthis, who came from the Shaw Botanical Gardens in St. Louis in 1907 and remained as the gardener for eighteen years. He not only created a campus with a wide reputation for beauty but was also active in developing playgrounds, tennis courts, and baseball diamonds as well as a large gardening project for children in the Training School. In his greenhouse, he was able to grow as many as 385 different species and varieties of plants, including such exotic ones as bamboo, pineapple, coffee, and banana. So highly was he appreciated for his creative role in beautifying the campus that the Board of Trustees in their 1915–1916 report issued the following sentiments: "The grounds present a scene of beauty unsurpassed in Illinois. Walks, drives, bridges, sunken gardens, trees, plants, flowers, a water expanse and the unchanged wilderness of a good part of the original field make a notable possession for an educational institution."

Additional buildings were slow in coming and during the interval between 1899 and the 1909 appropriation of $75,000 for a new training school, considerable repairs and minor additions were made. In 1904, a small grandstand was built to satisfy the athletic interests but in 1905 it was hit by a bolt of lightning and burned to the ground; the next year, with a $1,000 appropriation, it was rebuilt. In 1907 a bowling alley was installed in the gym along with some equipment for Swedish calisthenics.

In spite of the need for more housing for the women students, the first new building on campus was planned for the Practice School. Cook's decision that a new training-school building was more essential than a girls' dormitory indicated quite clearly the importance he placed upon the Practice School. He not only wished to have better facilities for the teacher-training program but he was also eager to secure the space in the east end of the building that the Practice School had been occupying since the opening of the school.

Tentative plans were developed by McMurry, Gilbert, and Cook for this new building and submitted to the state architect. His specifications were put out for bid and the construction firm of Allen and Son, of Peoria, was awarded the contract with W. T. Phillips, of DeKalb, as the resident superintendent.

The building, later named McMurry Hall, was completed in time to be occupied by the opening of school in September 1911. Like the main building, it was designed with two floors and a basement, with the first floor for the lower grades and the upper grades on the second. The plans called for an eight-room structure but to each of the classrooms was added a smaller room, making it possible for critic teachers to take charge of two rooms. In the smaller ones the student teachers began their teaching with a few pupils. As they progressed in handling small groups, they were advanced to the larger room, where they took over a regular class comparable to those in a city system, thus anticipating their future work.

In the basement were the domestic science and manual training rooms, a swimming tank, showers, lavatories, and the fan room through which the building was ventilated. Lighting in the building was somewhat unconventional, with the light coming only from the left side of the pupils. On the front of the building were two towers which suggested a slight kinship to the "Castle."

No sooner had they moved into this new building than a campaign was launched to secure from the legislature an appropriation for a women's dormitory. In the arguments for this structure, Cook placed the very welfare of the Normal before the Board:

One condition stands across the way to the growth of the school and must be removed or we must content ourselves with practically our present numbers. This is the severe limitation which the character of the town offers in the care of our students. . . . Our students cannot find board in private families. People are willing to rent their rooms in the part of the town near the Normal School, as many of the houses have been built with the plan in mind. These rooms are now practically all utilized. Meals are furnished in four student clubs and in certain parts of the year they are crowded to their extreme capacty, while at all times they have little room for more.[22]

Further evidence was mustered to show that many students were obliged to room in one house and get their meals in another and by so doing they were "denied the privileges of a real home. The boarding hall, when properly conducted, furnishes a real home and affords an opportunity for a training in matters of social conduct that is not otherwise available." It

Stone Club Boarding house students in 1900

was this latter point that Cook emphasized, for it had been nearly fifteen years that the school had been without any place on campus that could serve as a home for a large number of girls as well as a center for the social and cultural life of the campus.

In 1913, the General Assembly finally appropriated $125,000 for this building and the contract was let, in June 1914, to a local firm, Skoglund and Wedberg. During that same month, the foundation was staked out and construction was begun. By September 1915, the "house for women," as Cook called it, was completed, and 119 girls were housed on its four floors with 40 double and 47 single rooms. There was no discrimination in selecting the applicants, for the policy of "first come, first served" was the practice. The building had a number of attractive features: a large living room with a grand piano where the girls could meet and entertain themselves or their company in informal parties, and also an adjoining dining room that afforded the whole college a place to hold its special dinners and dances.

Williston Hall, as it was named, was placed in charge of a matron and several faculty advisors whose duty it was to supervise its operation and to see that each girl received nursing care in case of illness as well as "proper consideration while absent from home." From the beginning the principle of self-government was employed, and living in this modern building was indeed a luxury; however, the rules were more closely observed, and it was not so easy for the girls in the Hall to have their lights on after hours, or to take moonlight walks or to eat "spreads" as it was for those in the clubs or private homes. But even with these handicaps, the Hall soon became the mecca of college life where many of the social activities of the school were held and it never lost its attractiveness, for there was always a list of names waiting to be accepted.

In the literature of this period, it is notable how little mention is made by the faculty members of their salaries. This phenomenon, however, does not mean that a great amount of conversation did not take place off the record at the common meeting places, as it always has where two or more are gathered together, since it is a universal topic among teachers. Official discussion, however, was not wanting, for at the Illinois State Teachers Convention at Rockford in 1916, one sectional meeting was completely devoted to a thorough analysis of normal-school salaries by participants from these institutions.[23] Salary increases were almost nonexistent until the inflationary influences of World War I were felt; then, through the combined efforts of the normal-school faculties, some minor increases were finally secured from a parsimonious state government.

No doubt the salaries were held down by the low educational status of the normal schools at that time. Supply and demand also worked against them, for teachers could easily be replaced. Most of all, Cook was not nearly so forceful in fighting for large budgets as he was in preventing political influence; in fact, he often remarked how proud he was that the Board of Trustees had never reduced his budgetary requests. The implications of such a boast from the standpoint of salaries are quite clear.

Salaries of the faculty were based entirely upon the judgment of President Cook. The range of annual salaries for the first instructional faculty was between $900 and $1,500; by 1920, this range had increased to between $1,200 and $3,000. The president's salary of $5,000 was never raised during Cook's incumbency. In relation to the presidents of other normal schools, his salary was not only larger but the extra amount added to his income by free rent for his home gave him a decided advantage. Moreover, upon his retirement, the Normal School Board, "in view of his long and distinguished service in the interest of education," recommended that he be retained by Northern as a nonresident lecturer and that he be given a salary of $2,500 per year. For that salary, he was to lecture as desired at the several normal schools and also to attend teachers' institutes and other educational gatherings to offer his services. One might conclude that his total income from all sources while at Northern was of respectable dimensions. Even before he left Illinois State Normal, he had delivered many commencement addresses as well as other speeches over the years; he drew royalties on public school textbooks, and he was a frequent consultant and inspector at other normal schools.[24]

Upon what basis Cook determined the salaries and rank of his faculty is not clear, for we find no distinct method except that there was a noticeable difference between women and men teachers. All of the latter were listed as professors and the former as assistant professors—at this time there was no associate rank—even though they all assumed the same responsibility in their teaching.

A comparison of two department heads, Mr. Page and Miss Simonson, over a nineteen-year period illustrates the disparity. The percentage difference of their salaries in 1901–1902 was as high as 55 percent; by 1920–1921 that difference had decreased to 21 percent. Before Cook left the institution, opposition had developed not only to the high cost of living and the low salaries but also to the continued discrimination against women. He finally addressed himself to this double standard as follows:

This crying injustice ought to be remedied, but it is my understanding that no arrangement has been made for such relief. The women do just as much work as the men, and do it just as well. In the budget which follows, this old discrimination is still maintained. It will, of course, be useless for me to make any change unless the others do the same thing.[25]

To assist in influencing the Board a frank resolution was drawn up and submitted by twelve of the women faculty at Northern, requesting that sympathetic action be taken to resolve this grievance in the budget.

We have shared in the building up of the school and loyally worked for its welfare, some of us since the beginning of the school, and during this time have had assurance of efficiency in our positions.

Those of us who are heads of departments have been expected to measure up to the standards set for men in similar positions; but our salaries have continued to be $700 a year less than theirs, although four among us have served from nine to seventeen years. . . .

We appreciate the present consideration of the members of the Board in their plan for a 25 per cent raise of salaries generally, but still we wish to ask their attention again to what looks like an injustice—the proposed plan of classification.[26]

They also felt that to continue the classification of women faculty as assistants would be unfair, especially for those who were heads of departments. President Cook, in order to correct this injustice, asked the Board to reduce the minimum salary for professors in the new salary schedule that was being considered so that he could elevate some of the women to that rank and remain within his budget.

The salary increases presented by the five normal-school presidents in 1918 averaged 24.8 percent; however, after the Budget Committee and Governor Lowden had gone over it carefully, they decided to lower it to 10 percent. This action quickly aroused the faculties to concerted action, but they could do nothing to restore the higher figure. The 20 percent increase listed for the presidents was also finally denied on the grounds that "it is a larger salary than is paid to any normal school president in the country; that the present salary of $5,000 is higher with two or three exceptions than any other paid."[27]

When J. Stanley Brown became president of Northern in August 1919, the inflation brought about by World War I was playing havoc with those on fixed incomes. He summarized the plight of his faculty after the first six months by reporting to the Board that he already had several faculty resignations and that

there are other members of the teaching body whose resignations may be expected during the summer because of our inability to make any change in the salary schedule for next year. If we are to fill the positions thus made vacant, at the salaries which we have to offer, we shall either fail utterly to get anyone or be compelled to lower the standard of qualifications for such teachers.[28]

President David Felmley of Illinois State Normal also gave a gloomy picture, for he already had twenty resignations because of low salaries. "As a consequence," he said, "I hav [simplified spelling] spent a large part of my time this summer in efforts to capture a 2000-dollar teacher with a 400-dollar salary." Moreover, he also reported that his faculty had low morale, for they were being paid in real wages that were worth a little more than half of what they had been five, ten, or twenty years ago.

So serious were these privations and so unwilling were the legislature and governor to cope with the plight of the normal schools that their faculties began in earnest through the Normal School Council "to unite to bring pressure" upon these agencies not only to increase salaries but to support these schools financially in a more respectable manner. This Council had been organized in Springfield in 1902 for the presidents' exclusive "purpose of increasing efficiency in the training and education, and for promoting scientific method and spirit in dealing with education problems. . . ." In time, however, faculty representatives joined the Council in order to deal more effectively not only with salaries but also with a wide range of problems.[29]

Late in the General Session (14 June 1917) a bill was passed just at the time the new Department of Registration and Education went into effect, revising and improving the pension system for all public-school teachers, including those from the normal schools. That same year, the Board consented to pay traveling expenses for presidents and faculty members when they were sent as representatives to educational meetings.[30]

The faculty was free to take leaves of absence in case of illness or for further study, without compensation. In an analysis of these leaves for study, it is noticeable that most of the faculty went to the University of Chicago and a few to the University of Wisconsin; the era of Columbia Teachers College had not yet arrived. They usually left for a single year and the only exception was that of Charles McMurry. Those who were absent because of illness received no salary before 1918, when the Board established a policy of full compensation for the first two weeks and half pay for the next two; in case of a death in the family, one could be away without loss for a week. But no "member . . . may be absent from regular duties without a permit from the President."[31]

There were no written contracts or tenure rights, but no

evidence exists that Cook ever actually dismissed a teacher; nor is there any evidence that any of his faculty ever had a sense of employment insecurity.

It was true that Cook recruited his faculty with great care, investigating not only their professional ability but also such personal matters as drinking, smoking, as well as moral and ethical questions. He had strong views on temperance and he also believed firmly that all teachers should have an active religious affiliation. In the classroom, teachers had to submit to his close personal supervision; few showed any inclination to deviate from his teacher-training views. All administrative functions were his domain and at no time did he employ more than one secretary. His teachers were not called upon to do what he considered his work; however, many of them did perform yeoman service in behalf of the students and their activities. During the last year of his administration, when time and energy were running out on him, Newell D. Gilbert, head of the department of education, was appointed dean so that Cook might be relieved of the many burdens that he had carried alone for so long.

President Cook required his small band of somewhat timorous teachers to attend a weekly faculty meeting on each Tuesday afternoon from four to five o'clock. He was "painfully prompt" himself and he expected everyone else to be. The door was closed punctually and what went on within was of a confidential nature, so much so that no records were kept and it was always a topic of speculation and wonder on the part of the students.

Within the walls of the Faculty Room, however, it was not so mysterious: each faculty member was given the names of students to report on "as to the character of their work, their ability, their habits, their adaptation to the work of teaching," and even their social activities. The agenda also included time for criticism of existing conditions, suggestions for possible improvements, and opportunities for reports on ways of self-criticism of teaching methods. On occasion the meeting might

129

include a systematic study of education principles and practices with perhaps a guest specialist to present his views. Faculty members were required periodically to exhibit their skill in the conduct of a class recitation before their colleagues, after which it was freely discussed in the light of the institutional principles. Cook, in his evaluation of this faculty exercise, stated, "It is found to be a prime necessity of our calling to keep the surface of our thought agitated lest we drop into a deadening routine." [32]

Like everything else in the new Normal, the library had a humble beginning. By the spring of 1900, books had been cataloged and were made available to students, and the first library cards were issued. The library hours were quite limited: 8 A.M. to 5 P.M. on school days and 8 A.M. to 12 A.M. on Saturdays. Books and magazines were selected by the faculty with the approval of President Cook, and for a number of years certain publications of the United States government were supplied. Even with these two sources, in addition to various gifts, the library had by the close of 1921 accumulated only twenty-five thousand items.

The location of the library at the east end of the "Castle," where it "straddled the second floor hallway," helped to lure students into it since most of them had to pass directly through its center on their way to classes. This flow of traffic every 45 minutes obviously disrupted the peace and quiet in a room that had a capacity of fewer than one hundred students. The large single room had a rather homey atmosphere with an artificial fireplace and large mantel surrounded with pictures given the school by classes and various individuals, and a small bust of the library's benefactor, Jacob Haish.

Elma Warwick was the first librarian and Grace F. Babbit was her assistant; both remained but a short time. They were succeeded by Madeleine W. Milner, librarian, and Josephine M. Jandell, assistant, in 1901, both of whom had excellent training at library schools. The two of them were active in extending the influences of the library through lectures and book reviews as well as by sponsoring literary clubs and societies. Miss Milner was the first to offer library orientation lectures during the general exercises. In 1909, when Milner left, Jandell was promoted to librarian, a position she held until retirement in 1923. The new assistant librarian in 1909 was Eva I. McMahon; she succeeded Jandell as head librarian.[33]

During the twenty years of the Cook administration, all students were required by law to devote as much time to teaching as they had in attending the Normal. There was no obligation on the part of the school to find positions for these students, since it was in no way a teachers' employment agency; however, all effort was directed toward filling positions to the best advantage of the school and the candidate. The problem of placement was not a serious one, for generally by the time of graduation a high percentage of students had already been placed. Cook estimated that less than one percent failed to redeem their teaching pledge.

There was always a sizeable number who left to teach before they finished their work; some returned to the campus at a later date for the final year. A good example of this practice was found in the first graduating class, where fifteen of the sixteen became teachers but thirty other students from different classes were also placed in village and country schools. This large number of placements was due to two factors: first, there was a clear indication of definite appreciation of the superior value of the professionally trained teacher; and secondly, the unprecedented scarcity of teachers produced an unusual demand. For example, in 1904, Cook was not able to fill more than one-tenth of the calls made upon him for teachers.

There was indeed a tremendous number of positions for trained teachers in all sections of Illinois, for most of those already teaching had not been graduated from a normal school. Floyd R. Ritzman reported the findings of a study of this potential reservoir in a section of Illinois:

There are three thousand five hundred teachers . . . and but one hundred and thirty-five of these are State Normal graduates. Thus but one teacher in twenty-six begins her work with professional training. The proportion does not vary greatly for the sections served by the other Normal Schools of the state. For the DeKalb field it is one in twelve; for the Normal field, one in twenty-two; for the Charleston field, one in twenty-five; for the Carbondale field, one in twenty-seven. The Normal Schools are not furnishing more than enough trained teachers to fill the new positions created, due to the increase of population.[34]

For most of the years of Cook's administration he assumed personally the task of placement as well as the duty of following up on his students; however, other faculty members such as McMurry, Gilbert, and Ritzman also gave him valuable assistance.

In the spring of the year, all roads led to Cook's office, where members of school boards and their principals came in pursuit of teachers. "By our system of room teaching," he said, "school authorities can come and investigate our young women by seeing them at their work of instruction and management." Most of the placements were in the elementary grades; however, on occasion a few members of the graduating class would accept a secondary position, especially if they were trained in domestic science, manual training, art, or public school music. This practice was regarded as a miscarriage of purpose and was discouraged, but it continued to increase nevertheless, for by 1916 as many as 11 percent of the placements were in high schools generally and another 8 percent in the above-mentioned specialized fields. Some of the young men became principals of village schools and a small number of graduates, usually men, transferred to earn their bachelor's degrees.

Cook, in placing his students, emphasized their practice-teaching experience. The letters he wrote for them to his long-standing acquaintances often were full of hyperbole: "admirable," "persistent," "excellent," "kind-hearted," and a "down-right good fellow." He described one candidate as "large-minded and large-bodied and large in enthusiasm and in everything that makes for good things." In replying to a candidate who wanted a supporting letter, he reveals the personal nature of his recommendation: "I will . . . tell him that if he does not take you he is making the mistake of his life and that both in this world and in the next he will be punished for it." [35]

In the spring of the year when the first superintendent appeared on the campus it was only moments before all the students were suddenly stricken with fear.

One of these neophyte teachers has left her reactions to this experience:

You are in your classes, when the telephone suddenly rings. You are wanted in the office at once. Your appointment has come. . . . You wonder what town he is from. "How fortunate it is that you have on your becoming blue dress! . . ." You fix your hair. . . . "Shall you say seventy-five dollars if he asks you?" You reach the office and meet, not one man, but apparently the entire school board. . . . With fear and trembling, . . . the interview is carried on. When your life history is exhausted, they tell you that you will know the outcome in a week or so. You leave them with your mind in a daze. . . . Oh, I do wonder if I made a good impression.[36]

For some it was not a good impression and the ordeal had to be repeated until they were accepted. Salaries paid to these beginning teachers ranged, during this twenty-year period, between $40 and $80 per month.

Cook always gave his undivided attention to the various student activities, and much of his energy was spent in helping them to succeed. However, he considered fraternities and sororities, then becoming popular in colleges, an intolerable nuisance and declared that they should never have been permitted to get started and that once they were in existence they should have been sternly repressed. To him, they were wholly undemocratic and un-American organizations that fostered class distinctions and made snobs of their members. [37]

From these uncompromising views, it is not difficult to predict his views in respect to disciplinary matters. He was

133

without doubt a firm believer in administering the rod, figuratively speaking, to students if they did not abide by the rules; however, he rarely had to resort to severity of enforcement. When he first arrived in DeKalb, he notified the citizens that a normal school had an entirely different class of students from those in colleges and universities and if at any time they had any complaints of a student's conduct either in public or private they should immediately report to him and he would "design them for some other work" by seeing that they made themselves conspicuously absent at once.[38]

To carry out his rules of conduct, the faculty was assigned counseling duties and the students were divided among them; the women members were given a much larger number of students. It was their duty to see that their charges observed the prescribed regulations on and off the campus. Students' rooms were also to be inspected, and the advisors were to cultivate students' acquaintances on a personal basis and report at the faculty meetings on each concerning his behavior. Students also were closely supervised in the study hall where seats were assigned; if anyone was found not to be occupying his seat, according to his signed pledged, he was then deprived of it and given another place to study under closer surveillance.[39]

Other rules were more severe; for example, attendance at public dances was "absolutely prohibited" unless permission was granted by the counselors and also by the president. This rule caused some violations, and as a result the culprits had their deportment grade reduced by as much as one-half on the first offense; in the case of a second infraction it was reduced to zero and the student was requested to withdraw at once. If these offenses took place in the senior year the student was not recommended as a teacher.

At times the discipline seemed somewhat severe when one attempts to adjust the crime to the punishment; however, this was not the age of permissiveness. Two such examples might be cited here: a girl had cut her classwork for a day in order to go to "Champaign on a pleasure trip" with the consent of her parents. In a letter to them Cook gave his idea of such an infraction:

We regard the cutting of her work here as one of the gravest of faults. If students can simply go away at their pleasure there is no telling whether we shall have a school or not. . . . If there is one thing above another that our young people need to acquire it is a sense of responsibility toward their duties. Ethna will be penalized . . . by a sharp reduction in her deportment.[40]

A second case was the dismissal of a girl on the basis of a different violation; in relating her conduct to the father, Cook said:

She has been guilty of very gross misconduct at the railroad station where she goes to wait for the train. . . . This misconduct consists of profane language and general rudeness. I think I need not say to you that a Normal School is no place for a girl who is so far forgetful of everything that constitutes propriety as to be guilty of profanity.[41]

Northern was a low-cost school compared to private colleges and universities, and this economic advantage made it possible for the lowest income families to secure educational opportunities for their children beyond the common and high-school levels. The major costs in 1899 have already been mentioned, but over the years they had all slowly increased except for tuition, which remained at $6.00 per year. By the 1918–1919 school year, fees were beginning to show wartime inflationary tendencies; board and room at Williston Hall had increased to $6.50 a week, and in the boarding clubs from $6.25 to $7.00, while the expense for books and stationery rose to $12.50 per year. In the case of a room downtown, it was not only the rental cost that worried the student but also that if he found it to his dissatisfaction he "could not change . . . without facing Dr. Cook" and, according to James E. Ackert in his "Educational Reminiscences," "no one ever did." Some of the other normal schools used the textbook rental system and one of them charged as low a fee as $1.00 per quarter and $1.50 per semester per student, a cost considerably lower than that at Northern, where Cook required his students to buy their books from the downtown stores.

A few students always found it impossible to continue their training to the point of graduation because of lack of funds. To assist these worthy individuals, the first student loan fund was established in 1900 when the Northern Illinois Teachers' Association gave $300. Following that grant, Mrs. Fred L. Charles established a loan fund of the same amount in her husband's memory in 1912, and four years later the Alumni Student Loan Fund was created by the class of 1916. These nominal contributions, plus a few smaller gifts given by friends, were lent to needy students, especially girls, since it was nearly impossible for them to work for all their board and room. It was different with the boys, however, for of an enrollment of forty-six in 1913–1914, twenty were paying all their expenses from money they had earned during the summer months, and one young Danish immigrant, Soren K. Ostergaard, who spent four years at Northern, not only financed his entire expenses but when he was graduated with his two-year diploma was able to show a bank balance of $300.[42]

In 1916, a bachelor farmer near Newark, Illinois, Andrew Brown, bequeathed in trust to John W. Cook his entire estate "to be used by him to assist worthy students of that school, who shall not be addicted to the use of intoxicating liquors or tobacco, in any form or manner." Each borrower "shall refund the amount . . . when they shall become financially able to do so," in order "to assist other such students . . . in the same manner, so long as the fund shall last." Cook administered this estate until 1919 when it was finally sold for $22,000. In the 1924 report by President J. Stanley Brown, the total value of the funds from this sale was listed at $23,990.50, of which nearly $3,000 accruing from interest payments was lent out to forty-three students.[43]

In October 1903, there landed in California some one hundred boys between the ages of fifteen and twenty from the

Filipino student basketball team (1905 Norther)

137

Philippine Islands to attend schools for four years at the expense of their government. In order to increase their proficiency in English, they were divided two by two among families in southern California, where they attended secondary schools for almost a year before finally being sent to colleges to train in the areas of their choice. Thirty of them decided to enter the teaching profession, so the director of the movement, after consulting with Cook, allotted six of them to Northern in 1904, two in 1905, two in 1906, and one in 1907. Of these eleven, only one had a high-school diploma, and the others were mainly graduates of the common schools. Four of the number were graduated from Northern in three years and one in four years, with the two-year teaching diploma; the others failed to complete their requirements.

These young men were, as Professor Page observed, "good students and men of fine character." In spite of their handicap with the language they had no trouble carrying their course work, since they were a selected group from their home islands. They were especially adept at playing their native games, and they displayed an extraordinary talent when entertaining the students and faculty with the yo–yo, spinning tops, and bamboo flutes.[44] With just enough players, they organized a baseball team which was called "The Fierce Filipinos" and frequently played the faculty and local high-school teams.

When they returned to their native land most of them were placed in supervisory positions in order to upgrade the rather primitive school system with the ideas they had learned in America. By so doing they hoped to stem the increasing tide of emigration to other countries. In time, some of them were elevated to higher positions in education and industry.[45] All remained staunch friends of the DeKalb Normal and never failed in their frequent letters to Cook to express their gratitude for the many advantages they received and friends they made while they were in school.

President Cook had experienced many problems in the operation of his young normal school, but as he approached the twilight years of his presidency, he was faced with a World War that was to influence greatly not only his own institution but all of American education. By the school year 1916–1917, he had built his enrollment to a high point of 424 women and 58 men; but with the war he saw that figure reduced to 223 women and no men in the fall of 1918. Many of the men volunteered their services in 1917, with almost the entire baseball team enlisting as a unit in the Hospital Corps of the 129th Infantry; others were excused so that they could return home to work on their farms. Three faculty members and the superintendent of buildings withdrew for various types of services, while those who remained behind devoted extra time to gardening and going about the communities speaking as "Minute Men." With all male students gone from the institution, Cook made no attempt to initiate any military programs; however, in examining changes in the curricula offerings for the war period, one notices that greater emphasis was placed on geography of countries involved in the war, and in the description of the literature and history courses more attention was given to those events that express

ideally the call of country and the spirit of the patriot in war and in peace: stories, poetry and drama that show these in our own land throughout our national life and in other lands; that relate to the interests and ideals of the Allies in the Great War; that set forth the meaning and work of citizenship, and that foster ideals of loyalty.[46]

Faculty women and the girls both took up war activities in the Red Cross with enthusiasm, "measuring, cutting, folding, turning, pressing, stacking and sewing" gauze bandages with regular quotas that they mailed out each day to the lads in khaki "Over There." Others became so interested in knitting sweaters and socks that no matter where they went they took their needles and yarn with them. One reporter noted that it was not an uncommon sight to see on the campus a "lad and lassie" wandering around the footpaths, one knitting and the other holding the skeins. The girls also spent a great deal of time making candy for the soldiers and sending them gifts,

139

Christmas cards, scrapbooks, and letters. The class of 1917 was so thoroughly entrenched in this work that they referred to themselves as "the nineteen seventeen regiment" which had been called out for real duty on the "Normal Training Battle Fronts."

The student body took on a number of fund-raising assignments, working endless hours at peoples' homes, putting on dances, plays, benefits, and saving their money by eliminating unnecessary recreational expenditures. Efforts also were made to follow the dictates of the "Hooverizing" campaign to eat only barley bread and to follow the slogan when at the table: "A clean plate is the first line of defense." On the walls near the home economics department, where luncheons were served, hung many posters recommending corn as a cereal; cooking classes also planned meals with various substitutes.

The senior class had so many of its members in the war that after long and serious reflection they finally decided there should be no *Norther* volume for 1918. As Ruth Lineberry so beautifully expressed it, "This year our memories are bound in France." In place of it, they went to work and raised $800 to buy a fully equipped ambulance through the American Ambulance Corps in France.[47] An abbreviated version of the *Norther,* containing some brief write-ups of the class along with their pictures, however, was published in the *Northern Illinois* so that there would not be a complete blackout so far as their class history was concerned.

On Lincoln's birthday in 1918, a service flag was dedicated by E. C. Page at a special program as a symbol of the struggle for democracy, past and present. The training school children sang a number of patriotic songs, Cook read the roll call of those in the service, and some talks were given comparing the current struggle with the experiences of Lincoln.[48]

During the war various speakers spoke to the students at the general exercises, sometimes stirring their "imagination to fiery, heroic ambitions." Cook's feelings were also somewhat affected by the reports of the German military machine on the Western Front; during one of his darker moments he asked his audience the gruesome question: "How should we behave as a German Colony?" These various talks were sobering influences to some, and others felt that there was need of a sounder discussion of the war. One student editorial asked if they might not have at least one assembly meeting each week when the faculty could discuss current events as well as the war. Baccalaureate and commencement addresses revealed the war influences. Newell Gilbert gave the commencement address in 1919 on "Making Democracy Safe for the World," and Cook gave his baccalaureate sermon the same year on "The Struggle of Civilization to Survive."

Student life soon began to reflect the influence of the war. Girls' hemlines and hair length both moved upward before the anxious eyes of their mothers. In this new age of the "flapper," such favorite pastimes as dancing took on a state of confusion in the gym; what only a short time before was the waltz, two-step, and Virginia Reel now resembled the "jumping jacks." The new ragtime dances no doubt seemed wayward and perverse to the establishment, and especially to those responsible for the placement of teachers; but, if so, it was only the prologue of student emancipation on the dance floor, for the advent of the Jazz Age with the free-wheeling Charleston was well up over the horizon. Youth could not be stopped from entering the "roaring twenties."

A serious problem came on 20 October 1918, when Cook had to close the school. "It is useless," he said, "to try to continue when there was so much anxiety with regard to the 'flu.' When we shall begin again is a matter for the future to decide. One of our girls died, another is seriously ill. There is nothing that seems of consequence now but the war and the epidemic."[49]

Of all the local citizens who made sacrifices during the war years, no group was more deprived than the faculty members. Prices shot upward from 50 to 100 percent while wages and salaries in the industrial plants responded accordingly, but the Normal teachers and maintenance people received only a 10 percent raise, and none was given the president.

The wartime problems, added to his fifty-four years as a teacher and normal-school president, finally brought Cook to the full realization that his energies were no longer commen-

surate with the increased demands of his office. For a number
of years he had been afflicted with periodic attacks of lumbago,
or what he chose to describe as "a lot of little devils picking away
in the small of my back. . . ."[50] Besides this ailment he was
totally incapacitated at different times by falls, eye troubles, and
severe complications of the heart. All these in connections with
his proclivities to overwork and his advanced age of seventy-
five years finally determined for him that the time had come to
"surrender this important trust" to someone younger.

By the opening of the fall term in 1918, it had become quite
apparent to those closest to him that this would be his last year,
and in January the *DeKalb Chronicle* revealed this disquieting
news to the public:

*One sorrow that is in store for DeKalb in the comparatively
near future is embodied in the news . . . that this is the last year
that we are to have Dr. John W. Cook as president. . . .*

*While no formal announcement has been made and no
resignation has been presented, it is a fact that the current year
will close the connection of this truly great man with the
school. . . .*

*This fact has been no secret among his co-workers . . . for
some time and it has been tacitly understood that when the
coming summer school ends, . . . [he] will leave the helm to
some one else.*[51]

While the official resignation was not presented to the
Normal School Board until 12 May, extensive plans went
forward for the faculty, alumni, and students to have the
proper "leavetaking." On Saturday evening, 14 June, a large
farewell banquet was held in the gymnasium, and a number of
Cook's relatives from Bloomington were present. Further
recognition of his service was contemplated at the close of the
summer school, but on 16 July, five days before it closed, he was
stricken with a serious illness and it was more than a month
before he could be removed to his new home at 5644 Kimbark
Avenue near the University of Chicago.[52]

The Cook era had come to a close at Northern, but since he
had been retained as a nonresident lecturer, he had many plans

in mind for writing and lecturing. Unfortunately, he was unable to carry them out, for he was plagued with continued ill health, and much of his time was confined to the indoors "fighting off the long weary days," as he described it. In a letter to his sister Dell he revealed the monotony of this period:

The days drag wearily along, one after the other. The order of events with me is about the same for all the days. I get up about half past seven, dress, go to breakfast at eight, read the morning paper and then try to find some occupation to make the day endurable. . . .

What a dreary retrospect these last two years present! The afternoon finally finds an end and then the long evening begins. Finally nine o'clock arrives and then I reluctantly go to bed.[53]

In another letter to her he also described the spells of exhaustion that he experienced on occasion:

I not only have the pain of utter weariness but also the distressing mental prostration as well. I have heard it said that women get relief from crying once in a while. I have had instances of nervous breakdown when I have had no control over my emotions. . . . If you were a witness of such dreadful distress I am sure that your sympathy would be awakened for the poor fellow who is paying the extreme penalty of long over work.[54]

Only once during his three years in Chicago was his health sufficiently improved that he could return to DeKalb; it was in May 1921 that he and his daughter Agnes went out for two days. This gave him a deep satisfaction to be again amid the scenes where he had been so happy. The town and college treated him royally, with Mrs. Will Ellwood placing at his disposal her Packard limousine and chauffeur. At Northern, the entire student body and faculty held a general assembly to welcome him back.

The end came to this restless man on 15 July 1922. A funeral service was held at Hyde Park Baptist Church with

Charles McMurry coming from Nashville to deliver the funeral address. Interment took place in Bloomington. At Northern, a memorial service was held in the auditorium.

In reviewing the twenty years of Cook's leadership at Northern, one should consider his administration in the light of the quality of work done as well as the future of this type of institution in the educational system of Illinois.

By the time of his retirement in 1919, there was little doubt in the minds of most normal-school leaders that he had developed one of the better institutions in the nation for the training of teachers. In fact, he was himself so certain of its uniqueness that he refused a number of other presidencies so that he might remain in DeKalb. Wherever he went, it was his basic theme, in his speeches and writings, on committees, and in educational associations. He became so prominent as a crusader that he was frequently introduced by toastmasters as the "Best Normal School President in the United States."

One of the best illustrations of his wide reputation was in 1912 when the *Brooklyn Daily Eagle* polled one hundred prominent schoolmen in the nation, asking them to submit the names of five living educators worthy of special commendation. The votes returned were distributed among 103 names. Among the top names were Charles W. Eliot, 1st; Nicholas Murray Butler, 3rd; John Dewey, 4th; Booker T. Washington, 5th; Frank McMurry (brother of Charles McMurry), 15th; in the next group, those who were deemed to be of superior merit in service to the schools were Andrew D. White, 27th; Woodrow Wilson, 28th; *John W. Cook*, 31st; Jane Addams, 32nd; Edward J. James, 39th; and A. Lawrence Lowell, 54th.[55] Such an illustrious reputation made by a president of a small normal school in a small midwestern town among his leading contemporaries should have augured well for his normal school in the years ahead. But such was not the case, for even before he had left Northern's presidency the winds of change were already increasing. Actually, in spite of Cook's reputation, the schoolmen had little faith in two-year normals, and for that matter neither did a large segment of middle-class society. The universities penalized normal-school graduates by requiring from them, with few exceptions, extra work for a degree; liberal arts colleges also often discriminated against them in their student activity conferences and looked upon them as educationally underprivileged and low in status as far as higher institutions of learning were concerned. To have this reputation in the eyes of other institutions was indeed damaging, but perhaps the greatest shortcoming of all was the fact that for years the state government, in Illinois at least, kept a tight rein on them in comparison with the University of Illinois as far as freedom with their budgets was concerned. It also seriously restrained their operations with limited financial support.

There were several reasons these normal schools had such a low rank among educated people, and most of them are commonly known. Certainly the type of students attending them was one of the principal reasons, for they were generally quite limited in their educational goals. A high percentage of students had only the limited scholastic attainments that were afforded by the country and town school districts. In 1890, studies showed that only 22 percent of the normal-school enrollees had had schooling beyond the primary grades.[56] A few in each class were college graduates who came for the one-year course in order to qualify for teaching. Moreover, the normal schools were required to admit (in most cases willingly) almost anyone who wished to enter, thus making it necessary to instruct a diverse group of students that ranged from college to eighth-grade graduates.

Most of the faculties, too, in this type of institution, added little scholarly status beyond their own schoolroom walls, for they were mostly diploma graduates with a few having the bachelor's degree. An earned master's degree was quite rare. The principal criterion for recruiting these teachers was that they must have demonstrated their superior ability as teachers of children, preferably in a practice school.

Opportunities were given Cook and the other normal schools to modernize their institutions and thus eliminate some of the opposition to their schools. In 1907, the 45th General Assembly authorized the normal schools to confer professional

(Bachelor of Education) degrees upon their students who had finished courses of instruction of suitable quality and length.[57] This movement was begun principally by President Felmley at Illinois State Normal, who had been earnestly struggling for an expanded role for these institutions. He was not content that they should be limited to the training of teachers for the common schools as they were doing. He insisted that they should expand and "make provision for the adequate training of teachers fitted to direct or perform the work of every phase of the public schools from the primary grade to . . . the public high school." One of the arguments he used was that this expanding function was being taken over by the growing University of Illinois program in secondary education.[58] With such a development the normal schools would find themselves performing the limited function of training only elementary teachers, while the training of high-school teachers would take place at the University where the library facilities and academic departments were strong. Felmley's anxieties and arguments, however, had little influence with Cook or President Lord of Eastern, both of whom were genuinely interested in their two-year normals and were definitely opposed to the training of high-school teachers. The two normal universities, Illinois State and Southern, accepted the challenge and went ahead with their four-year programs.

But the forces outside and within the normals were growing ever stronger for a broader function. When Cook returned from a meeting of normal-school presidents in Detroit in 1916, he wrote his old friend, McMurry (in Nashville) that "on every hand there was the ambition . . . to build [teachers] colleges rather than Normal Schools." Those in opposition to this current trend, including Cook, were accused by their opponents of wanting "to juggle with a lot of devices" and "method" instead of giving themselves to scholarship.

Cook wrote further of these opponents and noted especially the program outlined by President Carroll G. Pearse, of Milwaukee Normal, who

suggested a vast curriculum for the Normal School, giving all of the known world and the unknown world, too. In it, however,

146

*there was not the faintest suggestion of anything professional.
It was academic from start to finish . . . so elaborate it outruns
the universities in subject matter. . . . If brother Pearse would
come to DeKalb he would not find a quarter of the things for
which he has made his plea. . . .*

*Oh, it beats the Dutch . . . how unwilling these people are to
settle down to the simple problems of the school.*[59]

By these "simple problems" he had in mind "the plainest of all
plain things, namely, certain points of technic, of class manage-
ments, of assignments, and instruction and organization of
material and inspiration. . . ."

But the time had come when this two-year commonplace
type of normal-school practice was not sufficient to satisfy the
educational leaders, nor in fact many of the students, for they
too wanted an institution in the form of a college instead of a
normal school.

So loyal were the faculty and the students of Northern to
Cook's ideas of a normal school that no moves were made to
broaden its curriculum to a four-year, degree-granting institution while he was president. However, Western Illinois Normal
had moved ahead with its degree program in 1917; President
Lord at Eastern Illinois Normal reluctantly inaugurated his in
April 1920; and finally Northern, nine months later, under the
presidency of J. Stanley Brown, likewise initiated one. Two
years later the three normal schools were legally renamed
teachers colleges, and thus closed a chapter on normal-school
education in Illinois. Few at that time believed that within
thirty-five years these new colleges would be transformed into
universities.

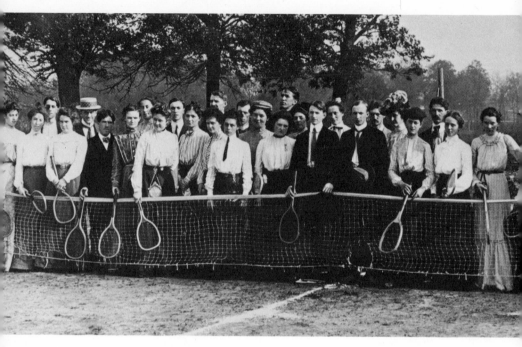

Tennis Association, 1901

5

Activities at the Normal School

STUDENTS in the new normal school were probably no different from students in normal schools anywhere; most of them came from rural areas and small towns, where they grew up under the prevailing mores and traditions of middle America. Their families were mostly white Anglo-Saxon Protestants with marked inclinations toward the Puritan ethic. Few students came from the larger cities, where more diverse standards and beliefs prevailed. These pre–World War II students created few problems for the administration, for the president and faculty were more or less of their own background, philosophy, and purpose. With such homogeneity of values, combined with a student body of mostly girls studying for the teaching profession, it is no wonder that such orderly social relationships prevailed for many years in work and in play.

A further factor that influenced these placid interpersonal relationships was the students' almost complete isolation on the outskirts of a rural town. Those who wished to shop or buy books had to walk nearly a mile to and from the downtown stores; thus students and faculty soon found themselves melded into a harmonious family group, with the various

149

organizations and extra-curricular activities their principal
source of social life. Most of the time, when they needed
individuals to speak or perform in programs, they had to
depend upon their own talents. No student was left out; for all
belonged to some organization, and each was responsible for
part of some activity.

Every morning during the first period of the day the faculty
and students assembled in the auditorium for the general
exercises. Cook preferred this term because he did not want it
to become a chapel experience but rather a meeting consisting
of a wide variety of programs interspersed with moral and
religious connotations. Like many other ideas and practices
borrowed from his alma mater, this custom arrived with Cook,
and throughout his twenty years it changed little in format.
There were basic reasons it was considered essential for the
normal-school process by both students and faculty. One of the
early reporters for the student yearbook saw it as

*the Melting Pot of our school. Of every type the students come,
with uncivilized customs and unorganized thoughts. There are
those who have not learned to wipe their shoes, those who do
not know enough to remove their rubbers at the door, those
who forget to lock their lockers, others who talk in the
library. . . . Many need to be told how to study. In this great
fusing place . . . they may sing the Normal songs and be fired
with the fervor and loyalty. . . . They may conform to the laws
of the Land . . . and be no longer barbarians but civilized.*[1]

It was also to many students "a respite, oasis from the strain
of recitations," a time of the day when all the people could
come together for a few brief moments to sing, to pray, to
think, and to listen. In these exercises, Cook was master of all
he surveyed. It afforded him the privilege to "institutionalize"
his charges, as he called it, within an ideological framework
using the whole gamut of his ideas, from patriotism, religion,
temperance, and morals to such matters as personal manners

Dr. Clyde Vedder lecturing to criminology class of 600 students in Altgeld Auditorium (1967)

and etiquette. The exercises were also an excellent opportunity for him to scold, praise, inspire, and even teach from time to time.

This was a compulsory exercise, the same as the regular class periods; if a student or faculty member were absent, he would have to clear it with the president. Cook had a hard and fast rule—"no excuse except for illness"—and in order to keep the students honest, seats were assigned, and various faculty members were given the task of proctoring attendance while Cook himself shepherded the faculty who sat in a semi-circle on the stage. Helen Gage recalled, some years later, that he was insistent that the student find his seat in the proper manner and that he also sit up and listen, refrain from writing or reading letters, or sleeping, whispering, or, in the case of girls, knitting; any infractions of the rules meant a lowering of the deportment grade.

Cook usually opened this daily exercise with a song or hymn; on occasion, he would follow with some literary or scriptural reading to convey a moral or religious attitude; and then a second song if time permitted, for he was a lover of music. After the songs were the most interesting parts of the exercise for the students, and they tended to listen with more care: Cook's announcements or pronouncements were followed by those of the faculty and students. By this time Parson or Lyon had completed the task of checking the attendance, and it was time for the program of the day. The content of the program varied greatly, as was Cook's intention.

Because of the variety of the program there was often a surprise for the student. It might be the president himself singing ballads or ditties, or telling stories of his childhood, reading plays or the Bible, essays from Emerson, or episodes from the lives of great political leaders. On occasion, he would use a series of meetings to read entire books such as *Colonel Grierson's Raids,* set in the Civil War, or one of Sir Walter Scott's novels.[2] He loved to write as well as to read poetry, and it was not unusual for him to offer his favorites to students. On many occasions he would share letters from former students who were out teaching or from the boys in the service. Again he would tell of the great educational leaders he had known and worked with, or he would devote some time to the educational conferences and conventions he had attended. It was not difficult for him to descend from the lofty to the lowly matters of life and offer his personal advice on how to study, how to succeed, how to walk, how to sit, and even how to take care of one's money.[3]

Besides Cook's role in the general exercises there was some participation on the part of the faculty and students. The musical organizations, the children from the Practice School who were in regular attendance every Monday morning, and dramatic and debate groups—all appeared in programs from time to time. Rose Huff was one of the popular faculty members who either directed musical organizations or appeared with Parson or Cook in duets. Sue Dorothy Hoaglin presented selections from Shakespeare's plays; Clyde Lyon read from the more modern plays, and other members of the faculty also shared in various programs. Edward Page was remembered mostly by the students for his lectures on patriotic subjects; Ralph Wager and Jessie Mann, for nature study discussions; and L. Eveline Merritt, for her stereoptican views of ancient ruins and art gathered from foreign lands.

Students also took their part in the daily exercise; many found it quite convenient to use as a forum to raise money for their enterprises. This was often done by performing a few stunts in order to create some interest in the college paper, or by holding an auction with a faculty member as the auctioneer selling all kinds of trivia to defray expenses of the yearbook. In time this participation led to singing the school songs, performing the yells, and holding pep rallies; and from these there developed an increase importance and influence of the athletic program in the whole life of the school. This began to appear with the advent of William W. Wirtz, who came as the athletic coach in 1910 and whose career and influence will be discussed later in connection with athletics.

Many outside entertainers, lecturers, prominent teachers, normal school presidents, clergymen, opera singers, and even imitators of birds and animals paraded across the general exercise stage. Cook was also able to secure many of his friends as speakers, and he would often attempt to return the compliment in some form, for there was little money for honoraria in those days.

With the opening of Northern, both faculty and students displayed a real interest in an athletic program even though there was no equipment or revenue to finance it. In spite of these handicaps, optimism prevailed, and immediately various faculty members were appointed to coach the following sports: John Keith, football; Fred Charles, baseball; John Switzer, track; and Swen Parson, tennis. Parson was also manager of the athletic fund, which was established to raise money and finance the activities.

Cook had mixed emotions about college athletics; however, he was willing to go along with a program, provided it could be organized and controlled by the faculty and also kept free of the evils common in many schools. He had apprehensions about the emphasis given to competitive sports, and in 1904 he expressed his views in a major address before the National Education Association:

We have suddenly awakened to the supreme value of athletics. . . . But I beg of you gentlemen, you of the universities, is it all sincere, this adoration of brawn and courage? It all seems like a gaudy poster, at times. Its advertising possibilities are enormous. We are cultivating certain of the brutal instincts, whose edge we have been trying to dull by the processes of civilization. Have we been growing effeminate, and are we attempting its correction by a cross fertilization with the spirit of the Roman amphitheater? We all know the topics that hold the center of the field of thought with the high school boys and university men in the football season. . . . But most of the institutions are too busy counting the number of students . . . to spend much time just now on a critical study of the relation of athletics to the national idea.[4]

In spite of his criticism, the young faculty coaches were able to organize teams in both major and minor sports that first year. Football was the most difficult, since there were so few

1902 girls' basketball team, with Coach Fred L. Charles

young men, and only with Professor Keith as one of the players were they able to field a team. Because of the size and inexperience of Northern's team, it competed mainly with the nearby high schools or private academies. Sometimes they played practice games against "town" teams such as the DeKalb Shoe Factory and the "Yannigans." The one team that soon became the one to beat and the one which aroused the students to the highest pitch of enthusiasm was Illinois State Normal, probably because it was Cook's alma mater.

Northern, with this humble beginning, was soon caught up in the sports fever of the time, which ebbed and flowed each year according to the number of young men in school and their ability to win or lose. The constant cry was the need for more players and more funds. Student organizations began to collect small fees for various activities, for makeup games between the literary societies or departments, gramophone concerts, minstrel shows, and candy sales. In time, however, the season ticket idea was introduced, producing more regular income and also attendance. Faculty members, too, were generous in raising funds by playing the college teams, and the alumni also often returned to play the regular players; on these occasions there was added enthusiasm as well as an increase in gate receipts.

The outcome of the first season augured well for the future, for it was not only possible to field a team and play a respectable game, but there was also a fine spirit and good attendance by students and townspeople alike.

A committee with Emma F. Stratford as chairman had selected yellow and white for the first school colors, which were proudly worn by the athletic teams, and these two colors remained for a few years until a change was made to cardinal and black.[5] A school song was not so easily secured; and during the first years various ones were composed by faculty and students; but none seemed to win any lasting favor until Neil Annas joined the staff in 1912 and began a long career of writing songs for the students and alumni.

1902 basketball team, with coach John A. H. Keith

Keith was coach for both football and basketball for several years at Northern before going to Illinois State Normal. This extra assignment must have been time-consuming since he had other duties in teaching the important field of pedagogy. He was considered quite successful as a coach even though many of his opponents were only high school or makeup teams. In the 1902 season, he had exceptional success, winning five, losing one, and tying one, after which Eastern Normal challenged his team to play for the championship. With the largest crowd in three seasons on hand, Northern defeated Charleston and declared itself the "champion Normal team of the State."[6]

In 1904, the team was coached by "Dixie" Fleager, who was paid with money from the athletic fund. He was an excellent coach, and the one year he was at the helm the team had its best football season. The following year found Harry Sauthoff as coach in both football and basketball. He was also an assistant to Mary Ross Whitman in ancient and modern languages, for it was in this department that there was an opening; and since no money was appropriated for a coach, whoever was selected had to be able to teach languages. Thus the three coaches between 1905 and 1918 were all members of that department—an incongruous record that no doubt would be difficult to equal in any other institution.

After Sauthoff's resignation Northern was able to engage Nelson A. Kellogg, who had a good academic record and was an all-around athlete at the University of Colorado. He remained at Northern for four years (director of physical training in 1908), and during that time he attained a good reputation as a teacher and faculty member, but his record as a coach was not an enviable one. School spirit began to ebb, and various things were done to stir it up, such as devoting sessions of the general exercises to this purpose. Competition, too, was increasing, for they were now scheduling a few of the adjacent colleges.

With the advent of William W. Wirtz as coach, one notes almost immediately an upturn in spirit for competitive athletics. Wirtz had not been an outstanding athlete himself, but he did have something even better—an excellent combination of body, mind, and spirit that afforded him the dynamics of

1921 football team

leadership not only on the gridiron but with the faculty as well. One of the students, Gertrude Kelly, described his personality in 1918 at the time of his resignation:

It seems to encompass everything it comes in contact with, from the smallest detail to the big things of our school life that require brain and energy in a leader. If it is but to make an announcement of a coming game, he convinces us that the only thing to do is to come and put some pep into the game . . . . Or if it is an apparently hopeless task [of raising] . . . an eighteen hundred dollar fund for the Y.M.C.A. he steps to the front and puts it over. . . . [7]

Wirtz believed at this time of his life in competitive sports as a good test for certain elements of character. If a young man lacked manly courage or was afraid of "bumps and hard knocks," the game would soon stamp him a "quitter," but if he had real character, it

is pretty likely to prove him a man. It does not take many evenings of practice to convince a fellow of a certain type that the football field is no place for him and that he would rather play tennis, and before very long we begin to notice an unused suit hanging on the hook in the dressing room. It takes a man with real backbone, with stamina, with some force of character to take his place regularly on the football field. . . . [8]

He had a charisma with young men, and through his training methods he stimulated them to their highest efforts. They soon learned that he was not only interested in winning games but that he also "wanted them to play the game and play it fair and square." Such ideals produced a fine spirit in the various sports that he coached during the eight years he was at Northern. By the time of his departure he, along with his predecessors, had established a definite athletic program in the usual sports, and with the exception of the war years it has been continuous.

In 1909, the Intercollegiate Athletic Association with seventy-seven colleges and universities present at their annual meeting demanded that something be done to reduce the "frequent distressing and sometimes fatal accidents." Many of these accidents were due to the frequent roughness and the inability of the referees to control the situation. Complaints were common that the rules against the use of profane language were also not enforced. Both were so common at Northern the first few years that it was necessary to warn all players and bystanders that the rule forbidding such violations would be rigidly enforced.[9]

The varsity teams generally excelled at home, but when they played away from home their victories were greatly reduced. Playing away from home was also often physically strenuous; games might be called early so the players could catch the last train back to DeKalb; sometimes they would have to run all the way to the station in their football suits.

One game that was played every year in October was the alumni game at the time the alumni assembled on the campus. Immediately following the first commencement the graduates organized an informal association, and beginning in 1903 they held their first meeting and had their first football game with the varsity team. This encounter continued annually until 1913 when it was discontinued because the alumni were no longer in physical condition. This occasion was referred to as "homecoming" for the first time in 1906, and at this time the alumni officially established a constitution setting the date for the meeting, the game, and the banquet on the second Saturday in October.[10] Provisions were also made for an alumni column in the *Northern Illinois,* with Jessie R. Mann as the editor.

In addition to playing the varsity football team, the alumni would on occasion return in February for a spirited basketball encounter. Soon an Alumni Athletic Association was also organized, consisting of representatives who had participated in the various sports during their college careers. Its purpose was mainly to "promote the athletic spirit of the school" by raising money among the alumni, faculty, and students and to get these groups to make the sports program more vital by attending all the games. "If all do this, if all *stand by*, if all show their interest in this work," they said, "who can measure the results? Man will develop a higher manhood, woman a higher womanhood, and athletics will then become a force for good."

The annual banquets that followed the game were also great

occasions. The "comebackers," as they were sometimes called, joined the faculty and President Cook, who acted as toastmaster, at the festive tables in the Library. Here he reigned supreme before the assemblage, reading letters from former students, expressing his witticisms, and reciting his annual alumni poem of which the following from 1916 is one of seven verses:

From near and far the loving mother calls
Her faithful children to her hallowed halls.
Her grateful towers, ivy-grown and gray,
Give voiceless welcome on this joyous day.[11]

Then came the several toasts from faculty and alumni; some wrapped in tears and others in humor. At one of the early banquets an alumnus recalled that "a friendly cornfield reached nearly to the back door [causing] . . . a witty member of the faculty once [to] give a toast to 'Our Fodderland.' " The climax of the occasion always came with President Cook's final admonition to his former students at the moment they were ready to depart: "Stand by, stand by, stand by." What this seemingly meaningless slogan meant to these former students was probably as much emotional as rational, but in general it has been explained that each person must perform his obligations in all aspects of his life no matter how much he may want to evade them. The slogan was frequently used in the Normal by those who wanted to improve all kinds of student problems, such as attendance at games and in organizations, to get students to serve on committees, to accept program assignments, and to be loyal to the highest ideals of the institution.

Men's basketball was mostly a home game during the pre-Wirtz period, with usually not more than four or five games at other places. With the coming of Wirtz the number of away games rose considerably. He was also able to entice a few more men to the court; and up until World War I, he usually had an increasing number of experienced players each year. In basketball as in football he consistently got the best efforts out of his players.

Girls' basketball got off to an early start with some forty players showing an interest in the game. Sue Dorothy Hoaglin took charge of the activity and organized an association with a membership fee of ten cents. A number of girls were experienced players, so almost at once they were able to have team competition. They became a rousing attraction for the students and townspeople. Over the years the girls won more games than the men, and there was always more competition for a place on the team.

For a number of years the girls' teams participated in intercollegiate games with several high schools and also with such colleges as Wheaton and Illinois State, but in the main most of the games were among the teams representing the various student organizations. When they did journey to the other towns they were often accompanied by a men's team and were given the opportunity to play the first game.[12]

The two literary society teams always brought out large crowds and created much excitement when either the girls or boys played. The Ellwoods with the purple ribbon and the Gliddens with the green engaged each other until these organizations passed from the scene during World War I. Team loyalties were soon forgotten, however, once the contest was over and everyone enjoyed the entertainment that usually followed the games.

From the beginning, opposition existed to permitting young women to play such boisterous, rough, and immodest games in public and, even more importantly, away from home. There was always the danger of their being hurt or of their health being impaired. The clothing they wore also permitted men to see their uncovered legs, which was certainly not yet tolerated, since women's dresses were still considerably below the high shoetops.

The first opposition to these games was taken at the high-school level when the Illinois State Teachers Association and the Illinois Interscholastic League both passed resolutions against the practice, especially when "the game is in the nature of a contest or for a prize." At Northern, the agitation toward restricting the girls' audience to students only began about midway through Cook's administration, and by 1915 they were strictly school affairs and were not open to the public.[13] Members of the school and any visiting friends, however, were entitled to attend. These games were followed by informal dancing—for students only. Because of this restrictive policy and the ever-increasing interest on the part of the public in male spectator sports, the pendulum continued to swing away from women's intercollegiate contests.

After the era of girls' intercollegiate basketball ended, other women's sports activities began to increase in importance. Baseball especially became popular, and even though most of the girls were totally inexperienced in the sport, it soon grew with "a great wave of enthusiasm." Various classes were organized into teams, and soon regularly scheduled games were a part of their activities.

On the opening of school in 1899, a minor sports program was also begun with the organization of the Tennis Association. Two courts had been laid out; and by 3 November, with Swen Parson as captain, the first tournament was completed. Prizes in the form of pins were donated by Fred Charles and were awarded to both men and women.

In the spring of 1900, Charles organized eighteen men into the first baseball team. Parson was the first manager, and other faculty members often formed a team in order to give the regulars some competition. The first season they played six games, mostly with local teams, and split evenly in the won-lost columns. Professor Switzer gave his services as coach of the track sports for the years he was at Northern.

For the next five years there was a different coach each year for both baseball and track, beginning with Alton J. Johnson. Henry A. Stiness, a junior law student at Northwestern University, was coach for baseball and track during the spring term of 1904; following him, the coaching of all sports was performed by the faculty members in charge of football and basketball.

At the close of each athletic season it was the custom to have a reception dinner for the teams. In 1906, the Athletic Association inaugurated the idea of awarding the N.I. monogram as an official athletic emblem. It was cardinal red on a black diamond. Each player was issued a star for each sport in which he

1925 baseball team; coach Paul Harrison at far left

qualified; it was attached in a particular corner of the diamond to indicate the sport. These were granted in the case of football to a player who had represented the school in at least three "halves" of regular "inter-school" contests. The girls were not issued a star for their basketball playing, but did receive the N.I. monogram and diamond. Cook encouraged these honors by bestowing them at a general exercise program. In 1907, it was a special occasion for the girls' basketball team: besides receiving the diamonds for a champion team—winning nine and losing none—they also had their pictures in the *Chicago Tribune.*

The president had had a keen interest in physical culture for young women even before he came to Northern, so, soon after he arrived, a systematic program in gymnastics was developed. Miss Hoaglin took charge of the forms then currently popular, the Emmerson Physical Culture and the Columbian rhythmical movements, while Inez Rice taught "free gymnastics and club swinging." In 1901, Jessica Foster was engaged as a regular teacher in physical culture, and she also offered courses in Swedish gymnastics.[14]

Physical training for men was a problem for some years since there were so few male students and the employment of a special teacher was not warranted. Some instruction was given by the coaches when they were not involved in a major or minor sport.

Physical examinations were late in coming, and it was not until 1919 that all students were examined by local physicians. This program was conducted without any expense to the school and was managed by the biology department. "It resulted," according to Cook, "in some remarkable discoveries of the existence of unsuspected physical deficiencies and set going efficient means for their correction."[15]

The postponement of some form of health program for so long almost borders on carelessness, for the campus was periodically struck by "plagues" that disrupted the normal operations, sometimes for days and weeks. On Christmas Day, 1906, DeKalb was stricken with an outbreak of scarlet fever, and the students were requested to remain at home. For nearly five weeks, bulletins and programs of study were mailed to

1902 track team; coach John Switzer (professor of physics and chemistry) at right

them. A few students returned unaware of the epidemic and said that the place appeared "an uninhabited island." Alice Swarthout stated in her description that "the streets are deserted, the Club Houses are empty, work has ceased and sports are fled. Only Tom Moore [the campus dog] remains with a melancholy wag of the tail. . . ."[16] Some neighboring critics attributed the outbreak (125 cases) to the lack of a sewage system worthy of the name, as well as the low flat land that was difficult to drain. Another epidemic struck the school in 1911, causing an excessive number of student absences with a variety of contagious diseases. The Training School was especially hard hit and one student reported that in her house they had cases of almost everything except "teething." The influenza plague also closed the school in mid-October 1918 for almost three weeks, and with the reoccurrence of the epidemic it was ordered to close early for the holidays.[17]

Upon the opening of the school, a board of managers under the chairmanship of Fred Charles had been established for the purpose of publishing the *Northern Illinois* monthly magazine. Alice Crosby was the first editor and Lewis Ragland was named business manager; sections were allocated to each of the classes, and a number of special columns were established for editorials, the Practice School, literary societies, athletics, exchanges, alumni news, and a humorous column appropriately named "Barbs." Emma Stratford, with her drawing skill, designed the front cover. A yearly subscription of eight to ten issues cost the students fifty cents, which was sometimes difficult to collect; the balance of the cost was raised from the sale of two or three pages of advertising to the leading business firms. This publication changed periodically in its emphasis before it became a semi-weekly newspaper in 1923. For a few years the literary section was prominent, with essays written by the faculty and stories, themes, and poems by the students; in time, the coverage of sports was given greater attention. Faculty activities were always popular with the students. Controversial issues or criticism of the town or campus were seldom expressed. The ever-popular "Barbs" column was used by those so inclined to indulge in the serious art of being humorous; their jokes or whimsical remarks about individuals were no doubt amusing at that time, but in the light of present standards they would create little reaction.

Another student publication was the *Norther* yearbook put out by the senior class. The volumes differed slightly in length and color during this period but were somewhat alike in format. The seniors "made drawings, wrote the verses and the stories, told the jokes on each other and the faculty." The editor and staff for each issue were selected in the fall along with the commitees to work with Ida S. Simonson, the faculty advisor for many years, in order to be able to complete the volume by Commencement Week. It was a treasure house and a monument to a class not only for the Normal students but for all friends of the institution. It was filled with pictures of the faculty, buildings, campus, and town, and was a complete mirror of school life gathered together in 200–250 pages. The editor in 1911, in presenting this "mirror" to her colleagues, expressed her hope that they would "often turn to these pages and live again these happy hours, to wander once more in our sunny gardens, under fine old trees, or watch the lazy river as you dream on 'things as they used to be.'"[18]

A third publication was a small but rather creative project developed by the printing class in the Department of Manual Arts and called *The Upper Case,* which appeared irregularly between 1916 and 1937. All the writing and printing was done by eight or ten students—both men and women—and it covered in a condensed style most student activities. Sports was its special interest, which inspired Coach Wirtz to say that it certainly was "about the best little booster of the athletic interests of the school that could be imagined."[19]

In normal schools as in private colleges, literary societies were created as educational activities in order to complement the instructional programs. All students were automatically members of one of two literary societies at Northern, and from them they received not only training in writing, speaking, acting, and parliamentary procedures, but also a certain sophistication in refined deportment. These societies also afforded a certain degree of social life for the student. Instead of following the usual pattern of classical names for the societies, they used the names of the benefactors, Ellwood and Glidden.

Membership selection for the societies was not left to the students but to President Cook. At the beginning of each term, during the general exercises he would divide the girls and the boys, then draw their names so that each society would receive an equal number of both. He also contended that such a method would assure an equal distribution of the talent.

The two societies were under the supervision of faculty members who acted as critics and general advisors. They met semi-monthly on Saturday evenings, and each student member was expected to participate; but being the "nightmare" it was for many of them, it was not always easy to fill out a program, and even then there was no assurance that all would appear the night of their assignment. At first they met in Chronicle Hall, but later they met in a room at the Normal set aside for that purpose. Townspeople were welcome for a nominal admission charge. Their programs varied over the years, but in the main they followed a regular pattern: debates, orations, and declamations were the core of each meeting, with other serious and humorous program items such as mock trials, poems, essays, imitations, musical and dramatic numbers, with the critic's report inevitably appearing at the close of the meeting. Procedure, or how a meeting was conducted, was usually considered by the critic more important than the program itself.[20]

An important adjunct of these two organizations was the Intersociety Literary and Musical Contest that was held annually in the spring. It created so much enthusiasm and rivalry among the students that not even the athletic contests were able to equal it. Starting in the fall, each society would begin to lay its plans for this mighty encounter, and for weeks the whole campus would be held in the grip of a competitive spirit. A senior reporter described its ecstatic nature in 1901:

There are many events of the school year that are of vital importance . . . but if we are seeking after the occasion which stirs the student life to its depths, which binds the . . . closest ties, and marks the floodtide of school spirit, we must turn to the society contest. Here each student finds a place. He is either on the platform or represented there, he waves his banner and claps his hands in the audience, and is kept busy between times bowing and smiling a welcome to the friends of other years . . . who come flocking back to receive a fresh inspiration and renew their youth.[21]

The evening of the contest found the auditorium festooned with green and purple banners and bright lights and generally filled to capacity. All contestants were seated on the platform, with six judges dispersed throughout the audience and Cook presiding at the podium. It opened with the school song, and between each part of the program the Normal Chorus would sing. The entire program was three hours in length, and the fact that it was able to hold an audience that long speaks well for the performers.[22]

Following the program, tension mounted while the judges marked their ballots. Cook delayed the decision as long as possible to create a suspense that "became almost unbearable." To the victor was given a special trophy: a beautiful bronzed statue of Perseus that the president and faculty had purchased for this occasion. When the enthusiasm and shouting subsided, it was time for the annual contest banquet in the gymnasium, where there were toasts by the faculty and judges as well as stories of previous contests by the alumni.

Changes in the intersociety contest gradually took place; the old system of so many entries and endless hours for practice "proved to be too much extra work for the contestants." It was the debate that always required the most time, so by 1915, with Clyde Lyon as the drama director, it was replaced as the principal entry by two popular plays by the societies that competed annually for Perseus.

The third major organization comparable to the literary societies was the Ionian Society, organized in 1899 exclusively for young women. It was divided into seven different study sections with a woman faculty member heading each group. Every two weeks some seventy-five members would divide themselves into their respective groups to study art, literature,

travel, magazines, current events, music, or illustrative drawing. On occasions they had combined programs.

Even before the ancient art of debate was withdrawn from
the intersociety contest, it began to develop as a separate
activity. With Charles Whitten as the faculty advisor, the first
intercollegiate debate was held with Platteville Normal in 1911
with Paul Moon, Arthur Norberg, and Jennie Whitten as the
representatives. To encourage and also professionalize this art,
the Debate Club was organized during the same year, and the
first annual declamation contest was held on 31 May 1913.

Public speaking was an important facet of college training,
and it was established early as a major activity. In 1896, Cook,
while at Illinois State Normal University, assisted presidents of
similar institutions in Kansas, Missouri, Iowa, and Wisconsin in
organizing the Interstate League of Normal Schools. This new
organization was created mainly because the regular collegiate
institutions were beginning to exclude the Normal schools from
membership in their associations. In 1902, Northern joined
and for five years participated fully in the activities before it
withdrew because the students lacked "interest in things oratorical." [23]

The first year, seventy-three students joined the League,
and each year a preliminary contest was carried out to select a
contestant to compete on the state level; the winner of the state
contest was sent to the finals, the location of which alternated
among the six member schools. These three contests were
enthusiastic affairs (at least for a few years) with a complete
program of various talents. At Northern, special judges were
engaged and the two winners were given the I.L. Ellwood prize
of $50 and the faculty prize of $25. Contestants in the regional
contest were escorted by students and faculty from their school,
along with athletic teams that engaged in various contests for
championships. The first year of Northern's participation was
at Emporia, Kansas in 1902, and Northern's orator, William R.
Mofet, with an oration called "Peter Abelard," received the first
prize of $100. James E. Ackert, one of Northern's most
illustrious alumni, recorded in his "Reminiscences" that Mofet
had won for Northern "its greatest victory." To celebrate
Mofet's achievement, two hundred people gathered at the

footbridge with a band. They made a noisy parade through the city, after which they returned to the site of an old windmill near the campus for a large bonfire. This was Northern's only regional first prize. However, her contestants did win two second prizes, and in the state contests they were victorious on the first three occasions.

Drama and musical organizations were much a part of student life at Northern from its earliest days. These, unlike the literary societies, expanded and became more important throughout the history of the institution. The first dramatic club was established by Sue Hoaglin in 1900 for the purpose of presenting from "time to time portions of the best dramas, thereby creating an interest in the highest form of literature." Jennie Farley assumed the position in 1902 and was at Northern until 1912, when Clyde Lyon became the dramatic teacher. He established this field as an integral part of school life. Plays, some serious and some farces, were also put on by many of the organizations. The school orchestra furnished music for these plays, which gave added atmosphere to the decorated auditorium. Following the senior play, during the final week of school, the juniors traditionally gave an informal reception for the seniors in the foyer. By that time the seniors were able to show off their *Norther* yearbook, as well as their class pins or rings.[24]

Before the close of the first year, there were four musical organizations: both men's and women's glee clubs, a band, and an orchestra. These musical groups soon became an essential part of school life, offering varied programs several times a year. The girls' glee club, or Treble Clef as it was named, soon became the most prominent of them all; however, the band grew in importance as athletic interest accelerated. Every Christmas season, after weeks of training and with many additional voices from the faculty and the city and with special artists from Chicago—all under the direction of Neil Annas—Treble Clef presented selections from Handel's "Messiah." At Christmas, 1912, at the general exercises, Treble Clef gave one part of the cantata "Queen Esther"; President Cook was cast in the role of Mordecai. This group of girls not only played a large role in the musical life of the college, but the organization also, in spite of its many exacting practice sessions every Monday night, had a fine social influence upon its numerous members. There were many lighter moments of fun and relaxation, the times they went on trips and the numerous picnics, bonfires, and other activities that came when the seasons finally ended.[25]

Another kind of social life was supplied mostly by clubs of all kinds. Some were associated with specific activities such as dancing, skating, hiking, traveling, athletics, nature study (especially bird-watching), and photography; however, many of the students found a pleasant social life within the boarding clubs in the "Ellwood Syndicate," as it was sometimes called. There were a number of different houses, and the following names were some of the more common ones: Benson, Hurt, Tudor, Rickard, Kilmer, Shafer, and Dadds. Each would have its regular parties, housewarmings, picnics, candy pulls, sleigh rides, hikes, dances, and faculty and alumni days. At the dance parties they blended such dances as the Virginia Reel with the Turkey Trot and the college orchestra also "knocked out" many of the ragtime tunes of the day.

A great deal of fun and good-natured bantering was exchanged in the boarding clubs about the quality of the food; one of the many sayings was: "H is for hash our club boarders know well, with plenty of pepper the taste to dispel." Contrary to this folksy wit, the clubs did serve good, ample, home-style cooking. The houses were usually booked to capacity, with a few single faculty members and boys also eating their meals with the girls. Each club had a boy who was the steward, and it was his task to represent it at the train station at the opening of school to interest the new students in becoming members.

By 1911, students at Northern were becoming restless and somewhat unhappy about their restricted social life. A little more sociability should be permitted by the administration, they thought, especially on Friday nights; for, as some of them said, DeKalb at night was about "as exciting as a cemetery." Up to that time no parties were permitted on Friday evenings, and as a result some students were tempted to go to places of a questionable nature. To correct this situation, a grievance committee chosen from the various clubs presented Cook and the faculty with a plan to utilize the gym on Friday evenings, when it was available, for social activities. All activities would be supervised by a committee chosen by the students. Cook, to the committee's surprise, immediately thought "it would be a good thing," and thereafter "Club Night" became an established event for games and dancing. Again in 1914 and in 1916 the students expressed discontent that they were more restricted than those in other institutions, and they asked the administration for a larger voice in their social activities. In fact they went so far as to call for a mass meeting to "find out if it is the pleasure of the student body that we have more social functions."[26]

Northern also had its student associations of a moral and religious nature, such as the Y.M.C.A. and the Y.W.C.A. Their emphasis was not so much religious as it was moral and character-building. They taught the need for personal service such as singing to the sick and aged, visiting the jails, teaching Sunday School classes, operating a non-profit bookstore, and helping the new students find rooms. The campus Y.W.C.A. was always much larger than the Y.M.C.A. It had regular programs in their "brown room" in the form of vespers, devotions, talks, receptions, Bible study, discussions, and meditations. They also sent delegates to the national and regional conferences. These organizations began to wane during World War II, and by 1948 there is no record of their existence.

Most of the students belonged to various Protestant churches, which maintained a rather close relationship with the Normal. Each fall the local churches gave receptions for the new students of their faith, and many of the ministers spoke at the general exercises. Periodically prominent evangelists came to the city for protracted meetings under the auspices of the churches, leaving deep impressions upon the students as well as the citizenry.

Cook wanted all his prospective teachers to be thoroughly endowed with the Christian spirit and to manifest in their lives the essence of Christianity; he did not wish, however, that they be inculcated with doctrine. Rather, he wanted through his educational program to close the gap between religion and education through an emphasis upon the spirit of Christianity. In spite of his sincere efforts, his institution experienced periodic violations of moral precepts; on occasion, even during one of the evangelistic services, he found it necessary to speak out on the subject of stealing.[27]

Graduation was a time when the seniors where honored by both the community and the school. For twenty years President Cook was able to secure the cooperation of most of the DeKalb churches in holding the baccalaureate services in the auditorium. In recognition of the importance of the Normal to the city, churches and the school joined hands in this annual affair. With Treble Clef furnishing the music and Cook preaching the sermon, it was an occasion long remembered by the graduates. The one thing frequently emphasized in the news reports was the general consensus of praise for his addresses; it was often related that he had a singular ability to take a scriptural text and interpret it in such a way as to please his audience. In 1915, the *Chronicle* reported these sentiments by saying that his sermons seemed to "grow better year by year. . . . There is nothing prosy or pedantic . . . but they are always brimming with good advice given in a sparkling manner that removes it from any suspicion of dullness. . . ."[28]

Commencement Day closed the final week for the seniors with the program always held on a Thursday morning. For a number of years it was somewhat weighted with the reading of a number of senior theses that all graduates had to write. The only compensating factor for these scholarly renditions was that they replaced the commencement speakers who might have been worse even if briefer. By 1912, however, the program was revised, and instead of the theses some prominent friend of Cook was usually engaged as speaker, and the valedictorian spoke in behalf of the class. Each class also wrote and composed its own song and music, and a few were able to purchase memorials for their alma mater.[29]

At the close of this major event came the popular president's reception for the seniors, either in the foyer or at his spacious home on College Avenue. Ten days before the reception "dainty white envelopes" were sent to the seniors. Music was provided by the orchestra and by Vera Wiswall, an accomplished vocalist on the faculty. Neil Annas was also always generous with piano solos at such occasions.

Faculty members were often brought together in various social activities. Young and physically active, some often went on hikes together: "On almost every Saturday some of these enthusiastic hikers traverse the country roads. Be it the short distance to a friendly orchard, the walk around the four-mile square north of the Normal, or the eleven mile stretch from Waterman to DeKalb—each is fearlessly undertaken." At other times several families would go as a group to a lake for swimming, fishing, or a summer vacation. On other occasions the whole faculty would meet at the president's home and then journey to some prominent farmer's grove for a faculty picnic, there to set a precedent that lasted over the years that certain male members would fry the steaks and brew the coffee. Following dinner, some would engage in sports, such as baseball or shooting matches, while others chose a less strenuous exercise in hunting for nuts or picture-taking.

Faculty groups on other occasions also visited prominent farms, industries, and historic places, and sometimes they even went to Chicago to see or hear something special in the entertainment world. DeKalb had little to offer its faculty culturally; however, the one redeeming feature that it did have over its sister Normals was its proximity to Chicago for those who might wish to see a play, hear a concert, visit the galleries and museums, or improve themselves in the excellent libraries.

Faculty dinners, parties, and recitals were enjoyed periodically at the different homes, and at times they were lively affairs with games and music by the orchestra or from the popular Edison phonographs. On occasion Mrs. Swen Parson invited groups to a piano recital by some promising artist. President Cook's birthday on 20 April always called for the largest reception of the year by both faculty and students. Honoring him on his tenth year at Northern, the faculty presented him with a beautiful silver loving cup with a long, engraved inscription bearing their deepest sentiments. In 1931, the class of 1920, which was the last class at Northern while he was still president, had a bas-relief bust of him—the work of his daughter, Agnes Cook Gale—mounted above the fireplace in Williston Hall.[30]

By 1918, the faculty was beginning to feel the need for a more formal organization, not only to afford them opportunities to meet socially and professionally, but also to furnish the "means whereby the collective influence of the membership may be brought to bear upon any question or problem, and to afford opportunity for the formal discussion of the same. . . ." With the coming retirement of President Cook and the inadequate salary situation for normal-school faculty members, the Faculty Club united with those in the sister schools, along with the alumni chapters who were brought into the group in order to assist in publicity matters such as writing letters to the senators and representatives to request larger budgets for the normal schools.[31]

The Faculty Club was more than a pressure group; it was a vehicle for social gatherings. A small membership fee was assessed, and with it flowers were sent to the sick or to newlyweds, outside speakers were secured, and the expenses of their representatives were paid when they attended the inter-faculty club meetings. Many of the programs were put on by the members themselves in the form of plays and farces or serious debates such as the pros and cons of the League of Nations.[32] There were indoor parties and outdoor picnics as well as an occasional reception such as the one for J. Stanley Brown when he was chosen president.

An aerial view of campus, circa 1930

J. Stanley Brown
second president, 1919–1927

6

The Decade of the Twenties

WHILE the American people were engrossed in the settlement of the war to save democracy, one small segment of the population was practicing on a local scale what might be considered a miniature sample of the "democratic procedures" similar to those then being used at the international peace conference. When Cook announced his retirement, the Normal School Board appointed a committee of three (Shepardson, Goddard, and Blair) to consider the question of his successor. Twenty-one days later, at the next Board meeting, Chairman Shepardson reported that "a very thorough canvass had been made," consulting normal-school faculties, superintendents, and principals of high schools and grade schools, and the "unanimous opinion of the committee was that Mr. J. Stanley Brown, of the Joliet Township High School—a member of the Normal School Board—was, from every point of view, the best man to succeed President Cook." They thought he ranked above all other candidates in scholastic and professional education, experience in normal-school work, and more especially "in developing one of the greatest high schools, not only in the State of Illinois, but in the Nation. . . ." Not only was he the unanimous choice of the Board, but the presidents of the other four normal schools concurred in the decision, including Cook, who "expressed himself as highly pleased with the selection of his successor." [1] With this unanimous opinion, J. Stanley Brown was given the position, and he began his duties on 1 August 1919, at a salary of $5,000 per year.

Certainly on paper this man seemed qualified for the position. He had been born near Cumberland, Ohio, 13 September 1863. At seventeen he became a village school-master, a position he held for three years before he entered Denison University. After six years there he was graduated in 1889 with an A.B. degree in classical languages. His first teaching position was in Kentucky, where he remained just one year as a classics instructor; in 1890, he moved to the presidency of Arlington College in the same state for three years and in the first year there he received a questionable M.A. degree from Blaineville College. [2] Feeling the call of the West, he journeyed to The Dalles, Oregon, where he accepted the principalship of the normal school for one year. After that he returned East to become principal of Joliet Township School, where he was when offered the presidency at Northern. [3]

It was at Joliet that Brown discovered his real challenge and where the qualities of his visionary leadership were nurtured to the fullest extent. This was the period when the junior college system was developing out of the reforms by William Rainey Harper, president of the University of Chicago. J. Stanley Brown almost immediately became involved with Harper in this movement and within a short time had added two years of training to his own school system; to make it more effective and attractive, he launched a building program in 1901 that was considered one of the finest in the nation. His background in the classics kept the courses and instruction on such a respectable level that the graduates were fully accepted by such institutions as the Universities of Illinois and Michigan. [4] Joliet Junior College is often recognized as the first of its kind in the nation.

Unfortunately, Brown's aggressive leadership at Joliet finally created some tension between him and his Board of Education about large increases in taxation, but this problem was relieved when he was called to Washington, D.C. during World War I to become director of the Thrift and Savings Campaign for the public schools; soon after his return, he was selected for the presidency at Northern.

His difficulties at Joliet did not detract from his leadership as a prominent educator. He had already achieved distinction as an officer in state and national associations and as author of several research studies. He was widely known for his vision and courage in trying out new ideas, some of which were exceptional contributions; for example, within ten years after his departure from Joliet, ninety-two junior colleges had already been established on his pattern.

J. Stanley Brown brought to his new position a vastly different type of personality from that of his predecessor. He was more reserved, more formal in appearance, and lacked the warmth or personal charm of Cook, and even though he was vastly more lenient with students, their impression of him was, according to one prominent student, that he was "pretty much a 'stuffed shirt.'"[5]

His wife described him affectionately as the "Big Man"; and indeed he was, with at least two hundred pounds not too equally distributed over a five-foot, ten-inch frame. He was not only big in size but he also had a big voice with a deep and clear tone that reverberated throughout the auditorium when he was speaking.

He gave the faculty greater freedom in their teaching, and never did he visit their classrooms as Cook had done. There was less supervision generally on his part, and the faculty as well as the students enjoyed a higher degree of flexibility in purpose and philosophy as members of the institution.

When he made his first appearance before the faculty, many of his staff knew him personally and were aware of his proclivity at times for saying the wrong thing; this occasion was no exception. Swen Parson recorded this *faux pas*:

I remember the new president's remarks at the first faculty meeting. He started out by saying that we must not expect him to do things the way Dr. Cook had done them. No two men can do things alike. . . . He hoped that we could all work together harmoniously. He then informed us that he had three college degrees. "One, the bachelor's degree, a perfectly good degree from Dennison [sic] . . . University, and a master's degree that I do not think so much of; a doctor's degree also from Dennison for a piece of work that I did in my high school at Joliet."[6]

This unfortunate remark left a somewhat cloudy impression about what Brown had in mind, and it was not until his administration was nearly over that the faculty was fully aware that his master's degree was such an illegitimate one that he was compelled to drop it from his credentials.

His social and political philosophy was in line with the "Old Guard" of the Republican party and the conservative Baptist church, both of which he ardently embraced. He taught Sunday School classes and served as a member of the Board of Education of the Northern Baptist Convention from 1915 to 1935. He also served for fifteen years in the Joliet Chamber of Commerce and in 1916 was president of District XIX of the Rotary International. He frequently spoke out against the liquor interests, and his praise of the prohibition amendment was often couched in eloquent terms. At one time he had the famous Reverend Clarence Wilson, executive secretary of the Board of Prohibition, Temperance, and Morals, as speaker at the college, and when the orator had finished the students too were firmly convinced that Prohibition was one of the most important achievements of the century.

Following the war, with the serious problems of labor unrest, he often spoke in various Illinois cities, expecially to the chambers of commerce, where he emphasized the true worth of thrift in solving such national problems. He believed that the public had lost its true sense of values and that

extravagance is becoming more and more a national characteristic and that its increase and practice will tend toward national weakness. . . . It is imperative that thrift should become a national characteristic and that to this end the teaching of thrift must become a serious and universal part of our educational system.[7]

In order to bring this recommendation to fruition on his own campus, a committee, with Brown as chairman and four faculty members, was established to formulate a course in "Thrift Education" for prospective teachers.

Some of Brown's other values were espoused in one of his speeches on Defense Day at the general exercises, 12 September 1924. He read informally two brief excerpts, one from President Coolidge and the other from the universally known celebrity of comic strip fame, Andy Gump. Coolidge's reverence for the flag was noted in these patriotic words: "He who lives under it and is loyal to it is loyal to truth and justice everywhere. He who lives under it and is disloyal is a traitor to the human race everywhere. What could be saved if the flag of the American nation were to perish?" Gump's ideas and style were perfect for the mass mind, as were his comics: "A man's country is his greatest treasure and you can't blame a guy for wanting to guard it——I claim a country worth living in is worth fighting for——Any time you don't think this a great country, buy a geography book, and try to find a better one——After you look all through the book, you'll see that you wasted the dollar you paid for it." [8]

One of J. Stanley Brown's principal interests was community planning, and he sponsored community-college conferences and concert benefits at the Normal in order to raise funds for this purpose. At the initial conference dealing with community problems, four sessions were held during the day with representatives from such organizations as the Parent-Teachers Association, Rural and Village, and the Woman's Club. For the evening session, two able exponents of this new community emphasis, Professor R.E. Hieronymus, of the University of Illinois, and W.G. Eckhardt, of DeKalb, a prominent leader in rural life, were secured as the main speakers. J. Stanley Brown presided at the sessions and gave the closing talk on the topic, "Fusion of Community Interest." [9]

J. Stanley Brown was not content with community planning and public relations on the home front alone, for his interests were also devoted to the idea of creating a new form of organized cooperation among the teachers colleges in the state.

At various times, meetings had been held with delegates and with the presidents alone for the purpose of discussing important issues. However, President Brown recommended a new plan of organization for the five faculties, which was to consist of day programs to be held at some central place in the state. Prominent speakers could be engaged, and group sessions of the faculty members in their particular specialties could be held. The first such meeting was called for 1 April 1927, at Springfield, with 338 members in attendance and Professor W.C. Bagley, of Columbia Teachers College, as the principal speaker. These meetings were apparently not of sufficient merit, however, to satisfy the faculties—even though they offered two days of vacation—so in 1929 they were put on a biennial basis. This pattern was followed until faculty interest ebbed to the point at which the meetings were finally abolished.

President Brown was vitally interested not only in promoting DeKalb's welfare but also in seeing that its citizens reciprocated favorably in making the college a better institution. In fact, on various occasions, he informed the local citizenry precisely what the college meant to them in terms of dollars and cents. In 1925, in a speech before the Kiwanis Club, he stated that in a single year the faculty and students spent nearly $500,000 in DeKalb. With this handsome amount being poured into the villagers' pockets, he did not hesitate to solicit from them their deepest interest in the "moral, religious, and educational development of the students." [10]

He was also one of the early Illinois educators to adopt the techniques of public relations that were developing at that time, and his experience in raising money in Joliet to carry out his expansion program better equipped him to promote his ideas at the college. So well did he apply the techniques of this new discipline that he soon became known as the "public relations president."

These promotional techniques were extended beyond the boundaries of his campus, for in 1922 the Teachers College Board was eager to bring before the people of Illinois the work they were doing. Thus Frank E. Richey was appointed chairman of a committee whose purpose it was to "direct the advertising and publicity campaign for the institutions devoted to the preparation of teachers for the public schools of the state." J. Stanley Brown, in an editorial in the *Northern Illinois,* supplied one of the first bits of information to be publicized by this new committee:

From September 1920 to September 1921, there were placed in the public schools of Illinois . . . 471 young men and young women at salaries ranging from $1,000 to $2,600 per year. The average of all these salaries was $1,440 per year. . . . It will certainly be a great stimulation to the graduates of four-year high schools—to enter one of these institutions and prepare themselves for the great work of teaching.[11]

He publicized with pictures and charts, as well as other devices made by the students in the industrial arts and home economics departments, at the county fairs and even at the American Exposition Palace in Chicago in 1924. He also did such things to dress up the annual catalog to give the college a more positive tone.

Brown's boosterism was used even in welcoming the new students. In 1926, for example, in a distinctive manner of positive thinking that almost equals the efforts of Norman Vincent Peale, he counseled them, "We must work together for a common purpose, strive together to reach a common goal. We must do positive things which make for advancement and help and eliminate as far as possible from our thought and work the negative forces which tend to destroy and nullify."[12]

To assist him in the task of promotion he employed a former city school superintendent, Clarence H. LeVitt, to head a newly formed public relations department in 1927. During the two years of LeVitt's tenure, many innovations were adopted in the catalog, with the use of words, phrases, poems, pictures, and eye-catching devices to describe the relationship between the college and the citizens of northern Illinois. "There must be," LeVitt said, "a constant lifting-power of service, and uninterrupted interplay of helpfulness between the College and those it serves. . . . Write to us—come and visit us—our latch string is always out." LeVitt was not lacking, either, in his ability to coin catchy titles and flowery descriptions for the prospective teachers looking for positions: they became the "Salesmen with the Soul of Service"; the "aspiring artist . . . of a thousand charms . . . intelligence shining through thoughtful eyes that glow with expectant vision." For the prospective and unwary male student he posed arresting questions: "Are you interested in Athletics?" "Do you want to be an Athletic Coach?" "Would you like to Teach Printing?" For those already employed, he asked, "Is your profession's Battery Dead?" "Is your School Tired?"[13] (Two years of this "enthusogram" publicity was about the limit of the second President Brown's endurance; and in June 1929, this position was eliminated.)

An additional way to demonstrate enthusiasm for Northern was to observe its silver anniversary during the twenty-fifth Commencement Week in May 1924. Anniversary Day was set for 24 May. The activities during the week included a Shakespearean play, the senior dance, a Treble Clef concert, pep meetings, a baseball game, the May dance, baccalaureate, and, in closing, commencement exercises. The alumni organization, which from its inception had observed its reunion in the fall, now changed it to the spring in order to observe the anniversary. All were met at the trains "by automobiles gaily festooned with streamers" and bearing the names of the classes along with their colors. Dr. Charles McMurry returned to the campus from the George Peabody College for Teachers to give the commencement address.[14]

With the development of John Dewey's educational theories of learning by doing, the administration soon adopted some of the current practices of student government and student participation through committee assignments. One of these innovations was the consolidation of all the several student activities under the Student Activities Committee consisting of three faculty members and three students. This system was not only to give the students some training in decision-making but also to help them to solve their money problems in connection with their activities. Many schools had adopted the "single tax" idea whereby each student prepaid a stipulated amount in the form of an activity fee to cover admission to athletic events, lectures, subscription to the school paper, and other sundry campus functions. It was hoped that such a new development might also restore enthusiasm for many of the student activities, for scarcely one-fourth of the student body was attending the football games.[15] Moreover, they hoped to enlarge the artist series, increase the number of issues of the student paper, and also put the sports program on a more secure financial basis.

An apportionment committee of students and faculty was appointed to distribute the funds. After the first year each student was issued a book containing tickets to all activities. Each activity drawing support from the fund was allocated a certain percentage of the total: in 1920–1921, 40 percent went to athletics, 30 percent to the entertainment committee, 13 percent to the *Northern Illinois,* 7 percent to the social committee, 5 percent to the Dramatics Club, and 5 percent to the Women's Athletic Association. Swen Parson, fund chairman, in commenting on the first year's operation, observed:

Since the plan was adopted there has been a marked increase in attendance and in enthusiasm of the student body at the games, plays, and entertainments. During the winter term the students were admitted to fourteen "events" upon their SA ticket, and they seemed well satisfied with the returns for their two dollars. . . . While the committee have had some anxious moments about the finances we find at the end of the year that "both ends meet." We are looking forward to next year with high hopes.[16]

Other committees were likewise created, on the principle of faculty participation in operating the college. One of the first, and certainly major, appointments for 1926 was the President's Council, consisting of five senior (male) professors. Also in the same year the president created the Committee on Athletics with four faculty members and two students; Neil Annas was chairman.[17]

Selection of the proper leaders for the various student activities was a difficult problem, for in such small colleges leadership often gravitated to a few, depriving many others of participation. To offset this tendency at Northern a quarterly "point system" was devised. A scale of points from 1 to 15 for all major and minor activities was drawn up, and no student could have more than 20 points per quarter; this spread the work and would not permit anyone to overload himself. For example, a person could not be editor of the *Northern Illinois* and president of Y.W.C.A. at the same time, for each carried a 12-point value. A subcommittee of the Student Activities Committee was established to supervise this system.[18]

The postwar period had brought a degree of restlessness to all American campuses which was not appeased by the appointment of a few students to a few committees with faculty members; they wanted some form of student government so that they could help solve some of their problems. The Northern students were no exception and continued their campaign, believing that it would increase their loyalty to the college, reduce the disciplinary problems now in the hands of the faculty, as well as stimulate all the students to greater participation in problem-solving throughout the institution. Control of the social functions was especially a source of complaint, for it still remained mostly out of their hands. All plans for any social function had to be cleared first with the president or a faculty committee. The supervision of dances was finally placed in the hands of a student group, and there is no evidence that their decorum on the dance floor reflected unfavorably upon the president's faith in them.

By the 1923–1924 school year sentiment had continued to increase for a student council to deal with a host of campus problems, then being discussed in the *Northern Illinois,* that were vital to students, not the least of which were smoking on campus, parking, pep meetings, foyer dances, noise in the halls, disappearance of library books, a campus cafeteria, and registration days. Northern students had their interest further increased when they discovered that Illinois State Normal had successfully developed a student government four years earlier, and that Western, too, had organized one less than a year before.[19]

After many more lengthy debates and discussions, a group of students finally submitted a petition to the president "for some form of student representation in school affairs which affect the student body as a whole." The matter was finally referred to a faculty group; and on 28 February 1927, it decided favorably upon the matter, a decision which became an important landmark in the life of the college. It was agreed that a council be set up, to be composed of thirteen members: three from the freshman class, six from the sophomore class, and four from the junior-senior group. Nominations were made by petition and submitted to the president for his sanction, after which the names were referred to the respective groups for ratification. The elected council members chose the first officers: Ruth Oliphant, president; Stanley Gritzbaugh, vice–president; and Evelyn Blomquist, secretary.[20] The Student Council then met with the president and his deans "to discuss matters relating to the general welfare of the college." A committee was created to draft a constitution.

After one year of the council's operation, it was decided to make some minor changes in its structure. But even with the revisions the student body enjoyed only a brief period of self-government. In 1928–1929 the classes failed to elect their representatives, and the president decided to appoint the representatives himself until the students finally acted upon the matter. They had earlier failed to elect members to the Student Activity Fund Committee, and he also appointed these representatives.

The rather sudden lack of student interest was probably because under J. Stanley Brown's successor there was no urgent need for a student council at Northern, since he was an able administrator and one who endeared himself to faculty and

191

students alike during the two years of his presidency. The catalogs make no further mention of student government until the Presidents' Club, which was formed in October 1932 to discuss student problems. This was a loose and informal organization with a limited and sporadic existence.

J. Stanley Brown had been head of the DeKalb Normal for nearly two years when the General Assembly changed the names of the three Normals to "teachers colleges." This was a change in name only, for they had already been authorized earlier to offer a four-year curriculum leading to the Bachelor of Education degree. It was a natural development for these schools, for the tremendous growth that had taken place in the American high school had resulted in greater demand for trained secondary teachers. Moreover, it had also become very clear to normal-school leaders that if they did not enrich and broaden their curricula to include the bachelor's degree, their very existence would be jeopardized by the universities and colleges which were then creating departments of education.[21]

The student assembly following the change to teachers college status was a historic one, for it was not only the first held under this new dispensation but it was also conducted in the same manner and place as the first assembly held twenty-two years earlier by Cook at the founding of the normal school. As President Brown read the Twenty-Third Psalm aloud, "a deep hush fell upon all the listeners" for they fully realized the significance of the event. The college song was sung and the brief but significant occasion became college history.[22]

A number of faculty committees began immediately to develop a four-year degree curriculum, deciding finally to offer it in music, drawing, domestic science, and an area called general curriculum—all intended for those who wished to teach mainly on the secondary level. The other level consisted of the old two-year normal-school curriculum, which now became the elementary department. A newly organized, four-year "high school" with a limited enrollment of not more than fifty students (which it never reached) was created for those without high-school diplomas, and it was taught by the college staff. It also served as the training school for those who wanted teaching experience for high-school positions. Unfortunately, it never had a good record, for it received mostly students "that couldn't get in any other school," and it was finally eliminated in 1927.[23]

The Bachelor of Education degree was conferred upon those who had a satisfactory high-school diploma and who had completed a four-year college course of at least forty-eight credits. One credit represented a subject pursued four or five times a week for fifty-minute periods during one twelve-week quarter. The academic requirements were sixteen credits in the department of the student's specialty, sixteen credits in a related field, and sixteen credits of elective work. The choice of the latter, however, was to be made by a committee whose chairman was the head of the student's major department, along with three other members representing the related fields. At least nine credits were to be taken in pedagogy and school administration, three of which were to be in practice teaching with the head of the student's major department acting as critic.[24]

Converting the normal school into a four-year college had certain immediate influences: the two-year students who had been called juniors and seniors now found themselves unhappily known as freshmen and sophomores; also, because the senior college had so few students and consequently no college spirit as yet, an increased burden of keeping the organizations and activities alive fell upon the shoulders of the lower classmen. They had to continue editing the publications, playing the games, and furnishing all the leadership.

A sharp and timely editorial in the student paper at the opening of school in 1927 raised some pertinent questions about what was wrong with the senior college. "As we enter upon our sixth year as a college, what do we find?" it asked. "The senior college is still a superimposition, a makeshift attachment, non-integrated, superficial, poorly attended—the weak sister of the vigorous and thriving junior college."[25] Why the previous administration used such "smug circumlocution and clever rationalization" in dealing with the situation was the question posed.

The *vox studentium* bore immediate fruit. In the following issue of the paper, an item was carried reporting that the senior college had elected officers, a student news reporter, and also a committee to investigate the advisability of appointing faculty advisors. Then, within a few weeks it was reported that the advisors were to be Swen Parson, Edith Bond, and the publicity director, who was to try to promote some genuine interest in this most important part of the college.

Some of the faculty "naturally and justly regarded the obligation of assuming the new duties and responsibilities [of a four-year college] . . . an imposition—a disturbing interference with the established order." It meant a tremendously increased burden of committee work and counseling, as well as the preparation of new courses to teach, and all with no immediate increase of staff. Increased budgets were also difficult to come by during the twenties. However, it was true that as far as salaries were concerned, the increase in 1922 and 1923 exceeded anything before or for several years thereafter.[26]

Expansion of new courses in both the junior and senior college curricula took place during this time; one field noticeably enlarged was that of rural education. With twice as many students applying for practice-teaching, President J. Stanley Brown arranged to take over two more rural schools adjacent to DeKalb, which he placed under the supervision of Helen Messenger, who was on the McMurry Training School staff. Special courses were offered in rural education, and Homer Hall, superintendent of schools in Boone County, was appointed director in 1929. Hall served a long and active career in upgrading teachers through his courses on campus and in extension work and summer-school institutes.

So much curriculum work was needed in the development of the new four-year program that the faculty soon felt the need for some expert advice on their aims and purposes. A leading specialist, Franklin Robbitt, was called from the University of Chicago. He held meetings on the subject "Curriculum, Construction and Planning," and it was well that he did, for it seemed that a very large number of faculty members were determined to include their specialized courses in the required lists. Older members seemed less eager to tear down the structure that had served them so well, but newer ones were looking forward to teaching their specialties to advanced students in the general curriculum.

There was a large increase of new courses such as logic, surveying, heredity, Latin American history, social psychology, calculus, and school administration, to mention only a few. Journalism, too, was introduced by Allan Wright in the English Department in order to better qualify students to publish their student paper. "It is hoped," he said, "that the *Northern Illinois* will undergo a decided change for the better by having trained toilers behind its columns."

Other innovations were forthcoming in this dynamic decade; often they were the result of a trip made by one of the officials to some neighboring college or distant convention. The findings of psychologists were being applied in the form of guidance and testing of the students, and several of the faculty members became interested in adopting these newer insights. Professors of education administered the ever-popular IQ tests to their students. For many years these scores were significant in placing students in teaching positions, and Helen Messenger, one of the earliest faculty members at Northern to explore this field, also applied them in the problem of college admissions. Her findings were so well received by teachers college presidents in Illinois that they appointed her to a state committee to investigate the subject. Her final conclusions were that the practice of selecting prospective teachers on the basis of grades was inadequate and that intelligence tests suggested a possible means of improvement, since those qualities considered valuable in teaching were found to be measurable by various types of tests. She went on to report that persons with low IQ scores should not be admitted to the colleges, for they not only make poor teachers, but training them is difficult and also more expensive.[27]

The deans, Neil Annas and Julia Hensel, also began to make use of new counseling techniques by inviting all students to bring their problems to them; for, as Dean Annas said, he was "ready at any time to share their confidence and help . . . in

195

any difficulties that might arise during the year." Dean Hensel, the girls' advisor, held daily consultations in the morning and afternoon. Many students were so pleased with this innovation that they asked the new president, J.C. Brown, for a counseling department that would consist of

A well-informed counselor, one of liberal mind and sympathetic understanding, keeping fixed office-hours in a private consultation room and prepared to meet by appointment . . . any student who finds difficulty in meeting the multifarious personal problems that follow thick in the wake of the process of self-preparation for . . . teaching—a provision of this sort would, we feel, meet the need in an adequate fashion.[28]

To create a more sophisticated grading system than President Cook's ten-point scale, J. Stanley Brown in 1919 had it changed from zero to one hundred, and then again in 1925 to the letters A, B, C, D, E. An honor-point system was also inaugurated, making it possible to receive points according to the numerical value of each letter grade. An "A" grade was worth three points; "B", two points, "C," one point; and a total of twenty-four points was required of those graduating from the two-year curriculum and forty-eight from the senior college. In other words, it took a "C" average to qualify for a degree. "D" grades could be balanced by an "A" or "B," but an "E" was worthless and carried no penalty except the loss of credit.[29]

The teaching load was decreased to sixteen hours a week, and class hours were increased from forty-five to fifty minutes with a ten-minute break between classes; each class generally met four days a week, and one period a day was a "floating" period for the general assembly, which was possible since different classes omitted it on different days. One change, no doubt welcomed by the students, was the scheduling of courses to omit the sixth and seventh period on Friday afternoon, making it possible for a larger number to leave the campus on week-ends. This satisfying innovation went into effect with the arrival of President J.C. Brown in the fall of 1927.[30]

The excuse system underwent a series of modifications, no doubt because of its abuse. A student could take his excuse, signed by his landlady, to the teacher in charge of his class and from this receive justification for his absence. The problem was that the teacher had to determine the authenticity of the excuse. This was changed so that the student had to take his signed excuse to one of the deans for inspection; if it seemed worthy enough to warrant an excuse for the class, the dean would then issue him a yellow card for every class he missed and these entitled him to full remissions. However, if there was some doubt on the part of the dean, an orange card would be issued, allowing the student to return to class until the matter had been investigated. In case of those who were unexcused, the absence was considered a cut, and a blue card was issued; with five such cards in a single quarter, the student automatically disqualified in the class. The modification underwent further changes, for it still "put a premium on the liar" as excuses were granted only on "sickness and death." Moreover, it "often forced the deans and president to break their word" when it came time to dismiss offenders from school. There was no easy solution to this problem, and it remained to haunt the college for several years before attendance was finally considered a responsibility of the student himself.[31]

J. Stanley Brown urged a number of other additions and revisions in the college so that he might attract more young men, a goal he claimed from the beginning of his presidency as his highest ambition. He had no interest, as some others seemed to have, in keeping it more or less a school for girls. He particularly tried to appeal to young men through enlarging the Industrial Arts Department and initiating a much expanded sports program. When he became president in 1919, there were only thirty male students enrolled in the college; this was caused chiefly, of course, by the war. To expedite this program, he engaged William Muir in 1923 as the college's first trained coach, and he also appointed Neil Annas to be the first dean of men. Moreover, he made an urgent appeal to the state for a men's dormitory and an industrial arts building that would also include a "men's building" with physical education rooms and a gymnasium. Such an expenditure, he reasoned, "would build a cohesion and spirit into the male students and add to the attractiveness of a Normal School Education, thereby attracting men into the profession."[32] The program was effective, for the enrollment of men more than doubled, from 66 in 1920 to 135 in 1926.

By the school year 1925–1926 the long wait was over, for the state finally appropriated $225,000 which was used for two of the three buildings which had been requested.[33] Milo Oakland, head of the Industrial Arts Department, was appointed the college representative to the state planning group, and after he redrafted the plans used at Normal and Carbondale, they were submitted to the contractors. Bids were opened in June 1927, but because of unforeseen problems the buildings were not completed until 1928, after J. Stanley Brown had left the presidency. The buildings were named for Edgar B. Still, the Board member from DeKalb.

It seemed that a series of "blunders" delayed the completion—blunders made either by the Department of Public Works or President Brown in locating the new buildings. Serious drainage problems developed, causing flow of water into the basement of the Industrial Arts building; in order to prevent this flooding, retaining walls had to be constructed along the outside. The gymnasium, too, was unfortunately located over an old sewer, and large accumulations of water under the concrete threatened the hardwood floor. These costly errors left no money for furniture, and, in addition, there was the costly problem of removing some 5,500 cubic yards of dirt from a single mound northeast of the buildings.

This was a restless period on the American campus, when students and faculty were beginning to refuse the quiet and passive roles of their predecessors; even the teachers colleges, with predominately girls in attendance, began to break with tradition. This manifested itself first in such customs as bobbing hair, rolling socks, abandoning corsets, and shortening dresses to the knees; for the young men, behavioral extremes were also manifested in wearing apparel, such as the raccoon coat. Complaints were growing common even among the girls that the boys were "rough and uncouth" and no longer had the consideration for them that they should have. Even though there were only a few boys enrolled at Northern, they created considerable noise and confusion outside the classrooms and in the library. One reporter remarked that if a stranger should enter the building, it would be "hard to tell whether this is an institution of higher learning or a zoo at feeding time." [34]

For years this growing expression of nonconformity had been interpreted by various writers as "an unproductive waywardness"; however, social historians today tend more to view the 1920s as a period of "amazing vitality, of social invention and change" and as the "formative years of modern society." It was a time of transformation in taste, habit, and beliefs.

The Northern campus was a microcosm of what the nation was experiencing after World War I: the automobile created not only a host of social problems, but spatial ones as well; movie houses brought Hollywood films, and radio sets carried jazz, sports programs, and popular amusements—all liberating and "troublesome influences" for those of an earlier generation. This social revolution was in full swing when J. Stanley Brown was chosen as Northern's second president in 1919, and it no doubt served as a catalyst in modifying his traditional tendencies to the extent that he was carried well beyond the point of security in his high position.

President Brown promoted the sports program by every means at his command and considered these activities a public relations vehicle to attract larger numbers of young men. By the time of his departure he had thoroughly established an athletic tradition that continued in future years to have a decisive influence on the life of the institution. In fact, it might be considered an athletic nemesis as far as his career was concerned.

He increased and formalized the accouterments of sports, sparing no cost (not even his own personal integrity, for that matter) in his efforts to glorify the program. In the weekly assemblies, at sports banquets, service clubs, and even Board meetings he extolled the virtues of "football and life." He quoted the great coaches of the day on how the game prepared a young man "to meet some of life's problems better than anything else. It teaches him how to play the game, whether on the gridiron or in life, hard and fairly. It gives to him the power of perseverance and that indomitable 'never say die' spirit." Coach William G. Muir also spoke freely of these same virtues, emphasizing the great influence competitive sports had on building character, making judgments, and coordinating the body, as well as developing loyalty to one's school and team-mates throughout life.[35]

Players were still scarce in 1920, and competition grew stronger, for in the meantime Northern had joined the Illinois Intercollegiate Athletic Conference. William Muir followed Paul Harrison as football and also as basketball coach. In basketball, he compiled a remarkable record during his three years; however, in football only his last season in 1925 really brought him popularity and that was with a specious championship team. That year, with twenty-six players, a few of whom were ineligible to play, Northern had perhaps the most exciting yet most disgraceful season in its entire history.[36] Until three of his "Four Horsemen" backfield players were declared ineligible, the team had won all their games, including the one against Illinois State Normal; even with replacements he was able to finish the season with only one loss.

I.I.A.C. Athletic Commissioner C.W. Whitten, who was a former faculty member at Northern and principal of the DeKalb Township High School, was meanwhile investigating the athletic situation in DeKalb and insisting that the president undertake reforms. Brown's inaction caused the revelation of a whole series of infractions, some of which Whitten had learned of earlier while he was still in DeKalb. He collected evidence that the college had used players who were not enrolled in the school, who were not in good academic standing, who had played too many seasons, and whose records had been falsified in reports to the commissioner.[37]

The evidence indicated that the president was mainly responsible for these infractions. Coach Harrison testified to Whitten that President Brown had personally instructed him to play a former Northern student who was at the time teaching in the high school at St. Charles. Furthermore, when Coach Muir used three ineligible players—in the second half of what became the infamous game with Northwestern College at Naperville in 1925—he reported that he had already agreed before the game with the Naperville coach not to use the players, but in the end he did so upon the request of President Brown who had relayed the message from DeKalb via one of his professors. Whitten later stated emphatically that J. Stanley Brown "not only knew of all the facts in connection with this game, but *he personally instructed* his coach to use the ineligible men."

When the president refused to follow the eligibility rules, the commissioner took his case directly to the citizens and students of DeKalb, who were for the most part wholly unaware of the duplicity then being carried out at the college. In the *DeKalb Chronicle* he presented his case in the form of a long letter indicting the college administration for violating the rules of competition and, more specifically, for deliberately falsifying the records in reports to the conference.[38] To avoid the eligibility requirements, the president had arbitrarily withdrawn from the conference in October. Official action was taken anyway; on 4 December 1925, the I.I.A.C. officially expelled Northern Illinois State Teachers College from membership.

A few months thereafter Coach Muir announced his resignation, hoping, he said, that he might secure a higher salary in a larger college somewhere "in the southern section of the country." R.A. Cowell, a graduate of the University of Illinois then coaching at Des Moines University, was engaged as Muir's replacement.

The athletic controversy was not the first of J. Stanley Brown's problems. Upon his appointment as president, he discovered that he had no home to live in, for the Board had not provided for his rent as it had done for Cook. Since he had no intention of paying rent himself, it was necessary for him to store his furniture and live in a private house until something better could be found. An appropriation was placed in an omnibus bill during the final days of the Illinois General Assembly session in 1919 to either build a residence for him or to pay his rent, but this failed to pass.

The first indication that Brown might be abusing his office came in the spring of 1923, when the Normal School Board investigated his residency in a remodeled apartment in the southwest corner of the first floor of Williston Hall. The hall had always been filled to overflowing, so obviously, with his presence there, several girls were deprived of a home. He argued, however, that he was unable to acquire a residence and that at the time he was engaged as president, it was his understanding that he was to be given a rent-free home. Thus, under these conditions he had appealed to the chairman of the Board and received permission to live in the hall at taxpayer's expense.

The initial complaint had come from a group of girls on his floor who clandestinely reported that they were receiving undue supervision from both him and his wife, and that at no time were they as free as other girls of the hall to move about. When the Board responded to their petition and the affair became public, the other four teachers college presidents also inveighed against this favoritism. The Board expressly denied that it had promised him a house and also stated that its former chairman had no right to grant this privilege and, henceforth, they also withdrew "any permit or permission . . . to the President of the school to live in Williston Hall." [39]

President Brown, in the early part of 1926, was confronted with some severe charges that were leveled against him through the Normal School Board by a group of school superintendents and principals. A committee of three Board members was appointed to investigate. The irregularities to which the Board committee gave its attention were as follows:

1. *Deliberate use of ineligible men in athletics and falsification of records to the athletic commissioner.*
2. *Falsification of academic records of the president and the supervisor of training in publications of the institution.*

1925–26 Faculty, President J. Stanley Brown is second from the left, first row.

3. *Misrepresentation of academic accomplishments of faculty members in reports to the North Central Association.*
4. *Mishandling of the funds of the institution including falsification of payrolls.*
5. *Granting of credits to students without requiring corresponding academic accomplishments.*
6. *Failure to keep abreast of the times in modern educational method.*[40]

One of the unsavory irregularities of Brown's presidency was the damaging charge of misrepresentation of academic accomplishments of himself and one of his faculty members. It was discovered that both of these individuals had listed at different times in college publications their attendance at the Universities of Chicago and Wisconsin. Commissioner Whitten indicated that upon contacting the registrars of these schools he found that neither of them had ever "matriculated or paid tuition or was in any way officially a student at either" of these universities.

This was a period when most teacher-education institutions were making great efforts to secure accreditation by major universities and newly formed associations, and one of the most important credentials was the training of the faculty. Thus some of these marginal colleges resorted to the embellishment of not only their faculty attendance records at major graduate schools, but also of academic degrees that were conferred upon them. The commissioner disclosed that at various times these same individuals had listed in the *Norther* and the annual catalogs academic degrees that were unearned or secured from "institutions wholly without standing in any accrediting institution or association." [41]

Perhaps the most severe charge against Brown had to do with financial irregularities in his administration. Even though teachers college presidents were denied by law the use of cash funds, he nevertheless always seemed, according to one faculty member, "provided with considerable amounts of cash." From time to time, he was able to pay the expenses of various faculty members to professional meetings as well as other sundry expenses. Athletic Commissioner Whitten also turned up evidence that Brown was "more or less systematically falsifying his payrolls" by certifying payments to some individuals who had not been teaching at all and to others who had taught much less time than was stipulated. It was alleged that the president in some cases endorsed the warrants thus obtained and cashed them at the bank. Commissioner Whitten never made the charge that J. Stanley Brown ever appropriated any of this money for his private uses, but he did state that Brown used it for paying "bills that were never presented to the auditor in accordance with the law." [42]

To add fuel to the fire, a "deplorable crime" took place in DeKalb when three young men, two of whom were students and one a graduate of the college, raped a coed. The event occurred on the night of 11 April 1926, and was first related to the public by the *DeKalb Chronicle*. The news spread quickly when the *Chicago Tribune* on 18 April featured and embellished it in a "revolting style." For days gory accounts were carried of this case, with reporters searching out the most minute aspects and continuously harassing anyone who might have the faintest idea of what took place. [43]

J. Stanley Brown was aware that things were going badly for him, since he was not only receiving "an awful kind of publicity" because of recent events at the college, but school superintendents were also beginning to look elsewhere for their prospective teachers. Moreover, the Board subcommittee to investigate the charges made against him had come to DeKalb in June and had called a meeting in Chicago for 28 September 1926 to formulate a report on its "thorough-going investigation." But the night before the meeting, President Brown called upon the Board chairman and tendered his resignation to take effect at the termination of the school year. [44] Brown was careful to draw to the attention of the subcommittee that this was a milestone in his career, for at the completion of his presidency he would be completing his fortieth year as an educator.

At the time that Brown made his announcement to the Board, he also released the news to the Chicago press—before the Board had a chance to hear or discuss the findings of its subcommittee. This created some irritation, for several Board members were interested in what the subcommittee had to report. Even though he had resigned, the findings were presented and discussed. Brown was invited to appear before the Board, at which time he made a statement

denying any responsibility or fault in most of the matters complained of by the committee of city superintendents and high school principals. He admitted his responsibility on two of the charges, namely, concerning the athletic situation and the endorsement of teachers warrants, but claimed that all his acts were inspired by no other purpose than what he conceived to be the best interests of the school.[45]

At their next meeting, the Board accepted his resignation as presented by him, effective 1 July 1927.

Immediately after this action, Brown called a special meeting of his faculty and related the move that he had taken. The faculty received the announcement with muffled pleasure, for, as Parson noted, there was so much dissension in the college by this time that not more than two faculty members were still supporting him. The student editor, Stanley Gritzbaugh, also recalled that in spite of the statement in the *Northern Illinois* that his resignation was "received with deep and sincere regret," many were delighted and relieved when it was announced.

Despite the president's resignation, Whitten soon observed that Brown was not content to step down, but was continuously putting forth "strenuous efforts to enlist political influence to secure his reinstatement." The commissioner, not to be defeated, appealed to the city superintendents to counteract the "persistent rumors . . . throughout the state that Mr. Brown's efforts were about to succeed." Whitten urged that they immediately get in touch with the three members of the Board's investigating committee, "stating what you think of the advisability of continuing this man in the office in which he has made such a conspicuous failure from every viewpoint."[46]

But Brown was not about to leave without carrying out the only retribution available to him in his last official act, namely the dismissal of two of his faculty enemies, Clyde L. Lyon and Allan T. Wright. The president gave no cause for his action; by the time these instructors received their discharge letters from him, he had already left the college. The actual reason, however, was that these two individuals had been mainly responsible for organizing the Faculty Club against the president during the crisis. Their dismissal was of short duration, for they were soon reinstated by the Board.

In the closing hours of Brown's career at the college, the faculty managed to muster sufficient enthusiasm to offer him and his wife an "appreciative farewell" in Williston Hall, and the students, also, on the following day at a special assembly tendered him their gifts and parting good wishes. He relinquished the presidency at Northern under a cloud of suspicion, returning to his old home in Joliet, where he was subsequently reported to be working from time to time as an inspector of teachers colleges until his death in 1939.

But retirement was no shield or protection from his irregularities, for no sooner had he settled in Joliet than others were revealed. For instance, "the canned goods scandal" was brought to light, revealing that J. Stanley Brown had stockpiled large amounts in the Williston Hall basement. Former students mentioned that various types of canned fruit could be heard to explode from time to time. This may have been a slight exaggeration, but when these stores were inventoried by President J. C. Brown, soon after assuming office, he reported to the Board that one grocery firm in St. Louis had agreed to cancel half of its order of six thousand gallons of canned fruit which, according to those in charge of the hall, "would last the institution for over seven years." [47]

J. C. Brown, in this same report, also called to the Board's attention the startling fact that his predecessor had received a payment of "$20 a month for handling the [Student Loan] Fund and in addition thereto a payment of $1,700. No such action had ever been reported to the Board by J. Stanley Brown or approved by it." [48]

Some six months before J. Stanley Brown's term expired, the Normal School Board appointed three of its members to select and recommend a suitable candidate as his successor. After five months of searching and examining qualifications of more than thirty-six candidates, six were finally selected for more careful scrutiny. Their names were presented to educational leaders over the country, asking them to express their candid opinions on the relative merits of each. The Board met on 19 May 1927, and accepted the committee's unanimous conclusion that Joseph Clifton Brown, president of State Teachers College at St. Cloud, Minnesota, was the "best person whom the committee recommended."

J. C. Brown was pleased to return to the state of Illinois, for, as he said when he was offered the position, it would be like "coming back home." The Board offered him an attractive salary of $7,500, and there were other appealing factors. Not only was he pleased with the larger enrollment at Northern, but also he was unhappy with the Minnesota governor's veto of an appropriation bill for two new buildings.[49]

The new president was born in Piqua, Ohio on 5 April 1879, and had graduated with a B.S. degree from Hanover College in 1901 as valedictorian of his class. He received an honorary A.M. degree from the same college in 1907 and an earned A.M. from Teachers College, Columbia University, in 1914.

His first teaching experience was in Noblesville, Indiana, where he taught from 1901 to 1903; then he was superintendent of the high school in Paoli, Indiana, 1903–1904, and a teacher of mathematics at Eastern Illinois State Normal School, 1905–1911. From there he left Illinois to head the Mathematics Department in the Horace Mann School in New York City until 1915, when he returned to the Department of Education at the University of Illinois for one year before accepting the presidency at St. Cloud, where he remained until 1927. He also taught summer sessions at the University of Chicago and the Teachers College, Columbia University.

He was probably best known in educational circles as an authority in the teaching of mathematics. He was author and coauthor of a number of textbooks in that field, but the ones he had collaborated on with Lotus D. Coffman, president of the University of Minnesota, were the most popular. He was also

Joseph C. Brown
third president, 1927–1929

well known for the important professional posts he held in the educational associations on the state and national levels and for his work in rating and accrediting teachers colleges throughout the nation.

This well-known administrator had varied talents, one of which was his ability as a speaker. While serving his two years at Northern he carried on a strenuous speaking schedule, concentrating on the northern counties of Illinois in order to build up the declining enrollment. His approach in speaking was often inspirational and he was schooled in the use of public relations techniques in recruiting students. His tri-weekly talks at the general assembly were miniature gems, sometimes sermonettes, book reviews, Bible readings, and an occasional talk on his favorite subject of astronomy. At times he opened his home to students for Sunday afternoon vespers and fireside singing. His versatility knew no bounds in planning and fusing new ideas to old forms, and it was exciting to the student body, who could never predict what was coming next.

He had an appealing personality with a gracious manner that attracted new friends. He was quick and bright, confident and genial, a combination that endeared him to faculty and students alike. Even though he was away from the college a great deal, he never failed to cultivate their acquaintance when on campus. Soon after settling into his new position he made this most welcome request: "My office," he said, "will always be open to the students and faculty and I hope you will take occasion to become acquainted with me very quickly."

With eleven highly successful years as president at St. Cloud, he no sooner had appeared on the scene at Northern than he began to carry out a similar program; however, his first real task was to heal the wounds his predecessor had left among the students, faculty, alumni, townspeople, and the schoolmen who employed the teachers.

No buildings were begun during his brief presidency, but he did carry to completion and dedicate the men's gymnasium and the industrial arts building. Important improvements were made in the "Castle" by adding new offices, club rooms, and shower stalls in the girl's gym.

From the beginning of his administration, all were highly impressed by his leadership. "The student body, the faculty, and the alumni," reported the *Northern Illinois*, "are all keenly enthusiastic over the manysided program of college development that is very rapidly and very tangibly progressing under the leadership of the new executive from St. Cloud."

President J. C. Brown inaugurated at his biweekly faculty meetings a plan for each member to study significant essays or books of a nonspecialized nature, then to report on them and to lead the faculty in a discussion of the basic ideas. At other times he had his faculty take up various topics such as, "What are the other teachers colleges doing that DeKalb ought to do?"

This development was shown in the efforts he expended in helping the students to organize clubs to enliven their activities. Evil days had fallen upon student spirit since the athletic debacle; all sports were at a low ebb, with a poor reputation of Northern's teams among outside colleges and little interest shown by students in whether the games were won or lost. Brown met with the students to help them organize pep clubs and select cheerleaders to support the team at every game with cheers and demonstrations. No doubt he had plenty of ideas for the students, since he himself was an avid football fan, taking pride on his own perfect attendance at the games in St. Cloud as well as those of the University of Minnesota.

He made immediate plans to restore membership in the "Little Nineteen" (I.I.A.C.) athletic conference, with a petition submitted in December 1927. During the two years that Northern was without membership, it had serious problems scheduling games, since it could no longer play conference teams; thus he awaited the decision with high hopes that Northern would be readmitted.

Northern's readmission and the boundless enthusiasm of the president did not carry over into victories on the football field. Coach Cowell's three-year record (one year of which was under J. Stanley Brown) shows nearly twice as many losses as wins; however, as basketball coach, his first season was an exceptional year, for his team lost only a single game, thus qualifying it for a trip to the National Amateur Athletic

Association finals in Kansas City. The combined efforts of the students and the generosity of the townspeople made it financially possible for the whole team, after some discussion, to make the trip. The team members, though poverty-ridden while there, acquitted themselves extremely well by winning the first two games, then losing the third when their best player fouled out in the third quarter. The *Kansas City Star* gave the "Redbirds" some fine compliments for their courageous efforts; and when they arrived home, they were loudly welcomed at the train by a large throng, a band, and a parade as well as a luncheon at the Kiwanis Club arranged by Professor Milo Whittaker, its president.[50]

J. C. Brown's administrative ability was also applied in raising academic standards to bring the college more in line with modern accreditation. One such change that helped to place the college on a strictly collegiate basis was the tightening up of entrance requirements. High-school students who did not rank above the lower third were requested not to seek admission to the college. Standardized tests were also inaugurated for class entrance purposes; students were excused from required courses if they were able to make certain scores and required to take non-credit courses when they fell below a certain level. It is interesting to note that the smallest number of freshmen excused from a subject in the fall of 1928 was in penmanship!

Ideas for facilitating the registration process were also inaugurated, and the school calendar was drawn up for the first time to cover the whole academic year. Student teaching was expanded. To meet the growing numbers of those in the rural teaching curriculum, one more training school, near Sycamore, under the direction of Grace Vincent, was also added. The curriculum for the senior college was enriched with science courses after the arrival of Howard W. Gould. Efforts were made in several areas of the senior college to reduce the number of professional education courses for those training for high-school teaching, and some departments even assumed the task of teaching the methods courses.

J. C. Brown had a keen interest in natural science and the outdoors generally; and when he came to Northern, he became interested in a scout-leadership training course. He inaugurated a sequence of activities that would enable a young man to receive a diploma from the national scouting headquarters. For teaching in this area, he engaged Walter E. Swarthout as a part-time instructor. This started a growing interest in scouting that was to continue over the years under the influence of Marion C. Hayes and which became embodied in the first and most important service fraternity on campus, Alpha Phi Omega.[51] The president's interests in physical education were also apparent in his requests that all men be required to take one year of physical education and all girls be required to have physical examinations with the hope of improving their posture and physical condition.

To warm the hearts of the faculty, three important financial matters were taken up by the Board in 1928 and 1929. These were essential improvements in order to provide incentives to retain teachers as well as to attract others to the campuses. Morale was low in the teachers colleges at this time because even Illinois high-school teachers as well as college teachers in other states were drawing higher salaries. The three Board policies enacted were an emeritus program with an annual income between $1,200 and $3,000, depending on the person's length of service; leaves of absence so that faculty members could continue their education; and, finally, a classification system of all faculty into the four regular ranks, complete with a salary schedule that provided for annual increments.[52]

There was also what one might almost call an obsession or preoccupation on the part of both presidents of Northern during the twenties to secure accreditation from universities such as Chicago, Illinois, and Columbia, as well as from the North Central Association of Colleges and Universities. They believed that such distinction would interest more students in the four-year degree course at Northern.

J. Stanley Brown was the first to receive such recognition when, in 1925, Columbia University accepted Northern's four-year graduates as possible candidates for the master's degree. Before this, most students were required to take additional subjects in order to qualify. Work on further accreditation was continued by J. C. Brown, and in December 1927, he announced that the American Association of Teachers Colleges investigators would arrive in January to rate the college. A thorough study was made, and at the Boston meeting of the association, Northern was given an "A" rating along with nineteen other colleges. The following spring efforts were made to secure accreditation from the North Central Association, in the belief that the recent high rating in Boston would carry additional influence; such was not the case, for, at the 1928 annual meeting in Chicago, Northern's inadequacies of physical facilities, of its library, and in the training of its faculty were pointed out. It was not until 1933 that a temporary rating was granted. However, by the time the college opened in the fall of 1929, the University of Chicago announced an "unreserved recognition of Northern Illinois credits." This, no doubt, was a direct result of J. C. Brown's influence with this institution, for he had not only taught there during some summer sessions, but he had also invited several of its prominent professors, such as Charles H. Judd and T. V. Smith, to the Northern campus as speakers on several occasions.

During the twenties, several faculty members were recruited whose work added notably to the life and stature of the growing institution.

Milo T. Oakland, a two-year graduate of Northern, began his career as a coach, athletic director, and assistant in the industrial arts department. He specialized in the teaching of printing, which was a special development in the Department from its inception; he went on to become head of the Department when Samuel J. Vaughn left in 1920. He served the college for forty-one years, meanwhile attaining a degree of prominence in his field.

Paul Harrison had the unique honor of being attached to the college in various ways for more years than any other faculty member. He graduated from the Training School, attended the high school, and received his bachelor's degree—all from Northern. During his faculty tenure of forty-five years, he served under five of the seven presidents. Following three years of coaching the football team, he became a full-time teacher in the Industrial Arts Department, where he served until President Leslie Holmes engaged him to restructure the long-neglected Lorado Taft's Eagle's Nest art colony at Oregon, Illinois, which had been assigned the college for an outdoor education field campus. Before completion of that work he was appointed its director.

Milo L. Whittaker came from Colorado in 1920 to be principal of the Training School. He had already gained some prominence as an author, community leader, and educator. After two years as principal, he was transferred to the college to teach in the social science department; upon the death of Page, he was appointed head of the department. During his thirteen years in this position he became somewhat known as an innovator in his field. He also secured a certain degree of distinction by recruiting a highly trained staff, most of whom were academically oriented toward the arts of teaching, research, and writing. He spent endless hours in community service as well as in writing textbooks in citizenship and character education and research bulletins for government agencies on rural life in Illinois.[53] On several occasions, Karl Langdon Adams, who became president in 1929, remarked that the "social science faculty was without doubt, my strongest department."

Helen R. Messenger began her career in 1920 in the Training School and some five years later became a member of the education department, where she devoted twenty-seven years not only as an instructor of elementary education but also as a leader of women in her profession. She was one of the state founders of the women's education honorary Delta Kappa Gamma society, and through her initiative the Alpha chapter for DeKalb and Ogle counties was founded on 23 November 1935. Besides her activities in this organization, she carried on programs of research and writing in her special fields.

Otto E. Peterson joined the staff in 1924 to fill Dean Newell Gilbert's place as head of the department of education and psychology; later he was appointed director of the placement bureau. Peterson had a solid background of training and experience; he had attended the Universities of Chicago and

Wisconsin and had served for a number of years as a school superintendent. He was considered an excellent teacher, and his friendly nature and leisurely methods of handling his responsibilities during his twenty-seven years endeared him to a host of friends in the college and city and among state school officials. He had far too many duties, which no doubt contributed to his untimely death in 1951.

George L. Terwilliger, another of the teachers who taught more than forty years at Northern, graduated from the college in 1925 and immediately became associated with Charles Montgomery as a teacher in the biology department. Upon the latter's retirement, Terwilliger was made its head and he served in the position until 1965, retiring from teaching in 1968. He was always keenly interested in student activities and, like his brother Bill and sister Mary, took a prominent role in athletic affairs.

In 1926, William B. Storm came from Joliet, where he had been associated as a teacher with J. Stanley Brown. Upon the retirement of the aging Swen Parson from the Mathematics Department, he assumed its headship and during his twenty-five years he became known for his expertise in the training of teachers for the elementary schools. He and his brother, H. C. Storm, were coauthors of studies in taxes and taxation, and some of his experimental work in the teaching of arithmetic also found its way into prominent textbooks.

Howard W. Gould arrived on campus in 1927 to take Charles F. Phipp's position in the physical sciences department; for the next thirty-seven years he played a leading role in building up this department. He applied himself with boundless energy to upgrading his staff as well as his own training, in strengthening the curriculum, in advocating the construction of a science building, and in serving endless hours assisting the administration on major committee assignments. He was also an active participant in various church, community, and service club organizations.

Other faculty members who were destined to leave their marks upon the institution were also added to the roster. Alma Anderson, not long out of the University of North Dakota with her Phi Beta Kappa key, was associated with Eveline Merritt of the Cook era until the latter's retirement; she was then made head of the fine arts department, where she carried on a broad spectrum of activities in teaching, painting, lecturing, exhibiting, and traveling.

Miriam Anderson, also from the northwest, came to fill the position in the department of physical education for women made vacant by the resignation of Edith Bond. She served a rapidly developing department for twenty-eight years and after her retirement was highly honored by being one of the few faculty members who have had their names given to a building while still alive.

Mary Williams was brought to Northern in 1928 from St. Cloud, where she had taught under J. C. Brown, to assist Clyde Lyon in the teaching of reading; upon the latter's departure in 1930, she was appointed head of the reading department where she remained until her retirement in 1950. She was not only a charming person but also an excellent teacher in her field. The writer recalls with pleasure many pleasant conversations with her as well as the not-so-pleasant hazards of weather shared while motoring to and from extension classes in neighboring cities.

Gus William Campbell joined the instructional staff in 1928 after an already successful career in teaching speech, debate, and oratory in Wisconsin. Though he remained for only ten years, his influence in these activities are still recognized by those who succeeded him, as well as by the many alumni he taught who went on to higher levels of achievement in education, law, and the ministry. He also organized the first department of speech.

Another young man, added to the teaching staff at the same time, was Romeo M. Zulauf, who had graduated from Carleton College only a few years before. While teaching in St. Cloud, he became acquainted with J. C. Brown and came to DeKalb to teach courses in the social sciences. Almost immediately he and Milo Whittaker formed a close friendship that remained throughout their lives as they worked together to advance the Department. He demonstrated early his capacity for administrative leadership, and when the dean's position was reestablished in 1941 under President Adams, Whittaker left no stone unturned to secure Zulauf's appointment to this office. Once in office, he applied himself in his typical methodical manner, sparing neither his time nor energies in the ever-increasing burden of growing enrollments and college expansion. Moreover, though he was plagued for many years with health problems, he not only continually bore the weight of his office with dignity and fairness but also periodically took leaves of absence to complete his doctoral degree.

J. Hal Connor came to the English department with a special interest in creative writing, drama, and poetry. He had a unique combination of personal traits that soon won him many friends as well as positions of responsibility. He was a pioneer in teaching methods and used various social science materials for theme writing, essays, and readings. He was also an author and coauthor of various publications in the field of English literature. During his thirty-two years at Northern, he served as teacher, head of the Department, acting dean, dramatic coach, and editor of professional publications. He will long be remembered by his many friends for his appropriate eulogies delivered in behalf of deceased colleagues.

E. Ruth Taylor also joined this department at the same time as Connor, but in addition to her teaching, she assumed Russell G. Gage's position as faculty advisor to the *Northern Illinois*. She was excellently prepared for this special work, for one of her academic degrees was earned in the distinguished school of journalism at the University of Missouri. For twenty-eight years her high-level performance with the student paper, her scholarly teaching, lecturing, and writing gave her a high reputation on and off the campus.

Loren T. Caldwell, a young man and recent graduate student from the University of Chicago, joined the faculty in 1929 to teach in the geography department. In 1951, President Holmes, himself a geographer, created an earth sciences department with Caldwell as its first head. He was active in a research program earlier in his forty-one year career at Northern; later, however, his interests turned to the educational aspects of the teaching of science.

A glance at the academic achievements of the regular faculty members during these two presidencies shows a marked

218

contrast with those of the original faculty under President Cook, of whom at least half had only a two-year diploma. Of the forty-six full-time members on the college staff in 1928–1929, all had secured at least their baccaulaureate degrees, with the exception of a few from the original staff or those who were only part-time instructors. In addition, seventeen had master's degrees. Marion C. Hayes was the only one to have the Ph.D. degree in 1927.

Suddenly, at the high point of his presidency, when recovery from J. Stanley Brown's last two years was an accomplished fact, J. C. Brown dropped a bombshell with the announcement that he was resigning to accept the position of superintendent of schools in Pelham, New York, effective 1 August 1929. This school system was in one of the wealthiest suburbs in the United States; and although he had not applied for the position, he was offered one of the highest salaries in the field of public education, which he found impossible to decline.

The Normal School Board met on 25 June and accepted Brown's resignation, appointed Swen F. Parson acting president for the interim, and chose a committee to draft a resolution to convey their appreciation for his brief but valuable service. The following are a few lines of their sentiments:

Coming to the presidency . . . at a time when both its character and reputation had been impaired by previous maladministration, he brought to the great task of rebuilding this institution . . . a sound academic . . . foundation . . . high personal character . . . excellent intelligence . . . unusual administrative ability which insured success from the very beginning. The State Board wishes to record their appreciation of his wholesome and engaging personality, of his even and firm temperament, of his fearless courage and his unselfish devotion. We needed a man to 'carry a message to Garcia.' He did it. In addition to his great reconstructive work . . . his admirable presence on the platform, his engaging voice and worthwhile subject matter have carried him before . . . meetings, . . . clubs and organizations throughout the state, carrying the good news of a new day at DeKalb.[54]

219

Karl L. Adams
fourth president, 1929–1948

7

The Middle Period

THIS middle period of Northern's history was a time of gradual evolution away from the single-purpose institution of the past. Many have believed that because it was afflicted with the two great restraining influences (a world-wide economic depression beginning three weeks after President Adams assumed the presidency in October 1929, and a ravaging world war that lasted from 1939 to 1945), little of importance could have happened to the college. Notwithstanding these calamities, some basic changes took place that laid the groundwork for rapid expansion in the next administration.

With the sudden departure of J. C. Brown, the Teachers College Board was again faced with the problem of finding a successor. His resignation was handed to the Board in June to take effect on 1 August, thus leaving less than three months to find a replacement before school was to open in the fall. A committee of three Board members was appointed immediately to begin their search for suitable candidates. On 27 August, the committee reported to the Board that "since its appointment [it] had received the names and considered the qualifications of twenty-five different persons . . . [and] it appeared that the committee was unanimously in favor of President George Selke of the Teachers College, St. Cloud, Minnesota." [1]

The selection of Selke no doubt was influenced by J. C. Brown, who was his close friend and predecessor at the St. Cloud college. The committee, upon contacting President Selke, found that he would be interested in the position provided he could secure his release from his Board. Immediately he was accepted by the Illinois Board, and they awaited his final decision. On 3 September, word was received "that circumstances over which he had no control made it impossible for him to ask the Board to release him."

This called for immediate action, and the committee was requested to present further recommendations. Because the fall quarter opened on 9 September, the man they selected would have to assume the office several weeks late; thus to hurry the process it is highly probable that J. C. Brown and President Selke both came to the rescue of the Board by recommending another St. Cloud friend, Karl Langdon Adams, for the presidency. He was readily available at the time, for he had just completed the first year of his two-year leave at Columbia Teachers College and was planning to remain and continue his graduate work. He was offered the position on 17 September at an annual salary of $7,500, to take effect 1 October 1929. [2]

President-elect Adams was born 5 September 1888, in Lexington, Ohio. After attending elementary schools there, he entered the Ohio Military Institute—at that time the Grand River Institute—at Austinburg, Ohio, for two years; for his last two years he went to Franklin and Marshall Academy in Lancaster, Pennsylvania, from which he graduated in 1905. He then attended Ohio University, receiving a certificate in civil engineering and a Bachelor of Science degree one year later in 1909.

In college, his academic interests were largely in the field of science; his extra-curricular activities (besides Beta Theta Pi fraternity) were mainly football, basketball, and tennis. One year he was also a cheerleader. He played guard, center, and tackle on the football team but won only one letter in his senior year; in his sophomore year, however, he had won the campus tennis championship. [3]

This early interest in athletics remained with him in various ways throughout life. With the exception of his first year out of school, when he worked as an engineer, he not only taught school but also coached various sports until he went to St. Cloud in 1916. When he arrived at St. Cloud he soon became deeply involved in officiating games in the Big Ten and other Minnesota intercollegiate and high-school conferences.[4]

He rarely missed the games at Northern and usually found time every fall, along with faculty members and friends such as Parson, Peterson, Lyon, and Whitten, to attend one or more of the Big Ten games. It was especially appreciated by the students at Northern when he was able to forget "his official dignity" and join with them in their "cheers for N.I." So much was this a part of his life that many explained his personal characteristics of "decisiveness and clarity in decision-making" as springing from his sports training and officiating experience.

Adams came from a farily well-to-do, middle-class home, as did his wife, which afforded them the financial means for a way of life that was well beyond the reach of most normal-school teachers. Moreover, as a youth he was given an education in a military institute, a university academy, and a prestigious university that was well beyond the reach of most young men of that day. This background no doubt also gave him a professional and social advantage; during his years at St. Cloud, he was able to associate with the wealthiest families and enjoy the emoluments that accrued, most of which were not available to those with whom he taught at the college. Such a way of life tended to perpetuate his basically conservative tendencies. He was an active layman in the Methodist church, an official of the Kiwanis Club, and a director of the DeKalb Chamber of Commerce. His tastes in reading were somewhat circumscribed by his interests and background and consisted mostly of the *Chicago Tribune,* the *Reader's Digest,* and *School and Society.*

His usual brusque manner often caused timidity on the part of some faculty and students and gave the impression that he was insensitive to their needs; however, to many others he was a kind and sympathetic person, always ready to discuss problems with those who came to his office. Miriam Harms Dypold, a student reporter who had weekly interviews with him in the early 1940s, has only pleasant memories to relate:

223

*I never was referred to his secretary, no matter how busy he
was. He was always careful to give me background on his news
items, so that I could more easily write the stories. Occasionally
he had a little extra time just for conversation, and I felt
appreciative and maybe a little humble because I knew there
were many more weighty problems needing his attention. I
think he tried to be fair to students and listen to their concerns
and needs—I had a rather lovely thing happen to me on
Graduation Day . . . when I was handed my degree, President
Adams said very softly, "Congratulations, Miriam." It made my
day.*[5]

J. Hal Connor, one of the president's closest faculty friends
and advisors, likewise described some of his favorable at-
tributes: he was a person, he said, who "adhered scrupulously
to the principle that his office door was always open—both
literally and figuratively—to all, faculty, and students alike.
There was no dogmatic insistence on red tape. . . . If you
wanted to see the president, you saw the president. And when
your interview was over, whether you had gained your point or
lost it, you came out feeling better for having talked with a man
who treated you so frankly and so fairly." Connor also pointed
out that Adams was not one to withdraw or fail to help if a
faculty member found himself in trouble.

Having noted these commendable characteristics of Adams,
one must nevertheless in all honesty observe that on some
occasions he was not so considerate, fair, or democratic with
those with whom he differed. Under the influence of his wrath,
he wrote letters described as "offensive to say the least," by
Mary Butler, a prominent alumna who had incurred his anger
when she was president of the Alumni Association.[6]

Adams's basic educational interest was confined to teacher
training. This developed during his stay at St. Cloud and the
year he spent at Columbia. As soon as President Brown
employed him as a science teacher in St. Cloud's academy and
later as an instructor of government in the college, Adams was
inducted into the field of administration, where he became the
president's "right hand man." During his last four years at St.
Cloud, he served as director of the summer sessions. Following

these formative years he explored at Columbia Teachers College the theoretical aspects of school administration for his master's degree under Professor E. S. Evenden, who, according to Adams, was one of the leading authorities in this field. Adams became wholeheartedly devoted to the mission of training teachers for the public schools. He believed that teachers colleges must possess the same quality of professionalism that was used for training in the other professions; in other words, these colleges should be on a par with those that trained doctors, lawyers, and ministers. It was not easy for him, however, to hold to the single purpose of professional teacher education, for within a few years Northern's sister institutions were campaigning not only for state college status but also for permission to offer a master's degree program—both of which he definitely opposed. In regard to the latter, he believed that the addition of a fifth year's work to Northern's program would not "materially improve our service to the schools of our area." The other teachers colleges went forward with the master's programs while Northern's was delayed until 1951.

As a public speaker he was not so popular as presidents Cook and J. C. Brown, for he tended to be too serious and matter-of-fact and almost completely lacking in any form of humor. When he did make formal speeches, which was not often, he generally took time to do his homework, and as a rule was able to present his ideas with a degree of clarity and straightforwardness. He improved with practice; and even though he was not in great demand, he often spoke at as many as three or four graduations a year. Almost all of his presentations were involved with some aspect of modern education although he also enjoyed appearing on sports programs and at church meetings. One of his favorite topics was "The Rights of the Child," in which he developed his views on teacher training.

President Adams's ideas on certain subjects were often expressed in "pointed" terms; however, it should be noted that with the passing of time and the accumulation of experience, his disposition and convictions did mellow. One of those convictions was opposition to the idea of faculty research and writing. He was completely lacking in such a background himself, and had written and published only a pamphlet or so and occasional introductory statements for institutional publications. But this antagonistic view was tempered with the passing of time. In the following letter to the writer, his modified view is clearly expressed:

In reply to your letter . . . I wish to state that I shall be glad to help in any way I can to inform the Social Science Research Council concerning your writings so that you may get additional help to complete your data.

I believe that not only is this [research] good for the field of social studies, but I am sure it is good for you and if it is good for you, it is good for the college.[7]

The president's ideas on the education of teachers were quite firmly developed when he arrived on the DeKalb campus. To carry them out he began a program of reorganization of the curriculum to solidify a "foundation" of "academic experiences" in the form of a "core curriculum" for all students regardless of their teaching specialty. He was also eager to incorporate some of the ideas recently introduced at Columbia Teachers College, which at that time was the center of training for administrators in the public schools and teachers colleges in the United States.

One idea that he enthusiastically embraced was the integration of various subject matter fields; thus in 1933, he divided the geography department into two parts: the earth science courses, under Loren Caldwell, were placed in the newly formed physical science sequence and the others were placed in the social science department. William Gould, head of the geography department, was deprived of his position by Adams on the grounds that geography was not worthy of departmental status because it did not have a sufficient body of material to warrant its survival. But consistency may not always be a mark of virtue in college presidents, for a few years after the demise of the geography department, Adams organized a new department of speech by withdrawing its courses from the English department.

During these early years, Adams inaugurated other curriculum changes. A year of foreign languages that had been required for many years became an elective; an additional education course was added to the list of requirements for teachers; and in such fields as English, mathematics, and the social sciences, reductions were made in the required list for the secondary teachers.

Moreover, to satisfy the constant complaints of the practical arts departments that they were excluded from the general education courses and as a consequence had no opportunity to acquaint the student body with their fields, a survey course was created with the fine arts, industrial arts, and home economics departments, each having one-third of the responsibility for its instruction. Since it was the president's idea to maintain a teachers college curriculum that would include a foundation of "academic experiences" for all students, such substitutions for courses in the humanities and social sciences were hardly consistent with his goal.

Retention of the word "teachers" in the name of this type of college was for years vigorously supported by all the presidents and their professional faculties, but in spite of this singular loyalty to the education of teachers, there were undercurrents of change in and outside the institutions. As early as 1943, the state legislature proposed dropping the word "teachers" from the three remaining colleges so named, and one of the sponsors of this action was none other than DeKalb's own local senator, Dennis Collins. The main argument for this change, as discussed by the *Northern Illinois,* was that it would "improve the reputation of the teachers colleges," for with such a title they were still thought of as normal schools or a "factory for turning out teachers." The editorial also observed that making such a change—to just "college"—would certainly increase the number of students who did not intend to become teachers and surely "there can be no harm in . . . this for teacher training is no holy mission as some would make it." Moreover, such a move would also create sufficient prestige to make it easier for Northern's students to transfer to a university which "can often be a very difficult thing to do. . . ."

This particular legislative measure was not successful, but the enthusiasm it aroused did not subside and further efforts to

227

change the name were continued, especially by Eastern and Western; but Adams, who had by now become the senior president of the teachers colleges, used his influence to oppose the idea. He was indeed proud to say when the two sister schools finally became state colleges in 1947 that N.I.S.T.C. was the only one left by that name and it "will continue to follow the purpose for which it was originally dedicated." [8]

In spite of the president's opposition to this change, there was in the college a small but influential number of faculty members—dehorners of sacred cows as they were sometimes called—who had arrived on the scene in the late 1920s and early 1930s and who held quite different views on this subject. A few were intellectual mavericks, and their influence upon students, especially, was effective. These few individuals became the nucleus in opposing the single-purpose idea of teacher training, and, as already noted, some of the students also grew more vocal in support of a more academic training, especially the World War II veterans who were then returning to school. Along with these groups there were also the numerous journalists and writers in the metropolitan areas who often expressed their views not only in opposition to teacher-training courses but actually in favor of abolishing the schools of education altogether. [9]

One of the principal breakthroughs in modifying the purpose of the college was in 1943, when Adams finally consented to move toward establishing a two-year program of pre-professional courses for students who were undecided about teaching as a career. In the fall of that year, he launched such a program with the following commitment:

> . . . we have organized our faculty for a comprehensive study of the problems of a two year program . . . [to serve] as a background for any three or four-year work in other professions. . . . This study is causing a tremendous amount of interest on our campus and I believe will cause real growth. [10]

This historic committee of five members, set up to make the comprehensive study under the chairmanship of the leading "maverick," Hugh Jameson, reported to the faculty that the committee considered its primary mission to be that of creating a curriculum "with no professional features . . . to serve as a terminal education for those who want to go on into other fields of specialization." The final recommendations were in time reluctantly presented by the president to the faculty and the Teachers College Board, resulting in a long and protracted discussion before the plan was finally accepted and put into effect in the fall of 1945.[11] After a two-year trial period, the popular acceptance of this program was adequately illustrated by the fact that nearly 20 percent of the students chose to enroll in it; another interesting fact was that a large number of them, after this two-year period, decided to remain and prepare for teaching.

With this success the pressures began to mount for the four-year liberal arts degrees, but the opposition remained so strongly in favor of the bachelor's degree in education that it was not until 1955 that legislation was finally passed making Northern a state college with power to confer the liberal arts degrees. Important changes were made in 1943 when the old two-year diploma was abolished and the Bachelor of Education degree was re-named Bachelor of Science in Education. Extension courses for the purpose of upgrading a large number of poorly-trained teachers had also been instituted in many of the surrounding schools under the direction of E. C. O. Beatty.

From the beginning of his presidency Adams was challenged not only to improve the quality of teacher education but also to bring full accreditation to the institution. Preliminary steps had been taken earlier by his two predecessors in securing accreditation by the American Association of Teachers Colleges; however, there still remained the problem of obtaining recognition by the University of Illinois and the North Central Association of Colleges and Secondary Schools. The main barriers to qualifying with either of these were that various sub-collegiate courses were offered, and that a relatively large proportion of the faculty personnel were without graduate degrees—a few had no degree at all.

Initiative was begun with the University of Illinois soon after Adams arrived when he requested that a committee be sent to Northern's campus for the purpose of determining the status of Northern's students. An inspection committee made the examination and in their summary report pointed out that the University could not recognize Northern as a four-year institution. "A good share of the work now given as senior college work is, as a matter of fact," the committee stated, "no more advanced in character than that offered to freshmen and sophomores in most Colleges of Liberal Arts and Sciences." It reommended that provisions be made to increase laboratory and library facilities, to raise the level of academic training of the staff, and to reorganize curriculum offerings in several of the academic departments. These forthright suggestions were what the president wanted, and even though they had a disturbing influence upon the college faculty, for many knew that their lives and careers might be vitally affected, they served as a major stimulus for action.

After two years of real effort by the entire college, the University of Illinois committee returned to make its reinspection, and this time the outcome was favorable. Sufficient changes had been made in critical areas to warrant allowing Northern's graduates who had completed a sufficient number of hours of work in various fields to enter the University. To retain this rating, however, it was necessary to have a further inspection during the year 1932–1933.[12]

At the same time negotiations were being carried on with the University of Illinois, the North Central Association was also beginning to make its evaluation. After an inspection by examiners from the University of Michigan in 1931, Northern was taken from a limited status as an accredited teacher-training institution and given a Class A rating as a four-year, degree-granting college subject to reinspection in 1933. The report noted more or less the same improvements and weaknesses as in the University of Illinois reports.[13]

In 1933, the inspection was repeated. From all the evidence available, it would appear that it was perfunctory; as a result, it provoked Adams to respond with one of his plain-spoken reactions, saying that he was "disappointed at the action of the Board of Review in not giving to our college a clear rating. . . . The information contained in this report," he continued, "could have been collected by anyone without visiting the college at all."[14] Nevertheless the same rating continued as before with a reexamination scheduled for two years hence.

This third inspection involved an enormous amount of work on the part of the college in collecting the data requested in the manual of procedures for gaining accreditation. But it was worth the effort. Professor L. B. Hopkins, the inspector, stated, after he had carefully examined those sensitive areas listed previously, "I do believe this institution should be accredited without any condition or qualifications." The decision was submitted to the North Central Association and, on 19 April 1935, the accreditation was confirmed.[15] In some very real sense, Northern had arrived.

Another development in accreditation that added to Northern's stature was the establishment of a local unit of the American Association of University Women. In 1930, Mrs. Adams and Dean Blanche Davidson, along with forty-three other DeKalb and Sycamore women, initiated the first meeting. After a number of petitions to the national office, beginning in 1933, Northern was finally given full accreditation on 22 June 1939. President Adams, in relating the final approval to the Board, said, "It may be of interest to the Board to know that we are one of 15 teacher colleges in the United States so accredited, that we are at the present time the only one accredited in this state, and that we happen to be the only college on the entire list that is accredited with only a Bachelor of Education degree."[16]

These accreditations had a marked influence on Northern's history, for the process of qualifying for accreditation laid the basis for further developments. A building program was planned for a science hall and library, two of the greatest needs of the institution. Leaves of absence were also inaugurated for faculty members so that they could work on advanced degrees. Moreover, spirit among faculty and students alike, as one prominent alumnus recalled, seemed to lift "the ideas of a teachers college to a higher level." This spirit also expressed itself in a higher rate of placement, increasing until nearly 85 percent of the graduates found positions. At the same time enrollment also experienced a handsome rise: from 729 in 1931 to 1,165 in 1939.

One of the essential ingredients in the process of accreditation was the upgrading of the college faculty. It was one of Adams's principal ambitions to increase the number of master's and doctor's degrees among his faculty; in fact, it was such an obsession of his to sprinkle the faculty roster with doctorates that in one case, at least, he listed one faculty member in the catalog for two years with this coveted degree before he discovered that it had not been fully completed. Some members felt that he was pushing them too hard to go back to graduate school; others (in private conversations) thought that he himself should set an example by completing his doctorate. In spite of criticisms and pressures, much credit should be given him for his untiring efforts, especially during the worst economic crisis in the history of the country.[17]

He was given some help in upgrading his staff by having several early replacements and retirements from the faculty. When he first arrived, he found a few who had been employed as instructors of various instruments in the music department. They were local artists who could perform well but who lacked the necessary academic requirements for teaching; they were soon replaced by others who could not perform so well but who had the degrees. Moreover, the president still had three teachers on his staff from the John W. Cook period—Mann, Parson, and Simonson—who were now able to retire under a newly enacted emeritus plan.

By examining the faculty rosters in the annual catalogs, one can see to what extent he succeeded in upgrading his faculty. When he arrived, among the total faculty only one held a Ph.D. and 16 had master's degrees; at the close of his nineteen years as president, he left his successor with 21 faculty members with Ph.Ds, 1 Doctor of music, 5 Ed.Ds, and 65 master's degrees out of a total faculty of 122.

In the hasty efforts by Northern's presidents to increase the number of degrees they did not always demand that the faculty pursue courses of study relevant to their teaching fields. It was not uncommon, especially for older academic instructors and even heads of departments to take their doctoral work in the Teachers College at Columbia, or in the departments of education at Northwestern and Indiana, or in the College of Education at Greeley, Colorado. They then returned with a doctorate in education, and even though it was perhaps less distinguished and had required less time and effort to secure than the Ph.D., it did nevertheless serve the same purpose since the administration accorded it the same value as far as salary and promotions were concerned. Northern had not yet reached that level of sophistication where anything more than "a degree" seemed important.

Although Adams was considered a strong executive, he still felt the need for an administrative staff as well as a number of committees to assist him in carrying out his policies. His began like most administrative staffs elsewhere, with a few members who often continued to teach part-time; as the years went by the number of full-time administrators increased. His committee system followed somewhat the same pattern with the exception that when he began as president he reduced the existing number of committees from eight to five.

President Adams, in making his appointments to the various committees, made it clear to the appointee that the faculty was not to substitute for administration in operating the college. He was a member of all faculty committees and usually acted as chairman of the one dealing with the curriculum. He was also for some years, because of the Brown scandals, largely in control of the athletic committee. Moreover, there was always to be a representative from his office to serve as secretary on all committees.

Some of the more important committees, bureaus, and councils created during this period to deal with the emerging functions were the Homecoming Committee (1935), the Assembly Program Committee (1935), the Public Relations Committee (1937), the Administrative Council (1939), the Student Activities Fund Committee (1940), the Internal Budget Committee (1944), and the Health Council (1947).

To serve on these committees was not only an honor but also a ladder by which individual faculty members could receive salary increases and climb to full-time administrative assign-

Leslie V. Burkett Blanche Davidson   Grace E. Nix A. Neil Annas

Karl L. Adams   Donalda E. Morrison   Otto E. Peterson Frank W. Phillips

Administration and Faculty 1935–36

Frank W. Phillips   Otto E. Peterson   M. C. Hayes   Homer Hall

Hellen Messenger Marina Phillips   Ethel Woolhiser Mary William

Education Faculty in 1935–36

Lillian Cobb   Gus Campbell   Maude Uhland   William Angus

B. Mae Small   Mary Prissinger   Grace E. Nix   E. Ruth Taylor

Foreign Language and English Faculty in 1935–36

Bernadine Hanby   James Livingstone   Katharine Neptune

Olive Johnson   Bertha Pratt   Norma Pearson   Eva McMahon

Librarians and Business Staff in 1935–36

Charles Montgomery Leslie V. Burkett   George L. Terwilliger   Norma Stelford

Loren T. Caldwell William Storm   Ira Jenks Eugene Hellmich   Howard Gould

Science and Math Faculty in 1935–36

Birchard Coar   Charles E. Fouser   L. Eveline Merritt

Alma Anderson   A. Neil Annas   Vera Wiswall

Fine Arts and Music Faculty in 1935–36

236

Industrial Arts and Home Economics Faculty in 1935–36

Physical Education Faculty in 1935–36

ments. For years, committee work was one of the principal criteria used in evaluating the teaching faculty, second only to the extent of service rendered to the community and northern Illinois. These data were collected by the administration as the time approached to determine the amount of annual salary increment. Under these conditions, there was never a dearth of applicants for committee assignments.

Notwithstanding this phenomenon, there were two individuals whose services on committees over a period of time should have special mention. All activities in public relations were for a number of years placed in the willing hands of Paul Street. At different times he was the alumni director, sponsor of student publications, a lobbyist and college representative, as well as holder of a host of other special duties that only a man of his stamina and personal qualifications could perform. During his nineteen years on and off the campus, he became one of the best-known and respected members of the faculty; but when his keen sense of justice caused him to speak out as president of the Illinois Education Association against the parsimonious Teachers College Board, he found it necessary to sever his connections with Northern. The following sentiments convey the feelings of students who worked with him:

The journalism office, where the Northern Illinois was prepared each week, was one of my favorite spots. Paul Street had a wonderful sense of humor; puns seemed to run rampant in that office; and it seemed the best in everyone came to the fore as we frantically attempted to meet deadlines. Paul Street believed in people and accepted their humaneness, he listened to our heartbreaks and triumphs and always kept encouraging us. He spent long hours in that office.[18]

The other member of the faculty whose service was given to many of the major committees was Charles Howell, who arrived on the scene the same year as Street and who worked closely with him as well as teaching a sixteen-hour load in the social science department. Howell had an omniverious interest in every facet of the college, and, with his expertise in the behavioral sciences, nothing escaped his penetrating analysis.

For twenty-seven years this tough-minded person worked on committees both at Northern and throughout the state on such social problems as discrimination, health, juvenile delinquency, public welfare, and civilian morale during the war. In time, his usefulness to the college became of such importance that President Holmes appointed him the first director of the Bureau of Research.

The fragmentation of administrative functions, a trend which has become so pervasive in educational institutions today, began at Northern during the Adams administration. Of the new administrative functions at Northern, the first were those connected with the health service, such as a doctor, nurse, and dietician; then came the student and academic deans, followed by directors or coordinators of the alumni, extension service, veterans, cafeteria, public relations, testing, and so forth *ad infinitum*.

Recruiting new faculty members was a simple process in the earlier years, for nearly all of it was done by the president himself. After once locating a candidate, he usually, but not always, consulted with the heads of departments. If the candidate was satisfactory to the president but not to the head, the latter might have to make an impassioned appeal if he hoped to persuade the president to change his mind.[19] When the president's ideas of governance were eventually democratized, following a serious confrontation with some members of the Board and faculty, he welcomed the appointment of a dean to advise and assist him in making decisions.

When recruiting, Adams had certain fundamental qualifications he expected of his candidates: he believed that his teachers should have either a teachers college background or a degree from a school of education, or at least some experience in public-school teaching. In rare cases, he might waive these requirements. He was staunchly opposed to employing graduates of Northern, and in only a few cases did he deviate from this policy, a practice that he characterized as "inbreeding." Some of the faculty at various times felt that he was partial to those who had degrees from Columbia Teachers College and that he had strong feelings against candidates who wished to carry on a program of research and writing unless it could be shown that it was complementary to their classroom teaching. He was just as decisive in advising new members on personal matters; for instance, he did not hesitate to tell them that he thought they should not buy their own homes. These convictions, like so many others held earlier in his career, gradually became less important; however, he never did build or buy a home of his own in DeKalb.

On his trips to various meetings, he occasionally interviewed candidates; in some cases, he relied upon university or commercial agencies for their services. For years, those who were called to the campus had to bear the cost of their interviews; however, by 1946 the Board finally adopted a policy that

the presidents be required to advise a candidate that in case he is accepted and given a position all travel will be at his own expense; and in case the candidate is not employed the college shall bear all necessary travel expense; and no expense shall be paid except where the president requests the candidate to come for an interview.[20]

Determining rank for a teachers college faculty was another of the knotty problems facing the president, for without advanced degrees it was necessary to use some other criterion, such as the total number of graduate hours. For example, the accrediting agencies had established the minimum of thirty semester hours or the master's degree for instructors and assistant professors; sixty hours for associates; and ninety or the doctor's degree for the professors. Where ninety hours were evaluated on the same basis as a doctorate, it caused certain faculty members to choose the former and thus by-pass such agonizing requirements as the dissertation and foreign languages, not to mention the various examinations, written and oral. Thus the accumulation of credit hours in easy fields and with less demanding instructors was a temptation. Such conditions soon created a disproportionate number in the professorial rank; for example, in 1941–1942 it ran slightly more than 27 percent of a total of seventy-eight faculty.[21]

With this weight in the upper rank, it was necessary to establish ratios for the various ranks so that rank would mean approximately the same in all five state teachers colleges. Moreover, the Northern budget would not afford the money necessary to pay so many high salaries. Thus the number of professors was limited to between one-eighth and one-fifth of the total staff, or not more than ten. The associate and assistant ranks were set at one-fourth to two-fifths each; and the instructor rank (unclassified group) at not more than one-fifth.

This limitation on the upper rank brought about demotions of a number of its members; while some were moved into the administrative category, four others—Hellmich, Hainds, Hayter, and Howell: the "4-H Club" as they were called—were lowered to the associate rank, where they remained for five years before they were again promoted. Other efforts were made to enhance the professor's rank by appointing a major committee to draw up suitable criteria to use for subsequent promotion into it. Some of the faculty opposed the committee's recommendation in 1945, especially those who had already earned their ninety hours, for they would no longer be eligible, since the new criteria made the minimum requirement the "earned doctorate." A few in the assistant rank, especially some of the older members such as Evans and Oakland, with only a master's degree, were also unhappy, for they were ineligible for promotion to the associate rank unless they returned to graduate school for more hours, or unless exceptions were made in their cases. The latter action was decided upon by the president and Dean Zulauf, although some members of the Administrative Council opposed the action.[22]

The annual contracts had more in them than just the rank and the nine-months' salary figure; on the reverse side were other stipulations which appeared at various times from the early thirties until the late fifties which revealed the evolutionary trend from normal-school practices to university procedures. For instance, beginning with the year 1932–1933, they specified that "every faculty member . . . is expected to earn at least five semester hours of approved graduate credit in his chosen field every three years." Moreover, all faculty members were expected to be expert teachers and at all times should "welcome the chance to demonstrate and to improve their teaching skills." If any one were not in "full sympathy with this point of view," by all means he should not "enroll as a member of this faculty." Another stipulation was one that met with a certain degree of opposition, for it strongly urged that the entire faculty "become members of the Illinois Education Association and the National Education Association." The president's goal was full membership in at least the I.E.A. at its annual meeting in Dixon, Illinois, which all faculty members were required to attend unless otherwise excused.

This goal was not always an easy one for him to attain, since there were a few reluctant joiners on the campus who had to be prodded at the last moment for their dues. There were others, too, such as Lillian Cobb, who were always reluctant to give up any class days, especially for such a purpose. But for those reluctant ones it was not a day entirely wasted, for the meeting was held in early October when the Rock River scenery was at its best, thus making it possible for many to attend the general assembly, eat at some historic spot on the Rock River, and then return home along the scenic river drive. A few, however, who were more courageous went directly to the pheasant runs or duck passes in search of the wild fowl; still others, such as the coaches, often found that they had their athletic duties to look after. The rule finally eroded until one might have seen on that particular no-school-day any number remaining home to winterize their houses or to attend to some other important domestic duty. By 1964, this "Rock River Division Day" finally passed into history, and all faculty members henceforth were at last free to stay at home and pay their dues to their own learned societies, instead of to one in which they had no professional interest.

The faculty during this period consisted of about an equal ratio of men to women; however, when it came to salaries, there was quite a noticeable discrimination. Only a casual examination of salary contracts would be necessary to draw this conclusion; with everything else being equal, such as rank, training, and experience, the differences were sometimes as much as $500 a year. Even though this was some twenty-five years before the women's liberation movement, discontent was beginning to appear not only in the area of salaries but also in respect to rank, headships, committee appointments, and positions on the administrative staff—and in the case of heads of departments, only four out of fourteen were women.

Nepotism was extremely rare, if not impossible; never were a husband and wife to be employed on the faculty during this period. Married women were expected to live with their husbands; if a wife were to accept a position at Northern, she would obviously either have to have her husband come and live with her in DeKalb or have the difficult task of commuting back and forth from her home. When there was any possibility of nepotism arising, it was only by a special Board decision that the second member of a family could be employed.

The system of tenure had been given little, if any, consideration during the preceding presidencies; however, with the passage of the tenure law for the public schools, action was soon begun to establish the same principle for the teachers colleges. There was little need for a tenure policy in the past, for almost anyone appointed in a normal school or a teachers college had a strong feeling of security—in fact too much to satisfy some critics. Rarely was anyone dismissed outright.

Tenure was first officially placed in the faculty contracts for the year 1949–1950, although it had been approved by the Board as early as 1943. The following statement appeared on the contract: "New faculty members attain tenure only after satisfactorily completing a minimum of three years of teaching at Northern . . . unless specifically stated otherwise in this notice." In President Adams's report to the North Central Association the year before, he noted that out of his total faculty, fifty-eight members were acceptable for tenure and twenty-six were not; of this latter group, nineteen were instructors.

A few of the Board's other 1943 salary schedule provisions should be noted. In regard to academic freedom, it stated that the teachers were entitled to full freedom in research and in the classroom in discussing a subject; they should be careful, however, to avoid introducing into their teaching controversial matter which has no relation to the subject; as a citizen, the teacher should exercise appropriate restraint and show respect for the opinions of others. Promotions and salary increases were to be determined by automatic increments, teaching ability, professional growth, and general educational service to the institution. Sex was not to be a factor in promotion. Sabbatical leaves were extended on the basis of one teacher out of twenty-five each year at one-half pay after five years of service with the obligation to serve at least two years following the leave. Sick leaves were granted at full pay for two weeks and half pay for six additional weeks.

As for actual freedom in the classrooms it should be stated in all fairness to both President Adams and his successor that rarely was there any overt attempt on their part to censure or penalize individuals for what they said or did in their classrooms. There were times, however, when one heard of adverse feelings expressed more or less privately about a particular professor's grading practices or attendance records, and periodically a wave of reform to improve teaching by classroom visitation would strike the campus.

By the time Adams assumed the presidency, considerable sentiment was developing for an improved retirement system; as the members of the Board observed in 1928, they had already been placed at a disadvantage in attracting teachers of high quality because of the low salaries and the inferior pension and retirement plan. In 1934, the Board appointed a committee of presidents and Board members to create an emeritus system that would include compulsory retirement at seventy years of age. The enactment of this plan afforded an annual pension of $1,200 for instructors and assistant professors; $2,400 for associates and professors; and $3,000 for presidents. Retirement was possible at the age of sixty-five.

This plan remained in effect until 1941 when the present State Universities Retirement System of Illinois was created. Representatives from the five teachers colleges and the University of Illinois and various scientific survey agencies participated in drawing up the plan, which was certainly a vast improvement. Its principal weakness, however, has been that the state government has continuously neglected to fund the system, creating a tremendous deficit and loss of interest, putting the system in danger of being dissolved or changed to federal social security, which offers fewer benefits.

The relationship between Adams and the two boards he served under can be divided into two phases: one quite congenial during the period of Republican governors and the other quite the opposite under Democratic governors. However, in good times and bad he had two loyal members on his consulting committee, Harriet A. McIntire and the Reverend Preston Bradley, who served for seventeen and twenty years respectively. They were about as opposite as any two individuals could possibly be: she, a loyal conservative Republican from the heartland of Illinois, and he, an active, liberal, humanitarian radio preacher. Miss McIntire was an occasional visitor in the Adams household, sometimes as an overnight guest; and on occasions, Adams and his wife were guests in her home near Mendota. No doubt Adams was responsible for the dedication of the *Norther* to her in 1946 as a reward for her untiring "efforts as a 'builder' in the name of teacher education." Bradley was a frequent guest speaker at the student assemblies and baccalaureate addresses, and Adams often attended services at his church in Chicago. Bradley rarely attended Board meetings; but when he did, it was often at a time when Adams was having difficulties in one form or another.[23] He was a capable member when present and could generally be relied upon to vote for the welfare of the colleges as well as to mediate disputes that arose from time to time. On one occasion when Adams was unable to get an appointment with Governor Horner, Bradley interceded and went with Adams to the governor's office.

A serious problem during Adams's presidency was that appropriations were made to the Board with the amounts for individual colleges unspecified, thus creating friction and misunderstandings among them in the struggle for their fair share of the funds. Adams, for a number of years, worked diligently for a science hall and library as well as for a dormitory (all combined in 1943 under a "Twenty-Five Year Plan"), but each time the Board decided upon its priorities, Northern was given no buildings, only small sums of money for land acquisition or renovation of property. As a result of this pattern Adams was often mentioned by the other presidents as the one whose buildings were in the best physical condition, which was no doubt true, considering his engineering background. His devotion to the long struggle to secure these needed buildings, at a time when the nation was in the throes of an economic depression and the Board was under the influences of a Springfield bureaucracy, was commendable.

President Adams was beset with patronage controversies during the Democratic administration of Governor Henry Horner. He was not only a staunch Republican but was also rather unfamiliar with patronage problems and especially so when it meant dealing with Democrats. It was easy for him when Republicans controlled the executive office and the Board, as was the case for two-thirds of his administration, but he was rather unrealistic and seemed totally unaware of the fact that Democrats, too, would expect patronage when in office. This was probably because the G.O.P. had held the governor's office continuously since the Civil War with the exceptions of two Democratic administrations and thus had filled the vast number of patronage offices with Republican office-seekers. Adams had become completely adjusted to one-party rule. He innocently gave no recognition to the fact that "to the victor belongs the spoils" when Governor Horner came to power in 1933.

The president's first controversy developed when a Democratic member of the Board asked for the removal of two Republicans, James B. Livingstone, business manager at Northern, and Arthur Johnson, the supervisor of buildings. Livingstone had been brought to Northern by J. C. Brown to take charge of this office after the peculiar purchasing and questionable accounting habits of his predecessor had resulted in the stockpiling of unnecessary foods.

In 1933, Governor Horner appointed Jacob E. Alschuler, son of a distinguished Aurora legal family, to the Normal School Board; soon thereafter the problems of political patronage began to raise its head in the form of a request for the removal of Livingstone and Johnson in order to make way for two Democratic appointees. The only black mark, outside of being a Republican, against Livingstone was that during the 1930s he had committed the unpopular act of dismissing a number of WPA workers from the campus lagoon project for loafing on the job, thus, ostensibly at least, antagonizing the Democratic leaders.

But Adams was not about to discharge these two loyal employees; and for several months he persisted in retaining them, without salary, while Alschuler was trying to persuade the Board to dismiss them. After some delay by the Board, Bradley and Alschuler finally went to the governor, who responded like Solomon in his judicial manner and recommended that "one of the men, the business manager, be discharged and the other man be retained. . . ." This compromise was unanimously accepted by the Board, and a Democrat, Franz Romeis, was made the new business manager. Adams's role in this case, however, did not endear him to Alschuler, and as a result the worst for him was yet to come.

Frank Phillips, the well-known superintendent of schools in Freeport, Illinois, was appointed director of training and superintendent of the DeKalb public schools in 1929, a dual position that had been separated since the departure of Floyd Ritzman two years earlier. Phillips had a fine personal background of family, education, and school experience; as a result he soon rose to a prominent position on the campus, in the city, and also in the state. He was an excellent representative of the college and, for most of his career at Northern, a close associate of Adams. However, in time, with the increased tensions and dissatisfactions among the faculty in respect to Adams's leadership, he was finally looked upon by one segment as a possible replacement for Adams. Another segment was critical of Adams but not willing to sacrifice him by any undemocratic method, whereas still a third but small group was neutral and did not wish to participate in what they considered a political dispute. As for Phillips, his status with the faculty, certainly at the beginning of the controversy, was high, and he was respected by most of his colleagues. The groups who complained most of Adams's administration "as a one-man institution" finally mobilized their efforts behind Phillips, thus causing a cleavage between the two leaders.

In May 1938, Phillips had accepted the Elgin superintendency of schools and thus tendered his resignation to Adams, who immediately accepted it. But because of some misunderstanding with the Elgin board, Phillips suddenly found it necessary to cancel his contract, at which time demands were made to have his position restored to him at DeKalb. A period of tension ensued between the two; however, Adams finally was willing to give him back his position.[24]

This cleavage continued to widen and the tensions to deepen following this dispute until finally a few prominent leaders, such as the two deans, Annas and Davidson, along with professors Storm and Oakland, took their complaints to Alschuler, who already had had his troubles with Adams. The following were only a few of the grievances they laid before him. Adams, they claimed:

frequently passes over the heads of his departments in the choosing of faculty members for their departments and arranging courses and often the department heads find out about them through a roundabout course. He has deprived department heads from doing duties rightfully belonging to them . . . and . . . he has acted with considerable favoritism in the handling of his faculty, rewarding those friendly to him and doing the contrary to those he seemed to feel were opposed to him.[25]

These and other charges were denied by Adams; however, Alschuler went ahead and laid them before the Board, at which time he also moved that Adams's contract be terminated the following year. However, he was unable to get the motion before the Board, and it was delayed for over a year until finally Alschuler succeeded in getting a motion passed to set up a committee to investigate these charges thoroughly. But the

Williston Hall Dormitory

Board procrastinated and the committee was never appointed.[26] During this period of stalemate, ample time was afforded the supporters of the president to mobilize their efforts to counteract the opposition.

The leaders of the faculty who finally took the responsibility of assisting Adams were Milo Whittaker, Romeo Zulauf, and O. E. Peterson. Whittaker, at least, did not undertake this task because he was friendly with or had been shown any favoritism by Adams—quite the contrary. However, he did abhor the undemocratic methods that were attributed to Alschuler, who (it was rumored) had already approached Phillips and secured his consent to accept the presidency upon the dismissal of Adams—a charge Phillips denied.

Whittaker was fully aware that most of the faculty would not assist in saving Adams unless he was willing to make some basic changes in the governance of the institution, such as giving the faculty more voice in its operation. With his promise of such change, they moved ahead quietly—even though if their efforts were to fail, their own positions would be in jeopardy. Whittaker interviewed all the faculty individually with a prepared statement indicating that everything between the two parties—Whittaker and the one he was interviewing—was strictly confidential and if the party signed or did not sign nothing would be said. Each member was polled; when the votes were tallied, over 80 percent signed the statement that they were "favorable to Adams."[27] The president's supporters also drew up an abstract of achievements during the nine years of the Adams administration which they used along with the poll to win support from prominent schoolmen.

Zulauf and Peterson organized the second phase of the plan by securing Carleton Washburne, of Winnetka, probably the most prominent schoolman in Illinois, to contact a number of his colleagues and inform them of what Alschuler and the Board were trying to do to the college and its president. Washburne painted a fine picture of achievements at the college under Adams to be used by the schoolmen in their letters to the officials at Springfield. They were specifically asked to send them to Governor Horner and possibly also to John Hallihan

Williston Hall Living Room, 1937

*of the Department of Registration and Education . . .
expressing your appreciation of Karl Adams, your regret that
there has been any movement to remove him, and your strong
hope that he may be continued in office. . . . May I suggest that
the letter be one which will enlist the sympathy and support of
the Governor and Mr. Hallihan, rather than antagonize them
in any way. . . .* [28]

Unfortunately, Washburne also cast some unfavorable opinions upon the activities of Frank Phillips, and soon after the
letters were mailed Phillips wrote to Washburne to protest that

*a number of statements regarding me which display unmistak-
able bias, and which do me a grave injustice. It must be
assumed that in collecting data for this communication you
conferred with those whose cause you have espoused and made
no effort to arrive at all the facts. . . . There is a heavy and
unique responsibility on your shoulders [for accepting such]
prejudiced information . . . [from] two members of the college
faculty who have busied themselves on both sides of this
question over a period of years. . . .* [29]

Following a series of letters and phone conversations between these two schoolmen, Washburne finally offered his
regrets, saying, "I failed to take cognizance of what the
communications . . . might do to you. For this I apologize." To
help undo the harm resulting from his communications he
transmitted the letters between the two of them "to all persons
to whom I sent the original communications." [30] Phillips
denied that he had ever sought the position, and stated that on
the one occasion that he was approached, he was asked only
whether he would "assume the acting presidency" until a
successor could be appointed. This he consented to do. [31]

In the final phase of the controversy, the Board appointed
two members to work out procedures for "an investigation of
the Northern Illinois State Teachers College and the administration of Mr. Adams [to] be disposed of by January 1, 1940." A
number of individuals, including several of "President Adams'

252

Williston Hall formal dance in 1937

faculty friends" appeared before the Board to give their opinions. When the final vote on whether to dismiss Adams was taken by the Board, he was saved only because one of the Democratic members—either John Wieland or John Hallihan—changed his mind, making a vote of five to four in Adams's favor.[32]

This action by the Board may have been due to the physical condition of the governor himself, who had become seriously ill. The Democratic Board members probably felt that no unnecessary problems should be created at this particular moment. In spite of the favorable vote for Adams, he certainly could have had no feelings of security, for this was a campaign year; if the Democratic candidate, Hershey, defeated the Republican candidate, Green, all probabilities were that Adams's fate would be sealed. Thus the Adams family and some of their supporters waited with bated breath during the early hours of election night only to see the Hershey vote soar well above his opponent's, thus causing an early and unhappy exodus of friends from the Adams home. But Mrs. Adams remained hopeful until the wee hours of the morning, when, at last, as so often happens in Illinois elections, the downstate vote began to turn the tide and finally Dwight Green was elected. Mrs. Adams called those friends who lacked her faith from their beds to report the good news.[33]

President Adams, having survived this ordeal, now turned his attention to the task of ridding himself of his principal adversaries. Biding his time for more than a year, he finally found himself in the comfortable position in which not more than two votes could be mustered against any of his requests to the Board, since Governor Green had already made several appointments that tipped the scales in his favor.

On his list for dismissals, besides the three finally selected, were such prominent names as William Storm and Neil Annas; however, through the intercession of Milo Whittaker, Howard Gould, Romeo Zulauf, and others on the Administrative Council, these two highly respected individuals were permitted to

Social Sciences Department in 1940–41: seated, left to right: Hugh Jameson, Charles Howell, William Gould, E. C. O. Beatty; standing, left to right: Earl Hayter, Romeo Zulauf, Milo Whittaker

remain, although Annas's deanship was transferred to Ernest Hanson and his salary was reduced sharply. Storm's and Oakland's salaries were not reduced but certainly the evidence indicates a lower rate of increase for several years. Those who supported Adams, on the other hand, received better treatment: Whittaker, the following year, received the highest salary of all the teaching staff; Zulauf was elevated to the newly formed position of dean of the faculty, a position Adams promised during the controversy he would create.

At the Board meeting on 19 May 1941, Adams requested that the Board terminate the contracts of the dean of women, Blanche Davidson, industrial arts teacher Carl Cramer, and director of training, Frank Phillips as of the close of the school year 1941. All of these members had served since 1929, and all had been employed during the presidency of J. C. Brown. In regard to Dean Davidson, the charges were that many difficult situations had arisen over her relationships with faculty, students, administration, and townspeople. Cramer was criticized for his incompetence in the English language and his poor teaching as well as his relationships with the faculty and administration. In referring to their dismissal, Adams noted that considerations of tenure conditions and the rights of adequate notice of dismissal compelled him to offer each a one-year extension beyond the usual termination date at the close of the current school year, provided they agreed to cooperate with him during that time. "The question of the cooperation would of necessity be determined," he said, "entirely by the administration."

At the July Board meeting Adams reported that since neither Davidson nor Cramer had accepted his conditions, he was recommending an immediate termination of their contracts. He felt quite confident of this action for he had already received the consent of his Board committee; when the motion was voted upon, Alschuler was the only one in opposition.[34] With respect to Phillips, his case was different in that his dual relationship with the college and the city schools made him only a part-time faculty member. Since both Adams and his principal of the Training School, Stuart Fink, were of the opinion that such a relationship was unsatisfactory from a professional standpoint and that the position should be changed to a full-time director of both the elementary and secondary training programs, Phillips's replacement presented no particular problem, for his position could be eliminated.

As far as the Board and Adams were concerned, the dismissal controversy had terminated, so he proceeded to replace Phillips with Oscar Chute, Davidson with Helen Moor, and Cramer with Lawrence Secrest. But for the three complainants the issue was definitely not settled; they had decided to take their case to the Cook County Circuit Court seeking a writ of *mandamus* to compel the Board to reinstate them in their positions with back salary as of June 1941.

On 29 June 1942, the suit was heard by Judge Allegretti whose court decided in favor of the plaintiffs. Rights to due process, the judge ruled, were violated in that the plaintiffs should have been given charges and a hearing prior to any dismissal; moreover, the hearing that was finally given was not carrried out with the proper procedure, for the right of counsel was not exercised. The attorney general, feeling that this decision had "set a significant precedent," appealed it to the Illinois Supreme Court, which on 21 January 1943 unanimously overruled the lower court on the grounds that the appellants failed to show a clear right to the writ of *mandamus;* payment of back salaries was also denied.[35]

Thus came an end to one of the longest controversies in the history of the college. The legal encounter still left unsettled the vital question of whether teachers college instructors had the same tenure rights as those in the public schools. It also served to create such uncertainty about this right that increased efforts were begun by the faculties to secure that which they previously had taken for granted.

The collapse of the American economy had no sooner taken place than the problem of academic freedom and the rights of the teacher to teach controversial materials increased in importance. This was a recurring phenomenon in American history, and the problem had never been satisfactorily resolved except perhaps in prosperous times when the public was less concerned about what was done in their educational institutions. It had not been at any time much of an issue in teachers colleges for the simple reason that their faculties were usually indifferent and did not have the urge or sophistication to criticize the existing order. Moreover, they had been too carefully selected with respect to their religion, politics, personality, and training, and also the larger part of their curricula was of a professional character. This group hardly fit the charges made by President Harding's Commissioner of education in the 1920s that "there is altogether too much preaching of these damnable doctrines of Bolshevism, Anarchy, Communism, and Socialism in this country today. If I had it in my power I would not only imprison, but would expatriate all advocates of these un-American doctrines."

These extreme views began to take on importance in the state of Illinois, and there were restraints of various ideas through the advocacy of loyalty oaths and censorship of textbooks and speakers. Certain reactionary elements in the state legislature were given an opportunity to attack the educational institutions. Northern's difficulties sprang largely from the activities of a few faculty members, more specifically in the social science department, members who were also independent in their thinking and had some talent for public speaking. Milo Whittaker was the leader, along with professors Zulauf, Jameson, and Beatty. All were constantly called upon to analyze current problems of the Depression at forums, service clubs, and other types of community organizations. By the latter part of the 1930s, two more young professors, Charles Howell and Earl Hayter, were added to this group, and in time they also made their individual contributions.

Two prominent state senators from northern Illinois districts heard of these activities and in time made efforts to investigate the college and especially the activities of certain social science professors. In the case of Zulauf, according to the recollection of the writer, they were doubly certain of his "subversiveness," if for no other reason than his name. Jameson, an outspoken student of the Constitution, on several occasions aroused local citizens with his somewhat less than literal interpretations of that document. On one occasion before the Social Studies Club he answered the bitter attacks on Supreme Court Justice Hugo Black (whose Ku Klux Klan membership in his younger years had been revealed) as only a clever trick on the part of big business and the Republican party to embarrass President Roosevelt.[36]

These encounters with the local citizens and their representatives in Springfield no doubt brought some anxiety to Adams; for he was fully aware that such political leaders, if sufficiently aroused, might bring about further reductions in his budgets. To ward off such untoward possibilities, he might have been expected to try to limit such discussions; however, at no time was any such move made. To the contrary, he and Dean Zulauf actually lent their support to prevent a legislative investigation of the writer's career during one of the Red Scares. He also gave further evidence of his courage when one of the conservative Board members from Bloomington, William R. Bach, suddenly became concerned about an editorial in the *Northern Illinois* by Loretta Skelly, the student editor, which he said indignantly was "allowed . . . to be printed."[37] She had written an editorial criticizing the validity of oaths of allegiance for teachers then being considered at Springfield. In reply to a letter from Bach to her, she maintained among other things that his ideas would also act to intimidate students and teachers in the classroom. Adams also entered the discussion with Bach on the side of his faculty and students:

> *I find no criticism to make of your point of view. I believe however, . . . that you miss just a little bit the feeling of students and of teachers that this requirement was directed toward them. . . . Teachers, particularly younger teachers, felt that this was a direct criticism of them. . . .*
>
> *While you and I both desire the same end, we differ rather decidedly, I believe, as to the means that would accomplish this result. I do not believe, that an oath of allegiance by teachers would be of any significant help in making better citizens of our teaching group. . . .* [38]

Bach devoted one more letter to Adams in a slightly conciliatory vein but still maintained most of his previous position. Following these exchanges the whole problem of subversiveness turned from the Board to the politicans in Springfield, where the 65th General Assembly created the Seditious Activities Investigation Commission which finally became responsible for legislation establishing the Broyles oath.

This committee, with Senator Paul Broyles as chairman, was only a miniature of the controversial Dies Un-American Activities Committee in Washington, which became rather ridiculous through its unfounded implications that various individuals and organizations were involved with communistic plots.

Broyles, through his hearings, called the presidents of the state colleges and universities to testify as well as to file with him a study of "the type of textbooks being used with regard to government, idealogy and 'isms' and personnel employed." This examination of such materials was to be done by a committee of one faculty member from each of the teachers colleges, and those members appointed, he insisted, should be veterans. J. Hal Connor, one of Northern's most prominent veterans, was its representative, and Dean Zulauf also assisted him in compiling a list of courses that related to "sound American citizenship" then being taught at Northern.

To assist Adams in his efforts before the committee, the professors at Northern arranged a meeting for the purpose of accepting a statement drawn up principally by Hugh Jameson. This was discussed by the other presidents who found themselves so completely in accord with its contents that it was included in the Board minutes under the heading "Education in Americanism." [39]

Broyles and his committee worked diligently on a bill that would guarantee protection to the state government from all subversives, but for several years he found that many of the senators, both Democratic and Republican, as well as the governors, were rather hesitant to sanction such a controversial measure. It was not until some further amendments were added, making it rather innocuous, that it was finally signed into law on 18 July 1955. Its basic stipulation was that all those who drew pay from the state treasury must swear or affirm that they were not members of or affiliated with the Communist party or knowingly affiliated with any organization which advocated the overthrow or destruction of the national government or state government of Illinois by force, violence, or other unlawful means. After several Supreme Court decisions in the late 1960s declaring such oaths unconstitutional, the Illinois law was finally discarded.

Academic freedom in the classroom survived the attacks made upon it, but the problem of who could speak and where on the campus he might speak continued to be controversial issues. Until 1931, the selection of speakers to appear before student or faculty organizations was largely done by a lecture board or student committees and their faculty advisors; this system seemed to work without any serious difficulties on or off the campuses. However, in that year two prominent lecturers whose reputations caused some anxiety in the community had been engaged to speak at Illinois State Normal University. One was an expert on the social and economic life of the Russian people and the other, Norman Thomas, was the Socialist party candidate for President. As soon as these names were announced, an unfavorable public reaction resulted in the cancellation of the two addresses.

This *cause célèbre* also involved William R. Bach. He called upon the Board to revise the policy of selecting speakers for the campuses in order to prevent such individuals from being engaged. His restrictive resolution drew several objections from his colleagues, especially from Preston Bradley, and a less stringent policy was finally accepted for all teachers colleges. It read, in part, as follows: "The matter of the selection of speakers who shall appear before the student body . . . shall be submitted to the respective presidents for their respective approval before any invitations are extended or contracts made."

When the great economic debacle finally hit the nation on that fateful day in October 1929, it probably did less harm to small institutions such as Northern than to the large universities. The normal schools operated for many years on dismally low budgets, since their reputations were such that state legislators tended to think lightly of them as seats of learning. Northern was no exception. It had never known prosperity and, from the day of its inception, was compelled to operate from hand to mouth, underpaying and overloading its faculty, overcrowding the buildings, and for years depriving some of its students of even a place to eat or sleep on campus.

Depression years only aggravated these hard times, for enrollments at Northern tended to inch upward, averaging about 750 per year while biennial budgets were forced downward as much as 23 percent in 1933–1934, thus necessitating a salary reduction of 10 percent for the faculty. Teaching members during this period were neither added nor dismissed. The total number decreased from fifty-seven in 1930 to fifty in 1936 because no vacancies were filled, thus placing a heavier teaching load on the regular staff. After 1936, however, with gradually increasing budgets, the teaching staff was finally restored by 1941 to its 1930 level.

As for Northern's faculty salaries, it usually had the lowest monthly average for full professors ($337 in 1937) of the five colleges. However, salaries of the next two lower ranks tended to be a few dollars higher than at the other colleges. If the cost of living had been considered, all the ranks at Northern should have been higher, for this section of Illinois had a higher cost of living. The highest nonadministrative professor's salary on a nine-month basis in 1937 was $3,650; the lowest-paid professor received $1,800 and librarians received as little as $1,600. These salaries were considered low in comparison with some of the better high schools. A number of the more ambitious faculty members were not averse to doing a little "moonlighting" by refereeing athletic games, working in the local factories, or even preaching in nearby churches. An intense struggle also went on each spring to get on the two-month summer-school payroll, for that was often the difference between making a bare living or going in debt.

But even with their low salaries and heavy work loads, one found few complaints from the faculty during the Depression period, for each was aware that he was fortunate to have a position of any kind; thousands were unemployed in the surrounding cities and millions were standing in breadlines or being cared for by relief agencies. Anxiety was very real—especially for those with families where the breadwinner might be laid off at any moment. Rumors were often current that the colleges might not only have to curtail the "fads and frills" (such as the kindergartens) but that they also might have to close altogether for want of state revenues. Economies were made wherever possible in student help, secretarial and janitorial services, travel expenses, and even in the use of college utilities.

Notwithstanding these wretched economic conditions, much effort was made not only to raise salaries but also to eliminate or modify other troublesome aspects of the teaching profession. Several salary committees in cooperation with the American Association of University Professors (A.A.U.P.) and such faculty leaders as Milo Whittaker, E. C. O. Beatty, and Charles Howell were successful in making contributions. These salary committees also cooperated with faculty from the other state teachers colleges; and out of their joint efforts, salaries were finally raised in the 1940s above the Depression level, and a certain flexibility was achieved for dealing with various inequities resulting from the increased cost of living during and after the war. The take-home income for teachers also had fallen at this time because they were now for the first time required to pay a federal income tax, according to a decision of the Supreme Court.

In 1948, the maximums of the salary schedule were increased $100 a month for the top three ranks and $75 a month for instructors. Qualifications and proportions for the various ranks along with the salary range were revised as follows: professor (doctor's degree; one-fifth to one-fourth in number), $4,950–5,850; associate professor (doctor's degree or equivalent; one-fourth to two-fifths), $4,275–5,175; assistant professor (two years of graduate work; one-fourth to two-fifths), $3,600–4,500; instructor (master's degree; not over one-fifth of the faculty), $3,150–3,825. This increase was certainly justified, for as many as thirty-five faculty members at Northern were already at their maximum and could not receive further increases.

Students, too, were caught up in the throes of this crisis, for their life and work on the campus underwent a metamorphosis during the Depression; halls, classrooms, assemblies, and boarding houses—all reverberated with opinions on the economy. The students were unable to insulate themselves in the ivory tower of extracurricular activities as their predecessors had; rather they themselves soon became an integral part of the emergency.

Student activities were at first centered on discussing methods and attending conferences dealing with the possibilities of creating an educational program that would establish a new order in society; but this idealism soon waned and a more pragmatic approach was taken. By 1933, a high percentage of the students were face to face with real financial problems; some were even forced to drop out for lack of funds. Part-time jobs on and off the campus that so many had depended upon were now becoming scarce; loan funds too were depleted, and the prospects of placement for the graduates were less hopeful. Many cooperative efforts by organizations such as the Alpha Phi Omega fraternity raised money from dances and other schemes for student loans. To pare costs to a minimum, many were compelled to do light housekeeping in very low-rent rooms.

By 1934, the federal government had enacted legislation to help keep needy students in school. When the fall term opened in 1935, eighty-five students were receiving as much as $15 per month and other more auspicious programs were to follow for youth both in and out of school. By 1936, Northern had fifty-three women and forty-three men (all with B average grades) earning a portion of their expenses under the National Youth Administration; however, with the upswing of the economy, these assistance plans were finally phased out.

On that fateful Friday, 1 September 1939, when Hitler launched his attack on Poland, he unleashed the forces of war that soon enveloped most of the civilized world. Student reaction on the American campuses to the war in both Europe and Asia followed a pattern that began with a high percentage of them believing that the United States should stay out of the conflict. Then, with the bombings of English cities and the horrors of the *blitzkrieg* in western Europe, sentiment changed to such an extent that a large percentage no longer felt that the American people could maintain a nonbelligerent position. With the Conscription Act and other wartime measures, combined with the Japanese bombing of Pearl Harbor, opposition to the war plummeted to an insignificant figure. During the next four years there was a constant exodus of students—both men and women—into the armed services and wartime occupations. Enrollment decreased sharply, showing 370 men and 638 women in 1941–1942 and only 90 men and 408 women in 1944–1945. With the large influx of returning G.I.'s in the fall of 1946, enrollment jumped to 901 men and 541 women, a significant event in Northern's history, for this was the first time that men students outnumbered women.

Like all educational institutions during World War II, Northern participated in a number of programs to enlighten the students and those in the surrounding areas not only on the serious problems of the war but also on the problems that would come with peace. The impact of the conflict created anxiety and frustration among students and older citizens alike; in an attempt to apply some reason to baffling events, discussion forums were held both at the college and in nearby communities. A Faculty Defense Council was established along with a Civilian Morale Committee under the chairmanship of Charles Howell, "to be responsible for the development of various services and for the mobilization of volunteer efforts of students and faculty members." One aspect of this program was the organization and maintenance of a comprehensive library of information for those who wished to enlighten themselves. This latter phase of the program was a significant development, for Northern was the first of some one hundred and forty colleges and universities in the country that had been granted an assignment to offer such services.

These initial efforts created a brisk demand for faculty and student panels, speeches, musicals, and plays. A news service was also located in the college, and the student paper and various books were sent to former students in the armed forces. Pictures of the service men and women were collected and displayed in the main foyer of the Castle for those visiting the campus. War bonds and stamps were sold during a tag day.

Faculty members also rendered yeoman services of various kinds. At Christmas time when the mails overtaxed the regular carriers, faculty members undertook the backbreaking task of delivering it to homes; others with more rustic inclinations literally put their hands to the plow and produced large and profitable "victory gardens," the successor of which later became known as the "Weed Patch," a communal undertaking appropriately named in honor of Professor Fred Weed, who staked it out in the area where the Neptune Hall complex now stands. Some members contributed their time to producing target drones and shipping cases at the piano factory and wagon works. Recreational courses and first-aid instruction were given by the physical education staffs for war workers, and a day nursery was established to serve mothers who wished to do defense work.

Only a small number of faculty actually left the institution to participate in the war effort. Three prominent teachers—Carl Appell, E. C. O. Beatty, and J. Hal Connor—were granted leaves to accept commissions, and Eugene Hellmich, Oscar Chute, and Durward Eaton accepted instructorships for military programs. This left more faculty remaining to instruct the four to five hundred students than was needed; when anyone left to serve in any of these areas, his position was not filled but rather absorbed by his department.

The college was able to secure a civilian pilot-training program under the direction of Milo Oakland and the Civil Aeronautics Administration. Accreditation was also granted by the Navy to enroll enlistees in the V-1 program which permitted men to remain in school through the sophomore year in order to take courses to meet the pre-officer training standards. Once these men were qualified by various types of tests, they became eligible to enter the V-5 program and to prepare to become officers. Those not meeting the specified standards went into the noncommissioned ranks.

Even though there was an effort to secure other military programs, President Adams entertained the hope that the original purpose of the college might be adhered to as much as possible, namely the training of teachers. He devoted a good deal of his time speaking before groups and on the radio on one of his favorite wartime themes: "Education—Our First Line of Defense." He felt deeply that education should not be neglected, for he looked upon it as the citadel of democracy. "It seems to me," he once said,

that expanding our military defenses, increasing our army, navy, and air services and developing and improving the production of machines and materials for war will not make us secure as a nation unless we do something that will really develop the total character and culture of our people.[40]

If the key to a nation's greatness was the school, then to President Adams the heart of the school was the teacher. It was the task of the college to strengthen and maintain a type of training that would give teachers the highest social and educational qualifications so that, through their leadership, the fundamentals of democracy could be experienced and learned by youth.

At the close of hostilities on 14 August 1945, the United States had suffered nearly 400,000 deaths; of this number, thirty-seven had been students at Northern. To honor the dead and to pay tribute to all Northern men and women who sacrificed their health as well as some of the best years of their lives, the Alumni Association established the Memorial Book Fund from which the first presentation was made at Homecoming, 10 October 1948. The plan was to raise some $2,000 which was to be invested and the interest accrued to be used to purchase books on the problems of world peace and international relations. These books were identified by memorial bookplates designating that they had been given in memory of these casualties. The design for the bookplate, drawn by a former Northern art major, Bettie Hall, was selected in a contest bearing a $50 prize.[41]

Those of the war generation, those who in President Roosevelt's words had had a rendezvous with destiny, returned in large numbers to the colleges and universities with a seriousness and intent that defied comparison with their counterparts of World War I: all seemed bent on securing an education. Millions of G.I.s received state and federal bonuses for education which probably far exceeded in value gifts of land and pensions given veterans following previous wars. In 1946, the 731 male and 11 female veterans made up more than 50 percent of the total student body of 1,442. For the first time in history, education seemed to have become an essential part of American life, a trend that has increased at an accelerated pace for the next twenty-five years.

This influx of older, wiser, and more mature students—many with wives and children—certainly created adjustment problems for a conservative midwestern college and its community. It was not unusual to have in a freshman class former commissioned officers who had assumed important wartime responsibilities. Such men were interested neither in the "rah-rah" campus activities nor the "mickey-mouse" approach of some of their instructors. But the main problems veterans experienced on this sheltered campus were the various restrictions placed upon their lifestyles; they had had enough of these restrictions in the services. They soon began to work for more freedom in the library, on dates, in selecting housing, in class attendance, for student participation in governing the college, and for much more open discussion of vital questions in classrooms. The veterans were opposed to racial discrimination on or off the campus—and they demonstrated to prove it in 1946 when two local restaurants refused to serve Blacks. They also devoted a good deal of effort to securing a non-profit student bookstore; but the Board opposed such a venture and the campaign failed.

The athletic program benefited greatly by the veterans' experience. In 1944 and 1946, Northern was the undisputed champion of the I.I.A.C. in football; and in 1946 it also participated in the post-season Turkey Bowl against Evansville College on Thanksgiving Day. Veterans were also important on debate teams, in dramatic productions and in musical organiza-

Vets bunking in Still Gym, fall of 1946

tions; and a number of them were especially successful in introducing expertise and realism into student journalism. During the 1940s, under the directorship of Paul Street, the *Northern Illinois* had a host of good reporters and columnists who contributed quality essays, poems, book reviews, short stories, editorials, and critiques that won for it numerous awards.

The veterans' influence was also effective in finding solutions to some of the more serious campus problems. From almost the first day of their return, the most critical problem they faced was the shortage of rooms. Many were forced to live "under almost impossible conditions: sleeping on cots and bunk beds [in the gym and] on the unused top floor of the science building"; DeKalb basements, attics, and garages became impromptu dormitories. This shortage was so acute that President Adams noted it in his post-war plans in 1943 and urgently requested an immediate appropriation to construct two dormitories (one for men and one for women) along with thirteen additional buildings and the necessary land to accommodate 1,500 students. However, the legislature chose to ignore the recommendations, and it was not until 1945 that some of the funds were finally appropriated for a library and one dormitory. The women's dormitory was finally occupied in 1949, but some three years more had to elapse before Gilbert Hall was finally a reality as the first men's dormitory on the campus.

In the meantime, while they waited for their dormitory, the crowded living conditions grew worse, and veterans finally organized a chapter of the American Veterans Committee to deal with this and other problems. The highly respected E. C. O. Beatty was its sponsor. Few groups have ever done more for the campus. A campaign was begun to find space in DeKalb, and one of the techniques used most effectively was a city-wide appeal for rooms carried by means of a tag attached to each milk bottle delivered to homes. Faculty members volunteered to canvass also, for they, like the veterans, held fast to the popular pledge that "there would be no forgotten generation after this war."

Relief in the form of surplus army barracks was not long in coming. In May 1946, the Federal Public Housing Authority

Gilbert Hall room in the Fifties

released nineteen temporary housing units that were set up on the newly acquired land at the corner of Lucinda Avenue and Garden Road. Soon thereafter a cafeteria building and the necessary surplus equipment were also secured from Camp McCoy, thus resolving the two most critical needs—eating and sleeping—for the time being at least. The cafeteria was probably most appreciated by the students as a whole, and it soon became the most popular social spot on campus.

"Vetville" also soon became a lively center, especially with the young married faculty and student couples with their ever-increasing number of children, so many in fact that the nickname "Fertile Valley" was sometimes applied to the area.

An evaluation of the influence of the veterans quite clearly shows that besides bringing to the campus a zest and maturity that pervaded college life, they also contributed an academic force that helped to raise standards of scholarship. When the senior class graduated in 1948, Edith Leifheit, the registrar, informed President Adams that this class had the highest scholastic averages in the history of the college.

Faculty participation in college and university governance was slow in developing. Beginning with the 1920s a number of educational institutions adopted formal organizations that permitted some participation in policy making, mainly in state universities. In Illinois, Northern was probably one of the first of such institutions to initiate such a project, arising largely out of the circumstances surrounding the controversy between Adams and Alschuler. In order to fulfill his promise to those who came to his rescue, Adams, in the fall of 1938, held several discussions with various department heads and faculty members and then appointed a five-member Faculty Council. On 20 December, he called the first meeting to discuss "the functions such a council might perform."

Following these deliberations a letter setting forth the purposes and relationship of the Faculty Council to the administration was sent with the approval of the president and the signature of the Council members to the entire faculty. One

Adams Hall room in the Fifties

line in the letter bore out the idea that this Council "should be considered a step toward developing a means whereby representative faculty and administrative opinion may be more effectively interfused." [42]

Soon thereafter a special faculty meeting was called to restructure the Council, for it had become obvious that it did not have the confidence of the faculty. Differences of opinion arose on the question of whether members should be appointed, elected, or a combination of both. To smooth out this point, the Council members submitted two plans for faculty participation; one suggested three elected members and two appointed, and the other called for five elected members.

Upon the opening of school in the fall of 1939, a special faculty meeting decided on the most favorable plan and it was immediately put into effect. This document, containing the by-laws governing the operation of the council, called for three elected and two appointed members; the elected ones were chosen from the three divisions of the faculty—Humanities, Education, and Arts and Sciences—for three-year terms. The president was to appoint the other two members for one-year terms, and he was to serve as permanent chairman.

The Council functioned informally and somewhat irregularly the first four or five years, with discontent increasing not only among the faculty but among the Council members themselves. Some complained that minutes of the meetings were irregularly kept; elections were not held for new members and new faculty were not allocated to their particular divisions; no agendas for meetings were prepared; and too often topics were brought up after the decisions were already made by the president. Moreover, Adams often did not brief the Council of his decisions when his final actions were at variance with its recommendations. There was general frustration from not knowing exactly what disposition was finally made of important matters. Such a situation made it difficult for Council members to report back to their constituents. In time, the president, did, however, agree to give a report of his final decisions before each Council meeting.

In an attempt to influence the president to correct further weaknesses, Dean Zulauf in a letter to him and the Council

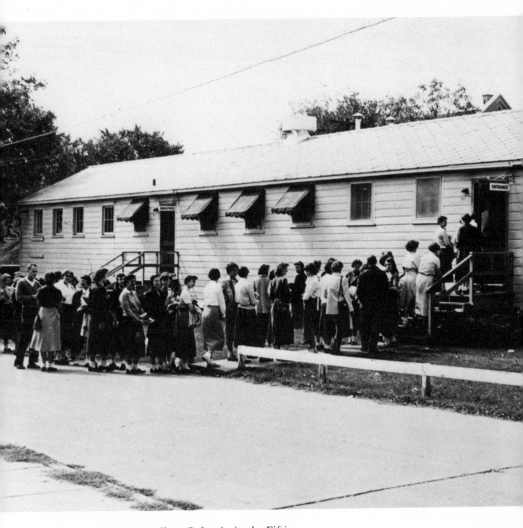

Waiting to be fed at the College Cafeteria in the Fifties

drew to their attention that there were a number of "essential things that must be done in order to comply with the By-Laws." Stuart Fink, an appointed member and a close advisor to Adams, also in a number of letters made it clear to him that if something were not done "there are some dangers involved . . . [that] the faculty will come to think of the Council as essentially a creation of the President's."[43]

These two appeals were effective, and they drew an immediate response from the president in which he set up a calendar of regular meetings each month with an assurance that a digest of the minutes would be circulated to the faculty through the *Faculty Bulletin,* which had been established to inform the faculty of college affairs.

Other problems continued to arise, and one of the more important ones was the fact that the number of teaching members on the Council in proportion to the number of administrative officers was too small. Thus when Dean Zulauf was reappointed in 1945, he mentioned the anxiety he personally had respecting his membership on the Council and even suggested that it might be well to leave him off. But the president had no such feelings, for he needed Zulauf's expertise and leadership, and as a result he was reappointed annually thereafter.

But this problem persisted and soon became a matter of increased concern. The humanities division took the lead and drew up some plans (most of the corrective ideas originated with that group) which were finally approved by the faculty and which provided for the dean of the faculty to be an *ex-officio* member and for an increase in the elected membership from three to four. One of the latter was to be a member at large and one of the two members appointed by the president was to be at least a half-time teacher.

In evaluating the work of this democratic instrument during its ten–year period, one must consider the administrative restrictions under which the Council functioned. For some time it was not privileged to exercise much voice in policy formation or decision-making. This was partly because of organizational weaknesses, and partly because the president did not favor such a role for this body; in fact, the president was not bound by Council decisions and no votes were ever taken. Although the Council was privileged to discuss almost any topic—if time permitted—the effectiveness of such participation is difficult to assess. Regardless of the limitations of such participation generally during this period, it was indeed a good beginning and one that helped lay the basis for future involvement that slowly and gradually developed into the present University Council.

Student involvement in the affairs of the college followed a pattern similar to that of the faculty—a quiet beginning during the administration of J. Stanley Brown but gaining increased recognition in the 1940s and a larger voice in subsequent years.[44]

In 1934, an Assembly Committee was first established to satisfy demands by the students. Gus Campbell was the advisor, and there was one representative from each of the four classes; upon Campbell's resignation this arduous and often thankless task was assumed by William O'Connell, who for many years faithfully struggled to secure with a limited budget the best available talent for student assemblies. The fact that this was a captive audience because of compulsory attendance did not make the committee's task any easier. However, under the new dispensation the students did have some choice as to whom they were to see or hear.

The Committee on Intercollegiate Athletics was also re-established at the same time, following a five-year interval during which the major sports of the college had been controlled exclusively by President Adams. This committee's membership consisted of three faculty members but no students until 1949, when it was reorganized by President Holmes into an Athletic Board with a membership of three instructors (two from academic fields), the head of physical education for women, the football coach, and five student representatives.

This long period without representation actually created little discontent among the students other than an occasional debate with the football coach over the spending of student athletic fees. Student columnists such as Sammy Guzzardo and Bernard Dahlin raised some embarrassing questions; they challenged not only the amount of money allotted to the athletic department, but also the disproportionate amount spent for football and basketball, while track and field activities were pathetically neglected financially. Other gripes they had were the tiny amount of money spent on assembly programs (which the entire student body was required to attend every week), or on the bank who entertained them at all sports events during the school year. These assaults (especially upon such "character-building" activities as the major sports) naturally sparked a retort from the department of physical education which at the time consisted of only George Evans and Carl Appell.[45]

Student representation existed on the Student Activities Fund Committee from its inception in 1920, but the number and ratio of students and faculty members varied. The total amount of the allotments as well as the number of activities increased as the student body grew in size; thus there was always a certain amount of competition for the limited funds, causing from time to time the restriction or the removal of various activities from the list and the acceptance of new ones.

Further democratic changes in student government also took place as a consequence of the broadening of intellectual horizons during this period. The liberal-progressive ideas in American society inspired some revolts against small-town democracy and puritanism as well as the traditional practices in American schools and churches. A long line of vociferous writers, with Henry L. Mencken heading the list, exposed "with melancholy faithfulness the fatuousness and vulgarity of contemporary American life." This school of writers especially influenced a generation of young writers and a sizeable segment of the nation with its iconoclastic views; and had it not been for the sobering effects of the economic collapse of the thirties, this intellectual ferment no doubt would have had much greater influence.

Only a few of the young people who came to the Northern campus during the thirties and forties, however, had come under these influences. Nevertheless, in spite of the tendency of most students to protect the "status quo" during these years, there was generally available a group of liberal students who were determined to arouse the student body to greater participation in forming school policy concerning their activities.

Marjorie Mann, one of those crusaders, argued convincingly that participation in school government was necessary in order "to produce a more unified school spirit, to develop an intelligent leadership among the student body, and to broaden the thinking of administration, faculty and students in the exchange of ideas." To affirm this concept of shared responsibility, she turned to the lessons of history for an analogy with which she used to prophesy, with more accuracy than she probably realized, the student turbulence of the 1960s.

Just as the neglected English peasant revolted in 1381 against the policies of the feudal baron, so too will the neglected student revolt against the policies of an administration that are made without direct consideration of the student opinions. It is true, to be sure, that the execution of these policies must be in the hands of the administration; but student government asks only for a voice in policy making.[46]

In spite of these arguments and prophesies, President Adams had not the disposition or background to bend easily to this democratic trend; he would listen, however, and he was more often amenable to student than to faculty opinion.

After the short and unsuccessful life of the Student Council during the two Brown presidencies, sporadic movements for its restoration appeared in the thirties, but to no avail, for most of the students were content with a loose and informal organization of representatives consisting of the presidents of the various clubs who, outside of an annual off-campus meeting with the deans to discuss student social problems, were somewhat inactive. This group, however, cooperated in vain attempts to have the student body ratify a proposed constitution for a council during the year 1937–1938, but it ended as a

279

complete failure because of "passive resistance when the election was held." Reaction in an editorial to this student inertia revealed that such behavior was not confined, as we sometimes feel, to our present generation. This is made clear in the following:

Less than a year ago the students of N.I. killed one of the most important movements ever to start at this school. . . . Here was a subject, advertised for weeks before, talked about in most of the classrooms . . . ballyhooed, bombasted, built up and torn down, . . . till everybody's head swam. And then at the election practically nobody was even interested enough . . . to vote either for or against. They were too apathetic to even step across the hall after assembly to cast a vote.[47]

Another try was soon made to ratify the constitution, and even though there was a much larger turnout, it failed by 74 votes—another disappointing blow to the reformers.

In the meantime, Adams, who had refused to accept the constitution on the grounds that it failed to receive a two-thirds majority, did make a gesture of accommodation to the pro-Council students by setting up a new Student Affairs Committee, still consisting, however, entirely of faculty. It was given wider scope to deal not only with social affairs but also with student problems of employment, discipline, elections, and other related matters. Moreover, it was empowered for the first time to function in the area of administrative policy, but, as he always warned, it must not "be considered a substitute for administration."

During the war years student life on the campus was concerned with more weighty problems than student government, and it was not until the spring of 1945 that the subject again became significant. Sentiment had grown stronger among both faculty and students that the latter were sufficiently responsible to have at least some representation on the Student Affairs Committee. A group of student leaders met with the president to discuss the issue. Following this meeting, he gave his reactions:

I was quite impressed, both with their thinking and the clear manner in which they expressed themselves. . . . I am planning next year to ask the faculty committee to include in its membership eight students—two from each of the classes . . . as the students suggest in their memorandum. I believe that such a committee would be more helpful and efficient, perhaps more understanding than a separate council with faculty advisors and faculty committees.[48]

This reorganized committee with its eight faculty and eight student members (a man and a woman from each class) began a new and enthusiastic period with the president leading the way, hoping that the students would feel a closer rapport with the administration. The committee immediately broadened its scope by providing a forum for consultation, discussion, and arbitration of student problems through a system of subcommittees. It was also planned that it would be a vehicle for counseling the administration on student attitudes as well as for developing cooperative relations between the two.

But even though this modification was an improvement, the idea of a Student Council persisted; a number of bright and mature veterans kept the project alive. In a courageous editorial, entitled "N.I. Needs a Student Council for Practical Experiences in Democracy," Jack Frooman presented a strong case: since the motto of this institution was "Self Direction Through Understanding," was it not time that the administration change this "meaningless phrase" by giving the right to students to participate through a representative council in determining student policies?

The Student Affairs Committee responded soon thereafter to this challenge by offering to increase the number of their sessions and also to permit students to have their problems discussed in open meetings. However, in order to put to rest any idea that the S.A.C. was to function as a typical student council, it immediately expressed its belief that a "small group of able representatives . . . could accomplish more than a large group. . . ."

This organization continued throughout the remainder of

Adams's administration; but with the arrival of President Holmes, the Presidents' Panel, which was made up of presidents of student clubs and organizations, was instituted to work with the three major student committees. The Panel and the S.A.C. were finally replaced in 1955 by the Student Senate.

When the college opened in the fall of 1947, plans were inaugurated to observe the semi-centennial anniversary during the year 1948–1949. Many of the faculty and students were excited by the idea of a Golden Jubilee to celebrate fifty years' service in the training of teachers for the schools in northern Illinois. This excitement was further encouraged by the fact that Northern was the last remaining teachers college in the state, and being so gave much pride to those who had struggled to retain that single purpose. Moreover, the college was growing rapidly with an addition of many new faculty members, a new cafeteria, the beginning of a new dormitory, and land acquisition for further expansion. These were exciting achievements that added spirit to the Jubilee.

President Adams established a general planning committee consisting of faculty, students, alumni, and townspeople, with Paul Street as its chairman. It was to use the whole school year of 1947–1948 to plan a suitable program and then have the entire year of 1948–1949 in which to carry it out. Subcommittees were created to deal with Homecoming, publications, publicity, a history, May Fete, the semi–centennial seal, academic activities, and, especially, the elaborate pageant which was to climax the Jubilee. Bernice Wolfson was made chairman of the pageant committee and Edith Rockwell, from the Bureau of Dramatic Activities, Extension Division, University of Wisconsin, was employed as writer and director.[49]

To initiate this anniversary program a special salute over the local radio station was introduced, with singing, speeches, and band music. A "Special Anniversary" Homecoming issue of the *DeKalb Chronicle* was published, recounting Northern's fifty-year history in thirty pages of pictures. A special football brochure was also designed by Owen (Bud) Nangle for the Homecoming game on October 9, and a brief history of Northern was written by faculty members who were especially familiar with the four administrations. Moreover, a contest for the winning Anniversary Seal was held under the chairmanship of Alma Anderson. The $50 prize was awarded to Norman Zander Fried, a graduate of the class of 1942.

A special "two-mile-long" Homecoming parade moved along the highway to the city where the "entire business district was a colorful spectacle" with flags and banners bearing the Golden Anniversary Seal in college colors. Professor Hugh Jameson, a master of the art of the clown, joined the march in his "old circus clown suit and gun," which warmed the hearts of those of other years who had returned to see him perform. The only thing that marred the Homecoming and saddened the overflow crowds at the game with "Old Normal" was Northern's defeat in spite of the heroics of Don Fortunato's superb passing and Bob Brigham's savage ground attack.

The final chapter of the Jubilee took place on 29 May 1949, with the staging of an immense outdoor pageant called the "Golden Guide Posts of NISTC," with a cast of one-third of the student body. Preparation was begun in December, and the production in verse, song, prose, and pantomime, was staged before an audience of more than 6,000 people along the banks of the Lagoon.

During the semi-centennial when President Adams was beginning his twentieth year (October 1948) of service, some of his closest friends felt it proper to show in some way an appreciation for his devotion to the institution. He had been honored a few years earlier as a distinguished alumnus from Ohio University in the form of membership in the Phi Beta Kappa scholastic fraternity; moreover, for a number of years, he had also had the distinction of acting as senior president of the five Illinois teachers colleges.

But these honors, though worthy, were hardly sufficient to overcome the embarrassing fact that Northern's president was the only one of the five who was without a doctor's degree. This situation provoked criticism from time to time as to why he had not completed his doctorate; in fact, when he was initially selected for the presidency it was reported that the Board committee actually believed that he already had "all the work for his Doctor's degree completed except his dissertation." [50]

But whatever the facts, it was too late at this point in his career for him to return to graduate school. As a possible substitute, a few of his closest friends, including Clara Sperling and Paul Street, initiated a campaign to secure an honorary degree for him. Street wrote first to President John C. Baker of Ohio University, inquiring whether Adams, as a alumnus, might be considered a candidate for an honorary doctorate. Baker replied that his Board of Regents had discontinued the practice and that he hesitated to bring the matter up again. [51]

Clara Sperling, the president's secretary, turned to President Charles W. Hunt, of State Teachers College, Oneonta, New York, a long-time friend of Adams, and made the following appeal to him for advice:

We think it would be a great climax [to the Jubilee] and a wonderful thing if he could be awarded an honorary doctorate from his Alma Mater, Ohio University. . . . We hope this can be done in June, 1948. This will surely make it THE YEAR of his life. We have written to President John C. Baker of Ohio University who replied that their board of regents had discontinued the practice. . . . This is certainly discouraging news to us.

I should like to ask your advice . . . on this matter. Is there anything we can do? I hesitate to put any more pressure on President Baker. . . . Is there any other way we could get such an honor for President Adams? [52]

The reply from President Hunt was also discouraging:

I have to say that I am not going to be of any use to you in your search for an honorary degree. . . . The awarding of honorary degrees is going out of fashion among our better institutions. . . . I do not think I should help to keep alive a process in which I do not believe. [53]

He suggested another way that they could honor him and that was to secure a number of letters from his colleagues and to have them bound into a memorial volume.

Miss Sperling, not to be discouraged in her efforts, made one final attempt nearer home to secure the prize for the president; this time she wrote President George D. Stoddard at the University of Illinois inquiring of him whether there was "any possibility that President Adams could be so honored for his untiring work in teacher education?" He likewise held out little hope, for the University of Illinois had a rather complicated system of a competitive nature: whenever such a degree was to be given, "others in the same category of professional position and distinction . . . must be considered. Honorary degrees would mean little if awarded in large numbers or without careful consideration, so we are always faced with the problem of choosing the few whom awards can be provided without offending others." [54]

Unable to secure the coveted honorary degree, Adams was nevertheless not forgotten: the Faculty Club celebrated his twentieth anniversary with a special party. Annie E. King, representing the faculty, presented the president with an exquisite leather-bound portfolio "in which he could keep his memoirs."

The year of the Jubilee was a demanding one on the president and doubly so when combined with the recognition of his own twentieth anniversary. He entered this period of celebrations already battlewearied by the years that he had struggled not only for his favorite cause of teacher education but against a miserly State Department of Education. He had spent far too much of his time and energy securing housing, classrooms, and library facilities, not to mention the task of recruiting an ever-increasing number of faculty members. During the last three years of his life, enrollment figures nearly tripled, yet for all his efforts he was successful in completing only one building (Davis Hall), though his faith in his task never faltered. To his neighbors and friends it was becoming apparent that he was exacting a heavy toll from himself physically by his busy schedule.

He was not destined to witness the completion of his own anniversary nor that of the Golden Jubilee. On Sunday, 5 December 1948, he performed his last community service in the form of a radio talk at the First Methodist Church, where he was an active layman. During the night he was stricken and died in his sleep at sixty years of age. His body lay in state in his office before his large chair where his friends could pay their final respects. At the funeral service, the Reverend Preston Bradley, representing the Board, delivered the sermon, and J. Hal Connor, who was so frequently called upon in behalf of the faculty on such occasions, gave a eulogy that is still remembered by those who were present. A special memorial issue of the *Northern Illinois* was edited by Tom Woodstrup, who also wrote a poem in his honor, which he called "We Who Follow."[55]

A memorial service committee made arrangements to honor the late president at the dedication of the new women's dormitory—which the Board agreed should be named the Karl Langdon Adams Hall. Dean Zulauf, who was acting president, reported that "The Karl L. Adams Award Foundation" had been planned by the Faculty Club and various committees throughout the area and that the first donation came at the time of the funeral. Today an annual award of $100 is given from this fund to a student in at least the fourth semester of study at N.I.U.

Adams Hall, 1949

Leslie A. Holmes
fifth president, 1949–1967

8

The Coming of The University

A T THE time of President Adams's death, Northern Illinois State Teachers College stood on the threshold of its final educational transformation. The institution had begun fifty years earlier as a normal school; now it was about to undergo an era of tremendous expansion of almost revolutionary dimensions. The faith of its founders and presidents, as well as the thousands of students who attended it, was that the "Normal-on-the-hill" was a special institution, that it served a special role in teacher education, and that no other type of institution was quite capable of rendering such a service. That being their faith, they surely never doubted that teacher-training would always remain its central purpose. Such was not the case, for the dynamic changes in society during the next two decades were so impelling that they made many of our sacred truths no longer sacred and caused many lights to fail.

The coming administration was to face a tremendous expansion, almost revolutionary, both within and outside the institution. There were changes, not only in the number of campuses, buildings, students, faculty and civil service employees, but there were also phenomenal academic and philosophical changes in aims, purposes, attitudes, and values that were to result in a major expansion in the number of colleges and departments, the variety of curricula, the health and security programs, sports and entertainment activities, as well as a multiplicity of personal and technical services for faculty, students, and those who resided in the larger community of northern Illinois.

So complex and impersonal were many of these institutional changes that some students, in confusion and frustration, finally reacted in the late 1960s in a way that led to aggression. The majority of students, however, still found personal satisfaction in conforming to the accepted pattern of behavior.

The Teachers College Board at its Chicago meeting on 17 December 1948, met to interview four prospective candidates who had made their applications after the funeral of the late President Adams on December 9.[1] Those who were interested in applying personally for the position or those promoting a candidate could waste no time, for it was rumored that the Board was anxious to fill the post before Adlai Stevenson, governor-elect, was to be inaugurated on 10 January. After that date, it could be expected that the Board would have not only a new chairman but probably some newly appointed members as well to administer and guide this imminent educational revolution—during a time that some might call Northern's Golden Age.

Four candidates were mentioned by the Board in the minutes; three can be identified: Dean Romeo Zulauf, of Northern; Leslie A. Holmes and Chris A. DeYoung, both from Illinois State Normal University. The two candidates from Illinois State had been highly respected by their president, Raymond W. Fairchild, and both had served in prominent administrative positions. In fact, DeYoung had been brought to Normal by Fairchild himself; however, in time, according to Richard G. Browne, a faculty member at Illinois State who later became executive officer of the Teachers College Board, Fairchild for some unknown reason had "cooled" to DeYoung's leadership and had begun to place more reliance on Leslie Holmes. As a result, DeYoung was never a serious contender.

290

"Fairchild," Browne related, "thought very highly of Holmes, mostly because he was intensely loyal and hard-working" and also "a very capable and popular teacher of geography . . . [who] took a genuine interest in his students. . . ." This high regard for his abilities set Holmes apart, and when the vacancy occurred at Northern he was Fairchild's nominee. Browne recalls the occasion when Holmes's name was first mentioned:

The first time I heard Les Holmes mentioned for the presidency at Northern was in an automobile riding back to Normal from the Adams funeral. Mr. Charles Goin Lanphier, then Coordinator for the Teachers College Board, was in the car and made the suggestion. Somehow I think the idea came from Pres. Fairchild.[2]

Browne, who had been Holmes's colleague for twelve years, was not unhappy with this nomination, even though Holmes did not share his views on the proper role of the faculty. It appears that their fundamental differences were largely based upon conflicting definitions of the roles of the faculty and the administration and the importance that each should have in governing the college. This was a period when the teachers college faculties were trying, mostly in vain, to secure even a small role of responsibility; Dr. Browne was one of the pioneer advocates of this effort. According to Browne, Holmes leaned toward minimum faculty participation in the administration of the college; this was evident in the fact that he "declined to join the A.A.U.P." Students at Illinois State also recognized the extent of his administrative loyalty; in one of their stunt night performances they had "a skit in which he was named 'Yeslie.'"

The third candidate, Dean Romeo Zulauf, was a reluctant contestant even though he had hurriedly been nominated with high recommendations. There was no faculty participation on the selection committee at that time; this practice came with the next president in 1967. Thus the faculty was limited to applying pressure on the Board and prominent schoolmen.

*The Peace Corps—The first group from N.I.U., 1961
Program for Malaya*

A small faculty group met at Paul Street's home where they formulated a plan to telephone various members of the Board, and also to canvass the faculty with respect to their sentiments regarding Zulauf.[3] A telephone poll revealed that a high percentage of the faculty supported Zulauf. He lost, however; probably because he still had not completed his doctorate; moreover, he had a liberal philosophy and quality of thought that might have been unacceptable to the rather conservative Board.

The decision in favor of Holmes was made so quickly following the last interview that Arthur Muns, his one-time assistant, related that the people in Bloomington heard it over the radio before Holmes actually arrived there. What was even stranger was that a prospective renter was waiting on the steps of his house when he returned from Chicago.[4]

None of the Northern faculty was in any way opposed to the selection of Holmes; actually only a few individuals knew him personally, and some had mistaken him for the other Holmes at Illinois State who was head of the speech department.

The president-elect was a native of upstate Illinois. He was born in the town of Freeport on 19 December, 1902, the son of a cattle broker. He attended both grade and high schools in Freeport, receiving his diploma in 1921. During these formative years he showed an early interest in nature study and science; in high school, he was active in basketball and football, with some lesser interest in track and the glee club. Later, at the University of Illinois, however, he did not follow up his sports interests; in fact, no activities are listed for him in *The Illio*. This may have been because of his personality, for even at this age he was somewhat shy and retiring; at least this seems to be how his high-school colleagues remembered him when they left the following line in the [Freeport] *Polaris*: "Dares to be true, and silently takes his part."

Holmes received a bachelor of science degree from the University of Illinois in 1926. He was then awarded a two-year assistantship in the geology department at Illinois to study for his master's degree, as well as an American Petroleum Institute fellowship, which he used for a third year of graduate work. This would surely indicate that his scholarship was well above average. A short note, tightly compressed between the pages of his personal copy of *The Illio*, reveals that this was probably true: at the conclusion of his final semester of work on his master's degree, one of his friends, W.C. Howard, sent him what must have been some highly encouraging words, "Your grades are all in and [Arthur C.] Bevan says that you surprised everybody, including yourself, by writing the best paper. . . ."

At the end of his third year of graduate work (1929) he accepted a position as a geologist with the Skelly Oil Company in Tulsa, where he remained until deciding to give up that career and to enter the teaching profession in 1931. He taught science at Argo [Illinois] High School and at Dodd-Harris Junior College in Chicago before becoming an assistant professor in geography at Illinois State Normal in 1936.

In Normal, he settled down with his wife and son to the arduous tasks of a teaching career with a heavy load of courses, carrying at the same time the additional burden of completing his doctoral degree work. In time, his love of travel and especially his interest in the outdoors afforded him a new experience through supervising geography trips during the summer months into Canada. These were called his "Red Bird Field Courses"; they became so popular that even after his retirement he continued to attend the "The Tripper Club" reunions.

After Holmes secured his doctorate (1942), President Fairchild appointed him one of his administrative assistants; he remained in this position until coming to DeKalb. As an administrator in a teachers college, he had to work more with the public schools and less in the field of science and teaching. One of these assignments—and one that he performed with unusual success—was that of recruiting prospective students. With his folksy and relaxed manner he was attractive in this work, and high-school students especially enjoyed hearing his pleasant and disarming expressions. Moreover, in a teachers college it was a *sine qua non* that administrators also be involved in community and higher educational affairs; thus by the time of his retirement Holmes had memberships in a number of fraternal, religious, and service organizations, and in as many as seven major educational associations.

Before a sketch of President Holmes's personal values and philosophy, gathered here and there in his small collection of letters, speeches, and publications, can be offered, it is necessary to enter some words of caution. The problem arises that as this history of Northern moves into the period of a living president and his staff, it becomes more and more difficult to secure objective information. Time has not properly sifted the wheat from the chaff, and it will take some years before the events of Holmes's administration fall into perspective. There is also a problem in securing information from the participants themselves. It is understandable that they would not wish to become too involved in evaluations of their own activities, and in most cases they have hesitated to offer much, if any, assistance for fear of being quoted—or misquoted. The college historian, armed with his tape recorder and note pad, seemed to present a frightening picture to a retired administrator!

Holmes was rather shy, reserved, and cautious with most people; he tended, however, to be more relaxed with small groups of students as well as with his staff, with whom he had an especially warm and kindred relationship. This amicable feeling existed throughout his administration, for he rated congenial qualities high on his list when making his academic appointments, sometimes to the extent of sacrificing professional and academic background.

Only rarely did any differences surface with those on his staff, the most notable one being the Paul Street controversy, which is discussed later in this chapter. His staff, or cabinet, was organized in 1954 and grew in size with the expansion of the college; it met once each month following the Board meetings to advise the president. The administrative structure was reorganized numerous times after 1954, each time affecting the whole university.

Holmes's relationship with the Teachers College Board and the Board of Governors, however, was at times quite the opposite of congeniality; here he and his colleagues faced those who controlled their destiny. This was especially true in the case of Royal A. Stipes, a long-time member and often chairman of the boards, who wielded personal power and prestige over all he surveyed, and who even encouraged dependence upon his leadership. Stipes's form of dominance soon taught Holmes, after a few unhappy experiences, not to get ahead of his Board with decisions and recommendations, or openly to publicize his views. Thus it was often difficult, for the faculty at least, to know exactly what the president's real convictions were on major issues, such as changing the name of the Teachers College to "University." For his own protection Holmes developed the technique of waiting until the Board had fully made up its mind before he took his position, at least publicly.

With the faculty, his relationship was one of mostly isolation, except in private conferences or on rare occasions when he acted as a speaker. Those he did associate with on a social basis were not the academicians, for with them he never seemed at ease. He was a kind and friendly person; but his reticence had a tendency to discourage meaningful conversation with him.

Holmes had no greater interest in public speaking, it seemed, than he had for social conversation or contract bridge. Rather like President Adams, he often began a speech with a definite theme but before going far in his discourse he would almost inevitably be drawn to his favorite topics of enrollments, budgets, and buildings. This was so often the case that he was humorously accused of playing the numbers game.

Other topics that found their way into his repertory were his favorite platitudes. When speaking to public-school teachers, at Boy Scout meetings, and especially at the freshman class orientation at the beginning of each year, he generally brought in some of the cardinal virtues. Since it was difficult for him, with a scientific background, to use philosophical abstractions or historical references, he would instead use the moral and ethical sayings or proverbs of such men as Franklin, Webster, or Dickens.[5] His speeches were never long and the same was true of his letters; both nicely subscribed to the Shakespearean dictum: "Brevity is the soul of wit."

Holmes was a believer in mixing faculty and town groups, and even though there were few facilities for entertaining until near the end of his career, he included some faculty and townspeople in many functions on campus. He also arranged for groups of office personnel to visit the Taft Campus, and he often had morning coffee with members of the operating staff and faculty.

In dealing with religious life on the campus, he encouraged a program for "Religious Emphasis Week" for all denominations, to be carried on in classrooms, dormitories, and the local churches. The University Religious Council put out an annual booklet with an introduction by Holmes in which he stressed the importance of religion for all, especially for "each in his own way." He also urged in his talks to students to "attend the church or synagogue of your choice" for by so doing "it can be the foundation and the basis for understanding your own life." He held religious affiliation of some sort to be of such importance that for a number of years when interviewing prospective faculty members he would make a point of inquiring whether the candidate was a member of a church.

President Holmes was the last of a line of Northern's presidents who might be described as having held somewhat the same general values, attitudes, and personal philosophy. All were leaders who espoused a type of conservatism that was expected of them if they were to serve as presidents of normal schools and teachers colleges in Illinois. Their lives were narrowly circumscribed by the roles they were compelled to live and by the standards they were expected to maintain with their students, faculty, and the public. Any doctrine or belief that did not conform to the basic tenets of Republicanism, Protestantism, and "Americanism" would have been interpreted as unsuitable for the classroom or the forum. Thus a tight rein was maintained on the lifestyles of the future teachers academically, morally, and to a certain extent religiously until recent years when serious challenges to these restraints were made.

For the first time in the history of the school, a new president was formally installed. The day was set for 13 May 1949, and a major committee of fifteen faculty members with Charles Howell as its chairman was established. The Golden Anniversary pageant and the annual baccalaureate and commencement exercises were also scheduled soon thereafter, thus making the final four-week period of the academic year 1948–1949 a very busy time.

On the appointed day, in mid-morning, an academic procession consisting of Governor Adlai Stevenson, several guest speakers, thirty-eight official delegates, the faculty, and the State Teachers College Board wended its way from the new science building to what is known today as Altgeld auditorium for the inaugural program. Speaking before some nine hundred guests, the governor made a few observations on the teaching profession, outlining some of the critical problems it faced—particularly, low morale and an apparent lack of interest in the profession. He especially called upon the teachers colleges to make every effort to interest competent young people in teaching as well as to "invigorate them with an enthusiasm to teach." Stevenson was fully aware that the state of Illinois and its people also had an important role to play in securing these goals by providing more revenue for the schools, which he was pleased to relate had already been done. "The proposed budget for the next two years," he said, "calls for an increase of some 70 per cent in . . . state aid to the schools . . . and an increase of 58 per cent in the operating appropriation of this college. . . ."

The morning ceremony was concluded when President Holmes delivered his inaugural address, pledging his "every effort to uphold Northern's ideals and traditions." He centered his rather brief observations and proposals around the general need for more classrooms, library books, land, dormitories, and faculty members, as well as for greater emphasis upon extension and adult education courses in order to upgrade older teachers. He also favored a few developments that were earlier opposed by Adams, such as the creation of a department of business education and the addition of a graduate program.

His principle new idea, however, was that of outdoor education. He believed, from his many years of experience in this field, that certain courses "should be taught where the students as well as the instructor can live the courses as they are being developed." Thus he recommended that in order to educate teachers properly, it was

necessary for the college to make available to certain of its
students and to the faculty, facilities that will permit them to
live with nature as they work with her. Only she can give the
best physical surroundings to achieve certain educational goals,
not the least of which is the goal of learning to live together in a
co-operative and congenial family. Too frequently teachers will
stress co-operation and democratic process to their pupils, but
either are not willing to apply it to their lives or do not know
how to apply it to themselves.

To implant the idea of outdoor education firmly in the
minds of all present he specifically called attention to the
wooded, hilly, and swampy areas of northeast Illinois, where
there were lakes "that could be ideally suited to the development of a field study camp."

The conclusion of the inaugural program consisted of
scholarly addresses by two outstanding former students. Professor Richard Meier, of the University of Chicago, spoke in the
afternoon on "Science and Freedom from Want," and in the
evening Professor Willard Wirtz, of Northwestern University
Law School, spoke on "The Conflict of Law and Power."

The key to the development of Northern from a small
teachers college to a sprawling university during the 1950s and
1960s is found in the population explosion in the twenty-one
northern counties of Illinois. The importance of this area, as
far as Northern was concerned, was brought to light by Martin
Bartels soon after his arrival as director of the Placement
Bureau. His 1952 study, "Supply and Demand Factors in
Teacher Education," revealed that population in the state of
Illinois for the decade 1940–1950 had increased 10.3 percent;
however, of that total increase, 86 percent occurred in the
twenty-one northern counties. His study further revealed the
importance and implications of this tremendous increase of
population for Northern in its role as a teachers college:

The answer is obvious, if three times as many elementary

teachers are needed as are available annually, with the demand heavily concentrated in northern Illinois, the facilities for teacher education need to be expanded. More dormitories, laboratory schools, and offices, as well as classroom facilities, need to be erected to meet the evergrowing needs.[6]

To give these data more significance as far as Northern was concerned, Bartels and Holmes in 1953, in their "Teacher Shortage: Crisis in Northern Illinois," applied them in projecting what would be needed in the way of additional teachers; they estimated a needed increase of "about 150 per cent over the 225 teachers NI now supplies each year." To meet this staggering demand they proposed a visionary model for growth that would permit the expansion of enrollment by an additional 3,000 students, or 150 percent more than the 2,000 the school was then equipped to serve.[7]

The sudden awareness of this meteoric increase in public-school population led to subsequent studies by the public relations and research departments that served to support the expansion program that was to follow. In time, a whole series of other additions were sought for a multi-purpose institution with its accompanying degrees and departments. It was argued that many of these northern Illinois students were interested in courses other than teacher-training. This expansion even reached Stateville prison, where Holmes inaugurated one of his most favored extension programs.

Long-range predictions of enrollments were drawn up, demonstrating with graphs, charts, and pictures the urgent need for enlarged budgets, new faculty, new departments, new colleges, land acquisition, and office and classroom buildings. These were used by Senator Dennis J. Collins and the local members of the Illinois House of Representatives with telling effect in Springfield, while Chauncey Watson, Northern's member of the Board, also used his voice and pen in behalf of the larger budgets.[8] This was a vital service, since enrollments always, it seemed, ran ahead of appropriations, and rarely did Northern get out of one crisis before entering another. However, as the administration soon learned, this predicament was not exactly harmful, for those schools with the largest enrollments received the largest share of the total appropriations. Northern was finally able, like the University of Illinois, to construct its budget on the basis of enrollments. By 1958, Northern's enrollment equalled those of Eastern and Western combined; by 1965, it had climbed to fourth place among universities in the state. Illinois State Normal, which for years led all her sister colleges, dropped to eighth place—a position not wholly unpleasant for Northern, which for years had lived under the shadow of Illinois State's size and prestige.

But even if it was less difficult to secure operating budgets based upon enrollments, it still was impossible to secure the enormous appropriations needed for capital improvements on the same basis from the state general revenue funds. To construct the necessary classrooms and office buildings as well as the desperately needed student housing, three techniques were finally evolved for raising the funds. One was a large bond issue in 1960 which was passed by a state referendum; the second called for the issuing of self-liquidating bonds to construct dormitories, the University Center, Field House, and Stadium; and the third involved the use of federal funds.

The ten-year expansion plan in the form of a bond issue was presented to the people of Illinois in November 1960, and each of the universities raised funds from its faculty to be used for promotional purposes. Northern was then allocated about $15,000,000 to cover the construction of ten buildings, two wings for the library, some rehabilitation, and acquisition of land.[9]

The housing situation became one of the most critical problems during this expansion period; but even though it was serious, increased admissions were permitted, provided the students could find rooms. Unfortunately, this condition turned many away or, on the other hand, forced them to live in unsatisfactory rooms or student houses. In 1964, the local A.A.U.P. took up this problem and criticized the city of DeKalb for changing the zoning laws to enable householders to increase the number of student residents per house. They also stated that the University did not have the necessary facilities to justify such increases; instead of numbers, the A.A.U.P. emphasized that the quality of education should be the main consideration—by "reducing, not increasing, student-teacher ratio which is now the highest of the six state institutions. Only by controlling enrollments can this ratio be reduced. . . . The University, we feel, badly needs planned, orderly growth. . . ." [10] These sentiments indicated that not everyone was completely captivated by the idea of quantity.

If numbers could not be controlled, the next best alternative was to inaugurate a selective admission policy. It was not until 1959 that the problem of setting higher standards at Northern was seriously considered; Illinois State Normal had adopted the idea some years earlier. The governor felt that teachers colleges should "tighten their admissions requirements," but the legislature could not agree: the Republican Senate passed a supporting measure but the Democratic House opposed it. [11]

Northern, which had established a policy in 1956 of reserving the right to admit freshmen on academic probation (if their high-school records so warranted), nevertheless went ahead and in 1959 decided to establish its first freshman admission policy by placing on probation all whose high-school records ranked them in the lowest one-third of their graduating classes and by also requiring that they take special entrance examinations. The first year, this policy was thought to have had a decided effect in reducing enrollments in the industrial arts, home economics, and men's physical education departments. [12] By 1965, high-school graduates had to rank in the upper half of their class for automatic admission.

In 1966, the pressures of enrollments caused the administration to warn that because of the shortage of housing, even those in the upper one-half would be acceptable only if they placed their applications on file by April 1. This was the first cut-off date, and in the next few years it was to be moved to earlier months. In 1969, the idea of eligibility was modified to the extent that a student could satisfy it by one of three methods: (1) a composite score of 24 or above on the American College Test; (2) a composite ACT score of 21 or above and a rank in the upper one-half of his high school graduating class; and (3) a composite ACT score of 19 or above and rank in the upper one-third of the graduating class.

From 1953, with a total of 2,285 students, enrollment figures continued to increase every year until reaching a peak of 22,819 in the fall of 1971. The decline of enrollment to

College Tea Room (later known as Student Union, Kishwaukee Hall, and Roy Campbell Hall)

21,070 the next year was a sobering experience. Such a sudden halt was no doubt due to a host of reasons, a few of which were the leveling-off of the birth rate, budget cuts, decline in job opportunities, unemployment increases, the planned expansion of junior colleges, as well as whatever loss, if any, that accrued from the student protest movement.

Besides the phenomenal growth in undergraduate enrollment, with the development of the graduate school in 1951, there came to the campus every year an increasing number of graduate students. The reservoir of graduate students seemed as bottomless as that of undergraduates to those predicting future enrollments. Indeed, from the beginning, projections were too low for both for many unpredictable reasons. In the case of graduate student enrollments the percentage increase was almost as high as that of undergraduates; for example, in the period 1962 to 1972 the number of undergraduates increased by 144 percent whereas graduates increased by 127 percent.

With the instatement of Leslie Holmes as president, it had been slightly more than a quarter of a century since the last title change for the college was made. Some time previously there had been, especially in some of the sister schools, a drive to drop the term "teachers" from the name. They would be simply state colleges, with authority to offer a four-year general education curriculum with liberal arts degrees as well as the regular professional teacher education courses. This aroused only slight interest at Northern, with one editorial in the student paper asking, "Why shouldn't N.I.S.T.C. be made a state college also? Our curriculum provides for more than just the educating of students for the teaching profession." Even though this was the extent of that effort, the other state teachers colleges went ahead and secured legislation to change their titles in 1947 while President Adams continued to follow the single-purpose concept for Northern. When Leslie Holmes arrived on the scene, he, too, followed his predecessors and issued the following statement:

A break from studies at the college cafeteria in the Fifties

May I take this opportunity to call to your attention the fact that the name of Northern was not changed when the names of the other schools were changed. In other words, we are still known as Northern Illinois State Teachers College and we believe the job is big enough for us here in teacher education so that we plan to continue this line of work.[13]

But wise men do change their minds, and it was not many years before he reversed his position and in his *Northern Alumnus* column, "Across the Prexy's Desk," he wrote the alumni that he was willing to inaugurate a multi-purpose institution provided it could be made "certain that teacher education does not suffer." He arrived at this conclusion after a long period of "serious thought and a great deal of concern," he said.[14]

Holmes was more fully convinced that university status would not interfere with the purpose of training teachers, as many claimed it would, after he sent out a number of letters to presidents of many schools that had already made this change. In the responses, there was hardly an exception to the reply that the move had made the teacher-education program stronger than it was before. Moreover, the respondents seemed to feel that the additional programs, such as the liberal arts, were helpful in enlisting an increased number of teachers.[15]

There was, nevertheless, opposition to this change-over by some of the faculty who were certain in their own minds that teacher-training, if not taken seriously, would ultimately become a "stepchild" to the other programs. On 8 January 1953, at a special meeting of administrators and several major committees, Holmes presented the question of broadening the program to include additional curricula and degrees. After a lengthy discussion, a motion was finally passed stating that the "college should not seek to perform other functions . . . [but] should continue to offer . . . general education and pre-professional work . . . in the teacher-education curricula." At a subsequent meeting, exactly two years later, before the entire faculty, the question of university status was again brought up, and after several efforts to amend the resolution it was finally carried without a dissenting vote. However, this assent was accompanied with the request that such a change be followed by the necessary financial support to carry it out.[16]

In spite of the unanimous vote, certain leaders had some misgivings. Wilbur Yauch, head of the education department, felt that competition from liberal arts programs would be keen and as a result "our future as a high-grade institution in teacher education may be endangered." It "can be effective," he said, "only when the whole college recognizes it and helps make it worthwhile. . . ."

More provocative questions and opinions came from James J. Martin, a rather irascible history teacher, who, in relating his reasons for resigning his position, vehemently condemned the assumption that it was possible to make a university out of Northern simply by naming it as such. He felt among other things that it would be necessary for the institution to be not only devoted to the intellect but also committed to the support of active scholarship, which Northern was not able to accomplish at that time. In the light of these facts, he believed, Northern should continue to grow on the college level "without becoming grandiose" and without surrendering "to the weight of sheer expansion. . . ."

To refute Martin's arguments, four prominent English professors—Paul Burtness, Warren Ober, William Seat, and Robert Wilson—collaborated in a lengthy rebuttal favoring the change to Northern Illinois University. They claimed Martin's objections were hastily concluded, for progress was already being made in dealing with some of its weaknesses; as to others, they admitted much still remained to be done and especially in the area of faculty participation at the Board level. They were quick to point out the progress made in selecting better students, retaining faculty members, and developing a liberal arts curriculum, as well as the possible advantages that finally would be gained under university status.[17]

Though opposition by the faculty was only a rear-guard action, Holmes faced on the Board not only the highly respected opposition of both William Reavis and chairman Lewis Walker but also that of his old friend and colleague Richard Browne, who felt the need for public-school teachers was too great to divert energies to training for other professions.

On the other hand, he had a staunch supporter in Chauncey Watson, the local member from DeKalb. Moreover, he also had, under the chairmanship of Kenneth Snyder, an energetic and well-organized campaign in DeKalb and its environs, the purpose of which was to enlist support for the idea of a university in northern Illinois. Finally, on his side was the able leadership of Senator Dennis Collins and six members of the Illinois House of Representatives—George Byrdia, Hubert Considine, Charles Willett, John Manning, A.B. McConnell, and Fern Carter Pierce.

If Holmes and his political colleagues were to win over the Board, it would be necessary to prove beyond any question that becoming a university would not in any way minimize the role of teacher education. This they tried to do by using more or less the same arguments that had been continually used in securing other expansion programs, namely that the millions of people in the northern twenty-one counties should have a university to serve not only increasing number of students preparing to teach at the elementary, secondary, and college levels but also larger numbers of young people who wanted four-year degrees. The concept being promoted was the development of a regional university at DeKalb for the thousands who would otherwise have to go elsewhere for pre-professional education.

The initial effort to publicize the idea of a university as well as a separate board for N.I.U. was initiated by Kenneth Snyder, a local business man, under the direction of the DeKalb Chamber of Commerce. Careful to absolve Holmes and the college from any criticisms for organizing the campaign, Snyder made it absolutely clear that he "was one of the originators, if not the originator." [18] However, two Northern students, Janice Hawkins and Johanna Eisenzoph, were members of both Snyder's Expansion Committee and the President's Panel which also took an active role in petitioning the legislature.

The activities of the College Expansion Committee, as it was called, soon conscripted many of the leading businessmen of the city. However, in time it was discovered that the issue was too involved for the local citizens to handle alone, so they turned to many of the leading figures in the twenty-one counties—not including Chicago. Several of these were newspaper editors who published materials supplied by the research team in DeKalb; in fact, one small brochure, called "A Northern Illinois University—Why?," compiled by William Froom, was distributed to as many as 40,000 citizens during the campaign. A few of the leaders prided themselves on the fact that before the campaign was over they had actually spoken throughout the entire area "from the river to the lake"; R. F. Greenaway, editor of the *DeKalb Chronicle,* at one time ran as many as seven editorials on the subject in April 1953. All in all, this was an enormous undertaking by these DeKalb citizens who expended not only an extraordinary amount of energy and enthusiasm—in a cooperative relationship not often seen between town and gown—but also a substantial amount of local funds as well.[19]

In time, the idea of university status for Northern struck a responsive chord in the minds of educational leaders and legislators in the state—even though the University of Illinois saw a definite possibility that such a development would compete with the new branch campus it desired to have in Chicago. Moreover, the University also had expectations that if a new university were to be created in northern Illinois, it could become another campus under its jurisdiction.[20] All of these possibilities produced further tensions among the factions.

Governor Stratton was not forgotten by the Expansion Committee; it was obvious to them that much of his policital power as a Republican governor lay in the twenty-one northern counties and therefore he should be responsive. Nothing was left undone to apprise him of their aims and purposes. Meetings were arranged in Stratton's office, and he spoke at the commencement exercises at Northern and at the fiftieth anniversary of the DeKalb County Court House in 1954. In the latter address, he committed himself "to give great attention to the education of teachers and in so doing, we must plan for the expansion of our teaching facilities. This is particularly true here in northern Illinois." As for the newly formed Commission on Higher Education, it was still uncommitted; but the Teachers College Board held out vigorously against the university idea, especially in light of the fact that the need for elementary teachers had reached an all-time high. It was willing to recommend only the same state college status that the other two sister colleges had been given a few years earlier.[21]

By 12 January 1955, there had already been several bills prepared in the legislature to make Northern a university and also to create for it a single board; but since the Board as well as the governor was unanimously against this move, there was little chance for passage unless their thinking could be reversed. Chauncey Watson, working with the president, tried to overcome this opposition with a mass of evidence containing well-documented statistics and experiences from other universities. But it was to no avail, for Reavis and Browne were not only highly competent but also well supplied with data. They were able to influence the Board and thus secure a vote against the university idea. To be sure that members of the House and Senate were fully apprised of their position, a copy of the resolution was mailed to each of them as well as to the governor and to his Commission on Higher Education.

Behind the scenes in the Illinois senate, things were coming to a head. The Education Committee had finally voted the bill out with an amendment to change the school's status to that of a state college instead of a university. Those who had come to testify—Holmes, Snyder, and Watson—had earlier agreed to this change, for the opposition was too strong in the legislature, and the prevailing opinion was that Northern was trying to move too rapidly.[22] In the light of this action most parties concerned seemed delighted with the title of "state college," since the bill did eliminate the word "teachers" and also provided for two liberal arts degrees and various vocational courses. But Senator Collins was quite disappointed with the loss of the university status and said frankly that he would be ready to initiate the same bill at the next session of the legislature.

These amended bills passed both houses and were signed by Governor Stratton on 14 June 1955, and a ceremony with several leaders from DeKalb and Springfield was held in his office; two prominent student representatives, Dorothy Horn and James Skipper, were also present. While the leaders at Northern waited two years for the next session of the legislature to meet, they busied themselves by constructing the three buildings—laboratory school, a classroom structure, and the Field House—that the legislature had granted them.

Following up on his promise, Senator Collins again introduced bills to change the name to "university." To assure the necessary support this time some sixteen senators—political leaders from such cities as Chicago, Rockford, Champaign, Evanston, and Downers Grove—were made co-sponsors. Many of the materials used to promote the idea two years earlier were still applicable; however, this time it was not necessary to overcome the opposition of the governor, for he had tempered his views. He promised the DeKalb leadership that if the bills passed the General Assembly without the separate board provision, he would definitely sign them into law. Further support also was given by the schools at Charleston and Macomb, who in the meantime had gotten on the band wagon and introduced bills for the same status for themselves. But the Board, hoping again to prevent passage, noted that the Collins bill continued directly or indirectly to advocate "diverse functions" other than the education of teachers which the Board felt were not "consistent with the long established purpose of the college." Therefore, by a vote of six to two the Board again expressed disapproval of university status.[23]

But this time the Board had no effect, for increased efforts were made to reaffirm Northern's intention not to forsake its original purpose. President Holmes, Dean Zulauf, and Professor Yauch, as well as others—all pointed out that with the tremendous need for teachers even university status would "have no effect on the purposes already established." Moreover, the bills prohibited any professional courses that would culminate in degrees in law, medicine, dentistry, pharmacy, engineering, or agriculture. To demonstrate how firm his convictions were to this purpose, Holmes, as soon as the bill was passed, sent a letter to all secondary educational institutions in northern Illinois stating "that as we broaden the scope of our educational service, I wish to give my personal assurance that we have no intention of minimizing our role . . . [of] preparing teachers for the schools of Illinois." However, there was an escape clause in the new charter which invested in the institution itself the responsibility for determining its educational

311

programs; and with the pressures for new curricula that soon arose, it was not long before a wave of expansion fever took over, as is so obvious today when one views the present catalog and physical plant. So rapidly did Northern Illinois University grow that it soon became the most rapidly expanding university in Illinois. But even with this growth, it would appear (statistically, at least) that Holmes's argument was more nearly correct than that of the Board, for the number of students entering the teaching profession continued to maintain a normal rate of increase following the granting of university status, and at no time did he or his staff lose interest in the training of teachers. In fact, he even extended his interest in teacher education to include the preparation of college professors.

The passage of the Collins bill was uneventful as it moved through the Senate and the House, for a great deal of work had been done by Collins during the interval between the 69th and 70th Sessions of the Illinois General Assembly. It passed the Senate with only David Davis dissenting, and it passed the House by a vote of 133 to 27. Governor Stratton signed the bill on 23 May 1957. Honoring Senator Collins for his "courageous support," now as well as in the past, Chauncey Watson gave him great credit for the outstanding leadership he provided in achieving this goal and also for laying the foundation that would ultimately make "Northern Illinois University one of the great American universities."

Acceptance of the idea of a graduate school at Northern was slower in developing than at the sister schools. This was not necessarily because these other schools had a greater need for the program but rather because President Adams and some of his faculty had been lukewarm on the subject. One valid argument against it was that appropriations were hardly enough to finance the undergraduate program let alone taking on the additional costs of graduate programs that would run even higher in per capita expenditure. Moreover, the teachers of the Northern twenty-one counties already had available several distinguished graduate universities that they could

312

attend where library and science facilities as well as the faculties were far superior to Northern's.

These and other arguments prevailed during the Adams administration with only an occasional reference or discussion of the subject until 1939 when Adams finally appointed a graduate faculty committee to work with the other schools; differences of opinion, however, were so pronounced that no plan was satisfactory to all concerned. Southern, Normal, and Western were able to work out a "five-year" program which they launched in a limited manner beginning in 1943; Eastern and Northern delayed their final programs until later.

The war and the rapid increase of undergraduates afterward further delayed action by Northern until President Holmes appointed a steering committee of eleven members in November 1949, "to set up the mechanics of getting a graduate program started." The Board in the meantime established some guidelines to follow: Northern must have an adequate library collection in each field in which work was to be offered; departments must have one-half or more of their faculty members with doctoral degrees; all offerings must be taught on the campus; and the degree was to be the professional M.S.Ed.

The Board finally granted permission in 1951, and the first graduate courses were offered by the departments of biological sciences, education, English, mathematics, physical sciences, social sciences, and speech during that summer session under the directorship of J. Robert Hainds and an advisory council. With this assignment Hainds began a long and vigorous administrative career that finally elevated him to the level of academic vice president.

The opening of the new library the next year added considerably to the new graduate school. Added space had been made in the Haish Library for books and students but during the post-war period a new and larger library became an absolute necessity. Under the direction of head librarian Bernadine Hanby, a committee developed plans for the new Swen Franklin Parson Library with the capacity to hold 150,000 volumes. On 10 December 1952, "85 tons" of books (83,326 volumes) were carried by hand from the old library to the new one by students, faculty, staff, and friends. Leading the proces-

sion, President Holmes carried the first load and others followed—all in a joyous holiday spirit.

The transfer to the semester system soon thereafter was
another encouragement if for no other reason than that the
long-existing system of mostly four-credit-hour courses could
now be re-evaluated.

Things did not run smoothly at first. An internal hassle soon
arose within the academic fields when it was discovered that
they would have to share sixteen of the forty-five credit hours
in all graduate programs with the education department. Some
departments actually refused outright to participate in graduate work if this requirement were not changed. The final
solution was that the departments could decide the student's
requirements within the framework of work the student had
already completed and what the law demanded in order to
secure a secondary teaching certificate.

Other difficulties arose over the problem of whether there
should be a written thesis. Anything that even resembled the
idea of "research" was frightening to those in the professional
education fields, so a compromise was made by calling it a
"qualifying paper." Efforts were also made at the outset to
establish that "those teaching graduate students should not
carry a load of sixteen hours [the usual undergraduate num-
ber], or have more than three [daily] preparations," but acceptance of these demands was slow in coming, for it had a
tendency to discriminate against that large segment of the
faculty which was ineligible (for lack of a doctorate) to teach on
the graduate level.

For some years, the graduate students were mostly part-
time; attending Saturdays, evenings, and summer sessions;
pursuing courses that led to teaching degrees. However, in
time, some departments began to urge that arts and science
graduate degrees be awarded in order to qualify holders of
them to pursue doctoral programs elsewhere. The Board
finally recognized the request but still insisted that the primary
purpose was to prepare teachers for the public schools.

The number of departments offering graduate courses had
increased to 23 by 1960, with over two hundred graduate
faculty members. By 1961 the University had evolved from
three "divisions" into four colleges, thus giving greater num-

bers of students wider choices of graduate programs. The College of Business, especially, under the widely experienced administrator, Dean Robert Thistlethwaite, had phenomenal growth in all of its departments.

Graduate momentum continued until Northern finally began thinking in terms of a limited doctoral program, but it was a long and arduous undertaking before this was ultimately achieved. The purpose of doctoral programs in the universities under the Teachers College Board was, according to Richard Browne, to supply

qualified persons with graduate training. . . . Our Universities have a particular responsibility to meet this need in two areas (1) the preparation of "master teachers" for colleges, universities, and junior colleges, and (2) the preparation of elementary and secondary teachers and administrators.[24]

Others reasoned that if a more scholarly faculty were to be recruited and retained at Northern it would be necessary to have a doctoral program.

The initial planning for this doctoral program began in 1957, but it was several years later before approval was finally given to the departments of business education, education, English, and history. The work was done by an all-university coordinating committee consisting of twelve faculty members with the academic vice president, J. R. Hainds, as its chairman. They were directed to make an in-depth analysis with the assistance of the Graduate Council and eleven subcommittees. This group carried out the gigantic assignment of examining and probing every phase of university structure and finally of preparing a 450-page report for the accrediting agency. At the same time, each of the four departments seeking the degree program—history, English, education, and business education—drew up its own proposal for a doctoral program.

To assist this coordinating committee in the evaluation of the program, Ronald Thompson, executive dean of Special Services at Ohio State University, and Robert Sullivan were appointed by the North Central Association as consultants during the final stages.

Some of the sensitive areas that needed revision had already been pointed out as early as 1953 in response to the request for accreditation on the master's degree level; namely that the college needed a complete reorganization of its administrative practices and procedures. It was felt that the administration wielded too much influence in policy-making, most noticeably on the Faculty Advisory Council, for which the president even served as chairman; this was also the opinion of Richard Browne, who had made a study of faculty participation in teachers colleges.[25]

The mammoth "Study," accompanied by an abbreviated "Request," was filed with the North Central Association in December 1961—well ahead of time, according to Hainds—with the intention of securing preliminary approval in time to offer the first program in the summer session the following year. But the submission was made with some lack of confidence, for at the last moment there was a desperate effort to secure Thompson's services for at least one more day; but unfortunately he was engaged elsewhere. When contacted by phone, however, he gave them a pep talk to the effect that they had nothing to worry about and they should by all means "exhibit full confidence in the excellence of your program and facilities"; finally, he cautioned Robert Hainds about what must be done the day before the visitation: The following are only a few of the "musts":

Walk through all the buildings and over the entire campus. DO IT YOURSELF. Look at the halls. . . . Are they swept? Are they scrubbed: Are the walls cleaned: Look at the windows. . . . See that there is no dust anywhere. Go into the washrooms. Sniff as you go in. . . . Go into each classroom. . . . If there are any ragged . . . shades, get rid of them. . . . Look very carefully at the professors' desks and see that there is no junk present. . . . If a professor has old yellow notes on his desk, hide them . . . see that everybody exhibits enthusiasm about the university—not be apologetic about the place.[26]

The four examiners visited the Northern campus in January 1962 and, after a rather perfunctory examination, reported to the North Central Board that it was "premature" to grant preliminary approval. They found numerous shortcomings in the library, faculty training, grading, teaching loads, classroom and office space, travel funds, graduate assistantships, quality of the graduate students, and admission policies.

The failure to give preliminary approval set in motion a series of responses. The University engaged Arthur S. Adams, former president of the American Council on Education, for a week as a consultant and visiting lecturer to meet with various groups for the purpose of aiding the administration in mobilizing their forces and especially of assisting the departments to develop doctoral programs. This latter phase was so important that Adams recommended that the administration bring an outside panel of impartial scholars to the campus; thus the deans of the graduate schools of Duke, Harvard, and the University of Illinois were brought in for conferences.

The unfavorable report by the examiners created a vigorous reaction, especially by Charles Howell, who claimed that it contained numerous false judgments, misinterpretations, and errors of fact. He even went so far in his "Comments on the Report of the North Central Examining Committee Report [sic]" as to say that

If one were to examine the report of the examining committee with the same degree of care that one would customarily give to the examination of a qualifying paper at even the Master's level—and this report has been so examined—one would come to the conclusion that, at best, it should be referred back to the candidate for correction of obvious errors and, at worst, rejected outright because of these errors.

He then proceeded to devote seven pages to specific errors that he noted in the "Report"; Hainds and F. R. Geigle, the executive vice president, also gave many hours to checking and verifying data against some of the examiners' statements.

A seven-page reply was prepared for President Holmes to present to the Executive Board of the North Central Association in which he prefaced his remarks by saying that when he read the examiners' report, it caused him to recall the second line of Marc Antony's famous funeral oration: "I come to bury

Caesar, not to praise him." The impression "conveyed by the report is that the request of Northern Illinois University for *preliminary* approval of doctoral programs might better be buried than granted." To show, however, that it should not be buried, he expalined that many of the criticisms of the examining committee were not well founded and concluded:

If the term premature is to be used at all properly here this morning, it should be used not in reference to the university's request but in reference to the many erroneous statements, impressions and conclusions set forth in the report of the examining team. In addition to the erroneous conclusion concerning prematurity already mentioned, the errors and misconceptions are so numerous that I can not possibly lay them all before you in the few minutes now allotted to me. I can . . . present most of the others to you in writing.

Besides his presentation to the Executive Board, he had also prepared a booklet of pertinent facts that "would have been given the examiners before they left the campus if opportunity had been provided . . . [and thus] it would have enabled the writer of the report to avoid the erroneous statements. . . ."

While the North Central Executive Board was giving their attention to the "Report of the Examiners" and also the president's rejoinder, two of the examining committee members were sent to Northern for one day to meet with the departments and to take one last look. With this information, their final judgment was sufficient to override the examiners' original recommendation, and a preliminary accreditation was granted on 19 June 1962, in ample time to offer the first programs in the fall.[27]

This was a real milestone in the history of the University. It was the "Coming of Age," remarked C. Norton Coe, dean of the graduate school; the "most significant step the university has made since its beginning," observed Robert Hainds with a justifiable pride, since it was indeed in large part his creation, if any one person were to be singled out for this honor.

The doctoral programs that were created in 1961 (history and English, Ph.D.; business education and education, Ed.D.)

318

with such urgency to supply what was believed to be an ever-increasing demand for professors by rapidly growing college and university enrollments throughout the nation were in a vastly different situation ten years later. Those completing their degree requirements after four or five years of graduate work found the job market drying up and employment difficult. Few students were able to complete their Ph.D. work within a reasonable time, largely because of the lack of fellowships; in fact, the first such degree was not granted until the fourth year of the program and a total of only fifty had been conferred through 1972. The number of Ed.D. degrees, however, has been much higher; the first two were granted during the second year of the program, and by 1972 the total number was 149.

No one doubts that these programs are extremely expensive when the total per capita cost is considered; on the other hand, for a university such as Northern which is attempting to move away from its earlier background and build instead a first-rate university of scholars and teachers, they are of inestimable merit. Those departments with doctoral students have already recruited a few reputable professors as well as young teachers with promising careers, mainly because of these programs. The problem is, of course, retention of outstanding faculty. Doctoral programs have also played a large role in the growth of the library during the last ten years; though its total holdings may still be pathetically low for a university of 22,000 students, one should nevertheless consider the change in its rate of growth. When the first masters' program was offered in 1951, it had only 79,000 volumes; by 1972, it had reached a half a million cataloged volumes. Moreover, it should be noted that myriad social and cultural aspects of college life have also found their way to Northern if for no other reason than the increased sophistication of its faculty. To recognize this contribution one need only to have lived through those earlier years.

The doctoral programs, and more especially the Ph.D. programs, were certainly wanted for their prestige value by most of the administrators; however, there were always certain misgivings by some that they might adversely affect the main purpose of the University, namely teaching. To further the cause of teaching and to counter the apparent over-emphasis on research and writing, the Committee of Nine, under the chairmanship of F. R. Geigle, initiated a program in 1966 to promote and reward outstanding teaching and to provide "encouragement and incentive for teaching achievement." Annual selection of faculty recipients for "Excellence in Teaching Awards" was initially made through the efforts of this committee. Each winner is awarded a $1,000 honorarium (funded by the Standard Oil of Indiana Foundation) along with a citation and listing on a permanent plaque. The first recipients were Donald E. Kieso, D. Richard Little, and Donald M. Murray.

The neglect of teacher education continued as a perennial subject for discussion; as late as 1965, Provost Geigle expressed to President Holmes his concern about the efforts of certain departments to ignore the subject: "Of course . . . the College of Education and this office," he said, "are aware of this situation and . . . the many facets of this problem. It is a problem that needs constant investigation if we are to maintain the primary objective of the university." Dean of Education Robert Topp always kept a close vigilance over his domain by defending the importance of teacher education against attacks from those both on and off the campus.[28]

Another byproduct of these doctoral programs was the development of a cleavage in the faculty over the issue of "publish or perish," a strange controversy indeed, for it was not an issue between good and evil but rather between two goods. For years, only a few faculty members had done or were doing any respectable amount of research; instead most of their energies were absorbed in teaching a heavy schedule of courses as well as serving on committees. Those few, however, who did pursue a regular research program were not entirely forgotten, even at this time, for Holmes had already begun to show recognition of them by having a shelf in his own office of books written by faculty members; and in one of his semi-annual messages to the alumni he specifically revealed his pride in being able "to list a number of authors . . . who have published textbooks, numerous articles in professional magazines, and periodicals."

Holmes's recognition of the value to the university of published research went beyond mere rhetoric however. A committee was set up under the chairmanship of E. Nelson James to investigate the feasibility of establishing a university press at Northern. The committee visited several nearby university presses and on the basis of what they had learned from them drew up a report that recommended the establishment of a press. The first meeting of the University Press Board took place on May 1965, and the manuscripts of three NIU professors were approved for publication. (HEARTLAND: POETS OF THE MIDWEST, edited by Lucien Stryk of the Department of English, was to be the first book published by the new Press in March 1967.) Jack Barker, formerly director of Northwestern University Press, became the first director of the Press in September 1965.

But the controversy persisted in the groves of academe when productive scholars were recruited and the requirements for professorships were determined on the basis of published scholarship and doctoral courses taught, along with direction of dissertations. These requirements were soon challenged by those who had earlier either chosen Northern purposely to escape what they characterized as a publishing "rat race" or to satisfy their primary interest in the education of teachers. Whatever the motives, the battle was soon joined by members from the liberal arts departments; and the infighting persisted for some time in various forms, resulting in severe strains on old friendships. In the end, feelings tempered, and there was an acceptance by the president and the Teachers College Board that research activities were an integral part of a unified program at a university.[29]

Research activities have now become well recognized; for a number of years each faculty member's list of publications was published by the Bureau of Research; the *Faculty Bulletin* also carried a list of faculty publications. Official policy also recognized the role of research by providing the necessary equipment for such activity, by reducing the teaching load to allow time for research, and also by providing small financial grants from the Dean's Fund for various types of expenditures. In addition to these recruiting incentives, a policy allowing scholars to secure the necessary transportation from the University motor pool for a daily hegira to the Chicago research libraries was established to overcome objections to the inadequate library facilities.

Hainds should certainly be remembered for the leadership he offered in building up the scholar-teacher faculty. If the critics of "publish or perish" wished to identify one who was responsible for its promotion, they need look no further than this tough-minded person, for he was already a productive scholar.

A good example of leadership was in the history department, where this writer had an opportunity to share with Hainds the task of securing its first head, Norman Parmer. Excellently trained but only thirty-three years of age, Parmer had some excellent credentials. He had traveled and studied widely and was a recognized authority on southeast Asian economic history with a published volume already to his credit.

Parmer's lifestyle was one of endless hours of work. He gave his entire self to the tasks of building a new department. At once he found a professional kinship with Dean Hainds; throughout the few years they worked together, out of their close collaboration came the basic ideas and personnel for the history department.

Parmer was personally an aggressive individual with many achievements. He was a leader in securing the Peace Corps training programs at Northern, in establishing the Center for Southeast Asian Studies, and in recruiting and developing a doctoral faculty. He was also in the forefront in establishing a nine-hour teaching load for research scholars, in determining curricula and research priorities, and in setting new promotion, tenure, and salary policies. When he left the headship, he left a department that was undoubtedly the strongest as well as the most controversial in the University. It has lost none of its prestige and controversial nature, for throughout subsequent years, under the chairmanship of Emory Evans, it has continued to move ahead with new programs and carefully selected new staff members.

Other departments also improved their programs and faculties as a result of Hainds's leadership, but unfortunately not always without friction. In time these conflicts, and his own ill health, made it necessary for Hainds to withdraw as academic vice president.[30]

To replace Hainds in this high academic position (redesignated provost), the president chose Executive Vice President Francis "Bud" Geigle, who had been a successful businessman, teacher, and administrator. After coming to Northern in 1951 as the first head of the newly formed business department, he rose rapidly; first, to administrative assistant to Holmes, then to executive vice president, and finally (in 1963) to executive vice president and provost. In these positions, he proved himself to be an excellent assistant as well as speechmaker, arbiter, academic adviser, and public relations expert. Geigle's work was considered so meritorious that in 1970 the Board of Regents appointed him acting president of Illinois State University for one year.

Several others also contributed to this compatible administration. Ernest E. Hanson came to the faculty in 1941 as dean of men and later became vice president of the greatly expanded Student Personnel Services Division. As one member of the "team of Holmes, Hanson, Dorland, and Geigle" said of him: "He was loyal, dedicated, and always intensely interested in doing a good job." Harold Dorland served during fourteen of these busy years as vice president for business affairs; his responsibilities included supervising the expenditure of nearly $100,000,000 for construction of buildings. Those who knew him best regarded him as a person who did his work well and without fanfare. Certainly he is one who deserves considerable credit for the successes of the Holmes administration. William P. Froom, director of University Relations, Charles E. Howell, director of the Bureau of Research, and Edith Adams Leifheit, registrar, also gave many years of service to this "era of good feeling." Perhaps much of the success of the period must be attributed, as Richard Browne related to the writer, to President Holmes's ability to select both capable and cooperative associates.

One of the brightest aspects of the Holmes presidency was his relationship with the students, especially during the earlier years. He began immediately the practice of meeting with the presidents of the various student organizations, and on occasion had them in his office to talk over problems and appeals from different groups. Whenever a problem arose, on or off campus, it was his policy to see personally that it was dealt with as soon as possible.[31]

As the years went by, however, more and more problems presented themselves; and Holmes tended to transfer student problems largely to an increasing number of administrative assistants and counselors, until in time, only a few students had personal contact with him. In a move to rectify the situation, he held a "Presidents Day" in the Pow Wow Room—during his last year at Northern—where he not only fielded all the various questions "much better," the student president thought, "than could really have been expected" but also had served at least "3,000 cups of coffee." He also invited the Student Association Board (successor of the Student Senate) to his private dining room.[32]

In spite of his attempt to revive the memory of his open-door policy that had been so effective with student officials during his early years, the later years of Holmes's administration brought increased pressure in the form of direct challenges for certain rights: coeducational dormitories, a bookstore not limited to classroom supplies, no dismissals for parking violations, abolition of the loyalty oath and housing discrimination, change in women's hours, new dress codes, dispensation of birth control pills by the Health Service, publication rights, stronger student government, freedom in selecting speakers and the right to hand out literature, and student representation on major committees.[33]

In respect to student publications, one of Holmes's first controversies was in connection with the *Quarterback, a Journal of Opinion,* which was financed on a tentative basis by student activity funds, was initiated by students who wanted a forum for both discussion of issues and creative writing. The *Quarterback,* which was published for more than a year until one issue planned a cover consisting entirely of graffiti, a unique cross-section of American life in words, symbols, sayings, mottoes, and statements, such as "To hell with Cuba," "Down with Books," "Nigger Go Home," "Read Your Bible," "Beer for All," "Hell," "Bastard," "Wop," and "Pinko." Some adults felt that such language was vulgar and in poor taste; but its creators claimed that they were only attempting to depict the melting-pot idea of a heterogeneous America. The May issue of 1963 was the last one, for this representation of Americana occasioned such reaction that the "administration refused to allow them to distribute their magazine. . . ." However, not to be undone and also to avoid such censorship, a group of students, faculty, and clergymen organized an independent off-campus journal, called *The Edge,* which was sponsored by the United Campus Christian Fellowship. For the first issue they included the controversial page of graffiti. But as was the case throughout the years with other independent publications with no regular source of financial support, it too expired after a few issues.[34]

Controversies over students' rights were persistent for the president, and he insisted that he was unable to grant more liberties because he personally was held in "strict accountability by the Board for the successful functioning of the institution."

Dissatisfaction increased at Northern, and in 1962 a Committee for Student Rights, led by Barry Schrader, drew up a "12-point" program which was supported by a demonstration of some fifteen hundred students in front of Davis Hall, where the president and his staff would have no difficulty seeing or hearing it. Action was soon forthcoming and some of these points were conceded; others, however, were "to be discussed further by a special committee" appointed as a result of the protest.

In 1965, a chapter of Students for a Democratic Society was organized at Northern. S.D.S., part of the "New Left," was considerably more radical than any previous campus groups, particularly on the issue of the war in Vietnam. Its membership was small, but it was aware of the methods of protest and confrontation. The writer remembers well when some N.I.U. administrators informed him in conversation that they believed the University was in imminent danger of violent destruction from such organizations; so real was the threat to them that they were somewhat surprised that he was so "unaware" of the revolutionists and their violent methods.

With most N.I.U. students, however, the S.D.S. was not popular, and it had little influence except perhaps in stirring their interest and convictions against United States involvement in the Vietnam war and in creating a greater desire on their part to compel the administration to solve some of the grievances that had been smoldering for some time.

During the two years of its existence under President Holmes, the S.D.S. activities were largely confined to marches, vigils, teach-ins, and sit-ins. A protest was instituted in front of Lowden Hall against the Dow Chemical Company, makers of napalm, whose respesentatives were then on campus recruiting graduating seniors. On another occasion, an S.D.S. literature and poster display was disrupted by veterans who were angry with the positions being advocated.[35]

On the lighter side, this organization in 1967 initiated the observance of "Gentle Thursday," a spontaneous and uninhibited form of picnic in the lagoon area where one could "do his own thing" or just listen to rock music; this has continued as an annual tradition.

Control over who could speak on the campus, who could hand out literature, and what could be published in the *Northern Star* was still left ultimately with the president. Since this was a sensitive area and attracted considerable attention from both the conservative and liberal elements in northern Illinois (as well as the Board), he kept a close watch on what was spoken, written, and circulated on campus.

The distribution of materials on campus was a delicate matter for Holmes; to protect the University from the distribution of offensive kinds of literature, the rule was that any student or approved student organization that wanted to hand out leaflets, pamphlets, or printed material had to get approval from the Student Activities Office and to file a copy there. Such restrictions provoked deliberate violations by the students as well as by representatives of outside groups. This situation soon led to a campaign to establish a definite location where all forms of literature could be distributed "without censorship by the University." Holmes finally granted the "free speech area," and for a number of years it has continued to serve as a gathering place for those enthusiasts who wish to propagate their views. In 1966, rights were also granted to distribute literature of a noncommercial type in designated areas.[36]

The right of "outsiders" to speak on the campus was a larger problem, and over the years attracted more attention and caused considerable controversy. Most speakers who came caused no particular disturbance, but for anyone with a "radical" reputation, a problem was often created.

One of the celebrated cases at Northern was that of a speaker by the name of James West, who was engaged by the Young Democrats Club in 1960. He was an officer in the Illinois Communist Party. He was denied an opportunity to speak, Holmes said, because "[I am] not willing to expose the students to the influence of an atheist and a Communist." Holmes's aversion to Communist speakers was apparently influenced by J. Edgar Hoover's *Masters of Deceit*—a book the president had recommended highly to his staff. His concern was further indicated by the profuse underlining in his copy of Hoover's "Communist Target—Youth," a report published by the House Committee on Un-American Activities in 1960.

Holmes had support in this rejection from both members of the Board and the citizens in DeKalb. Richard Browne, the Board secretary, felt that West should not be permitted to speak since his party was not legal in Illinois; Ben Gordon, a prominent businessman and president of the local Rotary Club, also praised Holmes for his "vigilance and forthright action in behalf of democracy. . . ."[37] The local American Civil Liberties Union, however, felt that this action was rather severe and "reflected a lack of confidence in the powers of discrimination of the students." The Faculty Advisory Council also expressed regret for the cancellation and felt that "college students are mature and intelligent enough not to be deceived by the Party line."

The next case that created considerable notoriety was the granting of permission to Elizabeth Gurley Flynn to speak in 1962, under certain restraints. This consent had been made possible by revisions in speaker requirements brought about by the Student Senate. Flynn had been an avowed member of the I.W.W. revolutionary union and had spent her adult life in and out of jail in behalf of the radical labor movement. Nevertheless she was careful to limit herself to a historical lecture on the subject of "Early Twentieth Century Radicalism." Holmes, even with the restrictions he placed upon her, received a number of letters, most of which were critical of him for permitting her to speak; however, the local A.A.U.P. as well as most of the students were generally favorable to the idea, if not to the speech itself.[38]

President Holmes attempted to keep the University neutral on all political matters. To this end, there was a ruling that all candidates running for office, including the highest ones, were denied the use of the auditorium and were permitted only the use of a classroom; for it was believed that if the auditorium were to be opened to such partisan groups that fact in itself would indicate they were actually "being University sponsored." Another unhappy restriction in this category was that all faculty members were prohibited from wearing campaign buttons or any other physical symbols of political campaigns in the classrooms or on the campus.

In the fall of 1965, there was a confrontation that unsettled the University, all because of the power of a five-letter word. The trouble began in connection with the proposal for the Corporation for Campus Media which had been carefully drawn up after a year's planning and placed on the agenda for Board action at the 2 February 1966 meeting. In the meantime, however, Holmes had become highly perturbed at the *Northern Star* for using the word "bitch-in" five times to describe certain student meetings in various parts of the country, as well as the one that was held at Northern, where some two thousand students assembled for three and one-half hours to voice various gripes. He also objected to "offensive movie advertising" by a local theater carried in the *Star* as well as a few errors of fact in news reporting.[39]

This one episode seemed to affect Holmes more profoundly than almost any other during his presidency. Rarely had he made such hasty decisions, but this time he immediately withdrew the campus media proposal from the Board agenda on the grounds that "he did not think NIU was ready for the corporation." He dismissed the fact that the idea had the backing of the University Council, the A.A.U.P., the Campus Communication Committee, and the Student Association Board. Holmes was supported by some faculty members as well as by Paul Stone, the Board chairman, who engaged in a sharp letter-writing exchange with Allen Weaver of the A.A.U.P. In one of his letters to Holmes, Stone expressed his strong feelings: "I have the utmost contempt for this man and all his ilk!"[40]

Holmes did not place the media proposal on the agenda again even though the University Council had discussed it for several hours and the *Star* also had explained why the five-letter word was used, namely to report the previous student events as news items. The *Star* also ran an editorial in which the movie ads were recognized as in poor taste and added that they had "taken measures to insure that [they] will not appear again." But the *Star* was not about to surrender its journalistic independence, in spite of its willingness to "try to comply with the president's wishes," for the editorial concluded with a solid affirmation to "continue to manage the paper as we see fit."

Near the close of Holmes's presidency, in spite of some of his concessions, students protested vigorously that the only power they had with the Student Association Board was "the power of recommendation, which had, needless to say, been unheeded. If we are to function as responsible members of the university community, we . . . had better unite and take heed of our present situation."[41]

Even though students were determined more than ever to press for more governing rights and personal freedom and the administration was ready to hold firm to the end, no violence occurred such as was experienced in other parts of the nation and which occurred after Holmes's departure from Northern.

This is probably because most of the major elements in the subsequent campus violence—the Vitenam war protest, the expanded draft, racial tensions, and the acceleration of violence on other campuses—were just beginning to develop under Holmes.

The college faculty, like other groups in society, was subject to many pressures, influences, and changes that were beginning to appear in the 1940s—a period which served as a watershed between the old and the new in respect to the ideas and practices in such important matters as academic freedom, tenure, rank, leaves of absence, faculty involvement, academic training, and salary schedules, as well as various social activities.

The development of some of these academic practices began during the Adams administration when enrollments began to increase and larger numbers of faculty were recruited. The first noticeable enlargement of faculty and students came during the post-war boom; this growth was anticipatory of enormous future developments that few could foresee at the time.

This rapid increase in the faculty posed difficulties for the Holmes administration as well as for the departments, which were slowly gaining participatory rights in the process of attempting to recruit qualified people—an activity that was increasing in difficulty since graduate school enrollments in the country had fallen off sharply during the war. To appreciate the magnitude of the recruitment problem for the undergraduate faculty alone at Northern, one has only to note the tremendous growth in numbers of students and faculty during this eighteen-year period; in 1948–1949 there were 122 faculty members and 1,668 students; by the time of Holmes's retirement in 1967, there were 1,026 full-time faculty and 18,057 on-campus students.

To attract a faculty with higher qualifications than had been customary in the past for institutions like N.I.U. meant that it had to compete with the better universities, thus making the task doubly difficult not only because of its normal-school antecedences but also because of the "cornfield image" that many graduate-school faculties and students had of Northern. There was a general feeling that the administrators of such teacher-training institutions (suddenly made universities) placed more emphasis on high moral qualifications than on intellectual and scholarly ones in a candidate. Moreover, the salaries, teaching loads, library facilities, housing (DeKalb was a high rent area), and other factors of a social and cultural nature were deterring elements when competing for qualified instructors. But, in spite of these negative aspects, there were a few features that favored Northern, such as its proximity to the Chicago metropolitan area and that during the Holmes administration, higher beginning rank and tenure were liberally granted to promising young candidates.

The Holmes administration began early to upgrade the faculty. No sooner had he become president than a master's degree program in education was inaugurated. The expansion of the graduate program made necessary a more highly qualified faculty; for some years the only prerequisite for faculty membership in the graduate school was the completion of a doctorate. Later, additional qualifications were expected, and every effort was made to upgrade the faculty, concentrating first upon those departments offering the doctorate, since it was spelled out in the accreditation process that it was necessary to have a few research scholars with higher salaries and lower teaching loads as part of the departmental program. Fortunately for the University, such individuals were available in the groves of academe, sometimes temporarily unemployed, or unhappily employed, or about to be dismissed for various reasons not connected with scholarship, who could be induced to travel west of the Hudson or east of Berkeley. One or two of N.I.U.'s better graduate departments today no doubt owe their initial reputation to three or four such individuals.

To illustrate the early upgrading of the faculty, one can cite the number who had doctor's degrees. At the time Holmes arrived at Northern, in spite of the great effort his predecessor had spent in trying to increase their numbers—even by the method of encouraging key members to take leaves to work on degrees and older faculty members to retire—still only about

331

Alma Anderson *Miriam Anderson* *A. Neil Annas*

Carl Appell *Jack Arends* *E. C. O. Beatty*

Bertha Bellis *Loren T. Caldwell* *Lillian Cobb*

John Collins

J. Hal Connor

Z. Harold Dorland

George G. Evans

Stuart D. Fink

Charles E. Fouser

Otto J. Gabel

Newell D. Gilbert

Howard W. Gould

333

John Robert Hainds   Homer Hall   Bernadine Hanby

Ernest E. Hanson   Paul Harrison   Eugene Hellmich

Charles E. Howell   Hugh Jameson   Josephine Jandell

Edith Leifheit

Charles W. Leslie

John Lloyd

Clyde L. Lyon

Charles A. McMurry

Lida B. McMurry

L. Eveline Merritt

Helen Messenger

Charles E. Montgomery

Celine Neptune

Milo Oakland

William V. O'Connell

Edward C. Page

Anna Parmelee

Swen F. Parson

Otto E. Peterson

Ida S. Simonson

William B. Storm

E. Ruth Taylor   George L. Terwilliger   Maude Uhland

Mary Ross Whitman   Milo Whittaker   Esther Williams

William W. Wirtz   Romeo M. Zulauf

one-fifth (26 out of 122) of the faculty had doctorates. By the time Holmes retired, nearly one-half of the faculty possessed some form of doctorate. Even though this degree is not necessarily indicative of high quality, it was nevertheless in this particular period an important qualification and was also indicative of a giant step forward for the University.

The basic problem was not only recruiting well-trained faculty members but also retaining them with the low salary schedules at Northern during the 1950s. When Holmes took over in 1949, a study had been carried out by the Joint Salary Committee of the state teachers college faculties in order to substantiate the higher salary recommendations being made to the Board. Here is part of their argument:

The comparison between college teaching salaries in the lower brackets and salaries in high schools in Illinois are tragic. The cost of living index alone would justify the entire revised schedule so that it will be available next year. . . . In this way we might retain our present staffs and be able to give . . . whatever cost of living increase our funds make available. . . . there is no single factor as important to the development of institutional morale as to be able to help our faculties take care of this increased living cost.[42]

In spite of this pleading recommendation and others yet to come, budgets were rarely adequate to give even those with the highest credentials the top of the salary schedule. For example, in 1949 President Holmes pointed out to the Board that with a maximum of $6,000 for professors in the salary schedule he had not a single one drawing that amount.

In the Fifties, however, times began to change for the better, prodded by the effects of creeping inflation along with the increased competition for better trained professors. Eugene Hellmich, who for several years served as chairman of Northern's salary committee, had a leading role in this struggle for better salaries.

A device was introduced in 1950 that was to allow better apportionment of inadequate funds while at the same time was to provide for retention of the more qualified professors. The

338

method was called the "block system," and it had three levels, A, B, and C, in each faculty rank. The "A" level in each rank was used exclusively for merit increases to be awarded only by the president, dean, and a faculty committee who had been supplied with documentary evidence that the individual being awarded had met the necessary criteria established by the faculty and the Board. Block "C" (lowest) received annual salary increases automatically; in Block "B," automatic increases could be withheld for various reasons. This was one way to provide higher salaries, for at least 25 percent of the faculty expected to be in the merit group.

In the first year of the 1952–1954 biennium, the merit system awarded twenty-eight faculty members special merit increases of $40 per month over the regular $20 increment, and about half of the remaining faculty were granted an extra $20 increase over the regular $20. The second year of the biennium, however, was not so promising, for there were sufficient funds to give only a regular $20 increment to the whole faculty. The perennial problem was simply that state appropriations were insufficient for adequate salaries.

This was not the case with the University of Illinois and to a certain extent with Southern Illinois University, for they were more successful with their boards and the legislature. A professor at the University of Illinois was receiving as much as $1,356 more than one of the same rank at Northern. Moreover, in comparative studies made of the salaries at the sister teachers colleges, Northern almost always found its salaries at or near the bottom. This same disparity was also true in a comparison of Northern's median salaries for 1957–1958 with national averages reported by the National Education Association. Salaries for N.I.U. professors were as much as 8.6 percent lower.[43]

So weighty was the salary issue during the Holmes period that the Joint Council on Higher Education (presidents of state-supported institutions of higher education in Illinois) in 1954 urgently called for salary adjustments, and again in 1958 it recommended that a schedule be devised that would double the 1956–1957 salaries during the next ten years.[44] Through persistent efforts, the administration was able to do more than achieve this goal; for some faculty members it was considerably more. For example, one professor's salary of $7,560 in 1956–1957 was actually raised to $16,200 by the academic year 1966–1967, exceeding all expectations considering the past history of salaries. But even with this doubling of salaries, Northern still received only a "C" rating on a national scale in an A.A.U.P. comparison with other colleges and universities. These higher merit increases were helpful in dissipating the inequities in the higher ranks; however, many complaints were still heard from all levels, because of the inflationary spiral.

Faculty members hardly lived by bread alone, for they did have many social and intellectual activities that over the years also underwent various changes. Slowly and gradually the traditional patterns of behavior expected of those who taught prospective teachers evolved into those of the greater society; but before this actually happened, the faculty members who wished to deviate often felt constrained to exercise their choices behind the walls of their own homes.

Poker clubs of major and minor league proportions made their appearances in this semi-secret fashion during the Thirties as the number of male instructors increased, and smoking and drinking also increased but was still less common than among the general public. The presidents of Northern, until the most recent two at least, were more or less of the old school in these matters, and even though they made no statements nor issued any directives concerning such personal habits, faculty members and administrative staff did not feel free to indulge in drinking in the presence of the president until very late in the Holmes administration.

One of the most popular and respected social functions for years was the autumn garden party held at the Edward Edel residence at Normal Road and Locust Street. It was an elaborate and painstaking affair in a most beautiful setting, with Dr. and Mrs. Charles Montgomery sharing the roles of host and hostess with other faculty couples. This annual affair served as the debut for all new faculty members who were introduced by the heads of their departments. This highly regarded custom extended well into the Holmes administration, ending in 1959 with the retirement of Edel, after which new faculty members were taken to the Lorado Taft campus for refreshments and a view of the scenic Rock River and the Black Hawk monument.

Plays and musicals with faculty casts and the ever-willing J. Hal Connor as director were not uncommon; operettas were also staged on and off the campus and one, the popular "Pirates of Penzance" by Gilbert and Sullivan, drew 1,400 people at the local theater. The theater parties, too, were numerous with various groups taking the morning train to Chicago to attend the theater or opera in the afternoon or evening and return home on the late train.

For many years the Faculty Club served as the heart of the faculty. This group arranged for retirement dinners, special lectures, and the annual picnics in Hopkins Park. It still performs a few of these functions in addition to others, such as monthly luncheons featuring a wide variety of speakers.

Faculty meetings were likewise subject to change, not the least of which was a change during the Adams administration to one meeting per month instead of two. In time the faculty assumed the responsibility of arranging for speakers and introducing the discussion of controversial issues. On occasion, talks were given by faculty members, such as by Charles Rohde on his experiments at the atomic energy laboratory at Oak Ridge, or by Lawrence Secrest on his experiences in Russia. But even with these innovations nothing has seemed to be successful in preserving the regularly required meetings that seem to have outlived their usefulness. The first shoe was dropped when excuses were no longer necessary for those who were absent; the second one fell some years later when meetings were put on a voluntary basis, causing the president to eliminate them entirely soon thereafter in 1961, retaining only one major meeting at the beginning of each school year. This meeting was a social get-together with a major speech on some institutional problem or policy such as the role of teaching, research, and writing in a multi-purpose university. During the most recent two administrations the format has changed again, and each president has used the occasion of the faculty meeting to address his audience on some important policy development or to indicate reactions to problems concerning the faculty.

In recent years, the faculty has fragmented into smaller and smaller groups based upon academic disciplines, and the traditional teas, dinner dances, and parties have given way to more informal talkfests with beer and pretzels. This affinity is also noticeable at the luncheon tables in the Pheasant and Blackhawk rooms in the Center where small groups isolate themselves. Fragmentation of faculty and students as well as departments and colleges into more and more units leads to a situation that once provoked University of Chicago President Hutchins to remark, in his own inimical manner, that about the only thing left in a university that holds the whole thing together is the heating plant.

Faculty members for years gave considerable time to lecturing in communities around the area, and the demand for this service increased noticeably during times of war, depression, and political elections. It was not surprising that many answered these calls to speak to some P.T.A. or women's club—even though the honorarium was rarely more than $30. Besides lecturing to local audiences, a few individuals found time to attend national and sectional meetings in their own disciplines—usually at their own expense—and on a few occasions one or two might actually have been invited to read or discuss a paper. This activity increased in the 1950s; by the 1960s, N.I.U. was often represented at such meetings, and expenses of program participants were paid by the University.

Politically the faculty has grown over the years from one participating in no such form of activity on the campus to one that is today actively engaged in speaking, writing, displaying badges, and handing out literature covering the entire spectrum of partisanship. Each administration down through the years has given ground on this question, from complete prohibition to complete freedom. Moreover, the faculty itself during the past seventy-five years has changed politically from its early one-party loyalty to a two-party character that began to appear in the New Deal period.

It might be thought from these brief sketches of faculty activities that it was mostly a congenial and harmonious group,

342

which no doubt it was for the earlier years at least; but beginning with the Adams period, the campus increasingly experienced controversies and rivalries common to most halls of academia. Since Northern was a professional single-purpose institution, disputes, debates, and sometimes even quarrels arose over such controversial ideas as progressive education, the core curriculum and group learning, as well as liberal arts courses versus those in education, and research versus teaching. With the increase of faculty members with more academic backgrounds, such debates grew sharper until in the 1960s these controversies took on statewide significance.

With the appearance of the recommendations of James Bryant Conant, in his book *The Education of American Teachers*, forces were set in motion to re-examine the whole subject of teacher education.[45] A small group of N.I.U. professors under the leadership of Ralph Bowen, Orville Baker, Lillian Cobb, and others organized the Illinois Citizens' Committee for Teacher Education in 1963; with a generous grant of $5,500 from the Robert R. McCormick Fund, a campaign was launched to reform certain aspects of the teacher-education program. With the election of one of its members, Michael Bakalis, to the office of superintendent of public instruction in 1970, and the appointment of another member, Orville Baker, to the State Teacher Certification Board in 1971, this organization began to achieve some influence.

Until 1942, all those in the organizational structure of the college, academic and otherwise, were directly responsible to the president. However, in that year the office of the dean of the faculty was created with Romeo Zulauf as the first appointee, and department heads were made responsible to him. This office ultimately evolved into the positions of dean of instruction, vice president in charge of instruction, academic vice president, and finally, in 1963, provost. The graduate school, with a director, was established in 1951.

To cope with further enrollment increases in 1953, a major administrative reorganization was effected by setting up four major divisions of the college: Instructional Services, under Dean Zulauf; Student Personnel Services, under Dean Hanson; Regional Services, under Director Paul Street; and Business Services, under Business Manager Emil Anderson. At the same time an Administrative Advisory Council was established in addition to the Faculty Advisory Council, which had existed for a number of years. These various structural changes were the results of basic revisions advocated by the John Russell "Report" and William Reavis's "Rules and Regulations." Besides these, another key recommendation in both studies was that the faculties be given greater opportunities through their organizations "to achieve democratic participation." [46]

By 1959, with the continued enrollment increases and university status, the Division of Instruction was divided into three colleges: Liberal Arts and Sciences, Fine and Applied Arts, and Education. The following year the College of Business was established, breaking away from the College of Fine and Applied Arts. By 1957, the Evening College was formed with Virgil Alexander as its director; in 1966, it became the College of Continuing Education.

By 1961, the Administrative and Faculty Advisory Councils were reorganized to constitute the President's Cabinet and University Council respectively. A complete revision of the University's committee system at this time made committees, for the most part, responsible to the University Council, which established the educational and academic policies of the University.

All the years that the administrative organization was pyramiding, the number of departments was also increasing by both division and creation. When administrative expansion began in 1942 with the establishment of a faculty deanship, the college had only fifteen departments; by 1967, when President Holmes retired, the number had doubled, and several of these departments were so large that assistants were added to help share the enormous burdens with the chairman or head. In fact, the English department with sixty-six members in 1972, was actually larger than the entire faculty (sixty members) of the college in 1942.

Two important events in the history of the Teachers College

Board took place in 1949. First, the Board's authority over Southern Illinois University—which gained its own separate board—was ended. Secondly, Governor Stevenson appointed W. W. Wirtz and the nationally known University of Chicago professor, William C. Reavis, to the Board; both became highly proficient members. A committee was soon appointed, with Reavis as chairman, to codify the Board's rules and procedures. The resulting governing policies, adopted 25 September 1950, went through several editions over the years and actually served as a form of constitution. The formulation of the "Reavis Policies," as they became known, was considered by some to be a milestone in the governance of these colleges. The second important development was in June 1951, when the General Assembly passed legislation making the Teachers College Board independent, i.e., no longer a division of the Department of Registration and Education. Formerly the director of the Department of Registration and Education was *ex-officio* chairman; under this 1951 change, the chairman was elected by the Board from its membership, and a full-time executive officer was appointed. Wirtz became the chairman, and Richard Browne, the executive officer.

In 1965, the altered names and functions of its institutions were finally recognized when the name Teachers College Board was changed to Board of Governors of State Colleges and Universities. Also at this time Illinois Teachers College–Chicago (formerly Chicago Teachers College) was placed under the Board.

In the fall of 1961, Illinois began an experiment "to impart a sense of unity and far-sightedness" in the administration of its institutions of higher learning and to insure the optimum development of all the institutions comprising the system. The Illinois Board of Higher Education (IBHE) was created as a compromise between those who wanted a strong, all-powerful body and those who wanted only an advisory group. The Board's first task was to prepare a "master plan" for the "development, expansion, integration, coordination and efficient utilization of the facilities, curricula and standards of higher education for all the public universities and for the public junior colleges of the State."

345

The second major role of the IBHE was to approve or disapprove the establishment of any new college, school, institute, department, or research program. This was to assure that the development of each institution accorded with the master plan and with a well thought-out program of allocating resources where they contributed the most.

A third major power was to analyze the budgets of the universities and to submit recommendations with respect to them to the budget agencies of the governor and the General Assembly. This power enabled the Board to review appropriations in relation to the co-ordinated plan for higher education without involving the Board in a series of detailed budgetary problems.[47]

With this authority, the IBHE was to become, during the 1960s and early 1970s, increasingly powerful in influencing the development of state-supported colleges and universities in Illinois. The University of Illinois and Southern Illinois University enjoyed an enormous advantage because each of these universities had the chairman of its governing board serving as a member of the IBHE. In contrast, six other public senior institutions—Northern, Illinois State, Western, Eastern, Northeastern Illinois State, and Chicago State—though there were profound differences in size and mission among these schools, had among them only one representative, the chairman of the Board of Governors of State Colleges and Universities.

Because of the inequities associated with this arrangement, the Faculty Advisory Committee of the IBHE unanimously recommended establishment of a single governing body for all public universities in Illinois, with the dissolution of the various boards existing at lower levels. An alternative proposal—establishment of a separate governing board for Northern, parallel to those governing the University of Illinois and Southern Illinois University—had been favored by many at Northern. On 6 May 1964, the elected members of the University Council voted unanimously (the administrative members necessarily abstained out of deference to the Teachers College Board) that the IBHE support one of these reforms in the pattern of governance: either (1) a state-wide governing board over all public universities, or (2) a separate institutional governing board for Northern, in addition to the existing boards, so that each of the three largest public universities in the state would have its own governing board. However, the IBHE decided not to support the plan for a single state-wide governing board and chose not to deal with issues of governance in its "Master Plan" (July 1964). As a result, faculty members at Northern, with guidance and encouragement from key administrative officers, launched an intensive campaign to secure a separate board.

The campaign climaxed during the legislative session of 1965. Senator Dennis Collins introduced a bill providing a separate governing board for Northern, and many faculty members and other interested citizens from northern Illinois lobbied virogously for months on behalf of the bill. When the bill passed by a wide margin in the Senate, its supporters redoubled their efforts in hope of securing passage by the House of Representatives. In a conference with faculty spokesmen, Governor Otto Kerner indicated that he preferred not to support the bill. However, he acknowledged that the arrangements for governing higher education in Illinois needed study and pledged to have the IBHE look into the problem during the following year.

Without Kerner's support, and with a lack of sympathy on the part of the Board of Governors, the IBHE, and other groups in the state, the bill eventually failed to pass in the House. As Governor Kerner promised, the IBHE, under the leadership of Executive Director Lyman Glenny, in 1966 developed and incorporated as part of "Master Plan Phase II" a new proposal for the governance of public higher education in Illinois. Under this arrangement, the General Assembly, in the spring of 1967, established a Board of Regents, which, as of 1 July 1967, was to govern Northern and Illinois State; in 1969, a newly created upper-division institution, Sangamon State University, was also placed under this Board.

The new systems concept involved state-wide coordination of budgeting, programming, and master planning by the IBHE for all public institutions of higher education, with governance of the individual campuses by four system-level boards over the senior institutions—the Regency System, the University of Illinois System, the Southern Illinois University System, and the State Colleges and Universities System. Another system-level board coordinated activities of the community colleges, each with a governing board at the local level. The systems arrangement reduced somewhat the advantage enjoyed by the universities at Urbana and Carbondale but did not resolve the underlying issue of having campuses with diverse character and mission governed by the same board.[48]

From the first day Northern opened as a normal school in 1899, there began to develop among the faculty, the students, and the townspeople, the idea that the campus itself was its major attraction. This idea has persisted throughout the years as its several caretakers have continued to improve it.

At first, there appeared on the scene to shape this virgin pasture land an expert landscape architect by the name of Walter Burley Griffin, of Chicago, whose work and reputation has been described in an earlier chapter. Following him was Frank K. Balthis, a botanist and creative artist as well as a remarkable person who for eighteen years developed the campus to a high degree of balance and beauty. Some years after leaving Northern he was engaged by the Garfield Park Conservatory, and his creative ability won for him the Macmillan prize of $1,000 for his book *Plants in the Home*.

It was a great loss when Balthis decided to leave, but his successor, William Swinbank (a nurseryman from Sycamore who had come from England in his youth), was soon able to fill this vacancy. Even though he was not a formally educated person, as his predecessor had been, he was nevertheless a gentle and kindly man who had learned much from experience and who soon endeared himself to the college in his efforts to beautify the campus. But this was only a part of his work, for he, like Balthis, worked with the children of the Training School in growing gardens and flowers; in later years, when they became students in the college, they still remembered him with the following feelings:

He is a friendly gentleman. His hair has turned gray to match his growing years. He seems as much a part of the landscape of our campus as is the gnarled oak in yonder wood. We can see him . . . bending at his desk—clearing brush, transplanting flowers and shrubs . . . . In the spring the tulip bed is his fancy; in the winter . . . he seriously toys with the tropical plants in the hot house. He is as much a part of the campus as the buildings themselves or the giant tree that he trims.[49]

At the age of eighty, after having served the institution for twenty years, he regretfully went into retirement. Following his death, his friends, wishing to remember him for his unusual landscaping services to DeKalb and Sycamore, fixed a bronze plate upon a large boulder at the big bend of Highway 23 between these two cities.

In 1950, Anthony Lorusso, a graduate of Rutgers University in landscape engineering, assumed this position. The job soon took on gigantic proportions, for Northern was not only on the brink of an enrollment explosion but of one in land acquisition and building construction as well. At first he was given the title of superintendent of grounds, with responsibility for a campus of slightly over 180 acres, nine regular buildings, the College Tea Room, the Home Management House, the temporary barracks, and proposed sites for a men's dormitory and a laboratory school. Today he is campus planning coordinator, and over thirty additional structures have been built and numerous older ones have been purchased. The DeKalb campus has expanded to 417 acres, and the Lorado Taft and Pine Rock campuses near Oregon add another 201.64 acres to the total. These latter two campuses were acquired by Holmes as a result of his outdoor educational interests which he had emphasized in his inaugural address.

Soon after Holmes's arrival he began to interest the Board in requesting the legislature to transfer the Eagle's Nest art colony (the Lorado Taft Field Campus) from the Department of Parks and Memorials to Northern for use as an outdoor campus. By the opening of school the next fall a bill for this purpose was passed under the leadership of Senator Dennis Collins and signed into law by Governor Stevenson. At the time, the original four buildings were so badly dilapidated that the state architect estimated it would require at least $80,000 to reconstruct them; however, Paul Harrison, director of the project, used his college classes in the building trades, employed only a minimum number of skilled craftsmen, and did the work for as little as one-third that amount.

A pioneer curriculum for outdoor education was developed by a regular staff with little assistance from other institutions, for few such programs had been initiated elsewhere. The primary purpose was for education majors to train in the "natural environment as a literal extension of the classroom" so that they could instruct children about the out-of-doors. In time, with more specialized instructors, it was possible to offer courses in the arts and crafts, camping, and field sciences at the Lorado Taft Campus. Today the department of outdoor teacher education offers a master's program. Education classes and groups of children from elementary schools in northern Illinois come to this campus, where they enjoy comfortable facilities for both dining and sleeping. This was probably the primary purpose of the project; but as time went on, it also became an attractive spot for small conventions, board meetings, and "think-ins." During summer sessions, courses from various departments are held there.[50]

This additional campus was one of President Holmes's proudest achievements and also one of his favorite spots where he could visit with his close friend, Paul Harrison. They enjoyed each other's company as well as the scenic "Woods and Templed Hills" made famous by the Eagle's Nest art colony and Lorado Taft's giant statue of Black Hawk on a point overlooking the Rock River.

The second off-campus area was the recently acquired Pine Rock Nature Preserve about five miles from the Taft campus on the south side of Route 64, east of Oregon. It consists of approximately 58 acres of native prairie, the level portion of which has escaped cultivation because of its poor drainage; as a result, it "has an excellent stand of wet prairie vegetation with many unusual kinds of plants." Dominating this area is a large outcropping of St. Peter sandstone about fifty feet high and several hundred feet in diameter. This "excellent area for the study and practice of natural conservation" was purchased in

350

1966 for $7,500 from the Illinois Chapter of Nature Conservancy.[51]

The architectural style and landscaping of the campus had stood up well under President Adams largely because he was never really overrun with students as was his successor. With his expertise in engineering and ample amounts of land, he had plenty of options in placing his few buildings. Moreover, he usually had plenty of time to plan, since it often took years for him to get his appropriations. During his administration he drew up a twenty-five-year plan that called for a total of twelve new buildings and fifty-nine acres of additional land to be used for an athletic field, field house, golf course, women's gym, and men's dormitory. His proposed sites on the original campus were well laid out, including the lagoon area and spaces for the music and fine arts buildings just north of the Arboretum, thus showing his desire to preserve the woods. It was also he who had the lagoon excavated. His plan called for the development of a quadrangle in front of the Castle and science building, and an outdoor theatre and lakeside improvement area that would include "woodland trails and reforestation around the lake" as well as a remodeled entrance gate. The total cost of his twenty-three major and minor building proposals was estimated at about six million dollars.

Soon after President Holmes arrived on the scene, he was confronted with a growing enrollment that placed an enormous burden upon the college for reconstruction of additional dormitories, classrooms, and offices as well as land acquisition for these building sites. There has been criticism that in the rush to acquire land and build the buildings in the 1950s and 1960s a landscape and architectural style emerged that bordered on over-all "architectural horror." William L. Fash, professor of architecture at the University of Illinois and director of Northern's Environmental Development Project, stated in 1972 that "the root cause of the physical and aesthetic deficiencies of the campus has been the absence of coordinated planning during the last few years to accommodate enrollment increases," resulting in "physical and visual problems" and "a serious circulation (pedestrian and vehicular movement) problem. . . ."[52]

The officials of the University, however, should carry only

351

part of the blame for these deficiencies, for the state architect, certain Board members, and perhaps others were also a part of the decision-making in this area. Heavy responsibility must fall upon the shoulders of Board member Royal ("Rooney") Stipes, who at times forced his will upon the university presidents. For instance, at Northern, efforts were consistently made to purchase the Listy property (where the Village Commons and University Plaza are today); but always to no avail, for Chairman Stipes insisted that the price was too high. In fact, money to buy this property was placed within the budget by Z. Harold Dorland, vice president of business affairs, so often that Stipes finally threatened that if it were included once more he would have Dorland fired.[53]

Stipes's dominant role in this land case accounts in large part for the reason private interests were successful in building a walk-in shopping center and the Plaza dormitory near the heart of the University. They had some assistance, however, from the DeKalb City Council as well as some leading citizens who were influenced by the belief that the University had gone too far in depriving local citizens of a share of the millions of dollars spent by the students for noneducational purposes.[54] This faction also resented the University's not paying its share of increased costs for city utilities.

In another important case, Stipes was responsible for locating the Field House where it is instead of where others felt it should be. One command from him (at the same time placing his foot with force on the exact plot of ground in question) was sufficient to settle what should have been an important architectural landscape question.[55]

Another exercise of power, though not connected with buildings, which demonstrates Stipes's influence, was displayed in 1955 when Holmes recommended to the board a redistribution of the responsibilities of the men's physical education department among "Chick" Evans and his two colleagues, William Healey and John Sohne. Evans, realizing that he would no longer be in complete command of the departmental activities and the coaching, quickly appealed directly to Stipes who, being a great admirer of coaches and athletes as well as an avid sports fan, was able to prevent this reorganization.[56]

1956 aerial view of campus shows abundance of trees before the combination of Dutch–elm disease and building construction eliminated most of them

Beginning in the 1920s, it was not unusual to read editorials and student complaints that there was not enough parking space on the campus for the increasing numbers who were commuting to the college. The need for more parking space and the need for building sites were constantly in competition with each other as long as there was so little land added to the original campus. The increased emphasis on sports activities created additional demands for parking, and this was especially true for the two major sports which for many years were performed on Glidden Field and in the Still Gym—both located in the congested area between the bridges. The congestion created not only parking problems but safety hazards as well. The streets on the campus were built during the horse-and-buggy days and were too narrow for parallel parking.

The 1930s and 1940s, instead of reducing the problem, only increased it as cars rolled off the assembly lines and concrete highways replaced the dirt and gravel roads. Rules and regulations were finally established in order to control the increasing problem. But even with these efforts, the parking problem grew to such proportions that the Administrative Council finally had to include it on its agenda; the Student Safety Council also publicized the problem by establishing a "No Accident Week." Who among former students or faculty can ever forget talks by both President Adams and President Holmes at the assemblies when with embarrassing frequency they mentioned the parking rules?

As the number of cars continued to increase, along with the added demand for building space, the need for land intensified the problem even further until finally it spilled over into town and gown relationships, producing one of the few serious confrontations with the city. This happened when it was no longer possible to use the campus lots without securing permits and registering vehicles; larger numbers of students decided to park on the city streets, which "tossed into the laps of city officials" a parking problem that brought about certain city council actions that strained relations to the breaking point. In the end the president and others finally worked out a solution—though Holmes was unwilling to forbid freshmen and sophomores from having cars. This particular restriction was not established until 1966.[57]

354

Parking was also an irritating ordeal for many faculty members, especially after the campus security department was established to enforce rules and issue tickets. Policies were determined by the Campus Internal Affairs Committee which had gone through more name changes perhaps than the University itself. It has finally become the Campus Parking Committee with a separate review board to handle traffic appeals. But the chief complaints leveled against this committee were that it did not have a majority of faculty members and no student membership at all to represent the latter souls, who for several years were dismissed following a certain number of violations. Grievances of the faculty were that the registration decals were no more than "hunting licenses" that permitted one to seek one of the scarce parking spaces; what they really wanted was a faculty parking lot separated from the student lots and as close as possible to the buildings where they taught.

Other complaints of a slightly different character were that faculty had frequent brushes with the campus police and some did not believe that these employees should be wearing guns except on special occasions. Moreover, a matter that was also frequently mentioned by the faculty was in respect to the membership of the committee itself; three vice-presidents of the University were members. Faculty members felt administrators belittled their positions "in the eyes of the faculty by being associated with punitive actions of such a petty nature." Geigle and his colleagues thought otherwise, however, because of the nature of the violations.[58]

As these complaints increased in number during the 1960s, some of the faculty actually refused to settle their fines and since enforcement by dismissal was not possible, as it was with students, the administration finally appealed to the Board attorney, Richard F. Dunn, for his opinion as to the action to be taken. The following is a part of his recommendation:

Simply fail to certify any offending faculty member for regular payment [of salary] until such time as the parking fines have been paid. . . . It seems to me that this might be a practical way to enforce the collection of fines. . . . I am sure that neither the Board nor the University want to tolerate faculty members who disregard reasonable . . . regulations, and in my opinion, fail-

355

ure to obey such regulations and pay fines would be sufficient reason to fail to renew the contract of a person without tenure and sufficient reason to justify termination of employment even though the offending faculty member did have tenure.[59]

The Council of Presidents of the five schools under the Board took up the matter and supported his position, agreeing that repeated faculty violators who failed to settle their fines and penalties "would be subject to release." There is no evidence that this action has ever been enforced by a president; although the reason may have been that the problem soon became more satisfactorily handled. More lots were added and were designed exclusively for faculty, students, or visitors, and those who wish to reserve individual spaces can now do so by paying a substantial additional fee. Students, too, are no longer dismissed for parking violations.

As the enrollment increased and more and more space was needed, it became evident to many that this frenzy of expansion was working a hardship on the few physical landmarks still intact as well as on the traditions and landscape architecture of the campus, as illustrated by the destruction of the Arboretum. The ancient biblical commandment, "cursed be he that removeth his neighbour's landmark," had little effect in the twentieth century and, consequently, the large murals depicting various phases of campus life on the wall in Altgeld, the fountain in front of McMurry Hall, the Theodore Roosevelt Speech Marker, the magnolia and birch trees, the large gate at the Castle Drive entrance, the beautiful life-sized statuary that graced the front of the auditorium in the "Ad Building," and the Jacob Haish bust that rested so long upon the fireplace in the Haish Library have either been lost, stolen, or destroyed.

Other landmarks, however, have had more success in the struggle for survival: the bronze plate still marks the final resting place of the Indian trail marker tree; the mosaic great seal—never-to-be-stepped on—with the insignia N.I.S.N.S. gilded into its periphery, has been removed from the Castle but has been restored and placed on display in the library until a new home can be found for it; the Ellwood and Glidden portraits are in storage; the bas relief of John Williston Cook that hung above the fireplace in Williston Hall and the one of

Fred L. Charles that once was on the stairway wall in Altgeld are fortunately in safekeeping against the day when they too may again be mounted. The wooden bridge that spanned the lagoon to the island—the I-Love-You-Bridge—has been replaced with one of concrete, but the stately flag pole installed by the veterans, the victory bell tower donated by Alpha Phi Omega, and the Freshman Bench are still attractive and awaken memories of other years.

Northern was never enriched with myths of ghosts like some colleges (nearer to cemeteries!) but in the 1940s one disembodied soul did suddenly appear. It seems that certain editors of the student paper, Betty Brough Prall and Mavis Eakle Williams, desperately in need of some last-minute filler, stood pondering their plight before the window of the journalism office when suddenly their eyes fell upon, of all things, a tombstone—with the name "John McGovern"—in a heap near the old greenhouse, the gleaning no doubt of some earlier college pranksters after a Halloween foray.

This was all that was needed, and from this initial ghost story came many embellishments throughout the years—a kind of "Kilroy" spirit that received the praise or blame for various campus incidents. John has been blamed for many of the mishaps on the campus—fires, flooded dorms, failed science experiments, and even the appearance of a mouse at play practice. But as with all ghosts, he also had his good side:

the exuberant spirit at football games, the nitwatchman's lonely keeper, . . . the unknown force that pushes the ball over the final touchdown, and the guy that props your eyes open in late eighth-hour classes.

John, however, considers Freshmen his special protege's [sic]. He is custodian of Freshmen Bench. . . . He will inspire you when you write that final theme . . . and will give you the strength to endure your . . . ability test in Phy. Ed.

. . . If you listen closely and watch ever so carefully, maybe you too, will see the immortal John McGovern.[60]

When sufficient time has elapsed, and the Holmes period has become an integrated part of the University's history, it will probably be interpreted as a period fairly free of controversies and confrontations. There were problems, but even with the problems and personal conflicts caused by an educational revolution, it seems to have been a period relatively lacking in institutional tensions among faculty, students, Board members and townspeople. Especially this seems so when comparisons are made with Holmes's immediate predecessor and successor. If this judgment is correct, the explanation can probably be found in economic and cultural characteristics of this period—a period that afforded institutions of higher education such unbelievable support.

President Holmes made every effort to avoid controversies personally, for he had a genuine abhorrence of them. When he did face potentially more explosive problems, he was particularly gifted with a keen sense of timing so that he could deal with them before they got out of hand. These personal qualities would have hardly been expected of one so cautious and retiring as he and of one who rarely ever put anything controversial in writing; yet he usually had a sense of who his friends were, where the danger spots were, and what strategy to use when the time came for action. A prominent faculty member who had contact with Holmes through various committee assignments once remarked that as an administrator Holmes had the keenest sense of the jugular vein of anyone he had ever known.

Others no doubt would explain this relatively quiet era as the result of a society enjoying not only an enormous post-war bonanza of economic development and world leadership but also an educational revolution whose momentum continued almost without abatement before finally peaking soon after the close of his administration. But this educational revolution was more than an expansion of numbers. It was a national hysteria, a faith, a belief that all young people should go to college. In a sense, it was an extension of the same cultural force that drove young people into American high schools a few generations before.

This faith in education gave to the thousands of students who came annually to Northern's campus (as well as to their parents) a sense of security as reflected in the behavior patterns of the institution. This behavior conformed to the folkways and mores of the period and with few exceptions caused little trouble for the officials. The Calvinistic restrictions were still present and functioned as a controlling device on student behavior.

Notwithstanding this pattern, the educational system had one severe shock, and that was in a questioning of the quality of education and standards of teaching which came after the launching of the Russian Sputnik in 1957. The shock, however, was more academic in nature and did little to disturb the basic values that were to be more shaken later with the student revolution on the Berkeley campus.

True, there were always instances of individual misbehavior. Cheating on tests, stealing and damaging of library books, smoking and drinking, sexual misbehavior, rowdiness and poor manners at student affairs, destructiveness, and an occasional brush with the city police—are perennial problems on any campus. Nevertheless, a tight rein was held over the students for many years, and it is only in recent times that it has been relaxed to allow students greater democratic participation in disciplinary matters.

Holmes had a few disputes worth noting with his faculty. One was the Paul Street dispute brought about over Street's presidential speech to the Illinois Education Association in which he criticized the Teachers College Board rather severely for failing to finance the teachers colleges adequately. This reproval was so shocking to President Holmes that his first reaction, according to Street, was to suggest that Street "resign as Director of Regional Services, . . . [and] enter the ministry." Street also recorded in his notes that Holmes felt that the speech had created such a relationship between them that he was "no longer valuable as his public relations officer [and moreover]," he said, "if I do not resign, he will dismiss me from the . . . assignment." In the same exchange Holmes also criticized Street's supervision of the *Northern Illinois* by claiming that he "consistently allowed too much freedom . . . to criticize things about the school . . . [and the] news reports are not always 'positive'"—i.e., a recent news story saying we lost six games and won four, rather than *won* four and lost six." Street countered that the paper should have the same freedom as the commercial press and at all times should exercise "the plainest kind of honesty and should never used the 'stacked deck' propaganda technique in reporting to the public."

A few days following the above exchange Holmes appealed to the College Personnel Committee to sanction Street's removal from the regional services position; the committee refused to do so by a nearly unanimous vote. Nevertheless, Holmes did secure from Reavis and Watson, members of the Board committee for Northern, consent for Board action, thus giving Street the option of either accepting a professorship in the English department as a part-time teacher of journalism while directing the student paper or accepting a full-time teaching position. Either of these would have no doubt meant a decrease in pay, for only administrators (then and now) were assured of a twelve-month salary. This aroused the faculty, the alumni, and the Illinois Education Association; all filed protests with the Board. Holmes insisted that there was no violation of academic freedom, for in this case Street was merely being given another assignment, and a president surely had the right to choose his staff members as well as the areas they will serve.

On 19 July 1955, the controversy resolved itself. Street asked for a two-year leave of absence to serve as director of the N.E.A. Centennial celebration in Washington, D.C., at the termination of which he accepted a position at the University of Kentucky.[61]

If the above case was not a violation of academic freedom, the case of Helen R. Miller certainly has all the earmarks of such a violation, even though there was no attempt to prove it as such. Helen Miller was considered for a summer session and a one-year appointment (1953–1954) in the English department on the recommendations of her two friends, Charlotte Whittaker and Leonard Parson, both of whom knew of her work at Evanston Township High School. J. Hal Connor, head of the department, had had her as a teacher and was highly impressed by her work. In addition, she was well known nationally, having taught in many prominent places such as the Universities of Illinois and Michigan and at Northwestern University. She also had an M.A. from Radcliffe, and a list of publications.

The first evidence that something was wrong with this appointment came soon after school opened in the fall when Holmes was contacted by some prominent members of the Board for a hasty meeting after which Holmes approved the idea of having Clara Sperling, his secretary, audit Miller's freshman class during the afternoons.

Some effort was also made to inquire into Mrs. Miller's personal life and work, especially under her former principal in Evanston. The evidence appears to indicate that the Board had been informed she had been a member of an organization on the U.S. Attorney General's "subversive" list; one must remember, this was the hysterical period of McCarthyism. Miss Sperling's report at the end of the quarter had only compliments for Miller's teaching ability and some interesting insights considering the onerous duty she was performing:

During these weeks, nothing was said by Mrs. Miller that would have led me to believe that anything was out of line. I personally felt she was an excellent instructor. . . . She has a fine sense of humor and knows how to handle younger people . . . . Personally, my relations with Mrs. Miller were most pleasant . . . . She always had valuable suggestions to give . . . [and] can be an excellent conversationalist.

In general, these weeks were pleasant except that I was present in class under false colors which, of course, nobody knew but I often wondered if Mrs. Miller suspected anything peculiar? She had told me that she was afraid I would be "bored" but I assured her that I certainly needed "refreshing" in . . . grammar and literature. . . .

The argument used by Holmes to secure Miller's release from teaching was the real possibility of a decline in enrollment over what had been predicted; in a letter to her he mentioned that "because of the continued trouble in Korea" a drop in enrollment was expected for the winter and spring quarters, and because she was not certified to teach graduate work without a doctorate, the Board had taken action to terminate her temporary contract at the end of the fall quarter; but he added, "if you are able to obtain work before this date, we will release you." She surrendered her contract, but (after some misunderstandings and a few exchanges between Holmes and the national A.A.U.P. office and a legal firm in Chicago) she was paid her salary for the next two quarters.[62]

There was another case in which President Holmes might be criticized for attempting to use too much influence in determining departmental personnel. At one time, he actively tried to control the type of individual the social science department should employ to teach sociology. But when the department almost unanimously took a stand in opposition to his position and signed a statement to that effect, the matter was finally dropped and never arose again.[63]

If President Holmes's administration has the honor of fewer disquieting issues than those of some other Northern presidents, it should nonetheless be noted that he did have the most prolonged and far-reaching one in the history of the University. An enormous number of people were involved, and the effects are still felt today and will no doubt continue to be in the years to come. In his own words, (in an interview on 13 February 1970), Holmes considered the "Arboretum Controversy" his most difficult problem during his presidency.

The Montgomery Arboretum, as the area came to be known after its dedication by Holmes in 1957, had been a part of the community and college life for many years and was from time to time known as the woods, the park, the picnic grounds, and even the place where "Teddy" Roosevelt spoke. It had also been used for many years as a laboratory by the biology department to instruct elementary teachers in the natural history of the area since it was a perfect sanctuary for the nesting of birds and an ideal spot for bird watchers in the early morning hours or for those who preferred the enjoyment of wild flowers. From the earliest days of the school, this area afforded some of the richest experiences in nature: who could know the number of young couples who were first awakened to a youthful romance while leaning against the old bur oak, the shagbark hickory, or even the pillar that marked the Roosevelt speech? All of these were a part of the heritage of the institution and one can see what a contentious issue was created when Holmes recommended to the Board on 16 February 1959—only two years after its dedication as an arboretum—that part of the seven-acre plot be used as sites for the science and administration buildings.

In brief, Holmes's basic arguments were carried to the Faculty Advisory Council under the following points:

(1) The area now constitutes a fire hazard. He read from letters from Chief Luoma of the DeKalb Fire Department and from Mr. Lorusso of the N.I.U. staff . . . [to that effect]. (2) The new science and administration buildings should be located in the central area . . . near the present science building. To purchase new land for their location would result in great expenditure and considerable delay in building. There is no suitable location, except Montgomery Arboretum, for the two buildings. . . . For example, the open area along Castle Drive is not . . . because the sanitary sewers there would have to be relocated at an expense of approximately $30,000. (3) Other areas on . . . campus and on the Lorado Taft Campus will provide facilities now provided by Montgomery Arboretum. (4) The wooded area was not originally planned as an arboretum . . . [but rather as a site for a] president's home. . . . (5) Plans for the location of . . . [these buildings] were made known at the time of the Governor's visit in December. (6) The name "Montgomery Arboretum" will still apply to the area along the lake and stream.[64]

To support these reasons he relied upon his staff for their complete loyalty. Charles Howell from the Research Bureau responded with maps, charts, leaflets, and a bulletin called "Yes Or No To Science In The Woods"; and F. R. Geigle on one occasion used his expertise as a bird watcher to try to assuage the indignation of such a prominent alumna as Eleanor Parson Zulauf.

Those in opposition to this action of the president and the Board consisted of the high and the low, the official and the unofficial. They fought not only by writing letters, taking pictures and drawing maps, but also by circulating petitions that were certain to be published in the DeKalb, Rockford, or Chicago newspapers, all of which gave ample space to the struggle to save the woods. Some were blunt and direct; others were more gentle in manner. Some appealed to Holmes's long experience in teaching outdoor geography classes and his contributions in developing the Lorado Taft Field Campus which had become the apple of his eye. W. W. Wirtz, former Board chairman and a close friend, finally intervened; but with his experience as a Board member and knowing first hand of the problems of this administration, he tactfully said: "I . . . cannot evaluate all the facets of this problem and for that reason will only express the hope that the board will at least reconsider and search even more deeply to see if some plan cannot be designed to 'spare that tree.' " [65]

Opposition also came from the three University faculty divisions, who passed resolutions requesting the authorities to reconsider their action. The Faculty Advisory Council took the same action when the president sought their advice. The Student Senate and a number of student organizations as well as the Alumni Association went on record in favor of saving the woods for its intrinsic value, which could not be measured in monetary terms. Signs were also posted in nearby yards and along the highways, and even a couplet from Robert Frost's "Stopping by Woods On A Snowy Evening" was effectively used to attract the attention of passersby:

The woods are lovely, dark and deep.
But I have promises to keep . . . (signed) Holmes

Another verse with a more direct and sharper barb was aimed squarely at the President:

As an alternate suggestion
Concerning trees or domes
Let's keep the arboretum
And do away with Holmes.

1960 Homecoming Parade

The spearhead of the statewide protest was the "DeKalb Committee for Saving the Montgomery Arboretum," which included doctors, lawyers, city officials, and even relatives of the original donor of the woods, Joseph Glidden. A great deal of effort was also expended by two biology professors, Jack Bennett and Robert Bullington, who furnished scientific expertise to help counteract the arguments denigrating the natural advantages of the Arboretum as well as statements about the fire hazard it presented and who pointed out the availability of other sites for the two buildings. Every argument was analyzed even to the amount of hose available for the fire department if water had to be pumped from the campus lake.

So great was the protest against the use of the Arboretum that at the meeting of the Board on 18 May 1959, they felt it necessary to rescind their earlier action of 16 March and instead recommended that the Arboretum area be preserved and that the administration should look elsewhere for other sites. This they did within the immediate area and the science building (Faraday Hall) was built by redirecting the utility pipes only a few rods north of the Arboretum; the administration building (Lowden Hall) was constructed about the same distance south of Altgeld Hall.

By 1965, the time had come to find sites for needed life science and mathematics-psychology buildings. President Holmes, with the recommendation of a Chicago architectural firm, again asked the Board that the Arboretum be used; they consented without hesitation. The lull of the previous five years was broken and the "Committee for the Preservation of the Montgomery Arboretum" was reactivated, calling for more funds and suggesting that all those "who love beauty" immediately send their protests to the Board as well as to Governor Kerner. However, these friends soon discovered that conditions now were not so favorable as in the earlier uprising. Homer Hall (an alumnus and retired faculty member), one of the leaders in this fight and a person who never slept when the welfare of the college was at stake, again came to the rescue, but he too noticed that there was a rather hopeless feeling. The *DeKalb Chronicle*, which had done such noble service in 1959, did not help the cause when it changed its position and

Library stacks preventing passage through the east end second floor corridor of the Administration Building (Altgeld Hall) in the late Forties

expressed willingness to use a part of the Arboretum; this, the editor said, was done in order to save the state of Illinois the cost of an additional land purchase.

Harvey Feyerherm, who had only recently been appointed head of the biology department, having failed with his suggestion of Glidden Field as the site for the life sciences building, now finally agreed reluctantly to support use of the woods for the following reasons:

I believe that Northern must have facilities that do not now exist in order to keep up with developments in biology. The sacrifice, if that is what someone may wish to call it, of a portion of that in order that we may move ahead in biology is surely not great. It is unthinkable that the future of biology depends upon an "untouched" woods. If given a choice between woods and building and less woods with building, there is no doubt in my mind how we should decide the issue. WE NEED THE BUILDING.[66]

Feyerherm also related other reasons for his decision; since there were only one or two individuals in his department who were interested in the woods as a teaching or research laboratory and since also the number of nature education classes (no longer required of elementary education majors) had decreased by 1966, he felt that the need for the Arboretum was much less than previously. Moreover, he described his department as rapidly becoming less interested in the natural history aspects of biology; newer members were more specialized and research-minded, not in flora and fauna but rather in fields more related to physics and chemistry, which required highly developed equipment and laboratories. Those, he noted, still interested in "plants and birds" were the few concerned with the instruction of elementary teachers.

Support was also secured by Holmes when the two daughters of Charles Montgomery, Ellen and Jean, wired the president thanking him for honoring their father by giving his name to one of the proposed buildings. However, they asked that as many of the trees be saved as possible.

Students receiving diplomas at Lagoon commencement, 1957

But there was still a good deal of fire left in the counter movement; letters appeared in the area newspapers and were also sent to the Board members and the governor's office by students, townspeople, and faculty organizations. The metropolitan papers also showed an interest and sent reporters. The action committee was able to secure meetings with the governor in Springfield as well as with the Board, after which a month's reprieve was granted by the latter to allow a subcommittee of three Board members—Morton Hollingsworth, Richard J. Nelson, and W. I. Taylor (chairman)—to visit DeKalb and meet with the "Friends of the Charles Montgomery Arboretum" and Kurt Biss, a town doctor, its spokesman. They spent one day on campus after which they recommended to the Board that it "reaffirm its decision to locate these buildings in the area approved. . . ." This recommendation was passed unanimously, although three members were absent, one of whom was Richard Nelson, who "had asked to be shown as supporting the resolution." [67]

Hardly had the action been taken than the president gave his orders to move into the Arboretum and clean it up; as for the Roosevelt speech marker, he gave specific orders to have it removed. It was one of the smaller gate-posts remaining from the large beautiful iron gates at the south entrance, and it shared the same fate as the bulldozed trees but not without some complaint.[68]

In the late fall of 1967, ground-breaking for Montgomery Hall took place, and its construction moved along without incident; many of the older trees were in the way and had to be leveled, and the hope that they would be considered more important than a parking lot was soon vanquished by those with a heady desire for such accommodations. After three years, this beautiful structure, which cost more than three million dollars, was finally dedicated, and today it houses, along with biological sciences, the school of nursing.

The mathematics-psychology building was much slower in developing. Delays in plans as well as a budgetary freeze by Governor Ogilvie postponed the ground-breaking exercise until early 1971, when the campus was experiencing the final phase of its student protest movement. Some protesters tried to

Faraday Hall Groundbreaking—May 1962

President Holmes, Senator Dennis Collins, Z. H. Dorland (V. P., Business Affairs), Harold Feeny (Head, Physics Dept.), Michael Jocich (Head, Chemistry Dept.), F. R. Geigle, R. G. Whitesel (Assoc. Dean, Liberal Arts)

halt the bulldozers and chain saws by physical intervention, and twelve students were arrested for climbing the trees or chaining themselves to logs and refusing to heed the repeated warnings to leave the area. The *Chicago Tribune* came to their rescue and ran a front-page editorial branding the removal of the trees as "an outrageous destruction of an irreplaceable asset—and unnecessary with a university situated on the edge of a corn-field." They also offered to pay the fine of one of the students as well as solicit aid for any others arrested during the protest. President Rhoten Smith, in a sympathetic gesture, stated that the cause of the "Arboretum 12" was a good one, and through him the University expressed informally the hope that they would not be penalized. He also stated (in a television interview for a station in Chicago, on 27 March 1971), that if he himself had had the original decision to make (in 1965) he would have done everything possible to find another location. Neverthe-less, he was convinced that it was necessary at this late date to occupy the site since it was the only one adjacent to the other science buildings and that any further delay in construction would only increase the cost.

Since the last faint hope for the woods had disappeared and the students had so gallantly made their last stand, the Board of Regents decided to make a serious effort to replace the tract with another grove of trees or a park that could be developed over the years by the students. To carry this out, plans were developed for the Northern Illinois University Ecological Park. The first "plant-in" was held at dawn on Arbor Day, 1971, with such dignitaries as Clayton Kirkpatrick, editor of the *Chicago Tribune,* present for the ceremony, in which 1,200 trees were planted. This section of the northwestern corner of the campus has had subsequent plantings, whenever money was available, and is today fast becoming a spot where animals (including humans) and plants alike may coexist.

On 6 September 1966, at the opening faculty meeting, President Holmes surprised many people when he announced that it was his intention to retire as president of Northern on 31

Lowden Hall Groundbreaking—August 1963
President Holmes, Z. H. Dorland (V. P., Business Affairs),
Arthur Muns (Asst. to President), F. R. Geigle, John Koach
(Alderman), J. Clayton Pooler (Mayor), Tom Cliffe (Alderman),
Senator Dennis J. Collins

August 1967, even though he would still have one more year before reaching the compulsory retirement age. This was a most timely moment for this action, for the American campuses were still quite peaceful except at a few major universities. For President Holmes, this exit from the campus was hardly different from his arrival in 1949. Both were equally well timed. On 31 May, at the Faculty Retirement Dinner, President Holmes gave his farewell address, "Looking Ahead," before a large gathering of his friends. In his speech, he pointed out many of the still unsolved problems at Northern as well as its future role as a multi-purpose university.

For Holmes, the thought of retirement presented no personal problem. For many years, with his wife Ethel, he had spent each vacation at their beautiful summer home on Butternut Lake in Wisconsin, where they entertained many of their friends and where they were able to enjoy themselves in natural surroundings, which were, after all, of primary interest to him as a geographer. Originally he had planned a return to teaching in a junior or private college near DeKalb while still retaining his residence there, but when a position was offered him in the geography department at Arizona State University, he accepted.

Three N.I.U. presidents meet: President Leslie A. Holmes, Board of Governors Chairman Richard J. Nelson, and President-designate Rhoten A. Smith in 1967

Singers at 1966 Madrigal Dinner in University Center Ballroom

9

Student Life and Interests

DURING its first seventy-five years, student activities at Northern followed the same pattern existing in other colleges and universities, even though it was a teacher-education institution for most of that time. In the beginning, these were few, but over the years they gradually increased in number, and they also changed in character with the changing times. Student bodies changed, and with the increase of male students in the 1920s, there was special emphasis on competitive sports. When social sororities and fraternities appeared in the 1940s, further adjustments were required. Moreover, wars and depressions altered student life, and the impact of these upon the philosophy, ideals, and values of the students left them, as President Adams observed, "in a state of flux." Then, in the early 1960s, appeared other major influences that suddenly flowed in upon the American campuses, leading writer Seymour Martin Lipset, a leading authority on student life, to characterize this phenomenon as *rebellion in the university.*

Who were the students? We know that many of them during the earlier decades came from farms, rural towns and villages located in the northern counties of Illinois, and few came from the larger cities. Their parents were from the middle or lower middle class, and for many years a high percentage of parents had less than a high-school education. This condition, however, changed considerably by 1960, when 45 percent of the students came from Cook County, and this figure increased each year thereafter. By 1970, a study revealed that at least 50 percent of the freshmen's fathers had had some college experience, and of this number nearly 23 percent were graduates or better. Another study of the freshmen's fathers at about the same time revealed that skilled labor was the leading occupation and commercial workers the second highest.

Since there are no empirical data for the earlier students, comparison of the intellectual ability of early students with those of later years is not possible; however, as admission policy became continuously more restrictive over the years, it is obvious that entering students have been of a higher quality academically. In 1971, the mean score of entering freshmen on the American College Test was 23.832 or near the level of 25 whereby a student can be admitted regardless of his high-school rank.[1]

Out-of-state students were always few in number, increasing from 13 in 1928 to 180 in 1961. Foreign students were even fewer, with only 127 in 1967 out of a total enrollment of 16,000. The foreign study program was also slow to develop, and it was not until 1956, through the efforts of Charles Howell, that the summer Oxford Seminar was finally initiated with nearly fifty students. Thereafter study abroad increased until today there are many students and some faculty members attending and teaching in various foreign university centers under the direction of Daniel Wit.

Racially, the student body was for many years white with only a few Black students coming from the neighboring cities, especially from Chicago. This is in contrast with today's representation of about twelve hundred Black students, twenty-five Black faculty members and administrators, as well as several minority programs such as Upward Bound, CHANCE, and the Black Studies program.[2]

Discrimination was an especially common experience for

the few early Black students. Some of them were compelled to live in Sycamore, where they were befriended by individuals such as William Day, a Black worker "who took them into his home, sponsoring them . . . [with] his own meager means and encouraging them by his own enthusiasm and faith in education."[3] Numerous confrontations by such organizations as the American Veterans Committee, the Inter-Racial Committee, and the American Civil Liberties Union were necessary before the local area was willing to recognize basic rights. The continued grievances of Black students today, however, are no doubt caused largely by the fact that they find themselves on a predominantly white campus in a wholly white community that has only recently accepted minorities as permanent residents.

Many students coming to Northern have found it necessary to earn all or part of their expenses. In 1938, it was found that nearly 20 percent of the males paid their entire cost; on the other hand, this same report listed over 33 percent whose parents financed the total burden, most of whom were probably girls, since campus jobs were fewer for them. These figures, however, do not reveal the whole picture; for some young men in this 20 percent group were forced to hold three to five different jobs in order to make both ends meet, and by so doing were probably compelled to sacrifice most of their extra-curricular activities.[4] Many of these students came to Northern because it was a low-cost institution; it was close to home, and many could return on weekends to work. A high percentage also received scholarship aid.

Religious tolerance was likewise a developing characteristic with the arrival of large numbers of Catholic and Jewish students from Chicago. This was evident, for example, when religious identification was finally eliminated from the registration records, thanks to Charles Howell's efforts. All major denominations developed programs for students which often included social activities and involvement in the civil-rights movement as well as worship services and theological discussions.

A gradual breakdown of older patterns of behavior was caused by what some critics like to believe was the development of permissiveness toward youth in both home and school, brought on by the "New Education." Whatever might be its basis, a counter-culture group did arise, thereby greatly increasing the discipline problems as the administrators continued to enforce the older rules and values upon those who were to be the teachers of tomorrow—rules that governed study habits, manner of dress, sleeping and dating hours, freedom of movement, and behavior—all for the reason that the conduct of future teachers was expected to be exemplary and in keeping with the established norms. Most of these rules were well known to all students, for they were listed in the annual "Handbooks." By the late 1950s, it was also becoming evident to the emerging subculture that many of these rules applied mostly to women, who were still unequally controlled by the age-old principle of *in loco parentis*.

Beginning in the 1950s, the dress habits of women on campus and in the classrooms and dining halls were an increasing problem for the deans, since certain forms of apparel such as bermuda shorts and slacks, heretofore worn "only for picnics and sports," were now beginning to appear not only on the campus but even on the downtown streets. Sunbathing also introduced the swimsuit to the campus, making its debut first on the more secluded lawns or roof-tops by those wishing to acquire an early suntan. This practice was not forbidden provided it was sufficiently secluded; however, the girls were admonished to be discreet and by no means to participate in coed sunbathing.

Williston Hall, the women's dormitory, served as the center of much of the campus social life for many years. Here the women students learned to live as a collective group under a set of rules created by the college and directed by two adult women. Two of the most prominent of the long list of its administrators over fifty years were Grace Nix and Donalda Morrison (dietician and nurse), who were well liked not only by the occupants but also by the whole faculty, who were their guests at never-to-be-forgotten Christmas parties. Miss Nix, who had an untimely death in 1941, has been remembered by her friends with a scholarship in her name. All other girls in the college either lived at home, commuted, or lived in approved private residences in the city, for Williston was the only

President Holmes with 1958 Christmas Queen and court

dormitory until the completion of Adams Hall in 1949. As a result, there were two main groups: the Dorm Girls and the much larger group of Town Girls.

Life in the Hall was for the vast majority a period of personal satisfaction and fulfillment, for it offered a microcosm of experiences that few forgot in their later years. For many years the students were required to be in their rooms by 7:30 P.M. on weeknights and 10:30 P.M. on weekends, with an extension of time for special occasions. By 1966, these hours had evolved to 11:00 P.M. Sunday through Thursday and 1:00 A.M. on Friday and Saturday.

Only occasionally was a girl dismissed from the Hall for misbehavior. Those who violated the smoking rules were often able to avoid detection by "stuffing a rug at the door sill." Smoking was the oldest and most persistent problem until the administration finally in the 1940s set aside smoking lounges in Williston and Altgeld as a replacement for "nicotine alley" and the parked cars. This only accentuated the problem, not only from the standpoint of enforcement of the rules, but also in maintaining some semblance of cleanliness and safety from fire. One student reporter noted that the "Sardine Lounge" in Altgeld was so congested that it took "a suit of armour and a pair of mastiffs to get through unscathed." By the time the tobacco problem was finally settled by establishing a more or less laissez faire policy, a new and more serious problem of marijuana began to raise its ugly head.[5]

As the college moved into the university stage and enrollments rose to unprecedented numbers, student infractions increased both individually and collectively. Theft of various articles became a problem, especially from rooms and lockers. In one year, over eight thousand pieces of silverware were taken from the various dormitories and eating places on campus; in downtown DeKalb, according to the chief of police, "shoplifters are a major problem in all business places . . . and the number of N.I.U. students arrested for theft each year . . . is high."[6] The library seemed to be the greatest target, and no matter what precautions were taken, means were generally found to circumvent them even after all exits were blocked and guards were placed at the main entrance.

1959 Winter Carnival Queen and court pose during coronation dance

Along with stealing, arose the problem of cheating on examinations or of filching them before they could be given, practices indigenous to most American campuses, especially in recent years when standards have been raised. At times this academic disease was so serious that it provoked various student editorials. But this was not a new problem. The Student Affairs Committee and even President Adams and his Administrative Council had devoted discussions to its solution, but to no avail, even in an institution where students were primarily learning the art of teaching.

School spirit was a part of the college life that underwent modification, especially in the 1960s and 1970s, when the students no longer demonstrated the same enthusiasm for "Old Siwash" with its yells, songs, colors, traditions, and fraternities (or even its alumni organization). However, they were still interested in their "thing," as they called it, which in the 1970s appears to include an increased awareness of public and personal responsibilities. On the American campus there is today a much greater involvement in student government and in such problems as equality of the sexes, campus security, discrimination, ecology, faculty selection and evaluation, as well as larger national and international issues. One would like to believe that this is a result of a higher quality of instruction and more sophisticated administrative leadership. In most universities, Northern included, the membership on many major committees, councils, and boards—which were until recently considered by administrators and faculty their private domain—includes a good representation of students.

The social activities of Northern students began to undergo a gradual transition following the Cook presidency, a transition characterized by a more relaxed atmosphere in which students began to guide their own affairs. Gradually, with fewer restrictions, there emerged not only new organizations but also proliferations in such areas as dramatics, forensics, music, honorary and social fraternities and sororities, athletics, and dances, as well as many special activities, picnics, parties, exhibits, and class events. For all of these activities, an open meeting date had to be found on the official social calendar that finally had to be instituted in the dean's office. When J. Stanley Brown became president in 1919, there were only seven organizations; when Adams arrived ten years later, the number had grown to twenty; and when Holmes took office after Adams's death there were forty-three organizations, which included national and local honorary societies, departmental clubs, religious groups, and social fraternities and sororities. With mounting enrollments and greater freedom for students, this trend has continued until in 1972 there were over two hundred organizations whose spectrum extends from the Gay Liberation Front to the Weightlifting Club.

Forensics was a good example of an expanding activity that at one time rivaled the athletic games in popularity. This occurred under the first professionally trained speech instructor, Gus Campbell, who arrived in 1928. Fortunately, he found a bevy of young men and women with excellent potential who helped him to mount a ten-year program that excelled in debate, oratory, and extemporaneous speaking. He also developed a discussion contest, named in memory of one of his outstanding students, George O. Strawn, along with a Forensic Club, Speakers Bureau, and a chapter of Pi Kappa Delta. His most prominent student was Willard Wirtz, who later became Secretary of Labor under President Kennedy. Several letters from students vividly described their coach with a kind of "rosy glow." Dorothy Youngblood stated that he was "the one person who had more influence on my life than any other teacher." J. Hal Connor, a colleague of Campbell, was also instrumental in contributing to the development of speech activities. He often coached students in various contests and directed and wrote drama productions.

Forensics continued to flourish under the able coaching of Paul Crawford, who previously had had a promising career with high-school championship teams. Two of his most gifted students at Northern, Margarete Baum and James Skipper, won national honors, and many others also excelled in debate and oratorical contest at the state and national levels. But his interests were wider than debate, for along with his colleagues he expanded the program to include parliamentary debate, after-dinner speaking, rhetorical criticism, and interpretative reading. In 1947, the first Jack Sellke Memorial Oratorical Contest was held with a $100 prize donated by the Rotary Club in Freeport. The program is still expanding under Crawford's successors, and in 1969 the University had the honor of hosting the National Debate Tournament formerly held at West Point.[7]

Musical offerings for many years were given by such organizations as the band, orchestra, choir, and men's and women's glee clubs. Orchesis, an interpretative dance group, presented an annual program in which participants "composed the dances, selected and arranged the music, designed and made the costumes, and planned the backgrounds and lighting." Professor Charles Fouser was the leading musician of a small department, a distinction mainly based on his many compositions and his numerous piano recitals. Neil Annas for many years directed the Treble Clef and the annual performance of the Messiah, and Professor Birchard Coar was director of the orchestra and the band.

Before the University gained some of its present reputation, it was difficult to assemble a first-rate musical organization, for most students were not from homes and schools where musical opportunities were afforded, and few, if any, scholarships were available. Moreover, those few who did choose such training were primarily interested in becoming teachers in the public schools, not performing musicians. In recent years, however, this has changed, and the University with its highly developed musical faculty and richer curriculum is now able to recruit more gifted students in greater numbers.

Besides the major organizations, there are a number of activities in which almost any musical interest can be satisfied, such as operas and operettas, string quartets, madrigal singers, orchestras, choruses, and ensembles. The music faculty includes a high percentage of performing artists who throughout the academic year offer many programs for the public. Perhaps the most noted musical group on campus is the Vermeer Quartet, which has a high national reputation. The Artist Series, which began when the student assembly was finally

Coach Carl Appell with 1949 I.I.A.C. championship track team

phased out in 1951, now presents a variety of programs of high quality, ranging from the Chicago Symphony Orchestra to Russian dance companies as well as famous individuals in many fields. Concerts sponsored by the University Center Board during the 1960s included such popular folksinging groups as the Limelighters, Smothers Brothers, and New Christy Minstrels—at a cost ranging from $3 to $5 per student.

There were many kinds of dances over the years, those at which jeans were worn and records played, square dances as a group, hobo dances with prizes, street dances, and those of the Sadie Hawkins Day variety sponsored each year by the Town Girls. The most popular dances varied with the period: from time to time there was the jitterbug, swing, bebop, and variations thereof. The Herbie and Dee Palmer Orchestra, a favored DeKalb group for many years, was usually paid around four to five dollars per player, but better known orchestras were paid up to $500 or $600 per night. Then there were the big-name bands engaged for the annual formals; such names as Art Kassel, Dick Jurgens, Ted Weems, Frankie Masters, and Griff Williams—all at large fees of $2,000 or more per evening— were scheduled at one time or another. The popularity of formal dances appeared to be losing favor by the late sixties, and as a substitute there were the small rock groups that gathered in dining halls, parking lots, verandas, or any open spot where it was possible to congregate in bare feet with patched blue jeans and workshirts just to listen. Steppenwolf, The Beach Boys, and Santana are examples of the best rock groups that drew capacity crowds in the Field House in the early 1970s.

The traditional senior class banquet and dance, which for years were held in some famous hotel or country club, and the practice of demonstrating gratitude to the alma mater by giving some form of class memorial or donation typify the kind of structured activities that were eventually terminated. Students with freer and less formal life styles preferred to gather in small groups with no distinction between sexes, meeting in apartment houses and rooms for parties with each paying for the beer, wine, or pot, depending on personal preferences.

Out of the growing number of student activities, two or three were rather unusual and very popular for many years. In

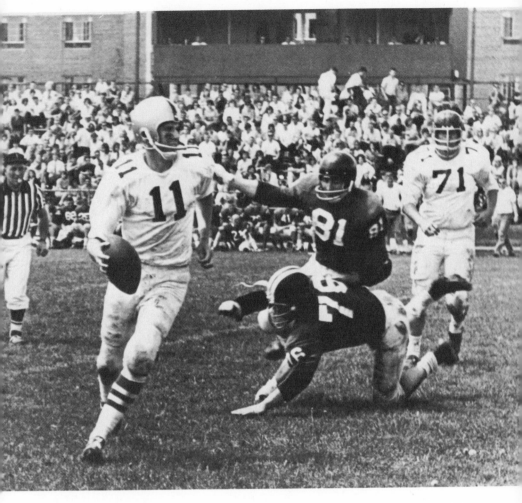

George Bork, quarterback of Northern's 1963 number–one rated college division team, in action at Glidden Field

January or February, when enthusiasm tended to be low, came the Winter Carnival with students from many organizations performing their skating feats or making snow sculptures. Other familiar events featured during this week-end were the crowning of the queen at the big dance, a floor show, and a Mardi Gras with booths for raising funds for worthy causes. In the 1958 carnival, one interesting sight was that of Dean Ruth Haddock's taking a "mean swing at a wrecked car" with a large maul.[8]

Stunt Night was a spring extravaganza first held in 1926, sponsored by Town Girls. It soon became so popular that multiple performances were necessary. Usually a number of organizations, including the faculty, used their talents to present some form of dance, revue, skit, pantomime, or melodrama. In 1931, twenty faculty members won second prize with their "Mother Goose" carnival, with President Adams taking the part of Little Boy Blue. A man of his rotund physique dressed in knee britches was a sight that was long remembered.

The idea of celebrating May Day was adopted early in the history of the college, first with a May Pole dance and later with a May Fete accompanied by various games, tugs-of-war, and other forms of contests, closing with an evening dance. It was held on the lagoon lawn and later on the island in the lake with the accompanying musicians nestled in the adjacent wood. Orchestras often assisted in dramatizing the story in dances, Treble Clef supplied background music, and on occasions the Training School children acted the roles of pipers.

The crowning of the queen and her accompanying king was added to the tradition, and the entire event was placed in the hands of the women's physical education classes under the able direction of Eva McKee, who for years performed the laborious task of producing the entire fete.

Gradually other events were added to the island acts and the royalty pageant: sorority and fraternity pajama races, bicycle and canoe races, street dances, tugs-of-war, picnics, and concerts were fused into the tradition. Today the May Fete has become rock concerts, lagoon festivals, and carnivals which seem to offer greater satisfaction to the present generation.

The best record in Northern's basketball history—21 wins and 4 defeats—was compiled by this 1971-72 team.

An example indicative of newer trends among students was the development of a "Humanities Week" program in 1972. A sum of $40,000 was raised by the Student Association and various campus organizations to have a whole week devoted to the process of humanizing the University community by pooling its many resources and by having speakers, concerts, dances, films, and in-depth discussions in the form of workshops.

Clubs were similar to the social activities: many were organized but few survived. In fact, at times there were so many clubs that to secure new members they had to "litter the halls" with placards and carry on marches as advertising techniques. One of these early clubs was the Varsity Club, organized in 1922 by Paul Harrison and Edward Shackley for the purpose of bringing better athletes to the campus, of maintaining closer contact with the alumni, and also for encouraging athletes present at the college. In this way, the organizers thought it "possible to establish a true and live college spirit."[9]

The Varsity Club grew rapidly as the sports program increased; in time it also promoted social activities and a formal dance. Another of its special activities was sponsorship during halftime at football games of the Greased Pig Contest. Former lettermen became the initial group called upon for contributions when the grant-in-aid program was begun. To encourage them in the art of raising funds and to give them confidence that their money was a good investment in athletic scholarships, George "Chick" Evans was quite adept at extolling the virtues and values of his athletic program. He stated on one occasion: "Our type of athletic competition fosters determination, poise, self-confidence, and team spirit, which are all vital to leadership. The grant-in-aid program helps fan the spark of leadership into flame, regardless of the students' financial circumstances." In 1969, the club was reorganized as the Alumni Varsity Club.

Another organization similar to the Varsity Club was the Women's Athletic Association: it differed mainly in that it lacked the finances or the intercollegiate competitive program that the men had. It was formed two years earlier than the Varsity Club for the purpose of fostering "good sportsmanship, scholarship, and physical efficiency, by creating an interest in gymnastics and athletics." All women were eligible if they could earn the required points in any one sport during a semester while also maintaining a C average or above. Through this association a large number of girls were introduced to sports and could freely participate on a regular basis. Over the years the Association also co-sponsored the cheerleading squad and staged an annual "Vod-Vil" of several variety acts which they claimed were "twin sisters to the Follies." In 1957, the W.A.A. was reorganized into the Women's Recreational Association, which sponsors both intramural and intercollegiate sports.

The Town Girls began as early as 1915 and continued until recently as a club to promote a sense of unity and "group development and accomplishment" for all those who lived off campus. It was the largest organization for many years, since, with only one campus dormitory, at least two-thirds of the girls in college were eligible. Their activities varied from the annual Stunt Night and formal dance to the Mother's Day program, special lectures, plays, and just plain fun, frolic, and free ice-cream socials.

A mysterious club—certainly one about which there is little information—was one exclusively reserved for male faculty and students, called "The Black Cat Club." It was created in the 1920s for the sole purpose of permitting men "to get away from the precise and the academic to create a little enjoyment for the few male students whose number they wished to increase." Meetings were "informal—no officers, no dues, not anything but good fellowship and animated congeniality." According to the best recollections by one of its contemporaries, the Black Cats completely expired after two meetings, which is probably somewhat understandable when one considers that part of the last program consisted of none other than the inimitable "Doc" Hayes giving a series of readings![10]

For a number of years, efforts were made to find space on the campus for the men similar to the lounge room used by the Y.W.C.A. members. Men students visiting other institutions often returned with glowing accounts of such rooms, but space was at a premium in the "Castle," and it was not until male students increased sufficiently that something was finally done to keep them from concentrating "during their free hours . . . in groups at stairways, lockers" or scattering all over the auditorium.

Soon after Illinois State Normal was able to set aside some rooms and provide some facilities, action was also begun at Northern. The Cavaliers (men's honorary) in 1939 proposed the establishment of a "men's union" to "bring about a closer bond of fellowship among the men students" and to give them a "better chance to really know one another." Moreover, the "union would be a powerful force in the breaking up of cliques, . . ." would offer "a constructive program of intra-collegiate activities . . . and would carry much weight in the securing of democratic privileges for every man on campus." This group, working with the President's Club, drew up a tentative plan which by 1940 finally cleared all the official hurdles.

A rather enthusiastic program was conceived by this infant organization, such as intramural contests in every outside activity including writing, music, and art; banquets, dances, and monthly get-togethers—all with the smallest amount of faculty supervision possible. This union was to be financed by assessing each male student a twenty-five cent fee. Burns Young, a highly capable and respected student (and today a successful dean), was the first president, and under his leadership the organization got off to a good start.

Unfortunately the Men's Union was born at the beginning of the war, and consequently social activities soon gave way to defense efforts; as a result, discontent set in over the lack of programs, games, and picnics, as well as the fact that they had no special room in which to meet. Some men students were beginning to worry about the draft and others were enlisting in the different services. Discussion arose as to whether or not the Union should be abolished. Dean Annas made every effort to hold it together and called a meeting at his home, but its numbers grew smaller and smaller. After the war, however, it was restored, and for several years it carried on regular programs centering around sports, films, and dances until 1957, when it finally expired and its remaining resources were turned over to the "Men's Loan Fund."

At about the same time that the Men's Union was organizing, women students organized the Women's League and developed a program for the opening of school in 1942. One of their main functions was the sponsoring of "Women's Week" with each of the various women's clubs having different duties to perform. They would take over campus functions, relieve faculty members in classrooms, speak in assemblies and faculty meetings, sponsor teas, and write letters to men in the service. They also acted as hostesses for speakers, operated a dating bureau, served Saturday morning breakfasts, and had a play-day for everyone.

As the years went by, this organization also seemed to lose some of its original enthusiasm; as its functions eventually became limited to such activities as teas, dances, and parties, it finally changed its name to Associated Women Students. Today it sponsors Mom's Day, the Bridal Fair, the Big-Little Sis program, and the Christmas Formal.

These organizations for men and women satisfied to a certain extent various expectations of college life, but for years there was still a definite need for some kind of building or suite of rooms that students could call their own. Only a small segment of the college men had such a place, namely the Alpha Phi Omega and the Varsity Club rooms; these privileges obviously caused considerable resentment, for both of these male organizations had restricted membership and represented only about one-fourth of the men students.[11]

While student sentiment was forming for some kind of center, there was also a plan forming in the mind of a young man by the name of Jim Lundberg, who planned and built on the river bank across the bridge "a handy and pleasant eating establishment." The College Tea Room, popularly known as "Jimmie's," opened in 1940 and was immediately taken over by the students as the place in which to stop on the way from town, after skating, to relax after work, or just have a Coke. When the end of the war brought a large influx of students, the college purchased the building and enlarged it into a student union where dancing and other activities were possible.

The "Tea Room," as they continued to call it, grew smaller and smaller in proportion to the growing numbers of students

—a 136 percent increase between 1953 and 1956—increases that made it almost impossible for a student to enter during a meal time or coffee break. The demand for recreational space became such a problem that a steering committee finally began to plan for a university center that could accommodate an enrollment of at least 10,000. The role of the University Center was to be a comprehensive one, as its title indicates: it was to be a center for the "community life of the college," a "hearthstone," as President Holmes wished it to be, and a "unifying force" that would hold the University together as it grew larger. For its many services, the University Center Board was created to administer the many programs that supply the increasing cultural, social, and aesthetic needs of the University family. By the fall of 1962, it was ready to open, and with its opening brought about a new way of life for the whole University. A few years later its size was doubled, and a 15-story tower was added, making it the main landmark of the campus. On the top floor, its Skyroom affords a magnificent, panoramic view of the University and its environs.

Regardless of the purpose of this worthy enterprise, it nevertheless provoked some complaints by townspeople and some faculty members for its "swank Pheasant Room," "plush faculty lounge," the president's "penthouse suite," as well as the guest rooms for dignitaries. Most of these feelings were generated from the fear of looming competition that arose in the minds of proprietors of the city bookstores, restaurants, haberdasheries, and others on the main street; others saw this sudden affluence on the campus as another spending spree with their tax dollars, even though it was paid for with student fees.

A campus bookstore was for some time one of the most controversial issues, with the students trying again and again to secure from a reluctant Board a cooperative or nonprofit establishment of their own. Finally the Board permitted the inclusion of a bookstore (as well as other profit-making enterprises) in the bond-financed University Center. In spite of objections by local merchants to the sale of items not directly related to the educational program, the bookstore was allowed to sell some competing items such as jackets, ashtrays, and mugs, provided the N.I.U. monogram was placed on them.[12]

Service fraternities first arrived in 1928 with Alpha Phi Omega, and its challenging programs and leadership soon made a mark on the campus that is felt even today. It required previous membership in a scouting troop or experience as a scout official and a good scholastic record before a student was eligible, and it soon became a large and well-functioning organization. One of its attractions was a spacious first-floor room set aside for its headquarters, in which was installed the only Coke machine and candy concession on campus at the time. Until 1943, APO members were given exclusive use of this room, and other students had access only to buy refreshments.[13] For many years this fraternity sponsored the Friday night Homecoming dance and the profits were used for a scholarship. An excellent example of its service to the University was during the bond issue promotion in 1960, when, to advertise to the general public the urgency of supporting the proposals, twenty-seven of its members joined marathon runners from other Illinois universities in carrying a torch to Chicago on the last leg of a 1700-mile run through the state.

Another popular activity was the Ugliest-Man-On-Campus contest held under the auspices of Alpha Phi Omega in order to raise money for worthy causes. To illustrate changing attitudes of what constitutes a worthy cause, in 1958 the fraternity decided to use the funds to mount the school's victory bell, whereas in 1972 the proceeds went toward defraying the expense of a "curriculum in ecology at NIU." In 1967, when Alpha Phi Omega held a bingo game, over $4,000 were raised.

Pleiades was an organization founded in 1937 as an honor society for senior women who ranked in the upper one-third of the junior class and had made an outstanding contribution to the college program. For years Pleiades promoted college loyalty, advanced a spirit of service, and created a warm fellowship among college women; this they did by sponsoring the Dames Dance, entertaining alumni on Homecoming Day, and raising funds for a scholarship. In 1971, Pleiades became a chapter of the national Mortar Board senior women's honor society.

Following the birth of Pleiades, the need for a similar organization was also felt by the senior men. To this end, ten men of the 1938 graduating class met and organized the Cavaliers with Dean Annas as advisor. To qualify as a member, each man had to demonstrate scholarship and show evidence of leadership ability and an interest and willingness to be of assistance in promoting worthwhile projects. For thirty-four years this organization maintained a fine reputation of service in many different areas of college life. As the *Norther* described it in 1942, it was "forever on the look-out for some needy cause which it may champion." In 1972, the Cavaliers made a decisive move, as had the Pleiades, and applied for national status by petitioning for membership in Omicron Delta Kappa. This application, under the experienced hand of Harold Aikins, the faculty advisor, was finally accepted by this most prestigious fraternity.

Other honor societies flourished over the years, and most departments eventually had at least one honorary. By 1972, there were twenty-three honorary societies on campus, with nearly twice that many departmental clubs and professional societies.

During the 1960s, on the initiative of four or five members led by Robert Hainds, preliminary moves were made to establish a chapter of Phi Beta Kappa. Upon Hainds's departure from the campus, other leaders—including Harold Aikins, Ralph Bowen, C. Norton Coe, and Patrick White—continued to work to eliminate objections to such a move. Some of these were derived from Northern's background as a teachers college which left many things to be desired: for example, there was no classics department, the library was poorly supplied with books and materials, and too few B.A. degrees had been issued in proportion to the large number of B.S. and B.S.Ed. degrees. Another serious barrier to the granting of a charter was the lack of funds available for scholarships in the liberal arts, although the University was permitting increased amounts to be spent for athletic scholarships. In time this small band of intellectuals was successful in securing unchartered status for an association of this renowned fraternity, and they were able to gather thirty-six interested members, sixteen of whom were from the faculty and twenty from outside the University.[14]

The Greek letter social fraternities and sororities were introduced mainly to provide smaller groups with a sense of personal identification in an increasingly complex college community and technological society. These organizations had their beginning under President Adams and his wife who were devoted members of Greek organizations during their own college days. Adams favored their recognition even though several members of his administrative council had some serious misgivings that they would bring a divisive influence into the college which would in time develop antagonisms between members and nonmembers.

The very first sorority was Sigma Chi Sigma which was formed around 1931 to promote "high scholarship, to uphold the ideals of true comradeship, and to achieve success through service." In 1944, they joined the national Sigma Sigma Sigma sorority, which for many years had chapters in first-rank teachers colleges.

A second group, organized in 1938 by girls interested in scouting, was called Sigma Delta Pi; Mrs. Adams and three faculty women were its advisors. In addition to assisting local girl scout troops, members sponsored an all-school typing bureau which filled a genuine need on campus. On 29 April 1944, with their thirty-five pledges, they were formally installed as the Alpha Omicron chapter of Delta Sigma Epsilon, becoming the first national social sorority on campus. (In 1956, Delta Sigma merged with Delta Zeta.)

After the appearance of Pi Kappa Sigma as a local sorority in 1945, a number of years elapsed before others arrived on the scene. Beginning with the 1950s, there was a rapid increase that reached a peak when seven new sororities and fraternities were organized in 1955 alone. In 1959, six more were organized; and by 1972, the University had a total of fifteen national and local sororities and twenty-two national and local fraternities listed in the annual catalog, only a few less than the University of Illinois.

These Greek organizations soon found it expedient to unite and form associations of presidents—the Panhellenic Council for women and the Inter-fraternity Council for men—whose functions were to serve as coordinators within each member group and to assist in developing common objectives. Considerable responsibilities were also delegated to each council to regulate and keep their own houses in order; that is, when violations occurred they were to step in and mediate problems between the students and the administration or the faculty. Specific problems were also to be handled by them in those areas connected with the rush system, initiations, leasing and buying houses, property damage, hazing, drinking, panty raids, and discriminatory practices.[15] Even with this form of democracy, the University still retained final jurisdiction and in some cases found it necessary to override decisions by cancelling a fraternity charter, dismissing members, and placing others on probation.

Besides these regular fraternities, the Flunkies Independent Organization was organized in 1952 as an intramural athletic team. In time it became a recognized social organization. Over the years, FIO was successful in winning all-school intramural tournaments in basketball and in winning the Alpha Phi Omega's all-school tug-of-war trophy during May Fete. The Flunkies also participated in "Showtime," an all-school variety affair, and sponsored the annual Miss Northern contest and dance. For their numerous trophies, a case was built and placed in McCabe's tavern in downtown DeKalb, where prizes were displayed for all to note their progress.

One of the requirements in the lives of all students for many years was attendance at general assembly programs. The first four presidents were responsible for arranging the programs, and each had his headaches in attempting to make them educational experiences, without creating certain disciplinary problems in connection with compulsory attendance. The ruling was that each student was permitted two absences per quarter, but the third one required justification or the student would be denied the privilege of registering the following quarter, unless he were pardoned by the president.[16]

The presidents, believing religiously that this aspect of college life must be retained, gave unstintingly of their time to secure not only educational but also entertaining programs. Every method was used and every novelty was sought to raise the interest level for the students. J.C. Brown not only used ingenuity and versatility in his own personal programs but he also adopted a plan of "true democracy" in having the students, through their organizations, participate to the extent of putting on their own programs. This same approach was continued by subsequent presidents, but it had its limitations in that the number of programs students could or would put on was few, thus leaving many others for outside talent.

For many years assembly attendance was required of both students and faculty, but at times it was quite spotty. When attendance was poor, it was embarrassing, especially when a prominent personage was on the program. Most speakers had two strikes against them before they started—for speakers were the most unpopular—and student reactions to them were often rude, discourteous, and "at times," as one reporter observed, "the din is so intense that the . . . speaker is scarcely audible." [17]

So great was dissatisfaction with the programs and the attendance requirement that in 1934 the number of meetings was reduced from twice a week to once, and students were given a greater voice in scheduling programs. Still the discontent and adverse comments continued until the fall of 1939 when enrollment exceeded the available number of seats in the auditorium, which held 1,008 students. Adams decided to require attendance at the assemblies only for freshmen and sophomores. This system was followed for a few years until it was was finally decided, with continually growing enrollments, that perhaps it was time to set aside the compulsory feature and make assembly optional for all students. The results were anything but pleasing to the president, who observed that at no time did attendance average more than 20 percent of the student body. Adams revived the old system and assigned each student an assembly seat for one of the two assembly periods each week, averring that he had always held "attendance at the college assembly as basic to the effective functioning of our college philosophy—self-direction through understanding."

When Holmes became president it was not long before the Student Affairs Committee informed him that the most sensitive area of dissatisfaction was the assembly and its programs.

401

In their amiable exchange of ideas they finally decided to do away with it on the grounds that the compulsory feature defeated its educational value.[18]

This at last brought an end to the "ancient, weekly attendance-required-or-out-you-go-ordeals" that students dreaded. In its place evolved the Artist Series which has a long and illustrious record of bringing high-level talent to the University community—talent that has included a list of great musical organizations and personalities from screen, stage, opera, music, science, literature, and politics, such as Henry Kissinger, Eleanor Roosevelt, and Van Cliburn.

The *Northern Illinois,* the principal student publication, began as a monthly magazine. In 1923, it was converted to a biweekly newspaper with changes in size and format as well as in purpose. This new format was to deal more satisfactorily with the up-to-the-minute news, activities of organizations, book reviews, sports, and matters of academic interest. Increased space was allotted to advertising, which in a short time made up at least half of the four-page paper. The paper was financed by advertising dollars and from the student activity fee, but it was necessary from time to time to restrict the number of issues in order to preserve solvency.

During Allan Wright and Russell Gage's period as faculty advisors in the 1920s, there was a gradual improvement in the paper's quality even though there was always a shortage of student writers, reporters, and finances. In an attempt to improve the quality of writing, Gage extolled the glamours of journalism by conducting weekly extra-curricular sessions in news-writing for those who wished to compete for staff positions. Quality was built into the paper, and this was shown by awards received from the Illinois College Press and the National Scholastic Press Association.[19]

In later years several feuds took place among spirited reporters; some good examples of these were the Guzzardo-Lorimer feud which gained such popularity that it inspired three other such journalistic battles—all flourishing at the same time: those between Riley and Lorimer, Countryman and Wiltsie, and Wiltsie and Rosenthal. The feuds created such interest that the feuders themselves claimed no partiality and were willing to take on all comers. These were the pre-war years—the Hitler period—that produced a large corps of provocative writers. In the 1941 and 1942 *Northern Illinois* there were three such columnists, Joseph Baylen, Oscar Matasar, and Don Riley, who produced, before leaving for active duty, some fifty discussions on the vital issues that were plaguing the American people—discussions on such topics as the fall of Britain, isolation, aid to China, Nazi brutality, the *blitzkrieg*, the Battle of Greece, and the draft, to mention only a few.

Other writers during the twenty-five years that Ruth Taylor and Paul Street served as advisors continued to bring awards to the paper. Muriel Mapes, Kenneth Bryson, John Wiley, and Shirley Ray—all wrote editorial essays of high quality. Over these years there were variety columns with such titles as "Larger and Better," "The Dust Rag," "The Northern Light," "The Critic's Corner," and "College Forum," to mention only a few. But of all the columns during the seventy-five year history of the paper the one that proved most popular was called "Griffins and Owls," inaugurated in 1925. It ran for over four years. The title was suggested "by some decorative figures and gargoyles which constituted a part of the architectural scheme of the main college building." It was a grab-bag of almost everything that flowed from the student pens and after it had proven its wide popularity, some of its clever and spicy features "of humor and beauty and love of romance—the spirit of the castle and tower" were published annually in a forty-page "Griff Book," edited by Stuart Engstrand (later a prominent novelist) until financial conditions forced it to discontinue.

The campus had, as did all such institutions, smaller publications outside the regular paper, but most of them died a-borning. One of the earliest was "The Rump Roast," a single sheet issued irregularly to convey student opinion on "whatever the writers think will be of value and interest to the school." Two years later a humorous sheet called the "T.C.

Annual Fibune: The World's Truest Newspaper" was created by three editors, Julien Peterson, Emily Cole, and Frances Papenhausen.

In 1939, the first volume of *Towers* was published; it was sponsored by Nu Iota Pi and Sigma Tau Delta, with Maude Uhland as the faculty adviser. There was a hiatus of nearly five years during the war when subscribers dropped from 1,000 to 394, making it necessary for *Towers* to be taken over by the student newspaper under the title *Budding Branches.*

With the growing increase in enrollment in 1947 and with Merle Weiherman as editor, *Towers* resumed publication and continued until 1964 as a single annual volume; however, in that year, with 200 contributors, it was necessary to begin publishing one each semester. By 1968, the circulation reached the 8,000 mark under the direction of E. Nelson James, who assumed this responsibility upon Uhland's retirement in 1956.[20] Four members of the English department have Sigma Tau Delta *Towers* awards named in their honor: J. Hal Connor (creative prose), Lucien Stryk (poetry), E. Ruth Taylor (critical writing), and Maude Uhland (freshman writing). The first three student award winners in 1965 were Patsy Kelley (Uhland award), Lavonne Mueller (Taylor award) and Mary Dale Stewart (Connor award).

By the 1950s, students were becoming rather dissatisfied with the name of the newspaper, for it was often confused with school and town establishments, and called for one that more closely resembled other college newspapers. The two names that were finally considered were *Northern State News* and *Northern Star*, and when the President's Panel decided on the latter; it became the official name in the fall of 1954. It had not only a new name but also a "new look" and a whole new larger format.

In 1961, with the arrival of Roy G. Campbell as the adviser, the *Star* began nearly a decade of steady growth and development. Campbell had had excellent training and experience on prominent dailies, and he introduced professionalism into every segment of the paper. Moreover, through the newly created journalism department under Donald Grubb, Campbell was able to secure trained reporters and columnists that brought in high awards and honors almost annually. Under Campbell's guidance, the *Star* was awarded seven Associated College Press All-American awards, and, in 1966, "Mr. C." was named "Outstanding College Newspaper Adviser" by the National Council of College Publication Advisers. In 1973, two years after Campbell's death, the Board of Regents re-named Kishwaukee Hall—home of the *Northern Star* and the campus radio stations—after him.

During the history of the paper, there were only a few occasions on which genuine controversies broke into the open in which presidents felt it necessary to interfere with what the students had published. This no doubt was because even though there were complaints of censorship by students, they did nevertheless know the limitations of their freedom to publish. Freedom in the earlier years pertained to such things as jokes, humorous remarks about the officials, and complaints about the food, too little time for recreation, library hours, dormitory hours, and too many rules and regulations, to mention but a few. Only twice did editors find it expedient to resign for reasons suspected of being connected with unpleasant restrictions.

However, student writers were introducing a new firmness and directness of style that gradually began to see results in problem-solving; and after the war, the veterans introduced to the campus a maturity and boldness that might be compared, only in a lesser degree, to the angry young student protesters of the late 1960s. The paper was finally becoming a vehicle in which the students could openly and freely discuss some issues of a controversial nature vital to their lives without fear of reprisals.

During the Adams administration, undercurrents of discontent began to appear over the rights of students to discuss problems of importance. When something was printed that he disliked, Adams's method was to call the "trembling" student into his office. Even though he was fair-minded, the student was scared to death, and it was, according to one who was called in, an experience that was long remembered.[21] In 1947, in reply to *Northern Illinois* adviser Paul Street's view that the "rights and privileges" of a college paper should be similar to those of the commercial press, Adams minced no words in stating his position that students should "understand clearly that their position on that paper is a position of responsibility. . . . The right to 'do as you please, to express any viewpoint' is a right that is subject to many responsibilities. . . . The interest of the college, the interests of teacher education, the interests of our American way of life are all which they, by virtue of their position, should feel obligated to support."[22] This was not the last president whose ideas on the role of the student newspaper differed from those of Paul Street.

In the years of the Holmes administration there were only minor skirmishes with the student press. In fact, an editorial in 1957 in reply to some criticism that censorship had been exercised in discussing the behavior of some coeds in a local tavern stated emphatically the opposite view: "There are no persons more independent than our columnists. They are in no way intimidated by administration, faculty, or the editorial board of the *Star*. They write what they want to write, and that is the way it will continue to be."

This view may have been somewhat idealistic, for suggestions did appear that more critical ideas should be expressed; however, it was true that student desire for greater freedom of the press was still so unformed that it seemed no great sacrifice on their part to stay within the boundaries imposed by the administration. There was give-and-take on some student reporting, but when it came to certain advertisements or four-letter words, Holmes found it quite impossible to compromise.

The *Northern Star* has experienced no opposition from Holmes's two successors so far as freedom of the press is concerned, and about the only controls are those of the student staff itself. The extremist writings of the right- or left-wing ideologists and the use of obscene or "four-letter" words are more likely to be seen in handbills or in such protest newspapers as *News From Nowhere* which was published from 1968 to 1971.

The second most important student publication was the school annual, or the *Norther*, which was issued the first year the college opened and has continued through the years to be one of the schools's best historical sources. The first twenty-one issues were published by the senior classes (two-year graduates), the next seven by the sophomore classes, the next four by a joint arrangement of sophomores and seniors and thereafter the staff was drawn from the entire student body. It was filled with literary efforts, jokes, pictures, affectionate accounts of those who taught, class activities, sports, and a calendar of annual events. It also featured individual faculty pictures; later, group photographs of departments were used.

For many years there was considerable anxiety in financing the *Norther*, since it was funded voluntarily by individual purchasers and as a rule a great number of subscribers would fail to sign up. Deficits at different times indicate a lack of student support. In 1929, the alarm was spread to all 701 students that there were only 460 signatures and that unless 140 more pledged their support—even if on the installment plan—there would be no yearbook. Nonetheless there was a yearbook—even though it failed by fifty-five subscribers—published on a limited-edition basis. The cost per student for many years was usually between $2 and $3. In 1934, to overcome this perennial task of securing subscribers, a new plan was set up whereby each student would get one book paid from his activity fee. In one year only was there no regular yearbook, and that was in 1918, when a small booklet was printed and the remaining funds were used to purchase an ambulance for the war effort.

In the late 1960s a growing dissatisfaction with the format of the *Norther* developed. The greatest change was its conversion in 1970–71 to a three-issue "yearbook in magazine format," for the purpose of "adding relevance, flexibility, and timeliness to tradition." The spring issue showed the greatest innovation, with such topics as "Gay Liberation," "Blacks," "Drugs," "The Radicals," "Anything For a Buck," and "Graffiti."

The college radio station had a slow development before finally becoming a reality. For several years it broadcast programs over the local WLBK station in DeKalb, which began in

1947. But a drive continued to secure for the college a station of its own, mainly on the basis of the public relations enthusiasm that swept the country in the 1940s. Finally, in 1954, WNIC–FM was licensed as an educational non-commercial station. In 1968, the call letters were changed to WNIU–FM. The station developed a full schedule with a large variety of programs that included the teaching of various courses and reports on activities of faculty and students; it also afforded many opportunities for students to gain broadcasting experiences in various fields. Opera and major symphony orchestras as well as recorded programs of national debates and lectures were made available to surrounding communities.

A student-operated radio station, WNIC–AM (later WNIU –AM) began broadcasting in 1957 with a signal that could be heard only in University residence halls. In 1972, the call letters were changed to WKDI, and an FM signal over a local cable was added to the AM dormitory service. This student-funded station presents popular music, news, and sports.

Commencement and baccalaureate programs followed a gradual tendency toward greater simplicity and less participation on the part of the students or presidents. During the Cook administration, commencement, especially, was an elaborate exercise, as has already been noted, and the baccalaureate was more or less a church service, generally held in the auditorium on Sundays, occasionally in the evening, with a local clergyman and music. In 1950, the senior class voted to eliminate the separate baccalaureate service.

Commencement speakers varied little and were generally not known for their scholarship or intellectual leadership; more often they were county superintendents, superintendents of public instruction, or normal-school presidents, with an occasional professor of education or of philosophy of education. Student involvement and interest continued to lessen, and perhaps their last genuine influence was in 1942 when they were finally successful in convincing Adams to have the exercises on the island in the lagoon. In the last few years even the compulsory rehearsal has been abolished, as has the president's reception for seniors and parents in the Home Management House gardens.

The exercises held on the island, hard by the Freshman Bench, if accompanied by good weather, would often draw audiences as large as six thousand people. A long winding line of faculty and students marched from the front entrance of Altgeld Hall down the walk to the island. It was a beautiful sight, but, during President Holmes's period at least, the president would invariably remark on what could be expected from the weather. The exercises were often a weary experience for the faculty (when they, too, were a captive audience), and they often tried to decide which gave more discomfort, the hot sun or the speakers. These were the years when every senior received some individual attention with his diploma and those getting the master's degree still more attention. But this ceremony, too, has undergone change: faculty members as a whole no longer were required to attend by 1959. The exercise in recent years has been held in the Stadium and student attendance is not required, for the diplomas are mailed directly to their homes.

The history of the Alumni Association began in 1900, when it was organized. For many years students met all trains, picked up and greeted the "old grads," who attended the business meetings, receptions, and especially the banquets. One new feature for 1919 was that five classes from preceding years were to be honored for the first time under the new reunion plan. At the banquets either the president or a faculty member generally presided with numerous toasts being given by the graduates; letters from absent class members were read, and there was a great deal of fun and laughter. At some of these meetings there was also a football game between the college team and the alumni. There also appeared, early in the 1920s, the Friday evening informal dance and a parade which assembled at the gate and was led by the Varsity Club followed by organizations, floats, and clowns. Then came the big game and the evening banquet. Thus arose the customs for Homecoming day which have continued through the years.

Change was inevitable, and the alumni programs over the years gradually shifted from the older ideas of the banquet as the center of attraction to that of a dance which was soon to become the culmination of Homecoming week. By the 1940s the banquet had been replaced by an alumni tea, an open house, or a buffet dinner. In 1938, an alumni panel was appointed to discuss the subject "Teachers of Tomorrow," and the comedy "New School for Wives," based on ultra modern notions of education, was staged. The influence of the approaching war was apparent in the Homecoming theme in 1940, a "Defense of the American Democratic Ideals." After the war, Homecoming returned to the patterns of the past; however, several new features appeared from time to time, such as the introduction of kings and queens in 1947 along with the accompanying coronation dance.

With President Holmes's arrival it was not long before these festivities were placed in the hands of the students with a faculty adviser. Many of the Homecomings during this period had dedications of buildings or ground-breaking exercises. For the 1960 Homecoming, the Alumni Association brought back from various parts of the country the "Collegiate Four," Dave MacKain, Cort Hulberg, Gene Anthony, and Jack Borden (1953 graduates who again thrilled the audience with their musical talents). In 1963, the popular Smothers Brothers packed the Ballroom to capacity; and in 1965, Williston Hall celebrated its golden anniversary, and the new Stadium was dedicated.

A second part of the Association's annual program was the spring alumni reunion held in the latter part of May, which at various times included a reception, business meeting, baseball game, May Fete, and a May Fete dance.

In 1926, the Alumni issued their first publication, the *Alumni Recall*, to all graduates, encouraging larger numbers to attend the spring meeting. This small magazine was issued once a year, at first in the spring, then, until 1939, exclusively in the fall, which indicated the growing importance of the Homecoming festival. Later publications to inform alumni about happenings at alma mater were the *Northern Alumnus* and *Rising Higher*.

At the spring meetings, most business affairs dealt with matters such as constitutional provisions, academic improvements, scholarships and loan funds for worthy students, reports from the presidents, and occasionally ceremonies such as the one in 1931, when the fireplace in Williston Hall was dedicated to John W. Cook. In later years it became the custom for class reunions to be held in June and the "Twenty Golden Years" group from the Cook period gathered at a special luncheon.

Later at spring meetings, the Association also presented annual awards. In 1967, it presented a Great American Award to Carl Sandburg, delivered to his home in Flat Rock, North Carolina, by an alumna. In addition, a small maple sapling was removed from Sandburg's sylvan retreat and replanted near the fountain of the "Alumni Court," which had been donated by the class of 1968. Other awards have also been presented at the alumni day banquets, such as the annual one to a distinguished alumnus, those for outstanding service, and the certificates of merit. President Holmes was honored upon his retirement by having a $2,500 annual graduate fellowship given in his name, and various scholarships honoring such individuals as Josephine Jandell and Paul Harrison have been established.

To handle the growing number of alumni (two thousand in 1921), it was necessary to engage a registrar to keep records, to trace the hundreds of addresses that were apparently lost, and to handle the increasing number of business transactions. For this position Josephine Jandell, college librarian, was selected, and for nine years she gave unstintingly of her time and energy. After she left there was a vacancy for a few years before Laura Tindall assumed the task of bringing the files up to date, for an annual stipend of $100. By 1938, the time had come for the alumni headquarters to be reorganized with additional space, and employment of a regular secretary. This was made necessary by the increased number of alumni chapters that had been formed since the first in 1920.

In 1938, the Alumni Association president Willard Smith, in cooperation with Adams and a committee, chose Paul Street to be secretary of the alumni office, combining this work with a part-time teaching position in the English department.[23] To these positions and later as director of public relations, Street applied his vigorous energies for seventeen years, endearing himself not only to the alumni but to the faculty and students as well.

Following him as secretary of the alumni office were a number of individuals for short periods of time until Thomas Woodstrup's appointment in 1966 as assistant to the director of alumni relations and development (shortly thereafter this position was re-titled director of alumni relations). A former student at Northern, Woodstrup had been an English major and editor of the *Northern Illinois*. He served as president of the Alumni Association in 1962–63. The problem facing Woodstrup was implementation of relevant programs for the ever-changing life-styles of students and alumni. The magnitude of this task is quite evident when one considers that over half of Northern's alumni have been graduated since 1960.

Since Northern was exclusively a professional school for teachers for over fifty years, it was necessary that some form of assistance be given in locating positions. To aid students in this nerve-racking experience, a placement service was created in 1922 with Floyd Ritzman as its director; before his appointment, placement had been handled from the president's office. Positions were not difficult to locate; in fact, the president had a perfect record in 1920: all members of the graduating class were placed at salaries ranging from $1,000 to $2,300; manual-training teachers, who were able to do some work in athletics, secured the highest salary. At the time, Ritzman mentioned, "We have literally hundreds of calls . . . [for teachers] which we cannot supply." [24]

For years it was rare that any graduate was unable to find a position. This was especially true in the twenty-one counties of northern Illinois, where the growing birth rate and increasing density of population produced an over-supply of positions, as was pointed out by Martin Bartels, who came as director of placement in 1951.

Teacher placement, like other forms of employment, was also affected by such phenomena as depression and war. In

412

1933, there were 244 graduates and only 159 were placed (about 65 percent); however, in 1939, when the Depression had abated somewhat, as many as 80 percent were placed. After World War II, all prospective teachers (especially elementary teachers) found the job market very favorable, but the salary situation for teachers was slow to adjust to this increasing demand. No sooner had salaries reached a respectable level in the late 1960s, than the declining job market narrowed the choice of positions—the bachelor's degree was no longer a guarantee of a teaching job. This declining market for teachers combined with the University budget restrictions and the elimination of the Laboratory School suggest that the heyday of teacher education and employment has already passed.

The University's expanding curriculum, however, has increased the areas that students can consider for their careers. During the 1960s and 1970s an increasing number of graduates were being placed in areas such as business, industry, nursing, library science, and government.

Of the large percentage of graduates entering the teaching profession—mostly in elementary schools at first, then later in secondary—some taught for only a year or so in order to pay off their school debts; many withdrew because of the low salaries that persisted for so many years. Low salaries seemed to be encouraged by the fact that many vacancies could be filled by women made eligible by an emergency certificate that allowed them to teach while they returned to college to get additional hours of credit. This lowering of standards actually brought hundreds of untrained people into teaching and at the same time held salaries down for those already in the profession. Even with these additional teachers, the ratio of vacancies to the number of prospective teachers remained high for many years. An excellent example of this disparity was in 1957 when the Placement Office received 14,475 reports of vacancies while placing 407 out of 550 graduates in teaching positions.

The financial situation of most students made Northern an attractive institution, since its costs have always been among the lowest in the country. For the first twenty-five years, only a $2

term fee was collected. A $2 activity fee was assessed quarterly beginning about 1920. In 1924, the registration fee was raised to $7 and the activity fee to $3 per quarter, or a total cost of $40 per year. Room and board in the dormitory were available to a limited number in 1924 for $9.50 per week, and approved places in the city or the clubs could be had for about the same amount. By 1931, a major change in costs was made when the registration fee was raised to $12 and a quarterly fee of $25 was included for those not intending to prepare for teaching. During the following years, between 1932 and 1937, the activity fee was raised to $6 quarterly. Starting in 1932, during the Depression, the registration fee dropped gradually from $12 to $9 where it remained until 1948. With more prosperous times it was once more raised (to $15) along with an increase in the student activity fee to $10. Beginning in that same year, there was also a $2 bond revenue fee per quarter, a financial device used for the first time to pay off bonded indebtedness on buildings not financed by the State of Illinois. In 1948 an out-of-state fee also appeared for the first time.

All three of these major cost items—registration, activity fee, and bond revenue—moved slowly upward during the 1950s until, by 1960 (when health insurance was added), their combined amount had risen from $25 per semester to $115.50. Along with the increased amounts in these three categories, by 1972–73 a bus fee of $10 and an athletic fee of $14 had raised the total cost for each student to $287 per semester. The out-of-state fee had climbed to $614.50 per semester, and room and board rates in the dormitories had been set at $1,130 for the two semesters.[25]

These costs no doubt seem extremely high for parents who have to pay them or students who work to earn part of the cost, but nevertheless anyone now attending Northern pays but a fraction of the total cost. For example, in 1971–72 the annual cost for the student came to a total of $568, but the per capita cost to the State of Illinois was nearly three times that, or $1,683.46.

To aid in reducing the cost of education for many of the less affluent students, a few loan funds and scholarships were available. However, there was little money for this purpose until 1919 when Andrew Brown's estate of $23,332.60 was donated, making it one of the largest single gifts in the history of the University. Down through the years other individuals and groups have offered scholarships and awards for students; many of these were to honor faculty members and presidents of Northern. The earlier student loan funds were usually small grants of $50 to $100 per year, bearing no interest charges and requiring only average academic eligibility. In recent years this type of assistance has been expanded, until scholarship and loan information covered nearly nine full pages in a recent annual catalog.

Competitive sports developed slowly under President Cook, but with the arrival of J. Stanley Brown a real effort was begun to attract more men to the college by putting greater emphasis on athletics. Northern violated the rules and regulations of the Illinois Intercollegiate Athletic Conference to such an extent that the school was expelled from the Conference. Northern joined this organization in 1920, was expelled in 1925, and was readmitted to full membership in 1927. It remained in the "Little Nineteen," as it was called, along with twenty-two other colleges until 1941, when there were so many withdrawals that only the five state teachers colleges remained as members.[26] These five schools made up the I.I.A.C. until 1950, when Eastern and Central Michigan both joined, and the name was changed to Interstate Intercollegiate Athletic Conference. The program was expanded at that time to ten different sports.

In 1955, Northern instituted a grant-in-aid program under faculty supervision in several sports, in order, as the administration reported, to aid financially "worthy students so that Northern can have representative athletic teams." Under the athletic grant program for 1956, total college expenses for a student were estimated at $810, which included room, board, books, laundry, and fees. Of this amount, the qualifying athlete would be expected to earn $405 per year. The grant-in-aid fund, which was to cover the other 50 percent, was to be made up from donations by former athletes, faculty, student organizations, and the Boosters Club, which consisted of local merchants, doctors, lawyers, and others who would give their financial and moral support in return for a special section of seats to be reserved for them at the games.

To visualize the growth of this program, one need only to

415

contrast the program in 1956 with the report of the Grants-in-Aid Committee fifteen years later. The initial plan set up twenty grants which would total $8,100; by 1971–72, the number of students receiving athletic grants-in-aid had increased to 214, totalling $250,318. This sum allowed 152 full grants—80 for football, 20 for basketball, and the remainder for the minor sports.[27]

The athletic grant-in-aid program continued to expand in importance year after year, but not without some opposition from students, alumni, and faculty who were not interested in catapulting the University into "big time" athletics. Fred Rolf, chairman of the Athletic Board from 1953 to 1968, along with President Holmes favored increasing the grants to the extent that it was necessary to withdraw from the I.I.A.C. in 1966. The reason for this attitude was expressed in 1956 by Holmes to a former student who warned him of the dangerous pitfalls of competing for athletes with the big schools who "bid for them as casually as a buyer would bid for a fine head of livestock."

We have been talking for more than two years of the athletic situation!!! Our agreement is that anything we do shall be above board, so with that as our starting point, we considered whether or not to drop our conference and play small colleges of several hundred student population, or stay in our conference which is composed of colleges similar to ours. In order to stay in the conference it becomes apparent that we must have better athletics, for we can no longer compete on an even basis with our sister institutions in basketball and football. We have been at the bottom for the last three or four years in both sports. This hurts the morale of the college, for our own students wonder what is the matter with us—staff and faculty. They can see no reason why, when our sister institutions can win their share of the games, we should be unable to do so. It is not our goal to win all the games, but a college with Northern's pride, wants to win half the games over a period of years.[28]

He was further disturbed for reasons other than the morale factor; it was becoming difficult, he said, to place graduates from the athletic department in coaching positions since superintendents were not interested in those from losing teams.

Soon after it was decided to support the athletic program more fully, Howard Fletcher was selected as football coach and Northern's fortunes turned for the better; her teams were again in the victory columns during the 1960s. Enrollments continued to move upward and the student activity fee, which was used to support the athletic program, was also raised to $18. By the 1960s, intercollegiate athletics appeared to be "at a point of major upgrading."

To capitalize upon this optimism, the president showed no hesitancy in asking the students to vote on a referendum for an increase of $8.50 in their bond revenue fees for the purpose of constructing a stadium. This they granted, though by a small popular vote; and within two years, in the presence of various dignitaries, a 15,000-seat structure was dedicated at the Homecoming game, 6 November 1965. To be certain that the old Glidden Field would not be forgotten, a block of its sod was transplanted in the new field.

This same spirit carried over in respect to post-season games; after lifting of the ban on such games by the Board, Coach Fletcher was permitted in 1962 to take his team to the Mineral Bowl at Excelsior Springs, Missouri, to play Adams State College of Colorado. N.I.U. lost by 23 to 20. Twice again, in 1963 and 1965, Northern was invited back to the same post-season bowl game, where his teams won the second engagement against Southwest Missouri, but lost the third to the University of North Dakota. The 1963 team (led by the legendary passing of George Bork to Hugh Rohrschneider) was declared National Collegiate Athletic Association college division champion by the Associated Press and the nation's top small college team by the National Association of Intercollegiate Athletics.

By now, a new spirit was in the air, and agitation had begun for moving into a more auspicious conference. According to the *Chicago Tribune,* in 1964, N.I.U. was already making plans to drop out of the I.I.A.C. in order to join the Mid-American Conference, a move which Northern's athletic officials (especially "Chick" Evans) believed was highly likely in the near future.

Notwithstanding these high hopes, there were certain prerequisites that Northern would have to meet; the major one was,

417

of course, an increase in the number of grants-in-aid to equal the number in other schools in the M.A.C. as well as the necessary finances to support them. An immediate campaign was begun by the Athletic Board to describe the real challenge that N.I.U. faced if it hoped to join this prestigeous conference. However, considerable opposition arose immediately to the idea of greater subsidization of Northern's athletes, even though funds were also to be granted for various other types of scholarships. The A.A.U.P. opposed it, and the students also insisted that they be given an opportunity to vote upon the issue. Moreover, the Student Activities Fund Board, the watchdog of all student activity fees and their allocation, was in opposition to the use of activity fees for athletic grants-in-aid.

These opponents, no doubt, appeared as a sizeable obstacle for President Holmes and his staff, but his Athletic Board chairman, Fred Rolf, assured him that the opposition was only the "critical attitude of a few unrealistic students and faculty members who are confused in their thinking as evidenced by the AAUP letter to the Board and articles in the *Northern Star*." He encouraged Holmes to go ahead with the plan by saying: "We [the Athletic Board] wish you to be assured that this is a splinter group which does not in any way represent the attitudes of the large majority of the faculty who solidly support you in your proposals for the improvement of our athletic program." [29]

Holmes took his case to the Teachers College Board where, without a student referendum but with the consent of the Athletic Board, he requested approval for an athletic fee not to exceed $10 per semester, effective in the fall of 1965. His argument to the Board was somewhat the same as his earlier one, namely, "Small schools feel Northern is too large; schools of comparable size, highly desirable competitors, feel Northern's teams are inferior to theirs because of current policies governing grants-in-aid to athletics." [30] The Board finally sanctioned this request and for the first time recognized the policy of paying for grants-in-aid for athletics from student fees.

At the close of the 1966 school year Northern withdrew from the I.I.A.C., still hoping, however, for an early invitation from the Mid-American Conference. Performance on the gridiron from 1962 to 1966 was more than could have been expected, and the monetary increases for grants-in-aid from various sources accompanied these athletic successes. However, these successes soon brought on heady ambitions for those doing the scheduling, and before long the career of Coach Fletcher was ended. His record was well above the average, but with the heavy investment in equipment, stadium, and athletics, the officials felt it necessary to engage a coach with experience at schools with a higher level of competition. Thus Richard (Doc) Urich, who had played and coached under some of the elite coaches in the country, was secured in 1969. But in spite of his excellent background, his career was brief, hardly long enough for the team to profit from his type of coaching and the better players that he was able to recruit; under him, Northern won only six and lost fourteen games. He suddenly resigned his position three weeks before the opening of the third season to become an assistant coach for a professional team, the Buffalo Bills. Urich's assistant, Jerry Ippoliti, became head coach and was able to profit from his predecessor's achievements with a fair season of 5-5-1. His second season (1972) was better, with a won-lost record of seven and four.

Between 1967 and 1969, two major decisions were made in respect to N.I.U.'s athletic future: one was a real disappointment; the other was considered a real achievement. In respect to the latter, application for major (university division) status in all sports was made to the National Collegiate Athletic Association. This was granted for basketball in 1967 and in football and other sports in 1969, making Northern the third school in the state to enjoy this recognition. N.I.U. teams and individual participants were then eligible for university division playoffs in all sports as well as automatic reporting of all scores and schedules by a statistical reporting service.

The unpleasant decision came in 1967 when the berth that had been actively sought in the Mid-American Conference was finally denied by the presidents of its seven schools on the basis that their "conference is not intertested in expansion at this time." [31]

Independent status did not place any serious hardship upon Northern's athletic program except it was known that any university going it alone indefinitely would have increasing difficulties providing adequate programs of intercollegiate athletic competition as well as receiving its proper recognition in awards. For this reason President Rhoten Smith got together with presidents of other institutions for the purpose of organizing a new conference. The conference consisted of Illinois State, Ball State at Muncie, Indiana State at Terre Haute, Southern Illinois, and N.I.U. On 22 September 1969, these five schools agreed to the title of Academic and Athletic Association of Midwestern Universities (A.A.A.M.U.); however, for intercollegiate athletic competition the organization was designated the Conference of Midwestern Universities (C.M.U.).

From the beginning, it was agreed that many other aspects of higher education should also be dealt with besides athletics. For example, there was a strong desire to develop relationships among the schools in academic areas by means "of associations to achieve certain research objectives, and for other purposes which the Big Ten Conference has been so successful in pioneering." Harold E. Walker was selected as the first executive director of the Academic Affairs Conference, with offices in Terre Haute.

The Athletic Conference provided for a commissioner of intercollegiate athletics, and the first one chosen was Jack McClelland, a former Drake University athletic director and North Central Intercollegiate Athletic Conference commissioner, who assumed his new position on 1 July 1970, with offices in Indianapolis. Commissioner McClelland's early efforts were devoted to the development of an ambitious athletic scholarship program that would provide a total of no fewer than 120 and no more than 220 full grants-in-aid by 1970–71, with between 20 and 24 grants for basketball and 75 to 100 for football, while other sports could be supported at any level determined by the individual institutions.[32]

Competition among the five members began in the spring of 1970 when Southern Illinois won the first championship in gymnastics; the following two years, championships were awarded in nine varsity sports with Southern taking first in all of them except for baseball and basketball, which Northern won in 1972 and golf which Ball State took in both years.

Because of the advance commitments of the five schools, no champion was to be declared in football until 1974.

The Conference was hardly in existence two years when Southern announced its withdrawal to take effect on 1 July 1973, leaving the other four members either to liquidate the conference or to secure other interested institutions as members. A major reason for Southern Illinois's withdrawal was that it had won fifteen of the nineteen league championships, and such domination in minor sports hardly created the type of competition desired. Whatever other reasons there may have been, the remaining members, after some deliberations as to their future, decided to dissolve the conference as of 30 June 1972, less than three years after it was organized.

No sooner had the Midwestern Conference expired than Athletic Director Robert Brigham began another attempt to secure membership in the Mid-American Conference. Richard J. Nelson, then president of Northern, gave his full support to the effort, believing that "being an independent is not a very good position for a university like ours to be in." He became involved in the negotiations with the presidents of the other Mid-American Conference universities, and on 7 March 1973, it was officially announced that Northern had become the ninth member of the Conference.[33]

In the summer of 1929, a young athletic coach was engaged by President J.C. Brown to take the place of Coach R.A. Cowell, who had just completed two disappointing years at Northern. George "Chick" Evans had been coaching at Boone, Iowa, his home town, and at the DeKalb High School before he was asked to take over the college position. Upon assuming this respnsibility he brought with him a few excellent players from his Iowa school, making his first year one of his better seasons of the twenty-six that he coached at Northern. President Adams, also a newcomer, was by no means a stranger to football, and the two of them developed a close and cooperative friendship while building an athletic tradition on the Northern campus. Evans took over teaching and coaching a one-man department of physical education for men with a total of 169 male students in the various courses and sports.

Evans was a large and vigorous man with a gravelly voice and a disposition and enthusiasm that constantly radiated athletic dedication wherever he was or whatever he did; in fact, sports were his entire life's interest, and he never lost an opportunity to relate their values to the public and students as a significant influence in the development of character and "a will to win" in life. He was always very positive in his athletic values, even if on occasion he had difficulty articulating them. He was not an individual easily persuaded by his colleagues, nor by his superiors for that matter.[34]

As a coach, he not only requested that all students become involved in backing the teams but he also announced, soon after his arrival, that he wanted "every man in school to be participating in some sport." "Our slogan is to be," he said, "Athletics for every man and every man in Athletics." He never lost an opportunity to expand into new sports or to increase the number of games, and he was frequently requesting from the Athletic Board more funds for his major sports.

Evans in his first year set a pace that was to mark his career for years to come. During his first nine seasons he failed to gain the coveted "Little Nineteen" championship, but in three of those seasons he had only one loss. In 1938, he led the "Profs" with Curtis Larsen as captain, John Young at end, and Howard Fletcher at tackle to this long-awaited prize. The following year Fletcher was named by the Illinois Valley Sports Writers Association as the outstanding Valley collegiate athlete. On these and other teams were such outstanding players as Reino Nori, John Pace, Ed Behan, Jack Mustapha, and Larry Brink, to mention only a few.

During Evans's twenty-six years of football coaching (1929–1954), his teams compiled a record of 132 wins, 70 losses, and 20 ties. The 1951 grid squad especially enjoyed outstanding success when it finished the season with a 9-1-0 record. Moreover, seven men from this team were selected for all-conference honors, particularly quarterback Bob Heimerdinger, who was named on most Little All-America teams. The 1948 team had a prominent player who later made a name for himself in teaching, coaching, and administration. This was Robert Brigham, who in 1968 was selected to succeed Evans as head of the department of physical education for men and director of athletics.

The undefeated football team of 1944 was only one of such honors in that year, for in basketball, baseball, and track where were also championships. This was indeed an historic event, for it was the first time that all four sports were won in a single year and also the first time that the football team's record showed all victories. This was all the more remarkable because at no time were there more than ninety men enrolled in the college. Such an eventful year called for a large celebration. There was a parade down the main street of DeKalb escorted by the fire and police departments, followed by a pep meeting, movie, bonfire, and dance.

Howard Fletcher, after teaching a number of years in the public schools, was engaged to take over as football coach at a time when the sport was in decline at Northern. It took him awhile to get back on the winning side again, and, considering the opposition that his teams had to meet in his closing years, Fletcher's thirteen-year record of 74 wins, 48 losses, and 1 tie, is commendable. He also took his teams three times to the Mineral Bowl, tied for the championship of the I.I.A.C. in 1964, and won it outright in 1965. On his teams he had such outstanding players as George Bork and John Spilis, both of whom went into professional football.

Evans also served as basketball coach for eleven years (1929–1940) during which time his teams won 125 games while losing 93. In 1932 and 1933, his teams added two more I.I.A.C. titles to Northern's trophy case. In 1940, he relinquished this task to Ralph McKinzie, an experienced and respected coach from Eureka College. In McKinzie's first year he succeeded in sharing the championship with Illinois Normal. In 1944–45, he repeated by winning a clear championship.

Between 1949—when McKinzie relinquished the position —and 1970, Northern had six different basketball coaches— Gene Fekete, Gilbert Wilson, Gilman Hertz, William Healey, Ev Cochrane, and Tom Jorgensen—who together compiled a record of 274 wins and 268 losses. In the 1972 season, Coach

Jorgensen's team won the conference championship, bringing joy to the hearts of some 4,000 fans who night after night during the season had jammed themselves into an overcrowded Field House.[35]

In addition to football and basketball, Evans also took over the coaching of Northern's baseball team. He and his successors, McKinzie and Darrel Black compiled only average records over a thirty-three-year period, although Black's star pitcher in 1963, Fritz Petersen, went on to fame with the New York Yankees. Only modest successes remained the rule until Tom Meyer became coach in 1964 and won for N.I.U. its first baseball championship; then, while Meyer's successor, David Mason, was away on leave in 1972, another young man, Wayne Franke, a graduate assistant in the department, surprised everybody with a second championship.

Baseball was the last coaching job for Evans, and the remainder of his career was spent as head of a large department of physical education and director of athletics. In spite of the sentiments of the athletes, coaches, and boosters who were on his side, Evans disappointedly had to announce his retirement when he reached mandatory retirement age in 1968. But he was well remembered by many of his old friends and students who gave him an excellent send-off with write-ups and testimonies to his prominence as a coach and administrator; in fact, he was held in such esteem by his dean, Robert Topp, that some months earlier Topp had recommended to the provost that Evans be granted a full professorship for his final year. But such a move seemed unwise to the officials and Evans retired as an associate professor, a rank he had received twenty-four years earlier.[36]

A year after Evans's appearance, a young athletic coach and teacher, Carl Appell, arrived at Northern. He was destined to make history with his accomplishments before he closed his long career in 1964. With a fine academic background from Oberlin College and experience in coaching elsewhere, his first assignments were mainly to assist Evans in developing the physical education department, which was Appell's chief interest, and also to help as line coach with the football team. Later he became the director of intramural sports. Track was also assigned to him as his major sport—a sport in which he himself had not participated at college and one that had little tradition at Northern. In the classroom he was the same taskmaster that he was on the track, demanding large assignments of all who took his courses; yet he was often witty and congenial as well as pessimistic and sarcastic; a combination of traits which can be quite effective in the teaching of young men.

With his first Little Nineteen championship in 1934, he credited this almost unbelievable achievement to the unlimited time and effort that his boys had "spent shoveling paths on the snowbound track" so that they could carry out their early training program. It used to be said that a sure sign of spring in DeKalb was the sound of Coach Carl Appell calling out times to the athletes as they circled the Glidden Field track.

With this type of leadership, Appell's teams won eight I.I.A.C. track championships. His 1958 cross-country team also won the N.C.A.A. small-college title, the first national championship in Northern's sports history.[37] Appell's most cherished award was the Helms Foundation plaque which entered him in the National Association of Intercollegiate Athletics Hall of Fame in 1961.

Among the outstanding athletes Appell coached and whom he always recalled with pleasure were Charles Hussung, Cy Perkins, Walter Peters, and Bill Terwilliger—who captured the national Amateur Athletic Union's decathlon championship in 1942.

The minor sports at Northern, as in most institutions, were what the name implies, and only in recent years have they been given a significant role in conference activities. For years tennis was a kind of white-collar sport coached mostly by faculty members and students.

Cross-country was introduced in 1937 by John Parson, a young Easterner whose one-year stay was altogether too short, considering his enthusiasm for the minor sports. It was not until 1950 that the sport was reinstituted by Appell. The cross-country coaches who followed Appell were J.D. Anderson (1964), Joe Hartley (1965–69), and Willie Kimmons (1970–1972).

Wrestling was introduced first by Evans as an intramural

sport and quickly became an attraction. During the coaching careers of Robert Brigham and Don Flavin, the wrestling teams won a I.I.A.C. championship in 1942 and several individual wrestlers won conference titles. The highest honors were achieved by Roy Conrad in 1960 when he was given the N.C.A.A. university division medal for winning the 177-pound-class championship. Johnny B. Johnson placed second in the 1973 N.C.A.A. 190-pound-class championship match.

Through 1971 the Northern golf team's record in dual-meet competitions was 144 wins, 114 losses, and 11 ties. In 1947, a team coached by John "Red" Pace captured the I.I.A.C. title just six years after the sport had been introduced; for some years thereafter, golf was coached by Nye LaBaw until Jack Pheanis took over when the former was appointed coordinator of intercollegiate athletics.

Swimming was a fairly recent addition to N.I.U., becoming a serious sport soon after the opening of the new University Laboratory School, which then contained the only competition-sized swimming pool on campus. For the first eight years (1960–1968) of varsity swimming, the sport was coached by Francis Stroup. In 1964 and 1965, his teams won the I.I.A.C. championships, and several swimmers also set individual and relay records.

Gymnastics likewise had a slow beginning, and the lack of enthusiasm shown for it during the first five years (1957–1962) was expressed in the over-all achievements: 3 wins, 17 losses, 2 ties; three coaches; and one year no team at all. With the arrival of Hubert Dunn in 1962, however, things changed immediately, for he was a pioneer in the gymnastics movement with numerous achievements in other schools. His teams were usually winners and, through 1972, had an over-all record of 63 wins, 49 losses, and 1 tie.

In 1962, Robert Kahler fielded the first soccer team, but the following year William Healey took over and for six years gradually improved this sport although he relinquished it to Dave Bucher in 1969. Bucher had an enviable record during the following four years.

Northern began early to offer the few men who were not participating in varsity sports opportunities to enter an intramural program of various types of games. By 1931, regular tournaments were held in "tennis, handball, horseshoes, playground ball, volley ball, basketball, wrestling, boxing, and golf." As the school increased in size and the varsity sports program was expanded, the program for intramurals was also broadened to include archery, ping pong, billiards, and bowling; in time touch football found its way to the campus and was almost immediately popular. Basketball was also popular, and for several years a group of faculty members would enter a team in the intramural league, usually dropping by the wayside before the end of the season.

In 1940, an Intramural Council was set up to make the ever-growing program more systematic by arranging the schedules and having everything in readiness before the season opened. During World War II, it was necessary to drop the program; but when it was taken up again, it was larger than ever, with as many as thirty-three teams in four leagues by 1947. Ralph McKinzie was assigned to direct the program with his department and students to assist him. In 1950, Nye LaBaw was made director of intramural sports. By the 1960s, additional funds and a greater increase in students had brought the program to such proportions that there was a desperate shortage of equipment and facilities. In 1965, Harold Wells became the coordinator of intramurals and under his direction the program continued to grow until sixteen champions were declared in 1971–1972.

When intercollegiate athletics for women was phased out during the Cook administration, the women turned to the Women's Athletic Association and its intramural rivalries in such sports as hockey, baseball, basketball, and many others closely tied to the physical education program. By the 1930s, a women's extramural program offered competition with teams at other schools. In 1936, a team went to the University of Chicago and tied them in hockey. Individuals from Northern also won medals at various meets: Mary Terwilliger was a member of the Illinois Women's Athletic Club team that won the National A.A.U. 440-yard relay four years in succession

(1933–1936); Jeanette Feurstein won the Illinois State Women's intercollegiate tennis championship in 1940.[38]

By the 1960s, the physical education department for women had an elaborate program of both intramural and extramural sports as well as recreational and special events such as ski trips, camping, picnics, horseback riding, and ice skating—all co-sponsored by the Women's Recreation Association.

The ladies, off for a gentle ride, circa 1902

Rhoten A. Smith,
sixth president, 1967–1971

10

The Agony of Change

IMMEDIATELY following Holme's resignation announcement in 1966, the Board of Governors of State Colleges and Universities adopted the procedure used in most other institutions for the selection of a new president. The ultimate responsibility and authority for the appointment of this individual was in the hands of the Board; however, the plan provided for the assistance and advice of an elected faculty committee consisting of eight members chosen from various groups and levels of administration and faculty. The Board selection committee members were Morton Hollingsworth (Joliet), W.I. Taylor (Canton), and Richard J. Nelson (Evanston). The members of the University selection committee were Arnold Fox (English), Donald Kieso (Accounting), Kerby Tink (Education), Julia Kilpatrick (Home Economics), Harold Husa (dean of men), Lyle Maxwell (head, Department of Business Education), Wayne McIlrath (dean, Graduate School), and Paul Burtness (chairman, English). There were also advisory committees made up of alumni, students, administrators, and nonacademic personnel.

This Board procedure was a definite reform in the selection of presidents, for it was no longer to be carried out behind closed doors. The only specific condition laid down by the Board was that "no member of the faculty or of the administrative staff at Northern Illinois University will be considered for this appointment." This provision caused some dissatisfaction, especially among certain elements of the faculty who had their favorite candidates. In fact, the University Council dispatched Paul Burtness with a request to the Board that it delete this provision from its resolution. He returned to report their reasons for this exclusion—and that the members did not wish to repeal it.

It was the University committee's responsibility to draw up a list of candidates, which finally included as many as two hundred names. From this list about sixty-five were invited to apply. At both Northern and Illinois State, where presidents were being sought simultaneously during the spring of 1967, the searches were made difficult because the new Board of Regents would not come into existence until 1 July 1967. The Board of Governors, under the chairmanship of Richard J. Nelson, had responsibility for selecting the new president, but the president would be serving from the outset under a different Board. The candidates were extremely uncomfortable, to put it mildly, to find that they could not meet the chairman and other members of the new Board of Regents and indeed did not even know who these members would be. The faculty members on the selection committee attempted to persuade Governor Kerner to make the appointment early and to name Mr. Nelson chairman of the new Board, for all the presidential candidates at Northern had been most favorably impressed by him. However, the governor felt he required Nelson's continued service on the Board of Governors; the names of the members of the new Board were not announced until shortly before the Board had assumed its responsibilities.

The University committee finally decided to invite five "premier candidates" to visit the campus. Following this, visits were made by various members of the committees to the candidates' institutions, and this final procedure reduced the list to three names in order of preference. A joint committee of Board and University members submitted the three names to the whole Board, which on 1 May 1967 selected the first choice of the selection committee, Rhoten A. Smith, dean of the College of Liberal Arts and Sciences at Temple University, as the successor to Leslie Holmes.

Dean Smith, according to the University selection committee report on 11 May 1967, was finally chosen for this position because of several facets of his experience and achievements. First was the high degree of respect, loyalty, and confidence his faculty had for him at Temple University. Moreover, Smith had "invaluable experience in the development of policy and in the solution of academic and other problems on a university-wide, as well as a collegiate, basis," and, as director of the Citizenship Clearing House of New York City, he had four years of highly successful experience in dealing with a distinguished board of trustees. Finally, the thoroughness and competence with which he explored the situation at Northern before he gave the committee his assurance that he would accept the presidency was impressive. The following describes his concentration and interest:

Dean Smith requested an opportunity to confer and did confer with Dr. Lyman Glenny, Executive Director of the Illinois Board of Higher Education, concerning the prospective role of Northern . . . in Illinois higher education; with Mr. Richard Nelson, chairman of the Board of Governors, concerning the prospective Board of Regents and the development of new policies for the Regency System; and with Dr. Frederick McKelvey, Executive Officer and Secretary of the Board of Governors, concerning relations among the State universities and concerning prospective institutional autonomy for the Regency universities. . . . Dean Smith also consulted Dr. Jack Peltason, Chancellor-designate of the Urbana Campus of the University of Illinois, concerning questions of state-wide planning for higher education. Finally, Dean Smith corresponded and conferred with a number of individual faculty members and university officers of Northern.[1]

Northern's sixth president was born in Dallas, Texas, in 1921; he graduated from Paschal High School in Fort Worth in 1938, and attended Texas Wesleyan College in 1940 and the

433

University of Texas from 1940 to 1942. After three years in the Air Force, he received his B.A. degree in 1946 and an M.A. in 1948 from the University of Kansas. In 1954, he received his Ph.D. (with a major in political science and a minor in American literature) from the University of California at Berkeley. He had served as an instructor at the University of Kansas while earning his master's degree and returned to that institution in 1951; he became an associate professor in 1957. While at Kansas, he also served as a research associate and consultant in the university's Government Research Center, the Kansas Legislative Council, and the Constitutional Revision Commission as well as advisor to the chairman of the Kansas Democratic party. In 1958, Smith joined the faculty of New York University as professor of politics in the School of Law and the Graduate School of Arts and Sciences. He also held the post of associate director of the Citizenship Clearing House in 1955–56 and was director from 1958 to 1961. In 1960, he served as consultant in the development of programs for the Ford Foundation. In 1961, he left New York University to assume the deanship at Temple University, where he remained until coming to Northern.

President Smith had fulfilled the various requisites in his ascendancy of the academic ladder. Besides his teaching and practical experience, he was the author of *The Life of a Bill* and *Republican Primary Fight, A Study in Factionalism* (with C.J. Hein) as well as some twenty other publications including contributions to books, journal articles, pamphlets, and an unpublished novel. His doctoral dissertation topic was "Majority Rule in American Democratic Theory."

When Rhoten Smith arrived at Northern on 1 September 1967, the University found it had a president with a background quite different from that of its presidents in the past. His doctorate in political science had been earned at one of the greatest universities in the world; his experience as a teacher and administrator was also in large public and private universities; his research and writing placed him high among his colleagues as a scholar; and his practical experience with political and citizen groups gave him a special expertise in dealing with governmental bodies.

There were other notable differences between Smith and his predecessors. His basic concepts of rights, privileges, and responsibilities in respect to students, faculty, and others who made up the university community tended to be liberal. He believed emphatically in expanding the rights of students to govern themselves, and when these privileges were granted and mistakes were made—even when violence was committed—there was no evidence of panic on his part. Students soon found his low-key personality and his genuine faith in them as adults especially attractive.

Smith met frequently with faculty and student groups for coffee, and he presented weekly "Chats with Rhoten Smith" over the campus radio. According to Dean Richard Bowers, the new president not only wanted to know the faculty and their problems but also had "shown marked concern for recognition of good scholarship and work by the faculty." John Lloyd, a member of the newly appointed Academic Planning Committee, was "quite enthusiastic about Smith, the quality of his ideas, the vigor of his manner, and the humor and wit with which he combines them all with his ambitions for the university."

Smith was also free in delegating powers to students; so much, in fact, that Jim Kiley, the president of the Student Association Board, was of the opinion that Smith would "go to any extent" in letting students run their own affairs and that he realized more than other administrators that students were adults. "He is a phenomenal man to work with," Kiley said. According to Smith's wife, Barbara, he had a very logical mind which at times could frustrate young people but, on the other hand, he was always willing to listen to all sides of every question.[2]

President Smith soon impressed the University community as well as the Board with ideas and goals other than mere expansion of facilities and a continual increase in the numbers of faculty and students. Paul Burtness noted, when he represented the faculty at the inauguration exercises, that under Smith there "is emerging a sense of the essential coherence which is proper for a university, a sense of a unifying commitment to learning and rational inquiry. Students, faculty members, and officers of administration are gradually developing the feeling of being engaged in a joint effort—a common effort—with the result that communication and understanding among these diverse constituencies are demonstrably improving."

On 4 November 1967, the Presidential Inauguration Committee under the chairmanship of William Seat had its first meeting and established the week of 19 May for the occasion. This committee and its many subsidiary committees gave their undivided attention and endless hours to the event. The result was probably the most elaborate ceremony in the history of the University and probably the last of its kind if present economic conditions in the state and nation continue.[3]

Beginning on 20 May there was a series of events that included speeches by Victor G. Rosenblum, president-elect of Reed College, and Percy L. Julian, director of the Julian Research Institute and member of the Board of Regents. Arthur Honegger's *King David* (symphonic psalm) was performed by faculty soloists and the University Chorus and Chamber Orchestra under the direction of Elwood Smith and Wilbur Pursley.

On 23 May, another highlight took place with the dedication of *Le Baron*, a contemporary nickel steel-plate stabile sixteen feet high and fourteen feet wide, by Alexander Calder, a leading American sculptor, recognized as one of the top three or four sculptors in the world. "Le Baron" is located on the southeast campus near the main entrance of the University among buildings of contemporary architecture, a position selected by Calder himself after examining campus maps and photographs. This stabile, selected by a committee under the chairmanship of Gilbert Fullington of the art department, was purchased at a cost of $50,000 (a figure many criticized as exorbitant), which included transportation from France and installation. The initial payment was made from a few faculty contributions and a $10,000 donation by the Student Association Board; the remaining $40,000 was due on 1 May 1969. Realizing that the subcommittee responsible for liquidating this balance would be unable to do so, the N.I.U. Foundation agreed to borrow funds to pay it off. This loan is being repaid by the income from vending machines in academic and administrative buildings.[4]

On Friday morning, the Inaugural Convocation was held in the Field House. The long processional of dignitaries included Governor Samuel H. Shapiro; Secretary of Labor Willard Wirtz; Richard J. Nelson, chairman of the Board of Governors of State Colleges and Universities; and Dr. Norris Brookens, chairman of the Board of Regents. They were followed by official delegates representing five foreign countries and two hundred and fifty United States colleges and universities, fifty-six learned societies and professional organizations, N.I.U. faculty and students, Northern alumni from each of the sixty-nine graduating classes, and residents of the northern Illinois area—a total of about fifteen hundred delegates and guests and an audience of about three thousand people. Special robes were designed by Patricia Foerster of the University Theatre for the president and members of the Board of Regents for this occasion. The president's robe was cardinal with black velvet panels and chevrons and an extra row of black velvet at the hem and sleeve. Added to this impressive robe was a newly created medallion designed by Eleanor Caldwell of the art department. This new symbol of the presidential office at Northern was given to Smith to signal his investiture in office as the sixth president. The medallion contains the letters "NIU" in a setting of 14-carat gold. In the lower section of the design is a 19-carat synthetic star ruby. The inauguration motif embodied in circular form the initials of N.I.U. "to bespeak the dynamic nature of an energetic modern university" and was designed by William T. Brown of the art department.

In his inaugural address, President Smith developed the theme of a "New University" that would incorporate two main goals, "Excellence and Opportunity." The second of these had already been experienced during the preceding twenty years to the extent that enrollments had increased twelve-fold, but the former goal—qualitative improvement in the educational experience of all the students—was yet to be realized. In spite of the formidability of the task, it was Smith's view that the necessary conditions must be provided for academic excellence without denying educational opportunities to the many. This was especially necessary since the college degree had become the "passport to achievement, to influence and affluence, to leadership in twentieth-century America. . . ." "It is my conviction," he said, "that the public universities can and must find ways to make more widely available opportunities for earning this passport to the good life. To fail to do so is to bar the door to a hopeful future in the very faces of those of our citizens who have least to hope for from life. Our abundant society cannot afford to bar that door." However, he did not suggest a lowering of standards but rather the development of newer and more sensitive methods in counseling, study-help programs, and admission procedures. "We find ourselves," he said, "in a position where we can assume leadership in forging what I shall call the New University," one that

will make better use of . . . the social sciences and will consequently find itself much more involved in the solution of social problems. The undergraduate curriculum in the New University will feature . . . more multidisciplinary work, less training for specific vocations, more attention to education for life in a world where change will be the only constant. . . . The New University will be dedicated equally to research and to teaching. . . . [It] will be a true collegium, with decisions resulting more from close cooperation and communication between faculty, students, administration, and the board than from confrontations based on conflict. With closer communication and with more openness and more candor on the part of all, the New University will have less hostility and suspicion among the various segments than seems to be the case too often today. At the same time, the New University will be a place of intellectual ferment and controversy, with respect for the opinions of all restored as the basis of intellectual exchange.[5]

"If all of this comes about," he concluded, "I believe the New University will once again claim the prideful allegiance of its faculty, students and alumni. . . . But this pride will be based not on nostalgia, sentiment, and football victories, but on continuing participation in the life of the mind."

438

As a memorial for this elaborate and costly inauguration, a sixty-four page book, *A New University*, edited by Professor Arra M. Garab and designed by Professor William T. Brown, was published by the Northern Illinois University Press. Five thousand complimentary copies were presented to friends of the University.

If the evaluation of current history might be compared to the writing of poetry (which Wordsworth noted "takes its origin from emotion recollected in tranquility") then one can expect little more than a casual description of such a recent administration from a writer who was so much a part of the scene. A more interpretative analysis of this phase of Northern's history is a task of the future.

It is also difficult to evaluate Smith's administration because so little time was given him to implement his program before national and local events began to affect his long-term program seriously. For the first time in its history, the Northern campus reacted to national political and social forces. By the close of Smith's first year, they were so distracting that his original plans had to be given lesser emphasis. Then, suddenly, at the beginning of his second year, he was stricken with a heart condition and underwent preventive cardio-vascular surgery in Cleveland, after which he was forced to recuperate for several months. During this time, the executive vice president and provost, F.R. Geigle, served as chief executive.

In spite of the impending student revolution, Smith was successful in inaugurating some of his ideas by increasing collective deliberations on various goals; he decentralized certain phases of administration to remove the "red tape" and to increase flexibility and established an Academic Planning Committee to cope with Northern's rapid expansion.

To facilitate communications with faculty and students, Smith opened the University Council meetings to these groups as well as to the news media.[6] He believed in an "open campus" and that a university ought to serve as an open forum for all ideas, and he was a firm believer in Oliver Wendell Holmes's dictum that "truth will triumph in the open market place of ideas." To help the students with their personal problems in the growing complexity of a computer society, a professional ombudsman position was created with Michael McDermott as the first appointee. Through McDermott's efforts, this developed into an important campus agency. Moreover, Smith made himself available on many occasions to students in the University Center and dining halls of the dormitories.

Under President Smith, the rights of students to determine policies in areas such as dormitory hours and visitation privileges were expanded. Moreover, a new role for students in governing the University was inaugurated when they were appointed to most of the important committees, and student advisory groups were created in various departments. But though these concessions were many, the students still found numerous unpopular restrictions in such areas as appropriations of funds, rules and regulations governing discipline, and the selection and retention of faculty members.[7]

With a new Board of Regents and a new president, there were new policies for the University. The time had come to revise many aspects of the University Council constitution then in use. The document made it difficult to inaugurate not only new policies of faculty and student participation but also structural changes. Thus a major committee was created in 1967 under the chairmanship of Paul Burtness; after nearly three years of work they presented a new University constitution to be ratified by the faculty, students, and Board of Regents. Following a lengthy debate, it was finally approved by the faculty and students. But the Board rejected the document because of one sentence concerning the selection of a new president: "No candidate shall be included for final selection if a majority of either Board representatives or a majority of university representatives oppose his inclusion."

In a second referendum, the faculty approved a new version with this sentence deleted. The second student referendum was declared invalid because of charges of irregularities in procedure; the ballots were destroyed, and a new election date set. This time the revised constitution was rejected by more than two to one.[8]

The main reason for the students' disapproval was that the leadership of the Student Association and the *Northern Star* claimed that numerous shortcomings were embodied in the new constitution, and they mounted a vigorous campaign to bring about rejection of the constitution on the grounds that a new one, more beneficial to students, could be drawn up. This defeat in the student referendum of 24 and 25 February 1971, was indeed a disappointment to the president, who only a few weeks earlier had announced his resignation.

While the proposed constitution was never ratified by all necessary constituencies and therefore never went into effect, a number of its provisions have been adopted by the University from time to time. One example is the inclusion of student representatives as voting members of the University Council. Another is the conception of departmental executive officers, not as heads serving indefinitely at the pleasure of the president, but as chairmen serving renewable terms of office and subject to a periodic review of their professional performance by their department and by the appropriate college dean. This change was adopted in the fall of 1969 by the College of Liberal Arts and Sciences. In spring 1972, the policy of establishing term appointments, with periodic review of professional performance, was recommended by the University Council for deans and vice presidents, as well as for departmental officers, and President Richard J. Nelson acted at once to establish these arrangements as University policy. This policy emphasizes the accountability of these officers of administration both to the faculty and to the officer of administration to whom the candidate for reappointment reports.

Jack Barker resigned as director of the University Press in June 1967 and returned to the Department of State for an assignment in Laos. The second director, Richard T. Congdon, took over the office in November. Ambitious plans to develop the Press were laid to rest soon after Governor Ogilvie was elected in 1968 and began his vigorous program to reduce the State budget for higher education in Illinois. Confronted with new financial strictures and harassed by rebellious students, President Smith had little time for the fledgling Press. Nevertheless, by the time he left the campus in June 1971, the Press had published twenty-two books.

A number of new curriculum developments were introduced to help more effectively not only the superior student

441

but also the average and disadvantaged ones. An honors program was initiated in 1969; and for the disadvantaged student, the "communication processes" courses in speech and English were instituted. A living-learning program was also developed, in which classes were held in a dormitory to give students an opportunity to blend academic and living experiences. The pass-fail grading option, developed for those who wished to select various courses "in order to explore interest areas which they might otherwise feel compelled to ignore because exploration might lead to poor grades," was adopted in 1969, and it continues to attract several hundred students each year.[9] The University also inaugurated a program called Sponsored Admissions, whereby academic departments may recommend admission of a limited number of applicants who do not meet regular entrance requirements. Another aspect of this philosophy of helping individuals unprepared for college was the probationary "restricted program" for students twenty-one years of age or older who had been out of school for at least one year and who were not otherwise eligible for admission.

The Northern Illinois State Teachers College Foundation had been incorporated in 1949 as a nonprofit charitable corporation to "receive, hold, and administer gifts of money, property, works of art, historical papers and documents, museum specimens, and other material having educational or historical value for the purpose of developing the facilities of Northern Illinois State Teachers College." The incorporators were J. Robert Hainds, Leslie A. Holmes, and Paul Street.

With the first professional audit of the records in 1955, the total investments, including current assets, were listed at $45,949.57, which were mainly gifts and scholarship funds invested in government savings bonds and bank savings accounts. By 1972, this figure had increased to $299,857.62. A considerable amount of the money was loaned to needy students through the years; in 1969–70, loans exceeded $30,000. During the 1960s, the N.I.U. Foundation borrowed from a Chicago bank in order to finance the purchase of land and property for the University. By 1970, the extent of these loans was slightly more than $500,000.[10]

The N.I.U. Parents Association, organized in 1965, has funded scholarships and other University needs through the Foundation. Since 1969, this group has sponsored an annual graduate fellowship named in honor of Earl W. Hayter. Several recipients of this fellowship have been able to carry out research abroad for their Ph.D. dissertations.

Under the direction of John Sayre, director of development, a methodical "Commitment to Excellence Program" was begun in 1968 whereby specific contacts were to be made in order to interest the DeKalb-Sycamore industries and nonindustrial groups in the development of the University. By 1969, there were seventeen corporations and persons associated with the Commitment to Excellence Program who had made gifts ranging from $25 to $2,000.[11] The Commitment to Excellence Program had a good beginning and was just gaining momentum when the campus unrest erupted, and the program's activities were reduced. John Sayre, the director, resigned shortly thereafter to accept a position at Western Illinois University.

Racial issues were beginning to become prominent at Northern by the late 1960s with the introduction of the "Black Power" movement. This movement was important in that it "took issue with the prevailing assumption that mainstream American culture was superior to other cultures." [12]

By 1967, the few hundred Black students on campus began to feel disenchanted with the lack of cultural diversity, and they organized themselves into the African and Afro-American Cultural Organization to define "what their problems are and to decide for themselves how their goals and objectives are relative to the well being of black humanity." This organization soon became the vehicle for Black unity and emphasized programs and educational experiences that would help Blacks explore their heritage.

443

In May 1968, shortly after the assassination of Martin Luther King, President Smith found himself involved in a confrontation with Black students in a sit-in at Lowden Hall. They made demands that seemed reasonable and just to him, and he promised to try to find solutions for their grievances. The students asked for a required course in white racism and African and Afro-American history. They also wanted the usual admission standards waived for Black students from the inner city who showed potential ability, the establishment of a center for African and Afro-American studies, and a bureau of Black student affairs. Finally, they wanted "the consideration merited by their unique position in a racist society, relative to flunking out," since the pressures from the white racist environment in which they had to live often hampered their success in school.[13]

Implementation of these demands soon took the form of a program for recruiting minority students, faculty, and administrators. Two new positions were approved immediately by the Board: William H. Brooks was appointed a special assistant to the president and McKinley "Deacon" Davis became administrative assistant for special projects under the vice president for student personnel services. Davis is still in charge of an expanded program, but Brooks left after a short time and was succeeded by John Mitchem. An interdisciplinary course, "Racism in American Culture and Society," was added to the curriculum. In 1971, a Black Studies program consisting of an academic minor with courses offered in several departments was initiated.

The CHANCE program (Complete Help and Assistance Necessary for a College Education) for disadvantaged students at Northern was directed by "Deacon" Davis and his assistant, Jerry Durley. It was their task to recruit students and to continue to assist them once they arrived on campus. This program was the backbone of the effort, and it used every resource possible to help the students stay on campus. From the program's beginning in the spring of 1969 through the fall of 1972, over one thousand students were admitted.

In spite of these constructive approaches to the racial problem, protests against racist policies and attitudes con-

Students engage Rhoten Smith in conversation at an informal coffee hour in 1968

tinued. There were demonstrations, threats, and disorders; Black students complained of dress codes in the dormitory dining rooms, the scarcity of Black policemen and doctors on campus, and neglect in naming any new buildings after their prominent leaders. Feelings grew tense with reports of various minor difficulties, but the climax of these tensions occurred on the night of 22 March 1969. A rumor spread that a young Black man had been apprehended while attempting to burglarize an apartment and that some white students had beaten the alleged thief while he was attempting to escape—all in the presence of the police, who also gave the victim a "roughing-up." In the ensuing violence, nearly two hundred policemen were called in. The Black students believed the worst. The campus grew tense with threats of violence, even though efforts were made by many groups to alleviate the hostility. The president appointed a committee of inquiry under Ernest Hanson to investigate the incident. (Apparently most of this was caused by rumor, for the University lawyer, John Templin, reported that the student was not hurt.) He also sent a letter to all parents explaining the disorders.[14]

Further Black protests came on 11 December 1969, when about one hundred and fifty students entered Lowden Hall in the late afternoon to consult with the president on a number of grievances—particularly the disposition of the Black Studies program which they felt was long overdue. What actually happened at this time has been variously interpreted. An anonymous letter to the local newspaper, apparently written by a University staff member, caused most of the controversial aftermath.

The president, in his official report of the sit-in, said that the students wanted a statement setting a target date for the Black Studies program. They also wanted the right to approve the director for this program. These demands, he stated, he was unable to grant. He reported that while they were in the building they lined the halls and kept the front doors locked to everyone else. They knocked over a coffee pot in a kitchen and left papers strewn on the floors. If other damage was done, he was unaware of it, for he was in his office in consultation most of the time of their stay. The campus police were ready, if

S.D.S. sponsored anti-war march from campus to Huntley Park, 16 October 1969

needed; but he did not call them for reasons that he later reported in a letter to the Lowden Hall staff.

You may also wonder why the police were not summoned to eject the students. This is an obvious response and one which I had in mind throughout the incident. It has been my observation, however, that the resort to force by the authorities, before there is real danger to persons and property, is as great a mistake as the failure to call for force when the danger becomes real. The line between the two may be a delicate one, but it is one I have to search for with earnestness and seriousness, because an error in judgment may have exceedingly regrettable consequences. In any event, it was my decision and I stand by it.[15]

The following excerpts from the unsigned letter in the *Chronicle* is a reply to the president's report:

The real reason for this letter is to bring out in the open the true facts of what happened and to let the taxpayers and citizens of DeKalb know just what sort of characters are being "mollycoddled" at the University. . . .

At about 3 p.m. a large group of black students . . . invaded the President's suite. During their complete take-over, they rifled desks and files; knocked pictures from the walls; overturned adding machines; stole money and a driver's license . . . overshoes and gloves . . . tore buttons from coats . . . left the kitchen in a complete shambles; typed obscenities and a threat to President Smith's life on one of the typewriters.

The writer further noted that harassment, terror, obscenity, and threats were leveled against some of the secretaries and at least four calls were made to the university police for help without any response. The writer concluded by saying:

We are all in sympathy with the philosophy that underprivileged Black young people be given a chance, but when their response to being given a chance is theft, violence, malicious mischief, vandalism, and intimidation we feel it is

S.D.S. sponsored anti–war march from campus to Huntley Park, 16 October 1969

time that the citizens of this community be told the truth, and that these young people be forced to face the consequences of their actions.[16]

The privilege of an unsigned letter gave the writer an opportunity to make the *cause célèbre* "sound," as Steve Newton reported in the *Star*, "like there was a marauding horde up here tearing up the place." Smith denied this emphatically and also noted in regard to personal danger that, according to his knowledge, "as one who was in the center of the occurrence throughout the two hours . . . no threats were made on my person or safety at any time. There was no damage to university property, as investigated by university inventory people the next day."[17] Some personal belongings and a small radio had disappeared, but these thefts were not witnessed by anyone. "What did happen is not condoned by me," he said, "or by anyone else," and he added that the "form of confrontation is one which we do not intend to tolerate again." However, he felt somewhat justified, for as he said,

large issues of university policy—stemming from pernicious national problems—were involved. No responsible official can allow an understandable moral outrage to cloud these larger issues. Rather, if we do focus our moral energies on the surface issues we shall miss the more profound ones and we shall make superficial and petty responses.[18]

The questioning of Smith's integrity in reporting the meeting and the chasm that grew deeper between him and some of his staff members (and some of the more conservative citizens in the area) was no doubt the result of differences in values and techniques in dealing with such matters. Nevertheless the basic issues at Northern were the same as those on the national level; specifically, to what extent and at what time should force be used to settle such violations. At Northern, the security police were held in readiness; at Kent State and Jackson State and Southern University the police were called in.

The Illinois attorney general's office suggested in 1968 that N.I.U. consider a program of police science education in the form of a "Regional Police Academy in Illinois." The plan was drawn up, and after some discussion and modification, Executive Vice-President Geigle indicated that Northern was interested. He commented that it would be "a great benefit to the people of Illinois and in the field of law enforcement in general."[19] There seemed to be no question that the need for better professional police training was urgent. N.I.U. had been holding semi-annual police institutes (all of which were oversubscribed); and many policemen from northern Illinois had to be turned away.

President Smith also indicated an interest in the program, but is was soon discovered that there was competition for this proposed college of police science; however, N.I.U. was in a good position to be selected for the site. Smith was careful to point out in his letter to Attorney General William Scott that such a program would have to be made an integral part of the University, "subject to the same canons of academic freedom and academic control of the curriculum which all of our other colleges enjoy," which meant that "neither I nor any other president can approve the establishment of a new academic program of any kind without the concurrence of the appropriate faculty committees and councils." Smith did have, in spite of these hurdles, "every confidence that the kind of school . . . described in this letter would receive the enthusiastic support of the faculty . . . but I cannot, of course, speak for them."[20]

To investigate the feasibility of such a program, an *ad hoc* committee was appointed to study "a degree program in law enforcement and corrections at NIU." In time the committee proposed a program in "law enforcement, corrections and related disciplines" that might be conceived as a "School of Social Justice." It was recommended that this program "should be sufficiently broad to include persons who seek careers in criminology, community relations, community organization, race relations, neighborhood services, social welfare and education as well as in law enforcement and corrections as these may be more narrowly construed."[21]

Great opposition to this report was expressed by students who urged that the program be defeated. The Student Association unanimously condemned the project, stating that it was being shoved down their throats. Some seventy students marched to Lowden Hall to express this feeling. The Blacks also saw it as another plot to increase the number of police and to give police greater control over the Black community. Four-letter words were flung about with fury, in leaflets and cartoons, portending what was to follow in only a few months. Several faculty members were also vocal in opposition to the concept.

The opposition, in spite of the emphasis on social justice, grew so hostile to the whole idea that the *ad hoc* committee finally voted against establishing any program. This decision was made on 5 May 1970, the day following the Kent State University killings.[22]

Until the late 1950s, security on campus had not been much of a problem. By 1958, the year authorization to carry revolvers was granted, there were still only three full-time police officers. In 1960, a major change was made in the Security Department when Donald E. Bruer was engaged as security and traffic supervisor of the N.I.U. police force, which at that time consisted of six officers and several students serving as courtesy patrolmen and desk clerks.

Bruer was professionally trained, and he installed an in-service training program, conducted by the FBI with some of the more modern electronic instruments, in order to modernize the service. He also strongly advocated the idea of a police training school at Northern, not only to benefit his force but other northern Illinois lawmen as well. By 1963, the force was increased to nine policemen and five full-time watchmen; for the first time they were given complete police authority and no longer had to depend upon the county sheriff for the power of arrest.[23]

When Bruer resigned in 1969 and James Elliott was made the director, the force had grown to over twenty-five employees, including the safety officer, seven nightwatchmen, and two meter-maids. In 1971, Diane Palombi made history when she was appointed the first female police officer at Northern after she graduated highest in her class in the Law Enforcement Basic Training Institute at the University. Elliott also inaugurated other changes such as "rap" sessions and workshops for officers and students. The Campus Security Advisory Board was created to receive and investigate complaints against the security force from students, faculty, and administrative staff, and to advise the president on various problems.

Though many things were done to keep the lines of communication open among the contending parties, much concern was expressed about campus police powers in respect to eavesdropping, use of electronic devices, and maintaining secret files on political and social ideas expressed in the University community. The question of the right of the campus police to invade student privacy was also a concern, especially after they "searched" or "inspected" the dormitory room of Charna Frank. The students called it the former and the police the latter; but whatever it was, it raised a civil-rights issue as to whether a student's room may be entered and, if so, upon what conditions. When the findings were finally completed on the case, President Smith decided that the room had not been searched, but inspected, and no one was to blame. He did, however, make changes in the student code regulating such matters.

Another controversy involving the Security Department took place soon after Richard Nelson came to the presidency. In January 1972, it was revealed that the department had employed an undercover agent, James E. Carlson, for sixteen months. In order to secure all the information possible on this case, the University Council asked that the Campus Security Advisory Board, under the chairmanship of Otto Olsen, make a thorough investigation. Members of this committee were handicapped in their investigation, since no records of Carlson's specific activities and reports were available. The Security Department insisted that Carlson was to seek out and report only "information on actual crime." Although Carlson had joined the Student Mobilization Committee, Elliott insisted that no records of a political nature had been given his agency or any other. The Advisory Board was highly critical of Carlson's assignment and expressed concern that political surveillance may have been involved.

One of the more controversial aspects of the committee's findings was that in the spring of 1970, John Gardner, assistant to the president, furnished the Security Office with a list of members of the Student Mobilization Committee because, he explained when it was discovered, "it was an object of curiosity." Elliott claimed he had destroyed the lists upon receipt; but his public relations officer, George Boyle, gave conflicting evidence, claiming that he was given them and still "personally retains copies of them." The committee claimed this action was political in nature and that it was improper for the administration to supply the lists and for the Security Office to accept them.

In concluding their findings, the committee called attention to a number of possible ramifications of this undercover work in the form of spying and reporting on activities of students and faculty members, actions that the University administration must prohibit in the future. Furthermore, it recommended that the president "should determine and administer appropriate discipline to the Assistant to the President [John Gardner], for supplying membership lists of a lawful student organization [the Student Mobilization Committee] to the Security Department, and to members of the Security Department who accepted those lists." [24]

President Nelson took no action on this recommendation until Vice President Richard Smith had completed an official account of the affair. Nelson's reaction then was that steps must be taken to prevent a recurrence of employment of undercover officers without his permission. He also informed the University Council that Elliott was "wrong in assuming the authority to hire . . . Carlson" for this purpose.

In spite of the president's closing remarks to the University Council that "a directive has been issued to insure that this will not happen again," some members who were not satisfied with this solution made efforts to censure or remove from office certain officials, but all such efforts failed. In the Student

Association, however, a motion did pass advocating that the president dismiss John Gardner; the president chose not to follow this advice.[25]

The ROTC issue on campus was not entirely a new question in the 1960s. As early as 1951, President Holmes asked for a vote on the proposition of a campus unit. With a large percentage of his faculty in favor of a temporary program, Holmes took the matter up with Leslie Arends, member of the U.S. House of Representatives, requesting tthat Arends inquire of the Air Force regarding the possibilities. Arends reported that there were no new units being developed at that time in educational institutions. Not to be undone, a few months later Holmes made further inquiry and was again informed that there was "no possibility of securing such military units."[26]

In the spring of 1968, N.I.U. was asked by the Fifth Army District to submit an application for an ROTC unit. Smith was unwilling to act on such a sensitive issue until he was assured of internal agreement; thus the idea began the rounds of an in-depth analysis from every point of view. It finally came before the University Council, where the elected representatives of the faculty voted 7 against and 6 in favor with 4 abstaining, whereas the appointed administrative members were unanimously in favor, making the total vote 17 for, 7 against, 4 abstaining, and 1 absent. Polls of the faculty in the four colleges had resulted in a distribution of 430 in favor, 155 opposed, and 28 with no opinion. The College of Liberal Arts and Sciences was almost tied on the question. The Council on Instruction held numerous discussions and finally voted unanimously in favor of application for an ROTC unit. The Student Association Board was opposed to it by a 7 to 6 majority, but a freshman men's opinion poll had only 1 in 5 opposed.[27]

A "Case Against the ROTC at NIU" was submitted by four history professors as a position paper for discussion of the issue: David Wagner acted as the chairman, and various representatives from other departments and organizations such as the American Association of University Professors and the University Council presented their views. But even such disputants, with highly documented arguments from respectable sources, were not able to secure even a delay in the start of the program.

With favorable reception from nearly all quarters of the University, President Smith finally filed the application. A sharp minority feeling, expressed by several professors and Jim Kiley, the fighting president of the Student Association Board, desperately challenged the administration, but the unit was approved by the Board.[28]

In the fall of 1967, a young instructor by the name of Peter Roman joined the political science department. According to various reports, Roman was an outstanding classroom teacher, and many of the more radically inclined students (those of the New Left) also found in him a real leader and protagonist for their causes. To promote the views of these activists Roman established an underground newspaper—*News From Nowhere* —which also served as a vehicle for his Marxian ideas.

With the opening of Roman's second year, after the political science department personnel committee had made its evaluation of him, Roman was notified by the department head, Dr. Daniel Wit, that his contract would not be renewed another year because he had not finished work on his doctoral dissertation and that this requirement was expected not only of him but of the other young instructors as well. Wit was especially careful to point out that Roman had not been fired, and this action did not have any bearing whatsoever upon his activities as a campus activist.

Immediately this action was attacked by some faculty members and students, on the grounds that Roman was an outstanding teacher and that it was absurd to lose the services of this dynamic person only because he lacked the doctorate. Roman at first seemed resigned to the idea, believing that he was not discriminated against for his personal views, since two other members of the department also received the same treatment. But in time he changed his position and took stronger measures to test the policy of retention.

He had plenty of assistance from friends, and soon petitions were circulated and presented to Wit asking that Roman be retained one more year. Other organizations, such as SDS, the American Federation of Teachers, the Student Association, the Faculty Committee for Social Responsibility, and the Associated Ministries Council, lent their support to various aspects of this case.[29]

As time moved along and no favorable action was taken, the pro-Roman faction adopted more extreme measures. They interrupted classes and held a rally in the University Center, with between four hundred and one thousand students present. A group also staged a sit-in at Lowden Hall for several hours.

By no means all students were in sympathy with Roman; most were more moderate and believed that if he had spent his time on his Ph.D. dissertation instead of selling *News From Nowhere* on the downtown street corners, he would have had no difficulty remaining in the department. Some anti-Roman students even circulated petitions to have Student Association president Jim Chestnut impeached for his actions in support of Roman.[30]

When appeals of the department's decision not to renew the contract reached the final stage—the University Council—some three hundred students (not all for Roman) were present at the meeting in the University Center Regency Room. Four student speakers, Jim Chestnut, Mike Haines, Steve Miller, and Frank Boehm, made strong indictments before the Council. Boehm said: "You men sit here publishing book after book, article after article and it's all meaningless. You men sit here judging Peter Roman and not one of you achieved as high a rating as he did in the [recently published] teacher evaluation." Steve Miller took a more direct approach in his statement: "Illegal as you are, we are going to, in the name of democracy, give you another chance to redeem yourselves. We are going to lock you in."

About two hundred of the students for Roman walked out, sat down in the hall outside the Regency Room, and blocked the door, leaving a paper padlock—three feet tall—on one door as a symbol of a lock-in. The University Council then proceeded to approve the Personnel Committee's report, by 23 to 3, confirming the original decision. When Council members attempted to leave the room, the protesting students decided to re-enter and, by encircling the Council members with locked arms, prevent their departure. These tactics failed, and President Smith with most of his colleagues escaped from the stage through a partition opening into the adjoining ballroom.

This was the final scene in the Peter Roman drama. The months of struggle, involving a large segment of the University, did have beneficial effects in that it stirred up the students and started them thinking about fundamental aspects of decision-making in personnel matters, promotion of faculty, tenure, research, writing and teaching, and departmental autonomy.[31]

Unlike earlier student protests at Northern, which were largely concerned with internal University matters, those culminating in May 1970 were similar to events occurring on other campuses across the nation.

There was a noticeable increase in protest as early as 1965, when students began to demonstrate with marches, counter-marches, and rallies for and against the war in Vietnam. At this time the "hawkish" students were so in favor of more participation in Vietnam that they wrote General Westmoreland, commander of the U.S. forces in Vietnam, to this effect. The Free Speech area was frequently used by advocates of the Student Mobilization Committee and the Vietnam Moratorium Committee, actively discussing withdrawal dates. Profoundly affected by the continued escalation of the war and the events of the 1968 Democratic convention in Chicago, the students at Northern followed the national trend of ever-increasing activism and protest.

By late 1969, feeling on Northern's campus had reached such a point that a moratorium of classes was observed by many students and faculty to support the National Moratorium Committee's demand that President Nixon set a date for withdrawal of troops from the war. On 15 October a large torchlight parade was staged with about two thousand marchers carrying *all manner of burning objects, including kerosene-soaked rags wrapped around sticks, rolls of burning toilet tissue, candles, flashlights, flares and railroad lanterns.*

Ten abreast and curb-to-curb, the paraders [some of whom were DeKalb citizens] filled Carroll ave. from the Lucinda ave. intersection to the post office Pagoda. . . . The march route moved north on Carroll before turning west on Lucinda toward the West Campus area. . . .

Participants seemed to be in good spirits, buoyed up the the large turnout and the knowledge that they were taking part in a nationwide movement. . . .

Returning . . . the marchers walked back to the University Center Carl Sandburg Lecture Hall where a capacity audience heard speeches. . . . [32]

A few weeks after the march, the Student Association allocated $7,500 to cover the cost of buses to take three hundred students to an anti-war march in Washington, D.C. Since this was a rather sizeable appropriation for such a relatively small group—at the expense of the many—President Smith for the first time felt compelled to exercise his right of veto. The Student Association called for a referendum on the question. When the final vote was counted, the funding was opposed by nearly three to one. Nevertheless, there was a hue and cry among students that they should control their own funds.[33]

As the University moved into the fateful second semester of 1970, more students were beginning to "shed their idealism" for a more direct approach to the solution of their difficulties. For some time they had believed they could work within the system to achieve peace, civil rights, economic and political justice, as well as academic rights and privileges. Now it was becoming obvious, not only at N.I.U. but throughout the nation, that the polarization of generations had at last created such disillusionment and cynicism that the only solution left, many students argued, was for the rebellious counter-culture to make a frontal attack on the old values.

This frontal attack was further accelerated at Northern by such campus speakers as William Kunstler, defender of the "Conspiracy Seven" in Chicago, and others less provocative such as Ralph Nader and Dr. Benjamin Spock. On Thursday, 30 April President Nixon added further fuel to the flame by announcing to a nationwide television audience that American forces and bombers were making attacks inside Cambodia. Additional outrage came suddenly when four students were shot and killed by Ohio National Guard troops at Kent State University on 4 May.

These killings served as a catalyst at N.I.U. The first reaction came when about one hundred and fifty students vandalized and broke windows in several buildings. A special Student Association meeting was held the night after the Kent State shooting. Some fifteen hundred spectators were present as the Kent State affair, ROTC, the war, and possible closing of the University were discussed. Following the speeches and discussion, a group of students marched to the downtown area, breaking windows in several businesses. They were finally turned back by local police and state troopers, and thirty-seven were arrested. After returning to the campus, students meted out further destruction, especially in the new shopping center on Lucinda Avenue.

President Smith decried these destructive acts as "simple-minded vandalism" and a very inappropriate response to what happened at Kent State. However, he did take cognizance that "students here at NIU, and elsewhere throughout the nation, feel . . . a great and profound concern for our nation and where it is going. They see a war they hoped to be ending, actually being broadened. They see a people ever more seriously divided, and they despair. They literally despair, I think for the future of our country." [34]

The next day, 6 May, he announced to the University Council a two-day moratorium for all classes so that faculty and students could reflect and examine the pressing campus and national issues. That night, the largest demonstration in Northern's history took place. An estimated eight thousand students marched "in opposition to all forms of violence." So well was it organized that it was later referred to by Smith as "the spirit of May 6." There were no arrests, injuries, or incidents of violence. Notwithstanding this peaceful march, there were still many who wanted to act on the issues instead of analyzing them.

In response to continuing pressure, Smith convened an all-University convocation (and University Council meeting) on 11 May. Before an overflow audience in the Field House, the president announced that he was calling for a student-faculty referendum on the retention of ROTC. He also announced that students were to be given greater decision-making powers. Five students would be added to the Council on Instruction, ten would be invited to sit with the University Council, and the University constitution, if voted upon favorably by students and faculty, would also place students representatives in the proposed University Senate. He concluded his remarks by saying that for Northern students to find it necessary to resort to force was an

enormous tragedy that none of us can overlook . . . . Regardless of who or what is ultimately at fault, the very fact that force is necessary to preserve an uneasy peace means that the educational system is failing . . . and there are those on this campus who are quite willing to smash this university out of their own rage and frustration.[35]

Smith reported to the Board in June that after several days of disruptions in DeKalb and on the campus, as well as continuing provocations from around the nation, one positive note had appeared at Northern: "Faculty members, few of whom have done much more than applaud or criticize after the fact our handling of previous student dissent, now began to come forward in encouraging numbers with offers to help, with ideas, with expressions of concern. In short, many of them began to realize the extent of their own responsibility to help see the University through this crisis." The moratorium had also cooled the campus community somewhat. Smith's endless hours of talking with students and his informative letters to parents were positive factors in an experience he later called "the most tumultuous I have ever lived through."

A short-lived peace followed the eventful Field House meeting. On 14 May, just as the president began to feel satisfaction and confidence, reports of the deaths of two Blacks at Jackson State set off a new round of trouble. An immediate response was forthcoming from both Black and white stu-

461

dents, requesting the same tribute for these victims as was given those at Kent State. This he granted in the form of a second two-day moratorium on 18 and 19 May, thus postponing the ROTC referendum until 20 May. According to Smith, this second moratorium evoked a storm of criticism against him much heavier than had been the case with the first one. There were many who wanted sterner methods used to keep the University open.

As for many of the students, they, too, were disturbed by the campus turmoil, which made classroom work and preparation for final examinations most difficult. Student senators, expressing the students' anxiety in this situation, voted for a suspension of classes for the balance of the semester, as Southern Illinois University had done. Northern's administration rejected this suggestion but did grant an emergency grading provision permitting instructors to give grades based on a modified pass-fail option. It also requested that "faculty members consider sympathetically all the options available to the student and . . . in courses where it is appropriate, assigning a grade on the basis of the student's achievement prior to the development of the current emergency." [36]

Monday night, 18 May, Father James Groppi of Milwaukee spoke on campus, and "blasted critics of student violence as 'hypocritical' in light of governmental violence in Southeast Asia, at Kent and at Jackson." He was invited to lead a march in memory of the Jackson killings over the same route the marchers had taken on 6 May. This march—of about fifteen hundred—was peaceful, for student marshals with armbands made every effort to keep it under control, arguing that any violence might subject Groppi to arrest under federal conspiracy charges.

Upon the return of the marchers to the University Center, Groppi left and all but about two hundred students dispersed. These remained in the Free Speech area and at about midnight decided to march to DeKalb. They were met by a line of police, who stopped them at the bridge on Lincoln Highway. The students began a highway sit-in. This brought about one of the most highly publicized and most dramatic incidents in the history of the institution. President Smith "was called out of

*President Rhoten Smith with students on Lincoln Highway Bridge during May
1970 protest sit–in*

bed" and immediately "donned a pair of chinos, a sweater and a baseball cap . . . and went down to the bridge" where he joined the sit-in group in front of "a line of about 15 policemen holding long riot clubs . . . while a gas machine could be heard warming up nearby."

He had gone to the bridge to try to convince the students to go home. This is his report of what took place:

I crossed the police lines and went among the students, many of whom I knew. The mood at this point was gentle and good-natured. When they asked me to sit with them, I did, moving frequently and trying to persuade them to clear the highway and regroup at the lagoon. At this point early on Tuesday morning, the group was leaderless, without any clear purpose, and essentially peaceful. If we could have talked them off of the street at this point all that followed that week might have been avoided.

As time wore on, however, the group was augmented by many others, mostly onlookers, but individuals who swelled the total numbers nevertheless. Also, many more militant students, black and white, joined the group, so that it became angrier, louder and much more volatile. Also the main participants became restive and less patient. By 3:00 A.M. it was clear the group could not be persuaded to move but would have to be dispersed by force.[37]

After the president gave up hope and departed, the state police moved in and warned the crowd to clear the highway within five minutes. As the police moved in, the protestors fled. Crossing the campus toward the dormitories, they regrouped frequently, with the police making more arrests each time. Windows were broken on campus and again at the new Village Commons shopping center, where several police and students were hurt. Thirty-five persons—not all students—were arrested.

Tuesday, 19 May, was quiet during the day, but that night hundreds of students gathered in Sandburg Hall for a "teach-in" on the ROTC question, which was to be voted upon the next day. Following the debates, a crowd gathered at the Center and decided to block the highway at the bridge. Again they were quickly dispersed by the state police with gas foggers. The hostile demonstrators moved to the West Campus where windows were broken, street barricades were built, signs were destroyed, and university vehicles were overturned or burned.

At the Village Commons shopping center, which had already been hit twice during the month, stores were broken into and some looting was reported, while back on the campus a firebomb went off in the old Still Gym. When police entered the dormitory area on the West Campus, rocks and bottles rained down upon them by students who had sought refuge by barricading the doors with furniture. Once more several students received minor injuries, and fifty-four were arrested, including several non-students. According to the president, this confrontation was the "first time we had a full-scale riot on our hands."

Wednesday was an active day, with a tremendous campaign to get the faculty and students out to vote ROTC off the campus. That night many gathered before their campus TV set to hear the results; the vote was 7,186 to 5,197 in favor of retention of the program.

This was a shock to the activists. A roving crowd committed some aimless violence in the Williston Hall vicinity where the ROTC had its headquarters; following this they started for Lincoln Highway, but, instead of going toward the bridge and downtown, they turned toward the University City shopping center where they inflicted considerable damage with rocks. This particular event was filmed and shown over Rockford and Chicago TV stations.

By Thursday, 21 May the citizenry of DeKalb was so aroused that law enforcement agencies and the city officials began to feel that whatever force was necessary to stop the vandalism should be used, even if the University had to be closed. Fortunately, there were only minor difficulties the rest of the week.

From 26 May to 2 June, the students were busy with academic matters, and it was hard to believe that the previous week's events had actually taken place. The only evidence that remained on campus and in the city as a reminder were some boarded-up windows. However, beneath the surface were unhealed wounds. Who was to pay the costs for damaged property which ran to approximately $54,000—more than half of that on the campus? The question of damages became a major issue and the DeKalb City Council attempted unsuccessfully to secure payment from the Board of Regents. The City Council also aroused the students the following September by enacting a curfew ordinance prohibiting persons, including local citizens and student press reporters, from being on DeKalb streets during a "state of emergency." [38]

Out of this uproar, the Illinois House of Representatives passed a resolution calling upon university officials to testify on the unrest and the reasons for the temporary closing of the schools. President Smith was selected to speak, along with presidents from Southern Illinois and the University of Illinois. Smith's presentation received the highest commendation of the three; in fact the *Chicago Sun-Times* editorially commended him for his informative speech and prudent leadership during the critical moments at N.I.U., comparing his leadership to that of the University of Chicago some time earlier. Pat McAtee, president of the Student Association, accompanied Smith to Springfield and spoke as a representative of the students. He told the lawmakers how national and international events during May 1970 suddenly aroused in the N.I.U. student body a sense of frustration and violence. One recommendation he made to them was to grant eighteen-year-olds the right to vote.

Following these speeches in Springfield, petitions were circulated—one endorsed by State Senator Dennis Collins, a long-time protector of citizens of northern Illinois from subversive ideas—requesting the General Assembly to enact several laws. These laws were to prevent the closing or opening of schools whose dates are predetermined; to prevent student polls from deciding matters of curriculum, including ROTC; to expel and deny re-admission to students arrested for unlawful acts on campuses; to ban all campus organizations which advocate violence against anyone connected with a university; and to restrict the distribution of "political literature" that advocated violence. The legislators claimed these laws were necessary to preserve the institutions that taxpayers were called upon to support; to back up this petition, the petitioners asked that

a joint committee from both political parties, and from both the House and the Senate be immediately formed to investigate the conditions at our universities, to re-evaluate the performance of those who lead the schools, to evaluate the faculty with which these heads of education have surrounded themselves and [to] immediately remove those who show incompetence, poor judgment, and those who through their actions have openly aligned themselves with these illegal and highly destructive demonstrations.[39]

Before the closing session of the Illinois General Assembly in 1970, a Joint Commission on Campus Disorders was created, with Senator William Horsley as chairman and Senator Collins as one of its members. The committee held a series of hearings at various locations, where faculty, students, taxpayers, administrators, and others were called to testify.

One meeting was held at DeKalb on 12 and 13 November 1970, with Senator Collins presiding. One faculty member from Northern, Sean Shesgreen, gave the committee his views on why students had "provoked a nationwide response" and also what the committee's obligations were in respect to it:

No country can afford to alienate its youth, for they are its only and its most valuable asset. It is the obligation of this committee, therefore, to respond positively and imaginatively to what the young people of America demand: a world without war, a country free of racism, a country which offers equal opportunity to all its citizens regardless of race and sex. This committee must remember that it is they and not the disenfranchised students who will be judged by the prophecy: "Those who make peaceful revolution impossible make violent revolution inevitable."[40]

The hearing did have some unpleasant implications. The local A.C.L.U. threatened suit for violations of the civil liberties of some witnesses. The advisory committee of the history department also drew up an indictment of certain violations and, especially, intimidations that posed a serious threat to the First Amendment rights of several of the witnesses. The hearings, according to the historians, were apparently undertaken "to pillory any member of a university community whose political and social views do not coincide with those of the committee . . . ," thus creating a fear of the consequences of what teachers taught or what social, economic, and political views they espoused.[41]

After three months of investigation, the Horsley committee finally submitted its report to the 76th General Assembly with mixed reactions from its members; two of its eleven Republican commisioners did not sign it, and all seven Democrats signed a dissenting statement. Perhaps the most intelligent reaction was by a Republican member, Senator Robert Coulson, who in a separate statement observed that the student problem was a national one and "calls for a long-range solution rather than short-range reactions. It has interrelations with a dozen other facets of our society which we have had no opportunity to examine." Senator Collins, to the contrary, termed the report "very important"; however, he did think that the faculty members were uncooperative.[42]

In the next legislative session Senator Horsley introduced fourteen bills granting powers to universities and colleges to control unruly students and faculty, but in the end none were enacted.

In the few years since the protests that peaked on that eventful night in May, many observations and evaluations of the "youth revolution" have been made. Some observers have concluded that, like most such phenomena, it was successful in accelerating various changes in educational institutions as well as in personal and psychological areas. For example, it appears that the "new generation" has adopted "an increased tolerance for diversity" in their ways of thought and their life styles, even to the extent that the older generation has chosen to emulate

One of the "Arboretum 12" being removed from tree during March 1971
protests

some of them. They are also devoting more time to their studies and private lives and less to political radicalism. One student writer said that they now have more interest in "burning the midnight oil instead of the ROTC building." Many also seem to have had a change in mood, especially the seniors, who appear to be running scared, looking for jobs, and complaining of the financial squeeze.

It seems apparent that the youth of today have a higher commitment to various progressive and humanitarian causes, such as ecology and conservation, local politics, and the poor, as well as greater open-mindedness, genuineness, compassion, and empathy for racial minorities, than previous generations. In politics, the citizen-students have become so alert within a span of hardly one general election that they are being wooed for some important local offices. Moreover, they seem more realistic when facing such agonizing human problems as abortion, discrimination, illegitimacy, and amnesty for army deserters and draft dodgers than do their elders.[43] C.A. Reich believes that many of these changes in youth are of revolutionary importance and are not a

passing fad or a form of dissent or refusal, nor are they in any sense irrational. The whole emerging pattern, from ideals to campus demonstrations to beads and bell bottoms to the Woodstock Festival, makes sense and is a part of a consistent philosophy. It is both necessary and inevitable, and in time will include not only youth, but all people in America.[44]

At the other end of the continuum, however, are other judgments of the revolution and the new generation. For example, two outstanding intellectual historians, Oscar and Mary Handlin, in their recent book *Facing Life: Youth and the Family in America* (1971) devote their final chapter to this revolution, in which they take a more critical view of the "troublemakers" of the 1960s who were "rebels without a cause" and "Student Radicals," who were "spoiled by permissive parents."

"Guess Who" play rock music in Field House, 1971

At the University Council meeting on 6 January 1971, President Smith revealed his plans to resign, effective 1 August, in order to accept the chief academic post at the University of Pittsburgh. He spoke frankly to a "stunned group of faculty members, administrators, and students," giving his reason as follows:

> I am leaving Northern for only one reason: I have been offered a new and especially exciting academic challenge, one which, I might add, I did not actively seek. After a truly agonizing period of weighing the opportunities for service and fulfillment, I have accepted. . . .

He concluded his statement on a personal note:

> It's going to be a very, very painful wrench for me and my family to leave here. We have heavy emotional investments, I find, in this university and its future and its success.[45]

As soon as the announcement was made, many in the University community expressed "great disappointment and not[ed] his departure represents a blow to the university." A.A.U.P. president Donald E. Polzin expressed his sentiments on what Smith meant to the University:

> We are suffering a great loss. He has certainly led us through a very difficult period of growth and done so admirably. While I wish him well, I regret he has decided to leave during this crucial point of development.
>
> One of his major accomplishments has been to open up the university. He has always respected faculty members and made every effort to involve faculty in his decisions. He always sought counsel from faculty and used faculty advisors in every major decision.[46]

President Smith was evaluated by other faculty members as a liberal, flexible individual who was able during his administration to liberalize as well as to enhance the values and the academic style of the institution. He was often praised for his

Vermeer Quartet in 1969: left to right: Shmuel Ashkenasi, Pierre Menard,
Richard Sher, Scott Nickrenz

excellent rapport with students and his understanding of their grievances. Some faculty members, however, felt that Smith's rapport did not carry over in his dealings with the faculty, and that he had too little contact with them; nor was his relationship with his staff sufficiently harmonious for him to carry out some of his policies. Perhaps the only widespread criticism of him was his decision to file an application for a unit of the ROTC.

Members of the Student Association, who had differed with him on many occasions, nevertheless "came to trust him." Gayle Maurovich, one of the ten students named to the University Council, felt that Smith had "done a lot to make NIU a better place, not just quantitatively but qualitatively. . . . I only wish he would have stayed at least until I had finished." Michael Maibach, a former Student Association senator, first student representative to the DeKalb City Council, and elected member of the DeKalb County Board, said of the president: "Rhoten Smith came to be a close friend of mine and of many students. During the riots, a time of raised voices and angry words, he retained his ability to listen to both sides and to then respond as a fellow human being." [47] Many in the Black community likewise expressed sincere regrets about his resignation; Smith had been a leader in promoting racial justice at Northern and in developing a Black academic program.

Evaluation of President Smith by the usual standards is difficult, for he served during the most abnormal times of any of the presidents. In addition to the disruptions of student protest, there were many other factors—including a statewide budget freeze on building construction—that stymied his program. Even though recruitment of new faculty declined, he was able to initiate the practice of offering higher salaries to retain good faculty members and maximum salaries for the employment of two or three outstanding scholars. Enrollment increases, too, began to decline, until by the fall of 1971 they came to a grinding halt. For the first time in nearly two decades the numbers game with students, buildings, and faculty members was over. No longer could statistics serve as substitutes for—or solutions to—massive educational problems in the "fastest growing University in the State of Illinois."

Commencement at Stadium, 1966

Richard J. Nelson,
seventh president, 1971–

11

Creating the Future

THE ERA of long-term college and university presidencies apparently came to an end during the turbulent sixties. No longer do universities expect to develop the life-tenured presidential "giants" of the past; instead, increasing numbers of institutions are constantly in search of new leaders. For example, during 1970 more than one hundred and seventy colleges and universities chose new presidents. In the first two months of 1971, there were one hundred and twelve schools looking for chief executives. Something seems to have happened to those ivory tower positions that were once looked upon as security "roughly equal to that of a Supreme Court Justice."

Today, in the aftermath of the student revolution, often highly qualified candidates are reluctant presidential aspirants. They are also more thoroughly screened and are expected to have vastly different credentials than formerly. One student of this subject has compared these positions

unfavorably with that of a pro-hockey referee . . . . The work is rough, physically exhausting, even dangerous . . . . A modern university president is expected to have practical vision, a good

477

*track record in administration, and national prominence as a
scholar. He must be a good public speaker . . . writer, analyst,
friend and colleague, manipulator of power, planner, co-
worker, persuader, and disciplinarian. He must have an attractive family and an indefatigable and effortlessly sociable wife.
He must be a Money Man, Academic Manager, Father Figure,
Public Relations Man, Political Man, and Educator. In short,
. . . as Herman B. Wells, former president of Indiana University, said . . . "He should be born with the physical strength of a
Greek athlete, the cunning of a Machiavelli, the wisdom of a
Solomon, the courage of a lion, if possible. But in any case he
must be born with the stomach of a goat."*[1]

Immediately upon receiving President Smith's resignation
on 6 January 1971, the Board of Regents and its chairman,
Gordon H. Millar, set up a selection committee to find a
candidate who would meet these new qualifications. The chairman was fully aware that a new president would not be easy to
find, for he must have "qualifications and capabilities broader
than have been traditional." There were "extremely difficult
problems to face with regard to the management of a $50
million enterprise"—especially at a time when funds were
becoming more limited. In the light of this urgency, he also
noted that "the Board would encourage both search committees [Northern's and Illinois State University's] to broaden the
aspect of the search, to take off the traditional constraints in
order to attract people to the university who may not have been
so attracted in the past. . . ."[2] Richard Little, the newly appointed chairman of the selection committee, also made a
rather prophetic observation, considering the candidate later
selected, by noting that for years individuals chosen for such
position had been scholars or those who had demonstrated
leadership in higher education but that now necessary qualities
"may very well be found in an individual with another range of
experience. . . ."

After considerable debate in the University Council as to the
best composition of a selection committee, it was finally decided
to include five faculty members (one from the University
Council and one from each of the four academic colleges) and

three students, along with three Board members. Richard Little, secretary of the University Council, was chosen by that body as the committee's chairman; Jack Arends (replaced by Eleanor Caldwell because of illness), J. Howard Nelson, Francis E. Stroup, and Alfred Young were elected by the faculty; Raymond Richardson, Renard Jackson, and Leslie Starks were chosen from the student body; and the three chosen by the Board were J. Robert Barr, Loren M. Smith, and Anthony Varese. This committee, after approval by the Board, immediately began to organize and to seek nominations. The committee also had six advisory groups, representing academic deans, students, faculty, operating staff, Black faculty and other minorities, and alumni. The committee was able to eliminate a certain amount of duplication by coordinating its efforts with those of the Illinois State University committee which was also in search of a new president. Nothing was spared to expedite the process: a house was fully equipped as an office, a secretary was assigned to the committee, and a budget of $16,125 was appropriated.

With the input from these several sources as well as the assistance of many faculty members, as many as 360 names were finally submitted. From this number the list was reduced to five, who were invited to the campus. Each was interviewed and observed for about a day and a half by individuals and by groups. When this was completed and the evaluation reports were filed from the six advisory groups, one name ranked highest on the list, and Richard J. Nelson was accepted by the whole Board of Regents on 16 June 1971.[3]

President Nelson was born in Chicago, 15 November 1915, attended the public schools there, and worked in a bank as a clerk before going to the University of Illinois. He was graduated in 1940 with a bachelor's degree in journalism. He then interrupted his career by serving five years in the army, in which he obtained the rank of captain, but remained six more years in the National Guard, where he rose to the rank of colonel. Following his departure from the regular army, he entered Northwestern University Law School, where he received a J.D. degree in 1948. For about a year, he was a member of a law firm in Chicago before he accepted a position as assistant attorney general in Springfield. The following year he became an administrative assistant to Governor Adlai E. Stevenson, whom he served until 1952. Next he joined the Inland Steel Corporation, where he served as manager of labor relations, director of public relations, and finally as assistant vice president for public affairs until his election as president of N.I.U.

While pursuing these several professional responsibilities, he still gave an enormous amount of time to educational, political, and civic-related activities. He served on numerous committees and boards in public schools, libraries, historical societies, and alumni associations and taught evening courses on collective bargaining for several years at both Northwestern University and the University of Chicago. His most important experiences in the field of education, as far as Northern was concerned, had been his numerous appointments to governing boards of higher educational institutions in Illinois. In 1961, he accepted an appointment to the Illinois Board of Higher Education (IBHE) and was a member until 1965. During this time he participated in the completion of the first two phases of the "Master Plan for Education in Illinois" and also served part of that time as vice chairman. In 1965, he was appointed to the Board of Governors of State Colleges and Universities (BGSCU), which governed N.I.U. until 1967. Nelson was serving as BGSCU chairman when Rhoten Smith was appointed president and was a member of Smith's selection committee. Nelson was on the IBHE a second time, between January 1967 and May 1968, as *ex officio* member because of his chairmanship of the BGSCU.

Politically he is a Democrat and has served as president of both the Young Democrats of Illinois (1950) and the Young Democrat Clubs of America (1951–1953). He served as chairman or vice chairman on various civic committees dealing with fair employment practices, constitutional revision, revenue problems, civil liberties, and human relations, and had received several awards for his work in these areas.

Richard Nelson was a firm believer in the civil liberties for all groups and individuals. This was no better illustrated than when he was the only member of the BGSCU to cast a favorable vote for the employment of Staughton Lynd on the faculty at Chicago State College. The Board ostensibly denied Lynd this position because he had defied the State Department in 1965 by visiting North Vietnam. Nelson regarded this decision as so important that he gave his colleagues on the Board an elaborate statement hoping to persuade them to protect the "hard won legacy of freedom" in higher education.[4]

Nelson was not one who restricted his libertarianism to education alone. He had at one time headed a committee in Springfield for the purpose of securing fair employment legislation, and, according to Franklyn Haiman, chairman of the American Civil Liberties Union in Illinois, it was his leadership that finally secured its enactment.

Inland Steel had an unusually liberal policy that all employees not only should participate in community, civic, and political affairs, but also were encouraged to hold elective office if they so desired.[5] Nelson, moreover, had an interesting point of view on the parallels between being an executive of Inland Steel and the president of an educational institution. He felt that the

basic goal of a corporation is to be efficient and to make money and it's not a democratic institution. The function of a university is not to make money. I think it has a responsibility to marshal and take care of the funds that it has and spend them wisely in its more fundamental objective of the search for truth through teaching, research and service. It's just a different ball game. And I think that as someone from the business community, a very important personal goal of mine is to make it clear to the faculty and to the student body . . . that I understand the differences and don't want to make an efficient business out of Northern Illinois University.[6]

The new president was oriented with exceptional sensitivity to student and faculty problems, and these groups were quick to sense this; however, in the case of the former it did not mean that Nelson always agreed with them. For example, when he was asked whether students should have rights to judge the qualifications of those who teach them, he replied with some-

481

what the same views as his immediate predecessor (and the A.A.U.P.) had expressed previously: "In terms of selection and firing," he said, "it makes more sense to me that students have a role in reviewing the capabilities of instructors and how well they've instructed, than judging whether or not they should be retained. . . ." He continued, "I'm not too sure about the competence of students in terms of reviewing professional credentials. It seems to me that this should be a faculty function."[7] As for the faculty, most of them would agree with Nelson's attitudes toward the regulation of teaching in a university; he expressed his opposition to the bills in the Illinois legislature that attempted to establish by law a minimum teaching load of ten hours per week for professors. This sort of thing, he felt, was not a problem for legislators, but rather "a matter of commitment to teaching and to students by faculty."

The concerns of this "silver-gray-haired executive" were disclosed in still other statements from time to time. One problem of the highest priority was the budgetary restrictions that had faced Rhoten Smith and were now squarely on Nelson's doorstep. Nelson made it quite clear that the University was in for a "belt-tightening and re-examination of goals" in 1971–72 because there is "not going to be enough money in Northern's budget . . . to take care of inflation" and that this "is going to cause people to look inward and reflect upon the quality and what they're doing with these dollars." In other words, he thought it would require the university leaders to "re-evaluate how their money is being spent" and subsequently would delay the introduction of some new programs or the support of some existing ones until the situation improved.[8]

He had just taken office when he was asked how he stood on the athletic program at Northern—his views on that subject were entirely unknown to some. No doubt he had given some thought to this widely discussed question before his selection as president, for his views reflected a degree of sophistication about national as well as local problems. The president cited limitations that he thought would result from an over-emphasis on intercollegiate sports. He felt that it is often necessary to compromise the educational functions of a university because of pressures to lower academic standards by accepting good athletes who are poor students. Once such a student is ac-

Aerial view of campus in 1973

cepted, pressures are used again on the faculty to "ease these people through school," thus creating a double standard of grading. In order to prevent such a situation, it was his firm conviction that athletics must always be subservient to academic goals. For Northern, he did not subscribe to the idea found in many schools that it is necessary to have a great football team in order to have a first-rate university.

Regardless of these reservations, Nelson was still favorable to athletics, but, as he said, he was "not an all-out supporter." His solution for Northern was to develop rivalries with other schools of comparable size and standards, not too far away geographically. The Mid-American Conference, he felt, would "try and keep athletics in perspective" and also keep the program in proper balance. He emphasized that he wanted a good academic university as well as a good athletic program.

When President Nelson is not struggling with controversial issues, he might be found cultivating his own hobbies at the president's home in the Woodlawn Acres addition of DeKalb where he and his wife, Shirley, live. They have two sons presently in college and a married daughter. One of his favorite ways to relax is with his extensive collection of books, especially those on the history of early Illinois and the old Northwest Territory.

President Nelson's interest in books has already manifested itself at Northern in that he has shown more than a passing interest in the University Press. The importance of the Press as an intellectual arm in public relations is never lost to him, but more than that—he takes genuine delight in being part of the publishing process that brings forth handsome, scholarly books. Although the economic crunch in higher education continues and university presidents elsewhere have sought to find some easement to their finacial problems by closing down their university presses, President Nelson has helped the University Press at Northern survive and prosper.

Another insight into the nature of this new president was revealed in answer to a query by a student reporter, who, after all the weighty and demanding problems had been taken care of, asked the simple question: "Why did you seek the job of NIU president?" The president's reply was likewise simple and direct: "I think it'll be fun."

Drawing of new library wing being constructed west of Swen Parson Library

On 3 August 1971, President Nelson performed his first official duty in the ground-breaking ceremony for the music building on the old Glidden Field. This was the only ceremony connected with his induction into office, for he "simply arrived one day at the presidential offices, greeted . . . staff members," then began moving into his Lowden Hall office.

During his first month in office he became fully aware of the economic difficulties that confronted higher educational institutions in Illinois as a result of the state budget cutbacks and the national wage and price freeze. The latter caused a delay in faculty and staff salary increases for several months. The limitations on state funds brought on a sudden review of the budget that forced the University to evaluate once again all programs and innovations in order to assess their importance. Some of these the IBHE had already placed on the "low priority" list. This problem of budget restrictions immediately became the tail that wagged the educational dog, and for the first two years of his administration Nelson was constantly plagued with various aspects of it.

His immediate reaction to the problem was that Illinois higher educational leaders must "accommodate themselves to a new ball game" by accepting the facts and adapting them to what had to be done. Nelson recognized the need to avoid expensive duplication of programs in the state, but nevertheless his concern began to mount as he saw the growing frustration of the faculty over the rigidities that were being built into the budgeting process for higher education through the increased role of the IBHE. It is "one thing to eliminate duplication," Nelson said, "but another to stifle innovation and experimentation."

This was a sensitive issue and it seemed to have two sides. Who was to serve as an independent judge in coordinating the programs in the ten competing universities with their four separate boards, if not the IBHE? Were they not committed to this role by law? Who would prevent the duplications of programs and services and control the expansion of new degrees, certificates, departments, and facilities?

It also seems to the writer (although fully aware of how unpopular this view might be), after observing the educational scene in Illinois for nearly forty years, that the universities have been able to carry on a certain amount of empire-building during at least the last twenty years. In fact, a day of reckoning may finally come when some of the existing developments (not to mention capital expenditures) are more closely controlled by the IBHE.

Former IBHE Director James Holderman faced this task, and in a speech before the Committee on Admissions of the Joint Council on Higher Education in 1969, he took the position that a primary concern of the IBHE is the necessity for "accountability" of how the educational dollar is spent: "If higher education does not figure ways to spend more wisely, others will do it for us. The public will no longer continue to provide money without questioning how it is to be used." In other words, he said, "The honeymoon is over for higher education," and the time had come when it was necessary to repair the public attitude toward all education. "The public," he said, "does not understand how a faculty member who receives $28,000 a year and teaches three hours a week can be contributing much to the University . . . . Much of the public does consider higher education to be the easy life. We have not done the job of educating that we should have. The legislature itself has a concern for what they consider the lush living of higher education."[9]

This idea was carried further in the conclusions and recommendations of a 1972 report of the Carnegie Commission, *More Effective Use of Resources: An Imperative for Higher Education,* when it identified a number of changes schools should make to stretch their budgets for the "lean years of the seventies." Lyman Glenny, former executive director of the IBHE, issued an even more discouraging prognosis for institutions like Northern. In his speech at the National Higher Education Management Seminar, he pointed out the "great transitions and upheavals occurring in postsecondary education today." These are reflected in present significant trends in enrollments, costs of attending universities, shifts toward the technical and training institutions, the decline in demand for graduate degrees, and, most important, the reduction of state and federal educational appropriations already in effect.[10]

In the process of meeting these budget reductions, a controversy arose between the IBHE and the universities as to who was responsible for determining where reductions were to be made. How much flexibility was to be given the schools in eliminating parts or the whole of a program and how much time was available to make the decisions? At first the stricken universities were told to deal with these problems within a few weeks. It was impossible to meet this deadline, for studies had to be made; otherwise, as President Nelson noted, decisions of such importance for Northern's present educational programs and its future development would be made without adequate analysis at any level.[11]

After a great deal of soul-searching controversy and hours of committee work, the first major cutback at Northern was the Laboratory School. This decision was made finally by the president himself on the grounds that he did not consider the school "an integral part of the instruction program of the University."

Besides the loss of faculty personnel, a substantial number of positions and offices were affected when two administrative divisions were reorganized: Student Personnel Services and University Relations. The former division was reorganized on the basis that it was time to move from an *in loco parentis* philosophy to that of a more "decentralized, student-centered organization geared to provide an atmosphere for the academic, social and personal growth of students." Included in this reorganization was the elimination of the positions of dean of men and dean of women. University Relations was abolished entirely, and a new position of assistant to the president for information and public affairs was created. The new title of vice president for development and alumni relations was created, and F. R. Geigle was appointed to this position.[12]

If President Nelson received adverse publicity during his first year for abolishing administrative units and instructional positions, it was nothing compared to what he received overnight when he banned the national anthem at home basketball games. His decision was made to avoid the racial tensions that had resulted the year before when Black spectators had raised clenched fists during the anthem and had then sung the Black national anthem. "The anthem should be a symbol of unity," Nelson said, "but if it becomes a symbol of divisiveness it serves no purpose." Word of the president's action spread quickly throughout the nation, resulting in letters of condemnation from private citizens as well as from such superpatriots as Georgia's Lieutenant-Governor Lester Maddox, who sent a two-foot-long telegram.[13]

On 3 June 1972, President Nelson adapted the graduating ceremony and his inauguration exercises to the economic difficulties by combining both into one. He had officially taken office on 1 August but had not been formally installed as Northern's chief executive. The installation ceremony was conducted during the evening commencement exercises in the N.I.U. stadium by Board of Regents Chairman, J. Robert Barr. Nelson's two-in-one speech was certainly what faculty and students had been dreaming of for years—brief and to the point. He told the nearly six thousand recipients of degrees that there were two things he felt strongly about after his first ten months as president:

First, I have never wavered in my faith in young people and particularly the young people of Northern Illinois University.

Second, that although we have experienced some very difficult times in terms of our budget, as have other universities throughout the country, . . . I believe we have been forced to take a look at ourselves and the way we operate and we are going to be a better university for the adversity that has been imposed upon us.[14]

In spite of these hopeful feelings, it was not long before Nelson as well as the faculty and students were all more pessimistic about higher education's future. What had happened in the preceding twenty-five years of higher education compared to what was happening in the 1970s was beginning to convince students that no longer would college degrees, be they baccalaureates or doctorates, assure them a good position. Instead, the obvious fallacy of such faith was developing "a lot of disillusioned young people." Less than two years earlier, the feeling of college students had been idealistic. Now they seemed disappointed and skeptical about the future. The hike in tuition costs plus the reduction in scholarships and jobs also contributed to this feeling.

Within the past two years the faculty too has felt the budgetary restrictions in delayed contracts, cuts in salary increments, threats to tenured positions, and, for some, the loss of livelihood. Perhaps the most serious was the tenure problem, not only for those who were working without tenure, but also for those who held administrative or departmental positions that were dropped. This brought up a question that had never before been dealt with properly: do faculty members relocated from an administrative or a departmental position retain tenure in some other area of the University?

Faculty women and minorities were especially concerned about the financial problems, for they had been discriminated against in the past and it could be difficult to protect their jobs when layoffs were necessary, since so many had nontenured positions.[15]

Such problems increased and there finally developed among a sizeable segment (not a majority) of the faculty the desire for some type of collective bargaining. For many years a certain percentage of the faculty had been represented in the traditional American Association of University Professors (A.A.U.P.), which was first organized at Northern in the 1930s. Although it has never enrolled a majority of the faculty, it has a good record in patiently and persistently keeping the basic problems of academic freedom, faculty involvement in governance, tenure rights, salary inequities, teaching loads, and a host of others before the employers. Some of these are perennial questions and never seem resolved; others arise periodically from the dynamic social, economic, and philosophical aspects of a changing society. A good example of the latter type of issue is the right of a faculty to govern itself, a right which recent presidents of the A.A.U.P. chapter at Northern, such as John Lloyd, Allen Weaver, and James Merritt, have believed to be an absolute necessity if it ever hoped to become a first-rate University.

A step in that direction was taken a few years ago in the form of a joint committee to establish a governance policy for the regency universities and a set of bylaws for the Board. After many long and arduous sessions with hearings and discussions, the committee's recommendations were approved by the Board on 4 May 1969.[16]

The more recently formed N.I.U. chapter of American Federation of Teachers (A.F.T.) with over eighty members has also concerned itself with somewhat the same issues. On numerous occasions its leader, Jack Bennett, and his fellow members have virogously championed the cause of dismissed instructors and the right to collective bargaining and have fought the widening salary inequities between "lower" and "higher" ranks within the teaching and administrative levels. To point up these disparities which Bennett has said created "bitterness and divisive feelings among us . . . [because of] incomplete knowledge, secrecy, and hearsay," A.F.T. distributed [1 January 1973] copies of the 1972–73 fall salary list to the entire faculty along with a table of the average monthly salary for each rank and the percentage increase compiled by the Provost's Office for the years 1963–64 to 1972–73.

A comparison of the average monthly salaries as taken from the list for professors, associate professors, assistant professors, and instructors over a ten-year period showed increasing divergence between the highest and lowest-paid faculty members. From 1963–64 to 1972–73, salaries for professors had risen about 78 percent; for associate professors, about 65 percent; for assistant professors, about 50 percent; and for instructors, only 34 percent. In 1963–64, a professor earned on the average of $1,253 monthly, or 60 percent more than an instructor's average monthly salary of $782; by 1972–73, the average salary for a professor had climbed to $2,235 per month, or nearly 113 percent more than the $1,051 earned by instructors each month.

This "list of university-wide average salaries," according to the A.F.T. cover letter, "omits the most glaring inequities: the salaries of administrative staff as opposed to teaching faculty." [17]

A third campus organization concerned with faculty problems is the Illinois Association of Higher Education (I.A.H.E.), which was organized in 1962 and already has a membership of about one hundred. The aims and goals of the I.A.H.E. have been stated chiefly as "academic freedom and due process, shared governance, expanded fringe benefits, merit over and above standard cost-of-living increments and last but not least collective bargaining." [18] Though there is a similarity between it and the A.A.U.P. and A.F.T., it nevertheless places greater emphasis upon various aspects of public-school education, the improvement of teaching, and problems associated with affiliated N.E.A.-I.E.A. membership.

Attempts have been made by the three organizations to work out common ground upon which to cooperate, but each group still believes that it is best equipped to serve as the bargaining agent. The I.A.H.E. especially emphasizes that its organization, already affiliated with over one million members in the N.E.A.–I.E.A., could be a greater force for professional negotiations on campus. The A.A.U.P., on the other hand, is apparently more popular with the faculty, for in a recent election to determine which was wanted as the agent for negotiations, it was endorsed by over one-third of the voting faculty. But since no clear majority has been given any of the organizations, there can be no bargaining.

In closing this summary of a few of the more important issues and events concerning the seventh president, one of his own statements relating to future goals of Northern seems appropriate:

At this particular juncture [August 1972], it is impossible to predict if Northern's great growth of the past 20 years has come to a halt, has already reached and passed its apex, or has only reached a breathing period.

Whichever ultimately proves to be the case, it appears the time has ended for just trying to cope with an ever-increasing quantity of students—if only temporary—and an era is beginning in which past gains can be solidified and increasing emphasis can be put on quality.

Northern's potential is enormous.[19]

Notes

Introduction

1. Clarence W. Alvord, *The Illinois Country, 1673–1818* (Centennial History of Illinois, vol I. Springfield: 1920), p. 1.
2. *DeKalb Chronicle Illustrated Souvenir*, 22 December 1894, p. 65. (Hereafter cited as *Chronicle Illustrated Souvenir*.)
3. *The DeKalb Directory* (Chicago: Interstate Directory Co., 1899), pp. 2–3.
4. For the development and influences of barbed wire fencing, see Earl W. Hayter, "Barbed Wire Fencing—A Prairie Invention," *Agricultural History*, 13 (October 1939): 189–207; and "The Fencing of Western Railways," *Agricultural History*, 19 (July 1945): 163–167.
5. Joseph M. McFadden, "From Invention to Monopoly: The History of the Consolidation of the Barbed Wire Industry, 1873-1899" (Ph.D. dissertation, Northern Illinois University, 1968), pp. 183–224.
6. *Chronicle Illustrated Souvenir,* 9 January 1892, pp. 9, 59–62; 22 December 1894, pp. 37, 94–96.
7. Ibid., 10 March 1900, p. l0.
8. Ibid., 22 December 1894, p. 106. DeKalb already had a few telephones by 1900 and a telephone exchange was to be installed in the spring of that year (*DeKalb Chronicle,* 11 and 25 January 1900).
9. *DeKalb Chronicle,* 11 August 1899. Interview, Ellzey L. Luney, DeKalb, Illinois, 14 April 1970. (Hereafter cited as *Chronicle.*)
10. *Chronicle Illustrated Souvenir,* 9 January 1892, p. 63.
11. *Sycamore True Republican,* 24 July 1895; *Chronicle,* 11 July 1899.
12. *Sycamore City Weekly,* 20, 26, 27 July 1899; *Chronicle,* 15 December 1902.
13. A model study of Muncie, Indiana, also a normal school town, illustrates the powerful influence rural beliefs had on American life with little change between the 1890s and the 1920s; DeKalb during that period showed many of the same traits. See Robert S. Lynd and Helen M. Lynd, *Middletown: A Study in American Culture* (New York: Harcourt, Brace & World, Inc., 1929).
14. These three philanthropists' deaths occurred in the following order: J. F. Glidden (1906); I. L. Ellwood (1910); Jacob Haish (1926), a few days before his one hundredth birthday. For sketches of their lives, see *DeKalb Review,* 11, 12 October 1906; *Chronicle,* 11, 12, 13 October 1906; 12, 14 September 1910; 19 February 1926; (Centennial Edition) 8 June 1956, Section 4, pp. 2, 4, 6, 9, 12, 13; *Northern Illinois,* February 1900, pp. 67–68; January 1903, p. 85; October 1906, pp. 26–28; October 1910, pp. 4–6; 26 February 1926, p. 1; *Chicago Tribune,* 8 September 1910; Alfred Bayliss to Cook, Springfield, 23 September 1910.

15. *Chronicle Illustrated Souvenir,* 22 December 1894, p. 24; *Sycamore City Weekly,* 10 August 1899.
16. *Chronicle Illustrated Souvenir,* 9 January 1892, pp. 16–18.
17. Harvey Wish, *Contemporary America* (rev. ed.; New York: Harper & Bros., 1955), pp. 41–48.
18. *World Almanac Encyclopedia* (New York: Press Publishing Co., 1913), pp. 717, 729.
19. *Chronicle Illustrated Souvenir,* 9 January 1892, p. 58; 22 December 1894, pp. 22, 100; 23 December 1899, p. 190.
20. *Chronicle Illustrated Souvenir,* 22 December 1894, p. 37; 4 May 1895.
21. Ibid., 22 December 1894, p. 37.
22. Ibid., 4 May, 5 September 1895.
23. *Chronicle,* 9 January 1892, p. 63 *passim*; 23 December 1899, p. 190.
24. *Chronicle,* 26 July, 27 September 1899; *Northern Illinois,* 12 February 1931, p. 1; interview, Beatrice Gurler, DeKalb, Illinois, 8 May 1970.
25. *Chronicle,* 30 September 1899.

Chapter 1

1. Superintendent of Public Instruction, *Biennial Report (1886–1888)* (Springfield: State of Illinois, 1899), p. LXII.
2. *Western Rural and American Stockman* (Chicago), 17 February 1877, p. 49.
3. See *Chronicle,* 12 January, 16 February, 2 March, 4 May 1895.
4. Superintendent of Public Instruction, *Biennial Report (1892–1894)* (Springfield: State of Illinois, 1894), pp. LVIII.
5. John W. Cook, "History of the Northern Illinois State Normal School on Its Twenty-First Birthday" (manuscript, N.I.U. Archives), DeKalb, 1920, pp. 4–5 (hereafter cited as "History of the N.I.S.N.S."). This all-out campaign was demonstrated at the Northern Illinois Teachers Association meeting at Joliet in 1895, when the normal bills were before the legislature. At that time, 1,400 teachers sent a dispatch which cost $35 to Speaker Myers at Springfield, urging him to assist in the passage of the bill. *Northern Illinois,* October 1899, p. 4; George W. Patrick, "A History of the Illinois State Teachers Association, 1854–1912" (M.A. thesis, University of Chicago, 1928), pp. 103–6.
6. Neil Thorburn, "John P. Altgeld: Promoter of Higher Education in Illinois," in *Essays in Illinois History,* ed. Donald F. Tingley (Carbondale, Ill.: Southern Illinois University Press, 1968), chap. 3, pp. 37–51; Josephine Goldmark, *Impatient Crusader: Florence Kelly's Life Story* (Urbana, Ill.: University of Illinois Press, 1953) pp. 40–41, 46.
7. Henry M. Christman (ed.), *The Mind and Spirit of John Peter Altgeld* (Urbana, Ill.: University of Illinois Press, 1960), pp. 51, 113–16.
8. *DeKalb Review,* 20 April 1899. DeKalb remained a Republican stronghold and it was only recently that Rosette's name finally was given to one of the public schools.
9. *Chronicle,* 24 June 1893.
10. Cook, "History of the N.I.S.N.S.," pp. 7–10.

11. Altgeld was overly enthusiastic in his estimate of Rosette's contribution to his victory in 1892. An analysis of the vote in both 1888 and 1892 does not show any appreciable change in DeKalb County. Returns indicate that the Democrats received only 93 additional votes in 1892, when Altgeld ran for governor, and that both county elections were resounding Republican victories. DeKalb County Poll Books, 6 November 1888; 8 November 1892 (N.I.U. Archives).

12. Swen F. Parson, Norma Stelford, and Charles A. Whitten, "A History of Northern Illinois State Teachers College" (manuscript, N.I.U. Archives, 1949), pp. 1–2.

13. *Chronicle,* 20 April, 21 July, 1895.

14. There were those who wanted the money given to "Old Normal" in the belief that it could become the best of its kind in the United States (*Chronicle,* 27 July 1895).

15. *Senate Journal,* 39th General Assembly (Springfield, 1896), pp. 50, 149.

16. *Illinois State Register* (Springfield), 5 April 1895.

17. Cook, "History of the N.I.S.N.S.," pp. 7–10.

18. *Chronicle,* 20 April, 4 May 1895. For a description of this institution, see *Dixon College Educator,* 3 (November 1900): 1–4.

19. *Chronicle,* 8 June 1895.

20. *Senate Journal,* 39th General Assembly (Springfield, 1896), pp. 312–13.

21. *Chronicle,* 4 May 1895; *Chicago Inter-Ocean,* 3, 6 May 1895; *Aurora Beacon,* 3 May 1895.

22. *House Journal,* 39th General Assembly (Springfield, 1896), p. 696; *Chronicle,* 4 May 1895.

23. *Chronicle,* 17, 29 July; 5 August 1895.

24. *Chicago Inter-Ocean,* 17 May 1895; *Chicago Tribune,* 22 May 1895.

25. Ellwood to A. J. Hopkins, DeKalb, 4, 24 March; 20 April 1895.

26. Ellwood to Hopkins, DeKalb, 20 July 1895. How much of his own money Ellwood used is unknown; however, it was his style to spend what was necessary. On one occasion he had 5,000 copies of the *Chicago Journal* passed around with an elaborate write-up on DeKalb (*Chronicle,* 20 April 1895).

27. State of Illinois, *Laws, Statutes, etc., 39th General Assembly* (Chicago: Chicago Legal News Co., 1895), pp. 227–28; *Chronicle Illustrated Souvenir,* 23 December 1899, p. 203. Enforcement of this pledge was, from its inception, quite lax, for many facets of it were subject to various interpretations. Consequently, by 1943 it was recognized that the pledge was unethical, and the Teachers College Board repealed it on 12 July 1943 (*Proceedings,* Springfield: State of Illinois, 1943, p. 137).

28. 22 May 1895.

29. *Chronicle,* 18, 25 May 1895; *Chicago Inter-Ocean,* 24 May 1895.

30. James Clark to Ellwood, Mattoon, 23 July 1895.

31. Ellwood to C. E. Wilson, DeKalb, 18 June 1895.

32. *Chicago Inter-Ocean,* 30 May 1895; Earl and Beulah Hayter, "In the Beginning," *Northern Alumnus,* 11 (December 1958): 9.

33. Ellwood to John P. Altgeld, DeKalb, 31 May 1895. Ellwood also had word sent to his townsfolk that he had "finally succeeded in wiping the earth with all his competitors and had the location committee appointed to his liking."–A. Fisk to B. F. Ray, DeKalb, 29 May 1895.

34. Ellwood to Altgeld, DeKalb, 17 June 1895.

Chapter 2

1. *Chronicle,* 8 June 1895.
2. Ibid., 13, 23 July 1895; *Freeport Journal,* 16 May 1895; *Chicago Tribune,* 27 May 1895.
3. *Chronicle,* 16 July 1895; *Rockford Register-Gazette,* 13, 18 July 1895. Population of these eight cities in 1890 was as follows: Rockford, 23,584; Aurora, 19,688; Freeport, 10,189; Dixon, 5,161; DeKalb, 2,579; Fulton, 2,099; Polo, 1,728; and Oregon, 1,566 (Eleventh United States Census, "Report of Population, Cities, Towns and Villages," 1890, table VIII, pp. 318–92).
4. *Aurora Beacon,* 24 June 1895.
5. *Rockford Register-Gazette,* 25 June 1895.
6. *Freeport Journal,* 13 July 1895.
7. *Chronicle,* 13 July 1895; *Freeport Journal,* 19 July 1895.
8. George W. Dicus to W. C. Garrard, Rochelle, 13 July 1895, in the *Chronicle,* 23 July 1895.
9. *Freeport Journal,* 27 June, 6 July 1895; *Chronicle,* 3 August 1895. The *DeKalb Directory* for 1899 listed as many as six saloons on Main Street.
10. *Freeport Journal,* 6 July 1895. Ellwood left an estate of $10,000,000 in 1910, according to his will, or the equivalent in purchasing power in 1969 dollars of about $60,000,000 (courtesy, Finance Department, N.I.U., 5 April 1970).
11. *Chronicle,* 13 July 1895.
12. Ibid., 8 June 1895.
13. *Rockford Register-Gazette,* 24, 25 June 1895.
14. *Freeport Journal,* 6, 16 July 1895.
15. *Chronicle,* 16 July 1895; *Ogle County Republican* (Oregon), 28 June 1895.
16. *Freeport Journal,* 27 June, 16 July 1895. The Fulton offer was about the same as the one by Oregon (*Chronicle,* 17 July 1895).
17. Parson et al., "A History of Northern Illinois State Teachers College," pp. 4–5.
18. *Chronicle,* 21 July 1895.
19. Ellwood contributed a small strip of 4.1 acres on the west bank of the river, increasing the campus to a total of 67.1 acres. Glidden's donation of 63 acres was estimated by the *Chronicle* to be "easily worth $15,000" (16 August 1895).
20. *Chronicle,* 22 June 1895. This second proposal may have been regarded as a safeguard, for, according to President Cook, Mr. Glidden was obdurate and refused to part with his land until Ellwood finally was able to reason with him and secure the deed on 5 July 1895, ten days after the trustees had visited DeKalb and ten days before the final decision (Cook, "History of the N.I.S.N.S.," pp.10–11).
21. A. W. Fisk to W. C. Garrard, DeKalb, 24 July 1895.
22. *Chronicle,* 19, 21, 29 July 1895.
23. Ibid., 16 July 1895.

24. 16 July 1895. Cook listed the cash figure at $30,000 and the $50,000 loan was given the trustees in the form of a personal check on 13 July 1895. It was to be used as a surety bond to guarantee building costs until 1 July 1896 when the first appropriation could be used legally. On several occasions Ellwood lent John H. Lewis, his son-in-law and board treasurer, different amounts in order to maintain credit balances (N.I.S.N.S. Board, Ledger-Book, No. I, N.I.U. Archives).

25. Parson et al., "A History of Northern Illinois State Teachers College," pp. 4–5.

26. *Chronicle,* 13 July 1895.

27. United States Weather Bureau, *Reports* (Champaign, Illinois), 24, 25 June 1895; *Sycamore True Republican,* 3 July 1895. May 1895 was reported the driest May in fifteen years (*Sycamore True Republican,* 5 June 1895). The Kishwaukee officially is called a river but probably would not be if size were the determining factor, for there are three creeks just south of DeKalb–Indian, Big Rock, and Shabbona–all of which carry as much water (courtesy, Geography Department, N.I.U., 19 March 1970).

28. Swen F. Parson, "Notebook and Diary" (manuscript in possession of Eleanor Parson Zulauf, DeKalb), pp. 247–49. The river was always a source of sportive jest among the Normal students in their verses, songs, and stories. One of the first poems dealt with this incident of raising the water level (*Northern Illinois,* November 1899, p. 24).

29. *Chronicle,* 12, 17, 29 July 1895.

30. Ibid., 5 August 1895. Unfortunately no issues of the *Chronicle* are available to help clear up what happened prior to this visit but Beatrice Gurler, who grew up in this period, remembers hearing her elders speak of this ingenious booster scheme (interview, 12 May 1970).

31. *Chronicle,* 29 July 1895.

32. Ibid., 16, 23 July 1895; *Freeport Journal,* 16 July 1895.

33. *Rockford Register-Gazette,* 15 July 1895; *Freeport Journal,* 16 July 1895.

34. *Chronicle,* 16, 18 July 1895.

35. *Freeport Journal,* 16 July 1895.

36. *Chronicle,* 20, 27 July 1895. Rockford, smarting from the defeat, recognized the celebration with this barb: "DeKalb will shoot off a few fireworks and open a case or two to-night to celebrate Gov. Altgeld's gift . . . to that town."–*Rockford Register-Gazette,* 20 July 1895.

37. *Chronicle,* 16, 18, 24, 27 July 1895.

38. Ibid., 23 July 1895. Within a few years Ellwood was promoted as a candidate for the United States Senate by political and industrial leaders but he declined the honor (ibid., 5 October 1899).

39. Ibid., 19, 25 July 1895.

40. Ibid., 18, 20 July 1895.

41. Ibid., 20 July 1895.

42. Ibid., 13, 23 July 1895.

43. Ibid., 20, 21, 23 July 1895.

44. Ibid., 18 July 1895.

45. *Rockford Register-Gazette,* 18 July 1895.

46. *Chronicle,* 20 July 1895.

Chapter 3

1. *Chronicle,* 4 April 1899. By October, the first complete map of the city was ready for distribution (ibid., 26 October 1899).
2. Ibid., 4 May 1899.
3. I. L. Ellwood to George O. Garnsey, DeKalb, 18 July 1895; Ellwood to Ralph Emmerson, DeKalb, 14 August 1895. The subcommittee of the Board consisted of S. M. Inglis, W. C. Garrard, and T. J. Sparks.
4. Northern Illinois State Normal School, *Annual Catalog* (DeKalb, 1900), p. 5.
5. Neil Thorburn, "John P. Altgeld: Promoter of Higher Education," pp. 50–51.
6. John P. Altgeld, *Live Questions* (Chicago: Geo. S. Bowen & Co., 1899), p. 957.
7. Ellwood to T. J. Sparks, DeKalb, 19 July, 10 August 1895; Ellwood to William F. Dose, DeKalb, 19 August 1895.
8. *Chronicle,* 26 August 1895. Brush was paid $9,590.40 for his plans and supervisory work between 1 November 1895 and 5 February 1900 (N.I.S.N.S., Account-Book, No. I (1895–1906), pp. 1–3). Brush was a graduate of the University of Illinois and had "built some of the larger business blocks in Kansas City."–*Chronicle,* 27 August 1895.
9. Board of Trustees, Annual Report (1895–1896) (unpublished), pp. 27, 32. The amount paid the McAlpine firm by the time it was finished, 3 February 1900, totaled $230,160.42 (N.I.S.N.S., Account-Book, No. I (1895–1906), pp. 1–3).
10. *Chronicle,* 17 September 1895.
11. Ibid., 29 July, 13, 20 August, 9, 19 September 1895.
12. A.W. Fisk to T. O. Thompson, DeKalb, 12 September 1895; Fisk to George F. Sisley, 19 September 1895; Fisk to A. G. Leonard, 16 August 1895; *Chronicle,* 29 August, 6, 7, 9, 10 September 1895; *Chicago Times-Herald,* 2 October 1895.
13. Ellwood to Gov. Altgeld, DeKalb, 20 September 1895; *Chicago Times-Herald,* 2 October 1895.
14. *Chronicle Illustrated Souvenir,* 1 October 1895, p. 3; *Chicago Inter-Ocean,* 2 October 1895.
15. Altgeld, *Live Questions,* pp. 497–501.
16. *Chicago Times-Herald,* 2 October 1895. Ellwood and Haish both served many friends at their tents and in their homes.
17. *Chicago Tribune,* 2 October 1895.
18. *Chicago Times-Herald,* 2 October 1895; *Chronicle,* 2, 5 October 1895.
19. State of Illinois, *Laws, Statutes, etc., 39th General Assembly,,* p. 227.
20. *Chronicle,* 5, 10 August 1899. For the decorative features and description of the interior, see ibid., 23 August 1899, and *The Norther* (1903), p. 32.
21. *Chronicle,* 31 March, 4 April 1899; John W. Cook, *Educational History of Illinois* (Chicago: Henry O. Shepard and Co., 1912), p. 245.
22. 11 August 1895.
23. *Chronicle,* 25 April 1899; Board of Trustees, *Biennial Report* (1899–1900), pp. 3–4; *Northern Illinois,* October 1899, p. 1.

24. Cook, "History of the N.I.S.N.S.," pp. 14–15.
25. *Chronicle,* 26 April, 21 May 1899. At this time there were two grade schools in DeKalb; the North Side and East Side Schools, along with a south side high school–grade school combination which burned on 27 January 1902, at which time President Cook gave temporary space for a city high school in the west end of the Normal building.
26. Ellwood to Allen C. Fuller, DeKalb, 20 May 1899; A. A. Goodrich to Cook, Chicago, 9 June 1899; Board of Trustees, *Biennial Report* (1899–1900), pp. 3–4.
27. Ellwood to O. F. Berry, DeKalb, 7 March, 22 April, 29 May 1899; Ellwood to Cook, DeKalb, 29 May 1899.
28. Cook to Ellwood, Normal, Illinois, 30 May 1899; O. F. Berry to Cook, Carthage, Illinois, 26, 29 April, 22, 26, 29, 31 May 1899.
29. Cook to Ellwood, Normal, 30 May 1899; Ellwood to Gov. John R. Tanner, DeKalb, 8 May 1899.
30. *Bloomington Pantagraph,* 2 May 1899; Cook, *Educational History of Illinois,* p. 245. The salary was $5,000 a year plus a $10,000 home built in the Ellwood Addition with the rent paid by the state (*Chronicle,* 15 April, 11 May, 14 July 1891).
31. Charles A. Harper, *Development of the Teachers College in the United States* (Bloomington, Ill.: McKnight & McKnight, 1935), pp. 171–86; William L. Leighly, "A History of Northern Illinois University: The Early Years, 1893–1919" (manuscript, N.I.U. Archives), 1967, pp. 16–25.
32. Interviews, Olive Swift Johnson, DeKalb, 16 May 1968; Lola Swift Faust, DeKalb, 24 May 1968.
33. Warren Madden to Earl W. Hayter, San Francisco, 20 April 1969.
34. Cook to Calvin Rayburn, Bloomington, Illinois, 13 September 1892; Cook to Ellwood, DeKalb, 30 May 1899. Cook was an admirer of Governor Altgeld and said on one occasion: "I should feel entirely comfortable in the event of his reelection. He did no end of work last winter in pushing the new Normal and in helping us to our new building."—Cook to F[rank] L. Cook, Bloomington, 21 January 1896.
35. For further information on the first faculty, see *Annual Catalog* (1899–1900), p. 4; *Northern Illinois,* October, November 1899, pp. 7, 25; Cook, "History of the N.I.S.N.S.," pp. 17–23; *Norther* (1900), pp. 23–28.
36. *Chronicle,* 11, 26 July, 16 October 1899; Charles A. McMurry, "Newell D. Gilbert," *Journal of Education,* 100 (16 November 1924): 462–63.
37. Cook to F. W. Shepardson, Chicago, 22 January 1920; taped interview, Clyde Lyon, Sycamore, Illinois, 22 June 1968.
38. Charles Francis Adams, *An Autobiography, 1835–1915* (Boston: Houghton, Mifflin Co., 1916), p. 36; Jessie M. Pangburn, *Evolution of the American Teachers College* (New York: Teachers College, Columbia University, 1932), pp. 22–24.
39. Normal School Board, *Proceedings* (16 September 1918), pp. 37–38. A resolution by the women to the Board analyzed this discrimination: women heads of departments on equal matters of training and experience drew $700 less per year; the women (assistant professors) had had only a $100 increase in salary in eighteen years (ibid.).
40. Frederick Rudolph, *The American College and University* (New York: Alfred A. Knopf, 1962), p. 294.

41. N.I.S.N.S., "To the County Superintendent of Schools" (pamphlet), DeKalb, 1 July 1899; *Chronicle*, 11 July 1899.
42. Student Entrance Record Book (1899–1918), p. 17; *The Norther* (1900), pp. 163–71. Specials were college graduates, seniors second year, juniors first year of the two-year normal course; others were classified according to their number of high-school credits.
43. Student Entrance Record Book (1899–1918), pp. 1–14.
44. Parson et al., "A History of Northern Illinois State Teachers College," p. 6; Ronald R. Rezny, "Reflections on the First Year of the Northern Illinois State Normal School, 1899–1900" (manuscript, N.I.U. Archives), 1966, pp. 4–5.
45. *Rockford Register-Gazette,* 22 September 1899; *Sycamore True Republican,* 27 September 1899; *Chicago Tribune,* 22, 23 September 1899.
46. *Sycamore City Weekly,* 28 September 1899; Cook, *Educational History of Illinois,* p. 248.

Chapter 4

1. John W. Cook to F. W. Shepardson, Chicago, 22 January 1920.
2. Lester M. Wilson, "Training Departments in State Normal Schools in the United States," *Eastern Illinois State Normal School Bulletin,* no. 66 (October 1919), p. 5l.
3. E. A. Sheldon to Cook, Oswego, N.Y., 31 May 1895.
4. Normal School Board, *Proceedings* (18 September 1930), p. 47; (26 June 1933), pp. 14–15.
5. Mary L. Seguel, *The Curriculum Field, Its Formative Years* (New York: Teachers College Press, 1966), pp. 7–46.
6. See the McMurry collection donated by the McMurry family to the N.I.U. Archives.
7. *Student Young Women's Christian Association: Seventy-Fifth Anniversary, 1872–1947,* (Normal, Ill.: Illinois State Normal University, 1947), pp. 3.–16.
8. Gladys M. Wetz to Earl W. Hayter, Roswell, New Mexico, 9 September 1970.
9. *DeKalb Review,* 8 May 1911; *Alumni Recall,* 3 (29 October 1927): 4.
10. *The Vidette* (Normal), 6 November 1906, p. 5. His debating experience at Harvard made him a popular speaker at teachers' institutes and student meetings.
11. *Northern Illinois,* January 1921, p. 16; 16 January 1930, p. 1. Inquiries were received from "all over the United States and from England."—*Annual Catalog* (1922), p. 13. It was also listed in the Illinois guide-books prepared by the Federal Writer's Project (*Northern Illinois,* 14 April 1938, p. 4).
12. *Northern Illinois,* 27 May 1937, p. 10; 7 October 1937, p. 1; *Alumni Recall,* 13 (24 September 1937): 3.
13. *Northern Illinois,* 18 March 1927, p. 2; *Norther* (1925), p. 41; Dorothy Youngblood to Earl W. Hayter, Portland, Oregon, 17 August 1968.
14. Following the Board of Trustees, Northern has been governed by the Normal School Board (July 1917 to June 1941), the Teachers College Board (July 1941 to June 1965), the Board of Governors of State Colleges and Universities (July 1965 to June 1967), and the Board of Regents (since July 1967).
15. The following DeKalb residents have also served on the various boards: Edgar B. Still (1923–1932), William W. Wirtz (1949–1952), and Chauncey Watson (1953–

1960). All three have been honored by having their names given to campus buildings.

16. Board of Trustees, *Biennial Report* (1913–1914), p. 8.

17. DeKalb, 21 April 1918; Chicago, 15 March 1919.

18. *Chronicle*, 31 July 1902; interview, Beatrice Gurler, 6 October 1970.

19. Northern Illinois University, "Enrollment Figures, 1899–1972," (N.I.U. Archives).

20. 2 August 1899.

21. Frank K. Balthis, "An Illinois School Campus," *American Botanist,* 31 (February 1915): 2–3. See Mark L. Peisch, *The Chicago School of Architecture, Early Followers of Sullivan and Wright* (New York: Random House, 1964), p. 96.

22. Board of Trustees, *Biennial Report* (1911–1912), p. 5.

23. *Rockford Register-Gazette,* 28, 29 December 1916.

24. Silver, Burdett, and Co. to Cook, Chicago, 1 July 1905; Normal School Board, *Proceedings* (12 May 1919), pp. 67–68.

25. Normal School Board, *Proceedings* (20 April 1918), p. 60.

26. Ibid. (28 October 1918), pp. 36–39.

27. Ibid. (14 March 1919), p. 57.

28. Ibid. (21 June 1920), p. 14.

29. Swen F. Parson to Felmley, DeKalb, 31 May 1922 (Felmley Papers, I.S.U.).

30. Normal School Board, *Proceedings* (20 April 1918), p. 61.

31. Ibid. (7 December 1917), p. 35.

32. *Norther* (1901), p. 142; (1913), pp. 30–31; (1919), p. 152; Cook, "History of the N.I.S.N.S.," pp. 33–34.

33. Daniel W. Lester, "The Haish Library in the Northern Illinois State Normal School, 1899–1921: A Preliminary Study" (manuscript, N.I.U. Archives), 1966.

34. *Northern Illinois,* November 1912, p. 19.

35. Cook to A. J. Reed, DeKalb, 26 April 1916; Cook to Robert T. McGrath, DeKalb, 26 April 1916.

36. *Northern Illinois,* June 1915, p. 175.

37. *DeKalb Advertiser,* 24 October 1908.

38. *Chronicle,* 12 May 1899.

39. Cook to M. O. Sutherland, DeKalb, 13 October 1913.

40. Cook to A. T. Rogers, DeKalb, 23 May 1917.

41. Cook to F. A. Drinkwater, DeKalb, 25 April 1910.

42. Cook to Homer J. Tice, DeKalb, 6 May 1914.

43. Cook to A. L. Brown, DeKalb, 18 September 1919; J. Stanley Brown to the Circuit Court of Kendall County, Yorkville, Illinois, 15 February 1924.

44. *Northern Illinois,* October 1905, p. 8; February 1907, p. 112.

45. Ibid., May 1917, p. 186; February 1922, p. 16.

46. *Annual Catalog* (1918–1919), pp. 24–25; Cook to Felmley, DeKalb, 13 September 1918.

47. *Northern Illinois,* March 1918, pp. 104–5; June 1918, 165. The seniors were encouraged in this action by a Sgt. DeViller from Belgium who visited the campus (interview, Lucile Martin Nelson, 18 April 1970).

48. This flag had 121 stars, four of which were gold (*Norther* [1919]), p. 9.

49. Cook to Dell, DeKalb, 20 October 1918.

50. Cook to Charles McMurry, DeKalb, 18 April 1916. This ailment forced him to give up the cranking of his car.
51. 14 January 1919.
52. Vera M. Wiswall to Alumni members, DeKalb, 1 May 1919.
53. 14 November 1921.
54. 20 May 1920.
55. 28 June 1912, p. 5.
56. Jessie M. Pangburn, *Evolution of the American Teachers College,* pp. 16–17.
57. Northern Illinois State Normal School, *Quarterly,* 6 (November 1908): 6. Only one Bachelor of Education degree was conferred during Cook's administration and that was to James R. Grant (in 1911) who came to Northern for one year with an A.B. degree from the University of Arkansas (*Annual Catalog* [1910–1911], p. 107).
58. Felmley to President E. E. James, Normal, Illinois, 21 November, 1910.
59. Cook to McMurry, DeKalb, 18 April 1916.

Chapter 5

1. *Norther* (1914), p. 51.
2. Cook to S.A. Forbes, DeKalb, 13 February 1909.
3. *Northern Illinois,* February 1907, p. 112; May 1907, p. 169.
4. John W. Cook, "Scrapbooks," XV, p. 30 (N.I.U. Archives).
5. *Northern Illinois,* October 1899, p. 9; May 1903, p. 173.
6. *Norther* (1903), p. 120.
7. *Northern Illinois,* May 1918, p. 172.
8. Ibid. December 1911, pp. 50–51.
9. *Rockford Register-Gazette,* 28 December 1909; *Sycamore Tribune,* 28 February 1908.
10. *Northern Illinois,* October 1906, p. 34; September 1907, p. 21.
11. *Norther* (1916), p. 105.
12. Interviews, Hazel Wiswall, DeKalb, 19 June 1968; Olive Swift Johnson, DeKalb, 12 November 1970.
13. *Northern Illinois,* December 1912, p. 45; December 1915, p. 61.
14. *Norther* (1901), p. 80; *Annual Catalog* (1903), pp. 37–38.
15. F. W. Shepardson, *The State Normal Schools* (Springfield, Ill.: Illinois Department of Registration and Education, 1919), pp. 1–11.
16. *Chronicle,* 27 January 1902; *Northern Illinois,* January 1907, pp. 86, 89.
17. *Chronicle,* 18 October, 11 December 1918.
18. *Norther* (1911), p. 9.
19. *The Upper Case,* 1 (21 January 1916): 1–4; (Christmas, 1916), p. 3.
20. *Chronicle,* 26 October, 3 November 1899.
21. *Norther* (1901), p. 44.
22. *Malta Mail* (Illinois), 11 December 1902.
23. *Northern Illinois,* March 1906, p. 121; November 1906, p. 56.
24. For a number of years a class pin or ring was placed in the Page Museum but unfortunately they did not survive the break-up of the collection.
25. *Sycamore Tribune,* 6 December 1907; *Northern Illinois,* November 1913, p. 25.
26. *Norther* (1911), p. 82; *The Upper Case,* 1 (11 February 1916): 2.
27. *Northern Illinois,* March 1907, pp. 134–35; April 1907, p. 155; October 1908, p. 8; February 1909, p. 113.

28. A few of the sermon topics were: "The New Profession" (1900), "Press Toward the Mark" (1905), "Be Strong" (1910), and "Planning One's Life" (1914).
29. See "Class Gifts" (N.I.U. Archives).
30. *Northern Illinois,* 23 April 1931, p. 1.
31. Faculty Club, "By-Laws" (1920), article II.
32. Ibid., "Minutes," 26 October, 10 December 1920. The economic situation of the faculty was so grave in 1919 that the club actually discussed the proposition of joining the American Federation of Labor; but when put to a formal motion, the members voted against such a move (ibid., 2 October 1919).

Chapter 6

1. Normal School Board, *Proceedings* (21 April, 12 May 1919), pp. 62, 69.
2. In October 1939, the *Denison Alumnus* listed this M.A. degree in his obituary although it had caused him embarrassment and was finally dropped by him from his academic credentials in 1926.
3. There is a discrepancy in his record on dates and places where he taught. The listings above do not correspond with his profile in *Who Was Who In America,* Vol. 1, *1897–1942* (Library Edition; Chicago: Marquis, 1943).
4. Robert S. Smolich, "An Analysis of Influences Affecting the Origin and Early Development of Three Mid-Western Public Junior Colleges—Joliet, Goshen and Crane" (Ph.D. dissertation, University of Texas, 1967), pp. 18–19, 23–29, 31–55, 71–77, 97–98.
5. Stanley Gritzbaugh to Earl W. Hayter, Rockford, 23 March 1969; interview, Homer Hall, DeKalb, 25 September 1970.
6. Swen Parson, "Notebook," pp. 307–14.
7. *Chronicle,* 5 January, 4, 24 March 1920.
8. *Northern Illinois,* 19 September 1924, p. 2.
9. Program, "Community Conference," DeKalb, 31 March 1920.
10. *Northern Illinois,* 3 April 1925, p. 1.
11. Ibid., March 1922, p. 3.
12. Ibid., 17 September 1926, p. 1.
13. *Annual Catalog* (1928), pp. 10, 28, 32, 35–36.
14. *Northern Illinois,* 28 May 1924, p. 1.
15. Ibid., March 1920, p. 4.
16. *Norther* (1921), p. 105.
17. *Biennial Catalog* (1924–1926), p. 14; (1926–1928), p. 20.
18. *Northern Illinois,* February 1922, p. 4. In 1922, there were eleven major activities and twenty-three minor ones (ibid.).
19. *Northern Illinois,* 2 May 1924, p. 2.
20. *Norther* (1928), p. 106; *Northern Illinois,* 11 February 1927, p. 1; 18 February 1927, p. 1; 25 February 1927, p. 3.
21. Normal School Board, *Proceedings* (22 April 1920), p. 30; Charles A. Harper, *Development of the Teachers College in the United States,* p. 308.
22. *Northern Illinois,* October 1921, p. 5.
23. *Alumni Recall,* 3 (29 October 1927): 2; George L. Terwilliger, speech to A.I.B.S. Chapter, DeKalb, 2 May 1968 (manuscript, N.I.U. Archives). The local township high school was also engaged for the practice teachers at $150 per month.

24. *Biennial Catalog* (1924–1926), p. 20.
25. *Northern Illinois,* 30 September 1927, p. 2; Parson et al., "A History of Northern Illinois State Teachers College," pp. 32–33.
26. *Norther* (1925), p. 80; (1927), pp. 69–72; Normal School Board, *Proceedings* (29 May 1923), pp. 23–24.
27. *Alumni Recall,* 2 (9 May 1927): 4.
28. *Northern Illinois,* 2 December 1927, p. 2; 1 February 1928, p. 2.
29. *Biennial Catalog* (1926–1928), p. 33.
30. *Chronicle,* 13 September 1927.
31. *Northern Illinois,* 17 April 1925, p. 1; 20 September 1928, p. 42.
32. Ibid., February 1921, pp. 4, 14.
33. Two new buildings were constructed below the East Terrace so as to afford enough space between them for a standard-size swimming pool when appropriations were forthcoming. The pool, however, was not built until some thirty years later, and then, of all places, in the new University Laboratory School.
34. *Northern Illinois,* 7 March 1928, p. 2.
35. Brown to Felmley, DeKalb, 10 September 1919; *Northern Illinois,* 23 December 1924, pp. 2, 3.
36. William Leighly, "The Presidency of J. Stanley Brown" (manuscript, N.I.U. Archives, 1969), pp. 32–48.
37. Much information about these infractions came from the private papers of Charles W. Whitten, given to the N.I.U. Archives by his daughter, Jennie Whitten, a prominent alumna of Northern.
38. *Chronicle,* 31 October 1925.
39. Normal School Board, *Proceedings* (7 May 1923), p. 4.
40. Ibid. (15 February 1926), pp. 17–18. The charges here listed were stated in Whitten's letter to Karl D. Waldo, principal of East High School in Aurora, 14 August 1926.
41. Whitten to Waldo, DeKalb, 14 August 1926.
42. Ibid.
43. Normal School Board, *Proceedings* (29 April 1926), pp. 16, 30; *Chicago Tribune,* 18 April 1926; *Sycamore True Republican,* 16 April 1926; 16 June 1926.
44. Normal School Board, *Proceedings* (15 February, 31 May 1926), pp. 17–18, 77.
45. Ibid. (29 September 1926), pp. 61, 62; *Northern Illinois,* 1 October 1926, pp. 1, 4.
46. Whitten, form letter to various schoolmen, probably January 1927.
47. Normal School Board, *Proceedings* (28 November 1927), p. 34; (23 January 1928), p. 12.
48. Ibid. (19 May 1927), pp. 23–24.
49. Edwin H. Cates, *A Centennial History of St. Cloud State College* (Minneapolis: Dillon Press, 1968), p. 178.
50. *Chronicle,* 18 March 1927; Normal School Board, *Proceedings* (21 March 1927), p. 25; interview, Thomas J. Huntzicker, DeKalb, 19 December 1969.
51. A charter for this fraternity was applied for by seventeen men with "Doc" Hayes as the faculty advisor in May 1928. Northern was the first college in Illinois to be chartered by this national organization (*Northern Illinois,* 23 May 1928, p. 1).
52. Normal School Board, *Proceedings* (24 September, 15 October 1928), pp. 30, 37–38. See Faculty Manuals, 1955–1967 (N.I.U. Archives).

53. On occasion, Dr. Whittaker gave readings of his poetry. Earlier in life he had published a history, *Pathbreakers and Pioneers of the Pueblo Region,* which he used for his M.A. thesis at the University of Denver. Today this is a rare book that sells for many times its original price. As a welfare worker he organized a community center in Pueblo, Colorado, which the city honored in his name (Hollis Whittaker Schelke to Charlotte Cummings Whittaker, Richmond, Indiana, 8 February 1967).

54. Normal School Board, *Proceedings* (25 June 1929), pp. 42–43; *Northern Illinois,* 28 May 1929, p. 2.

Chapter 7

1. Normal School Board, *Proceedings* (27 August 1929), p. 46.

2. *Chronicle,* 17, 18, 26, 28, 30 August; 1, 2, 3 October, 1929.

3. *The Athena* (1909), p. 33; *Ohio Alumnus* (January 1940), p. 10.

4. Edwin H. Cates to Earl W. Hayter, St. Cloud, Minnesota, 14 April 1969.

5. Miriam Harms Dypold to Earl W. Hayter, Ann Arbor, Michigan, 4 November 1969.

6. Mary Butler to Adams, Chicago, 20 August 1935, 31 July 1936; Butler to Earl W. Hayter, Chicago, 25 May 1970.

7. Adams to Earl W. Hayter, DeKalb, 24 January 1946.

8. *Northern Illinois,* 1 July 1943, p. 2; 21 July 1947, p. 3.

9. *Chicago Tribune,* 5 February 1939; *Faculty Bulletin,* 2 (December 1940): 4.

10. Normal School Board, *Proceedings* (8 December 1943), pp. 287–88.

11. Ibid. (10 May 1945), pp. 12–13.

12. G.P. Tuttle to Adams, Urbana, Illinois, 29 January 1932.

13. George F. Zook to Adams, Chicago, 4 April 1931.

14. Adams to George A. Works, DeKalb, 1 May 1933.

15. Works to Adams, Chicago, 19 April 1935.

16. Normal School Board, *Proceedings* (19 February 1940), p. 59.

17. Marie Alsager to William Lamperes, Tyron, North Carolina, 14 February 1969.

18. Dypold to Earl W. Hayter, Ann Arbor, 4 November 1969.

19. J. Hal Connor to Earl W. Hayter, Washington, D.C., 16 September 1969.

20. Normal School Board, *Proceedings* (22 April 1946), p. 63; (22 October 1950), p. 433.

21. R. M. Zulauf and S. D. Fink, "A Schedule of Salaries and Wages, 1939–1941" (manuscript, N.I.U. Archives), pp. 1–5.

22. *Faculty Bulletin,* 7 (May 1946): 1; Administrative Council, "Correspondence," 8 April 1944 (N.I.U. Archives).

23. Preston Bradley to Adams, Chicago, 23 October 1940; Normal School Board, *Proceedings* (11 September 1939), p. 132.

24. Carleton Washburne to the superintendents of schools, Winnetka, Illinois, 2 July 1938.

25. Normal School Board, *Proceedings* (11 September 1919), p. 120.

26. Ibid. (14 November 1938), p. 172; (11 September 1939), p. 120; (22 September 1939), p. 170.

27. Interview, Charlotte Whittaker, DeKalb, 18 September 1968; taped interview, Jacob Alschuler, Aurora, Illinois, 19 November 1969.

28. Washburne to schoolmen, Winnetka, 21 July 1938.

29. Frank Phillips to Washburne, DeKalb, 27 July 1938.

30. Washburne to Phillips, Winnetka, 29 July 1938.
31. Phillips to Washburne, DeKalb, 27 July 1938; taped interview with Jacob Alschuler, Aurora, 19 November 1969, in which this entire situation was discussed.
32. Normal School Board, *Proceedings* (22 September 1939), p. 170; J. Hal Connor to Earl W. Hayter, Washington, D.C., 20 May 1969. No record was kept by the Board and the *Chronicle* made no report of this meeting in Aurora; but several of the faculty members when interviewed remembered the occasion.
33. Interview, Charlotte Whittaker, DeKalb, 18 September 1968.
34. Normal School Board, *Proceedings* (19 May 1941), pp. 74–75, 84; (9 July 1941), p. 118.
35. Supreme Court of Illinois, "Abstract of Record," No. 26690 (November Term, 1942) [Appeal from the Circuit Court of Cook County], pp. 111–112. See also, *Reports of Cases at Law and in Chancery* (Bloomington, Ill., 1943; Edwin H. Cooke, Reporter), vol. 382, pp. 383–87; *Northern Alumnus,* 37 (September 1942):19.
36. *Northern Illinois,* 7 October 1937, p. 1.
37. *Northern Illinois,* 14 November 1935, p. 2; Bach to Skelly, Bloomington, Illinois, 17 November 1935; Skelly to Bach, DeKalb, 21 November 1935.
38. Adams to Bach, DeKalb, 18 November 1935.
39. Normal School Board, *Proceedings* (3 May 1948), pp. 218–20; (8 June 1948), pp. 276–77.
40. *Northern Illinois,* 15 November 1940, p. 4.
41. Parson et al., "A History of the Northern Illinois State Teachers College," pp. 71–80.
42. R. M. Zulauf, "Brief History of the Administrative Council, 1939–1952" (N.I.U. Archives), pp. 1–4.
43. Zulauf to Adams and Council members, DeKalb, 1 January 1942, and 1 October 1942; Fink to Adams and Council members, DeKalb, 18 January 1943, and 21 February 1945.
44. William Lamperes, "Student Life and Opinion, Northern Illinois State Teachers College, 1929–1949" (manuscript, N.I.U. Archives, 1969), pp. 1–46.
45. *Northern Illinois,* 24 March 1938, p. 3; 23 October 1941, p. 2.
46. Ibid., 12 November 1945, p. 5.
47. Ibid., 6 January 1938, p. 2.
48. Adams to Student Affairs Committee, DeKalb, 12 June 1945.
49. *N.I. News Items,* I (December 1948): 6–11; (March 1949): p. 3.
50. Normal School Board, *Proceedings* (17 September 1929), p. 61; *Chronicle,* 17 September 1929.
51. Street to Baker, DeKalb, 8 December 1947.
52. Sperling to Charles W. Hunt, DeKalb, 6 January 1948.
53. Hunt to Sperling, Oneonta, New York, 8 January 1948.
54. Sperling to Stoddard, DeKalb, 29 May 1948; Stoddard to Sperling, Urbana, 21 June 1948.
55. 16 December 1948, pp. 1–4; *N.I. News Items,* I (December 1948): 1–12.

Chapter 8

1. Teachers College Board, *Proceedings* (17 December 1948), 538.
2. Browne to Earl W. Hayter, Normal, 7 July 1969.

3. Paul Street to Earl W. Hayter, Lexington, Kentucky, 11 April 1968.
4. Interview, Arthur C. Muns, 6 February 1970. Holmes assumed office on 1 February 1949.
5. Interview, Paul Crawford, DeKalb, 16 February 1972.
6. July 1952, pp. 11–12.
7. *N.I. News Items,* 5 (May 1953): 2.
8. Chauncey B. Watson and Dennis Collins, "The Future Role of Our University" (N.I.U. Archives), 1957, pp. 1–3.
9. Bond Issue Committee, "Minutes," 16 December 1959; 14 April 1960 (N.I.U. Archives).
10. A.A.U.P. to Holmes, DeKalb, 13 May 1964.
11. Browne to Holmes, Springfield, 27 May 1959.
12. Charles E. Howell to Holmes, DeKalb, 14, 21 May 1960.
13. Howell to L. W. Hinton, DeKalb, 8 February 1949.
14. *Northern Star,* 9 December 1954, pp. 1, 2; *Northern Alumnus,* 7 (December 1954): 5.
15. Holmes to presidents of state colleges and universities, DeKalb, 27 January 1955.
16. *Faculty Bulletin,* 14 (February 1953): 4; see also (February 1955): 3–4.
17. *Northern Star,* 12 April 1957, pp. 3–4.
18. Kenneth Snyder to Lloyd Morey, DeKalb, 22 December 1954; Snyder to E. Edward Raymond, DeKalb, 4, 23 April; 17 July 1954.
19. Snyder to Governor Stratton, DeKalb, 22 December 1954; Reavis to Stratton, Chicago, 6 June 1954.
20. Vernon L. Nickell to Snyder, Springfield, 8 January 1955; Snyder to Robert W. Lyons, DeKalb, 7 May 1955.
21. Teachers College Board, *Proceedings* (17 January, 14 February 1955), pp. 238, 242–45, 246–47; Snyder to Peter L. Agnew, DeKalb, 21 February 1955.
22. Interviews, F.R. Geigle, DeKalb, 6 April 1972; Kenneth Snyder, DeKalb, 7 April 1972.
23. Teachers College Board, *Proceedings* (18 March 1957), pp. 277–78.
24. Ibid., "Executive Officers Report," no. 88 (18 October 1960), p. 22.
25. Teachers College Board, *Proceedings* (20 April 1953), p. 260.
26. Hainds to Cabinet and Council of Academic Deans, DeKalb, 1 December 1961.
27. See North Central Examining Association Committee Reports in N.I.U. Archives.
28. Geigle to Holmes, DeKalb, 30 September 1965; Topp to Benjamin C. Willis, DeKalb, 24 April 1964.
29. Teachers College Board, *Proceedings* (16 April 1962), p. 616.
30. Hainds to Earl W. Hayter, Wichita, Kansas, 27 November 1968.
31. Holmes to Ted Hennegan, DeKalb, 29 January 1954; Holmes to Ruth Kytte, DeKalb, 12 May 1953.
32. Ray Steele to Holmes, DeKalb, 21 April 1966; Holmes to Steele, DeKalb, 27 April 1966.
33. *Northern Star,* 13 April 1962, p. 1.
34. *N.I.U. News Items,* 13 (December 1961): 7; *The Edge,* 1, No. 1 (1964): 1–3. Interviews, Barry Schrader, DeKalb, 22 February 1972; Rev. Donald O'Hair, DeKalb, 7 May 1971.
35. *Northern Star,* 28 October 1966, p. 1; 3 November, p. 1; 4 November, p. 1; 17 February 1967, p. 1; 23 February, p. 1; 28 February, p. 1.

36. Ibid., 5 October, p. 1; 14 October, p. 2; 18 October, p. 2; 17 November, p. 4; 23 November, p. 1; 14 December, p. 4; 21 December, 1965, p. 1; 22 April 1966, p. 1.

37. Gordon to Holmes, DeKalb, 30 April 1960; Holmes's memo concerning Browne's statement, April 1960. Things changed in five years, and Herbert Aptheker was permitted to speak; however, the Security Office did make a confidential report for the University officials (D.E. Bruer, "Inspectors Report on Herbert Aptheker," 18 February 1965, N.I.U. Archives).

38. Blanche Houston to Holmes, Rochelle, Illinois, 19 October 1965; Holmes to Houston, DeKalb, 20 October 1965.

39. 21 September, p. 3; 12 October, p. 2; 20 October, p. 1; 26 October, p. 1; 9 November, 1965, p. 3.

40. *Northern Star,* 27 October, p. 1; 3 November, 1965, p. 1; A.A.U.P. "Minutes," 16 November 1965 (N.I.U. Archives); Paul Stone to A.A.U.P., Springfield, 4, 5 November 1965.

41. *Northern Star,* 11 October 1966, p. 1.

42. Teachers College Board, *Proceedings* (19 January 1948), pp. 30–31.

43. James E. Elliott, "Statement from the Northern Illinois University Faculty Salary Committee . . . Increases For the 1965–1967 Biennial Report" (N.I.U. Archives), pp. 1–12.

44. *Faculty Bulletin,* 19 (Supplement, May 1958): 4–5; Teachers College Board, *Proceedings* (20 September 1954), p. 83.

45. Earlier, Arthur Bestor's *Educational Wasteland* created a similar national concern and in an appearance at Northern he filled the auditorium to capacity in a debate with Wilbur Yauch.

46. Richard Browne to all faculties, Springfield, 1 December 1951.

47. *Education Today,* 20 (October 1961): 4–5.

48. Interview, Paul Burtness, DeKalb, 6 July 1973.

49. *Norther* (1933), p. 37.

50. Nancy C. Swanson, "The Acquisition and Development of the Lorado Taft Field Campus" (M.S.Ed. thesis, N.I.U., 1968), pp. 1–116.

51. *Education Today,* 26 (March 1967): 7.

52. *Northern Star,* 24 July 1972, pp. 1–2.

53. Interview, Anthony Lorusso, 1 March 1972; Harold Dorland, 8 May 1972.

54. T. E. Courtney to Teachers College Board members, DeKalb, 27 May 1965; Board of Regents, *Proceedings* (7 August, 2 October 1967), pp. 54, 126.

55. Interviews, Stuart Fink, DeKalb, 28 April 1969; Z. Harold Dorland, DeKalb, 8 May 1972.

56. Stipes to Holmes, Champaign, 29 January 1955; Holmes to Stipes, DeKalb, 4 February 1955.

57. *Northern Star,* 15 September 1966, p. 2.

58. James Martin to Geigle, DeKalb, 10 April 1962; R. M. Bowen to Geigle, DeKalb, 17 November 1961; Allen Weaver to Geigle, DeKalb, 20 December 1963.

59. Dunn to A. C. Muns, Bloomington, Illinois, 26 October 1966; F. H. McKelvey to Muns, Springfield, 9 February 1967.

60. *Northern Illinois,* 1 October 1945, p. 4; 29 September 1947, p. 2; Dorothy Bradish to Earl W. Hayter, Holland, Michigan, 11 January 1970; Sue Lorimer Parsons to Earl W. Hayter, San Diego, California, 3 November 1970.

61. See Holmes, "Correspondence" (Paul Street Papers, N.I.U. Archives).
62. Ibid., interview, Clara Sperling, DeKalb, 2 March 1973.
63. Interview, Hugh Jameson, DeKalb, 20 January 1973.
64. *Faculty Bulletin,* 20 (March 1959): 6.
65. Wirtz to editor, *Chronicle,* 20 March 1959.
66. Feyerherm to Holmes, DeKalb, 9 March 1966; Feyerherm to Dorland, 5 March 1965.
67. BGSCU, *Proceedings* (21 March 1966), p. 574.
68. Earl W. Hayter to Geigle, DeKalb, 1 May 1966.

Chapter 9

1. Bureau of University Research (Report No. 254-A-70-71 I) (July 1971), p. 3; *Northern Star,* 30 June 1967, p. 4.
2. Courtesy of Special Projects Office.
3. *Northern Illinois,* 24 September 1945, p. 9.
4. George Rommel to Earl W. Hayter, Charleston, Illinois, 9 July 1969; Miriam Dypold to Hayter, Ann Arbor, Michigan, 4 November 1969.
5. *Northern Star,* 28 February 1964, p. 5; 14 March 1967, p. 1.
6. Ibid., 9 February, p. 2; 6 April 1962, p. 1; 16 March 1966, p. 3. Richard Boardman, student bookstore director, estimated 2 percent loss of gross volume sales for 1967–68.
7. Paul Crawford, "Forensics at N.I.U. 1930 to the Present" (manuscript, N.I.U. Archives), 1969, pp. 1–3.
8. *N.I.U. News Items,* 10 (March 1958): 12.
9. *Norther* (1923), pp. 99–100.
10. *Northern Illinois,* 11 October 1934, p. 1; interview, Edward Fitzgerald, DeKalb, 13 June 1972.
11. *Northern Illinois,* 23 January 1941, p. 2.
12. *DeKalb Chronicle,* 29 March 1962; *Northern Star,* 6 March, p. 1; 4 April, p. 1; 16 June, 1967, p. 2.
13. *Northern Illinois,* 8 April 1943, p. 6.
14. J. Patrick White to Geigle, DeKalb, 22 October 1964; Harold Aikins, "The Northern Illinois Association of Phi Beta Kappa—A Brief History to Spring 1962," mimeographed (DeKalb, 1962), pp. 1–16. (N. I. U. Archives.)
15. C. M. Pike to Geigle, DeKalb, 29 November 1956.
16. Hanson to Holmes, DeKalb, 3 February 1950; Moor to Holmes, DeKalb, 16 February 1950.
17. *Northern Illinois,* 2 October, p. 2; 30 October 1941, p. 2.
18. John Twombly to Student Affairs Committee, DeKalb, 14 April 1950; W. V. O'Connell to Eugene Hellmich, DeKalb, 23 March 1950.
19. *Northern Illinois,* 15 May 1925, pp. 1, 2; 3 May 1927, p. 1; 1 June 1928, p. 1.
20. Maude Uhland, "[*History of*] *The Towers"* (manuscript, N.I.U. Archives, 1968), pp. 1–3.
21. Betty Brough Prall to Earl W. Hayter, Malta, Illinois, 27 June 1972.
22. Adams to Street, DeKalb, 24 October 1947.
23. Smith to Adams, Aurora, 28 March 1938; Adams to Smith, DeKalb, 12 April 1938.
24. Normal School Board, *Proceedings* (21 June 1920), p. 14. For data on placement, see the annual reports (1936–1971).

25. See "Student Fees, 1899–1971" (N.I.U. Archives).
26. C. P. Lantz, "A History of Illinois Inter-Collegiate Athletic Conference" (M. A. thesis, Pennsylvania State College, 1935); *Education Today,* 19 (3 March 1960): 1–2.
27. "Athletic Grant Program," 21 June 1956 (N.I.U. Archives); William A. Herrmann to Earl W. Hayter, DeKalb, 31 August 1972. The 1972–73 athletic department budget of $595,000 is divided into four major areas: 44 percent for operation-travel, 41 percent for grants-in-aid, 7 percent for equipment, and 8 percent for miscellaneous (*Northern Star,* August 1972, p. 31).
28. Holmes to Dorothy S. Stanger, DeKalb, 16 March 1956.
29. Rolf to Holmes, DeKalb, 27 May 1964 (Holmes, "Correspondence with Teachers College Board," N.I.U. Archives).
30. Teachers College Board, *Proceedings* (21 June 1965), pp. 797, 888.
31. *Northern Star,* 2 March 1967, p. 12.
32. *N.I.U. News Items,* 20 (October 1969): 8.
33. *Northern Star,* 8 March, p. 16; 21 March 1973, p. 11.
34. George G. Evans to Holmes, DeKalb, 21 June 1950.
35. Healey's successes were during the years he coached at Eastern when he won several championships, set records, produced outstanding players, and took teams to national tournaments. In recent years he has devoted much of his time to research and writing.
36. Robert Topp to Geigle, DeKalb, 19 January 1967; Geigle to Topp, DeKalb, 20 January 1967.
37. *Northern Star,* 23 September 1960, p. 7. The data for most of the various sports were secured from publications compiled by Owen "Bud" Nangle, director of Sports Information at N.I.U.
38. *Northern Illinois,* 3 March 1932, p. 4; 10 December 1936, p. 4; 16 May 1940, p. 3.

Chapter 10

1. University Selection Committee, "Final Report," 11 May 1967.
2. *Northern Star,* 10 May 1968, p. 31.
3. Presidential Inauguration Committee File (N.I.U. Archives).
4. Interview, R. E. France, secretary-treasurer, N.I.U. Foundation, DeKalb, 14 March 1973.
5. Arra M. Garab (ed.), *A New University* (DeKalb: Northern Illinois University Press, 1968), p. 55.
6. *Northern Star,* 6 October 1967, p. 3.
7. Students in an attempt to influence selection and retention of faculty members compiled a two-volume evaluation in 1968–69 of courses and instructors who were willing to co-operate with the project (*Query: A Student Evaluation of Courses and Teachers at Northern Illinois University,* DeKalb, 1968–69).
8. *Faculty Bulletin,* 34 (December 1970): 12–13; 34 (January 1971): 11–12; (April 1971): 19.
9. *N.I.U. News Items,* 20 (October 1969): 4; *Faculty Bulletin,* 32 (January 1969): 6–7; 32 (May 1969): 2–3.
10. R. E. France to F. R. Geigle, DeKalb, 15 April 1968.
11. John Sayre to Executive Committee, N.I.U. Foundation, DeKalb, 28 April 1969.

12. Fred Blakey, "The Creation of the Black Studies Program at NIU" (N.I.U. Archives), 1972, pp. 1–13.

13. *Northern Star,* 10 May 1968, p. 1; African and Afro-American Cultural Organization, "Proposal," 8 May 1968. (N.I.U. Archives.)

14. *Northern Star,* 25 March 1969, p. 1; 26 March 1969, p. 1; 27 March 1969, p. 1; 28 March 1969, p. 5; *N.I.U. News Items,* 20 (April 1969): 7.

15. N.I.U. News Release, 17 December 1969.

16. *Chronicle,* 16 December 1969.

17. *Northern Star,* 18 December 1969, p. 1; 8 January 1970, p. 1; *Chronicle,* 17 December 1969.

18. *Chronicle,* 17 December 1969; taped interview, Rhoten Smith, DeKalb, 7 June 1971. (N.I.U. Archives.)

19. William J. Scott to Geigle, Springfield, 18 November 1968; Geigle to Scott, DeKalb, 26 November 1968.

20. Smith to Scott, DeKalb, 19 June 1969.

21. Ad Hoc Committee of Police Science, "Preliminary Report," 6 February 1970; *Faculty Bulletin,* 33 (May 1970): 15–17.

22. *Northern Star,* 6 May 1970, p. 1; interview, James Banovetz, 25 October 1972.

23. Security Department, "Annual Report" (1963–64), p. 31.

24. *Faculty Bulletin,* 35 (20 March 1972): D 6–8.

25. *Northern Star,* 1 March 1972, p. 1; 2 March 1972, p. 2; 7 March 1972, p. 1.

26. Holmes to Browne, DeKalb, 23 June 1952; Browne to Holmes, Springfield, 2 September 1952.

27. *Northern Star,* 8 February 1968, p. 1; 27 February 1968, p. 1; *Faculty Bulletin,* 31 (February 1968): 10–15; 31 (March 1968): 4–6.

28. *Northern Star,* 21 May 1970, pp. 1, 3; 19 May 1971, p. 1; *N.I.U. News Items,* 22 (June 1971): 3.

29. *Northern Star,* 27 March 1969, p. 1; 30 April 1969, p. 2; 20 May 1969, p. 2; 21 May 1969, p. 1. See *News From Nowhere,* I (September 1968) to III (March 1971).

30. *Northern Star,* 5 March 1969, p. 5; 8 March 1969, p. 1; 18 April 1969, p. 1; 2 May 1969, p. 5.

31. Ibid., 22 May 1969, pp. 1–2, 4–5; *Chicago Sun-Times,* 22 May 1969.

32. *Northern Star,* 17 October 1969, pp. 1–2.

33. Ibid., 29 October 1969, p. 1.

34. Ibid., 6 May 1970, p. 2.

35. Rhoten A. Smith, speech, 11 May 1970 (manuscript, N.I.U. Archives).

36. Smith to faculty members, DeKalb, 19 May 1970.

37. Smith to members of the Board of Regents and presidents of Illinois State and Sangamon State Universities, 1 June 1970.

38. *N.I.U. News Items,* 21 (June 1970): 1–5; *Northern Star,* 6 May 1970, p. 1. Most of the persons arrested were bailed out with funds raised by students and their cases were finally dropped for lack of evidence. Dismissals from school were few.

39. *Northern Star,* 19 June 1970, p. 2.

40. Sean Shesgreen, "Statement to the Horsley Committee," 12 November 1970 (N.I.U. Archives).

41. Emory Evans et al. to members of the University Council, DeKalb, 19 January 1971; *N.I.U. News Items,* 21 (December 1970): 3, 6.

42. *Chicago Sun-Times,* 5 January 1971; *Northern Star,* 11 January 1971, pp. 4, 7; 18 June 1971, p. 2.
43. *Intellectual Digest,* 2 (July 1972): 80–81.
44. *The Greening of America* (New York: Random House, © 1970), p. 14. Reprinted by permission of the publisher.
45. *N.I.U. News Items,* 22 (February 1971): 2–3.
46. *Chronicle,* 7 January 1971.
47. Michael Maibach to Earl W. Hayter, DeKalb, 21 November 1972.

Chapter 11

1. Warren G. Bennis, "Searching For the 'Perfect' University President," *Atlantic,* 227 (April 1971): 40.
2. Board of Regents, *Proceedings* (17 January 1971), pp. 127–28.
3. *Chicago Sun-Times,* 16 June 1971; *Northern Star,* 16 June 1971, pp. 1, 3.
4. *Northern Star,* 27 September 1967, p. 1.
5. Richard Nelson, "New Civic Affairs Program," *Inland News* (January 1960), pp. 8–10.
6. *N.I.U. News Items,* 22 (August 1971): 4.
7. *Northern Star,* 16 June 1971, p. 1.
8. *Chicago Tribune,* 17 June 1971; *Northern Star,* 16 June 1971, pp. 1 ff.
9. Robert V. Remini to staff, History Department, University of Illinois, Chicago Circle (22 December 1969), pp. 1–2.
10. James B. Holderman, "Executive Director's Report (No. 108)," Board of Higher Education papers, 6 July 1972, pp. 1–2 (N.I.U. Archives); *Faculty Bulletin,* 36 (5 February 1973): 28–37.
11. Nelson to Board of Regents and others, DeKalb, 15 February 1972.
12. *Rising Higher,* 5 (May 1972): 1.
13. *Chicago Tribune,* 21 February 1972; *Northern Star,* 19 June 1972, p. 8.
14. *Northern Star,* 14 June 1972, p. 2.
15. *Faculty Bulletin,* 35 (26 May 1972): 5–8, 11.
16. Board of Regents, *Proceedings* (4 May 1969), pp. 144, 153–56.
17. A.F.T. to "Fellow Workers," DeKalb, 1 January 1973.
18. *Faculty Concerns* (leaflet) (June 1971), p. 1; (October 1971), p. 1.
19. *Chronicle,* 12 August 1972; *Northern Star,* 18 June 1972, p. 8.

Appendix One

Full-Time Faculty

(1899–1972)

1899—16	1924—56	1949—134
1900—19	1925—64	1950—152
1901—34	1926—62	1951—162
1902—32	1927—63	1952—177
1903—29	1928—65	1953—186
1904—28	1929—69	1954—197
1905—29	1930—64	1955—216
1906—31	1931—72	1956—236
1907—32	1932—70	1957—264
1908—36	1933—71	1958—322
1909—37	1934—71	1959—381
1910—38	1935—67	1960—421
1911—40	1936—70	1961—460
1912—43	1937—73	1962—527
1913—47	1938—71	1963—599
1914—49	1939—78	1964—695
1915—50	1940—78	1965—828
1916—51	1941—79	1966—926
1917—48	1942—76	1967—1026
1918—45	1943—74	1968—1151
1919—45	1944—74	1969—1248
1920—42	1945—79	1970—1320
1921—50	1946—92	1971—1278
1922—51	1947—114	1972—1270
1923—59	1948—122	Courtesy of the NIU Archives

Appendix Two

Part I: On-Campus Fall Enrollment Undergraduate Figures, 1899–1950

1899	173	1912	401	1925	692	1938	951
1900	217	1913	441	1926	557	1939	1,165
1901	220	1914	455	1927	514	1940	1,173
1902	234	1915	466	1928	654	1941	1,008
1903	218	1916	482	1929	701	1942	803
1904	220	1917	334	1930	760	1943	441
1905	261	1918	223	1931	729	1944	498
1906	297	1919	256	1932	837	1945	581
1907	303	1920	335	1933	792	1946	1,442
1908	318	1921	402	1934	743	1947	1,635
1909	316	1922	516	1935	715	1948	1,668
1910	359	1923	533	1936	768	1949	2,073
1911	366	1924	631	1937	769	1950	1,986

Part II: On-Campus Fall Enrollment Undergraduate and Graduate Figures 1951–1972

1951	1,705†	188†	1,893	1962	7,347	1,790	9,137
1952	1,780	220	2,000	1963	8,724	1,913	10,637
1953	2,040	245	2,285	1964	10,326	2,346	12,672
1954	2,313	256	2,569	1965	11,950	2,738	14,688
1955	2,899	361	3,260	1966	13,095	3,345	16,440
1956	3,674	451	4,125	1967	14,440	3,617	18,057
1957	4,278	466	4,744	1968	16,370	4,349	20,719
1958	4,940	717	5,657	1969	17,610	4,909	22,519
1959	5,125	987	6,112	1970	17,581	5,236	22,817
1960	5,747	1,295	7,042	1971	17,962	4,857	22,819
1961	6,458	1,653	8,111	1972	16,702	4,368	21,070

Courtesy of the NIU Archives
†Approximate Division

Appendix Three

Chronology of Buildings
(Occupied, 1899–1973)

Altgeld (John P.) Hall	(1899)
McMurry (Lida B. and Charles A.) Hall	(1911)
Williston (John W. Cook) Hall	(1915)
Industry and Technology Building	(1928)
Still (Edgar B.) Gym	(1928)
Davis (William M.) Hall	(1943)
Adams (Karl L.) Hall	(1949)
Gilbert (Newell D.) Hall	(1951)
Parson (Swen F.) Library	(1952)
Neptune (Celine) Hall, North	(1955)
Reavis (William C.) Hall	(1957)
Field House	(1957)
University School	(1958)
Health Center and Speech Clinic	(1958)
Fine Arts Building	(1959)
Physical Plant	(1959)
Neptune (Celine) Hall, West	(1959)
Neptune (Celine) Hall, East	(1960)
Neptune (Celine) Hall, Central	(1960)
University Apartments	(1960)
University Center	(1962)
Lincoln (Abraham) Hall	(1962)
Watson (Chauncey B.) Hall	(1962)
Central Receiving & Transportation	(1962)
Douglas (Stephen A.) Hall	(1963)
Faraday (Michael) Hall	(1963)
Graham (Ray) Hall	(1964)
Communications & Security Bldg.	(1964)
Wirtz (William W.) Hall	(1964)

Lowden (Frank O.) Hall	(1965)
Grant (Ulysses S.) Towers, South	(1965)
Stadium	(1965)
Grant (Ulysses S.) Towers, North	(1966)
University Health Service & Hospital	(1967)
Stevenson (Adlai E., II) Towers South	(1967)
Stevenson (Adlai E., II) Towers North	(1968)
Reavis (William C.) West	(1968)
Watson (Chauncey B.) East	(1968)
Reavis-Watson Lecture Hall	(1968)
Montgomery (Charles E.) Hall	(1969)
Visual Arts Building	(1970)
Central Receiving Building	(1971)
Computer Center	(1972)
Psychology-Mathematics Building	(1973)
Music Building	
Library	

Courtesy of the NIU Archives

Appendix Four

Degrees Awarded

Class	Two-Year Diploma	Bachelors Degrees	Masters Degrees	Doctors Degrees
1900	16			
1901	49			
1902	57			
1903	54			
1904	66			
1905	48			
1906	66			
1907	60			
1908	100			

Degrees Awarded

Class	Two-Year Diploma	Bachelors Degrees	Masters Degrees	Doctors Degrees
1909	76			
1910	92			
1911	82	1		
1912	105			
1913	125			
1914	144			
1915	162			
1916	123			
1917	198			
1918	152			
1919	101			
1920	103			
1921	125	1		
1922	164	2		
1923	173	4		
1924	197	15		
1925	207	15		
1926	234	7		
1927	214	14		
1928	183	18		
1929	191	14		
1930	219	34		
1931	163	34		
1932	146	64		
1933	176	68		
1934	149	69		
1935	151	88		
1936	133	85		
1937	135	105		
1938	128	105		
1939	105	118		
1940	134	173		
1941	95	197		
1942	72	201		
1943	35	185		
1944		120		
1945		97		
1946		128		

Degrees Awarded

Class	Bachelors Degrees	Masters Degrees and Certificates of Advanced Studies	Doctors Degrees
1947	172		
1948	222		
1949	316		
1950	374		
1951	417		
1952	381	28	
1953	354	84	
1954	342	121	
1955	381	66	
1956	411	86	
1957	550	118	
1958	688	105	
1959	741	129	
1960	814	158	
1961	843	185	
1962	903	243	
1963	1,012	244	
1964	1,221	283	2
1965	1,346	384	5
1966	1,670	461	10
1967	1,858	1,072	10
1968	2,457	1,023	21
1969	3,066	1,144	22
1970	3,304	1,357	18
1971	4,038	1,412	39
1972	4,313	1,709	66
1973	4,234	1,565	103

Courtesy of the N.I.U. Archives.

Appendix Five

Important Dates

22 May 1895	Governor John P. Altgeld signs legislation providing for a normal school in northern Illinois.
15 July 1895	DeKalb chosen as site for Northern Illinois State Normal School.
1 October 1895	Cornerstone laid with Governor Altgeld in attendance.
1 July 1899	John W. Cook becomes the first president.
12 September 1899	Opening day; students enroll in first classes.
21–23 September 1899	The 'Three Crimson Days," dedication of the new normal school.
October 1899	First issue of the *Northern Illinois* student paper.
10 November 1899	First football game, with DeKalb High School on Glidden Field, won by Northern.
Spring 1900	First issue of the *Norther* yearbook.
21 June 1900	First Commencement; sixteen graduate.
21 June 1900	Alumni organization formed.
6 October 1900	New York Governor Theodore Roosevelt and Ohio Senator Marcus Hanna speak in the "Woods."
October 1906	First mention of "Homecoming" in the *Northern Illinois.*
May 1907	General Assembly gives normal schools power to confer baccalaureate degrees.

1 July 1917	Board of Trustees of Northern Illinois State Normal School replaced by Normal School Board with authority over all five state normal schools.
1 August 1919	J. Stanley Brown becomes Northern's second president.
Fall 1920	Activities Committee of three faculty and three students created to administer the activity funds.
1 July 1921	Name changed to Northern Illinois State Teachers College.
Fall 1924	President J. Stanley Brown creates an Advisory Council consisting of five senior (male) professors.
1 July 1927	J. Clifton Brown becomes the third president of Northern.
1 August 1929	President J. Clifton Brown's resignation becomes effective.
1 October 1929	Karl L. Adams becomes the fourth president.
19 April 1935	Full undergraduate accreditation is granted by the North Central Association.
January 1936	Alumni Association incorporated.
Fall 1937	Extension program inaugurated.
22 June 1939	N.I.S.T.C. fully accredited for a local unit of the American Association of University Women.
18 July 1941	Normal School Board changes its name to Teachers College Board.
29 April 1944	First national social sorority, Delta Sigma Epsilon, installed.
19 May 1947	First national social fraternity, Phi Sigma Epsilon, installed.
1948–1949	Commemoration of the Golden Anniversary.
6 December 1948	Death of President Adams.

1 February 1949	Leslie A. Holmes becomes the fifth president.
31 March 1949	Northern Illinois State Teachers College Foundation incorporated.
22 January 1951	Master of Science in Education degree authorized by Teachers College Board.
7 August 1951	Lorado Taft Field Campus established.
Fall 1951	First men's dormitory, Gilbert Hall, opened.
10 December 1952	Over 83,000 books carried from Jacob Haish Library to new Swen Franklin Parson Library.
Fall 1954	Change from quarter to semester system.
9–10 October 1954	Twenty-five hour rain deluge floods NISTC campus.
1 July 1955	Name changed to Northern Illinois State College.
18 July 1955	Teachers College Board approves Bachelor of Arts and Bachelor of Science degrees.
1 July 1957	Name changed to Northern Illinois University.
17 November 1958	Teachers College Board authorizes Master of Arts and Master of Science degrees and the Certificate of Advanced Study.
19 January 1959	Teachers College Board authorizes Master of Music and Master of Fine Arts degrees.
July 1959	Three colleges established to replace the division system.
8 November 1960	Referendum approving the State Universities Bond Issue of $195,000,000 is passed.
July 1961	Illinois Board of Higher Education is created.
Fall 1961	Administrative and Faculty Councils reorganized into the

	President's Cabinet and the University Council.
20 November 1961	Doctor of Philosophy and Doctor of Education degrees authorized by Teachers College Board.
14 October 1961	NIU receives its first Peace Corps unit.
19 June 1962	Preliminary accreditation by the North Central Association for four departments to offer doctoral programs.
September 1962	Completion of the University Center.
Fall 1963	Football team is named national small college champion.
6 June 1964	First doctoral degree conferred on Herbert J. Bergstein.
26 May 1965	First meeting of the University Press Board
1 July 1967	N.I.U. is placed under a Board of Regents.
1 September 1967	Rhoten A. Smith becomes the sixth president.
23 May 1968	Dedication of the Calder sculpture "Le Baron."
1 October 1969	Debut performance of Vermeer Quartet.
18 May 1970	Protesting students rendezvous with President Smith at the Kishwaukee Bridge on Lincoln Highway at midnight.
30 April 1971	First planting of trees in Eco Park on Arbor Day.
1 August 1971	Richard J. Nelson becomes the seventh president.
5 March 1973	N.I.U. accepts membership in the Mid-American Conference.
15 March 1973	Groundbreaking ceremony for the new university library.
12 September 1973	Seventy-fifth anniversary year observance begins.

Index

529

Index